STAGES IN THE REVOLUTION

*Political Theatre
in Britain Since 1968*

1968 politicised a lot of people – not least new playwrights and other theatre workers: it marked a turning point in British theatre. The war babies of 1939–1945 had come of age and, discovering the real meaning of their 'inheritance', began to dismember it on stage with a violence that made the 'anger' of 1956 seem like mild distemper.

With cornerstone chapters on Arden, Bond, Mercer and Wesker, the spiritual forebears of the new political consciousness and its drama, this book follows the chain of events of the last ten years during which this politically aggressive generation of playwrights, directors and theatre activists have transformed the face of the British theatre.

As well as charting the work of writers such as Howard Barker, David Edgar, Trevor Griffiths, Howard Brenton, John McGrath and Barrie Keeffe among many others, the author highlights the influence of certain individual productions and theatre companies, stressing, for instance, the equal importance of the multi-million pound National Theatre and of shoestring touring groups like 7:84 and Joint Stock, and the avowedly socialist companies like Red Ladder and CAST.

The book documents the growth of a political theatre movement, the importance of which is only now beginning to be realised.

STAGES IN THE REVOLUTION

*Political Theatre
in Britain Since 1968*

Catherine Itzin

Eyre Methuen London

First published in 1980 in simultaneous hardback and
paperback editions by Eyre Methuen Ltd,
11 New Fetter Lane,
London EC4P 4EE

Filmset by Northumberland Press Ltd
Gateshead, Tyne and Wear
Printed in Great Britain
by Richard Clay (The Chaucer Press) Ltd
Bungay, Suffolk

ISBN 0 413 39180 9 HB
     0 413 46150 5 PB

For Wojciech

To Whom It May Concern

I was run over by the truth one day.
Ever since the accident I've walked this way
So stick my legs in plaster
Tell me lies about Vietnam.

Heard the alarm clock screaming with pain,
Couldn't find myself so I went back to sleep again
So fill my ears with silver
Stick my legs in plaster
Tell me lies about Vietnam.

Every time I shut my eyes all I see is flames.
Made a marble phone book, carved all the names
So coat my eyes with butter
Fill my ears with silver
Stick my legs in plaster
Tell me lies about Vietnam.

I smell something burning, hope it's just my brains.
They're only dropping peppermints and daisy-chains
So stuff my nose with garlic
Coat my eyes with butter
Fill my ears with silver
Stick my legs in plaster
Tell me lies about Vietnam.

Where were you at the time of the crime?
Down by the Cenotaph drinking slime
So chain my tongue with whisky
Stuff my nose with garlic
Coat my eyes with butter
Fill my ears with silver
Stick my legs in plaster
Tell me lies about Vietnam.

You put your bombers in, you put your conscience out,
You take the human being and you twist it all about
So scrub my skin with women
Chain my tongue with whisky
Stuff my nose with garlic
Coat my eyes with butter
Fill my ears with silver
Stick my legs in plaster
Tell me lies about Vietnam.

Adrian Mitchell, *Tribune* 16 April 1965

Contents

Preface

The main engagement took place in Sloane Square. There was a complementary action in the far east, at Stratford. These separate forces were never co-ordinated. The east relied very much on mercenaries recruited from another country. The west, although at one time there was an uneasy and short-lived alliance with France, employed the natives. The west once occupied the Palace and the Comedy, but these were not held. At this moment the east has taken Wyndham's and the Criterion. The situation is now confused. What exactly is written on that banner which the winds of expediency will so irritatingly fold? What are those charming business men doing on *this* side of the barricades? Is it true that some of the insurgents have been decorated by the enemy? They say the social realists and the experimentalists have fallen out. There are ugly rumours of unholy alliances. Even the citadel itself, the curiously named Royal Court, is threatened.[1]

In such a fashion did John Whiting in 1959 satirise the so-called 'revolution' in British theatre in the fifties. And then he asked: 'Are the fruits of revolution always conservative?' This question was echoed by John Russell Taylor surveying post-1956 British drama in his book, *Anger and After*, and its sequel, *The Second Wave*. But is it really a law of life that the revolutionaries of one generation become the reactionaries of the next? That the radicals of one decade become the pillars of the establishment of the next?

This was, of course, what happened to many of those hailed as revolutionaries from the fifties – like John Osborne and Harold Pinter. But it was not what happened to other writers of that period or slightly later – to John Arden, for example, or to Edward Bond. Nor indeed, for different reasons perhaps, to Arnold Wesker or David Mercer. More significantly it was not what happened to those that followed – to David Hare or Howard Brenton or Trevor Griffiths or John McGrath or Snoo Wilson. Nor to Steve Gooch, Caryl Churchill, Howard Barker, or David Edgar.

This was perhaps because that 'law' holds true only for those who accept the established system and its values, who accept that there is a 'room at the top' worth reaching. For those who reject the system – and for most that meant the capitalist system – the establishment is the enemy of the people and therefore *their* enemy. Not to strive for, but to struggle against.

And it was this attitude which characterised many of the writers

and theatre workers who made an impact in the British theatre in
the ten-year period from 1968 to 1978. They were not, for the most
part, just socially committed, but committed to a socialist society.
They were the writers of agitational propaganda and social realism,
who had not and who probably would not 'sell out' to or be sucked
in by the establishment.

None would be sufficiently naive or arrogant to claim to have
achieved a revolution either in the theatre or in society. Few would
even be able to agree on the best means to that end. And they were
acutely aware of the contradictions of having to work within a system
to which they were ideologically opposed, of biting the proverbial
hand that feeds. They lived the contradictions daily, and they, like
everyone, needed to eat. But they would almost unanimously regard
their work as part of the struggle towards a socialist society – as
a contribution, however small, to a revolutionary process.

Everything is political. All theatre is political. But the significant
British theatre of 1968–1978 was primarily theatre of political change.
In the words of John McGrath it was theatre 'that exists somewhere
within the shadow, or at least the penumbra, of the ideas of Marx
and Marxists; theatre that has as its base a recognition of capitalism
as an economic system which produces classes; that sees the
betterment of human life for all people in the abolition of classes
and capitalism; that sees that this can only happen through the rise
to state power of the current under-class, the working class, and
through democratisation – economic as well as political – of society
and its decision-making processes; that sees the establishment of
socialism not as the creation of Utopia or the end of the dialectic
of history, but as another step towards the realisation of the full
potential of every individual human life during the short time that
every individual has to live.'[2] In short – socialist theatre.

Richard Seyd, one of the founders of Red Ladder, admitted that
'if people don't think that capitalism is an absurd and damaging
way of organising society, then very little that one does is going to
change their minds'.[3] The theatre that is recorded in this book was
created primarily by people who *did* think that capitalism is absurd
and damaging, but who also believed that minds could be changed.
Their work was a contribution to that change.

Whilst there was nothing so dramatic as a state of revolution, there
were 'stages in the revolution' in the theatre in the seventies. This
book is a chronicle of that period, and a contribution to the debate
that took place. The book is structured chronologically in order to
reflect the dialectics of what generally came to be recognised as a

political theatre movement. Thus Edward Bond (to use one example) was less important in isolation than as part of – and a participant in – a series of events. What he wrote was important, but equally so was when and why, and its relation to other work and workers. This was true not only of playwrights and their plays, but also of theatre companies and their productions. The development of political theatre was lateral as well as linear. Howard Brenton, for example, wrote for Portable Theatre and Joint Stock as well as for the Royal Court and the National Theatre. Groups split and re-formed – Belt and Braces growing out of 7:84, Monstrous Regiment out of Belt and Braces and so forth. Thus the chronological framework is intended to give the content its context.

But the book is also sub-divided into sections (some long, some short), essays devoted to individual writers, groups and events. This is because there was a continuing process of analysis – within the work of individual writers, within theatre companies, between individuals, organisations and institutions. This process of discovering a *modus operandi*, of defining a philosophy, refining an ideology, was integral to the growth of political theatre, and an accurate history of the period demanded a format that enabled the issues to emerge and to be discussed. Thus the account of Red Ladder includes what they thought as well as what they did; of David Mercer, what he thought about what he wrote and its relation to the rest of theatre and society. So the consideration of each playwright, theatre company or event occurs at the approximate chronological point of its greatest public impact and is analysed there in some detail – though the origins may have been earlier and though the work was still in progress. Generally the essays on theatre companies are descriptive – historical accounts of their origin and development; the essays on writers are evaluative – dealing with their ideas as opposed to providing the usual series of play synopses; and the essays on issues (subsidy) and events (the opening of the National Theatre) are informative, occasionally deliberately provocative. For part of the history of political theatre in the seventies was the 'politics of the theatre' – the demonstrations, debates, strikes, campaigns – the battles fought on various fronts.

There were, of course, writers of stature and significance in the seventies who are not included in this book – Alan Ayckbourn, David Storey, Peter Shaffer, Peter Nichols, John Osborne, Harold Pinter, E. A. Whitehead, Simon Gray and more. They were excluded simply because their work was outside the scope of the book and its terms of reference. There were writers whose work was of only peripheral relevance – Tom Stoppard, Christopher Hampton, David Rudkin, Snoo Wilson. They are included in the introductions to each year. And there were writers whose work was often relevant, but which did not warrant the luxury of a long essay. They – Steve Gooch, Paul Thompson, Roger Howard, David Halliwell, Stephen Poliakoff, David Lan, Pam Gems – are also covered in the introductory material.

There were certain developments in British theatre in the seventies, important and 'political' in their own distinctive ways, but only peripherally related to the 'mainstream' political theatre movement. Peter Cheeseman, for example, who worked with Stephen Joseph's Studio Theatre at Scarborough in the early sixties (pioneering theatre-in-the-round), went on to create at the Victoria Theatre, Stoke-on-Trent, a regional centre of highly original historical documentaries, among them *The Jolly Potters*, *The Knotty*, *The Staffordshire Rebels* and *Fight for Shelton Bar*.[4] Cheeseman was motivated by a desire to create a truly local 'community' theatre: 'I wanted us also to begin to bridge the cultural gap which separates the artist from the majority of the community and which I believe to be a gap created by style not subject matter. I wanted to begin to develop a popular language, a style of our own which would make theatre livelier and more attractive than the current conventional play format.'[5] And it was thus he hit upon the idea of group-created documentaries about local subjects.

There was also the Theatre-in-Education movement which developed in the wake of the widespread politicisation and raising of political consciousness at the end of the sixties and was particularly characterised by its concern with social issues and social problems. The attitudes of the new TIE workers were radical. To them, children's theatre was a commitment; it was art in its own right; and it was a means whereby children could come to understand and control their environment.

As a movement, TIE began in 1965 with the Belgrade Theatre in Coventry which set up an independent team, attached to the main theatre to work entirely with and for young people both in the theatre and outside in schools. By 1970 there were dozens of theatres throughout Britain with similar TIE projects or programmes. By 1973, TIE work was taking place on such a scale that the Gulbenkian Foundation initiated an umbrella organisation – the Standing Conference of Young People's Theatre (SCYPT) – to respond to the needs of TIE work and workers. And then in 1976, Gulbenkian negotiated with SCYPT and the Theatre Writers Union a scheme whereby it funded writers attached to TIE teams.[6]

The development of TIE work was in part the result of the movement in the sixties towards progressive, child-centred education, in part a parallel to the theory and practice of drama-in-education, as expounded by Dorothy Heathcote and Gavin Bolton, who used drama as a teaching method in the curriculum. But it was also the result of the dissatisfaction of 'actors disillusioned with the lack of meaning in their work, the lack of control which they could exercise over it' and the desire to create something new – to change society at its youthful grass roots.[7]

The work of writers and of theatre companies – of the political theatre movement as a whole – had an important impact on organisations and unions in the seventies. So this book also provides a record of that, and particularly of the changing patterns and problems of subsidy. Some organisations – the Association of Lunchtime Theatres, The Association of Community Theatres, the Independent Theatre Council, the Theatre Writers Union, the British Theatre Institute, the British Theatre Museum – were new and grew up in direct response to the needs of the new theatre work being done. Some – Equity, the Writers Guild of Great Britain, the Greater London Arts Association, the Regional Arts Associations, the Arts Council of Great Britain – were not so new, but were forced to alter their activities radically in response to the new, 'organised' efforts of theatre workers.

There was no doubt, by the end of the decade, that the organisation and unionisation of the 'fringe' (as Equity still so quaintly persisted in calling it) had been one of the most significant developments in British theatre in the seventies. Significant in exemplifying the principles which underlay the political theatre movement. Significant in materially – and to some extent ideologically – changing working conditions (through the negotiation of agreements and contracts, in increasing subsidy and in lobbying for larger government grants to the arts). Significant also in creating collective forces which could influence future developments.

It is curious in some respects that a major chapter in the history of political theatre in Britain in the seventies should be a history of organisational effort, and that it should furthermore be such an exciting chapter – particularly as this kind of history is usually as boring as the bureaucracies which govern it. At the same time, 'organisation' in the seventies was, because of the political philosophy behind it, the 'organisation of workers' at the grass roots in a Marxist sense, with some of that political philosophy's revolutionary implications. It was indicative of the strength of the movement; and it was indicative of the failure of existing methods of organisation.

The seventies also saw the opening (and some closing) of hundreds of small theatre venues, important in mounting their own productions and promoting new work, and also in presenting the work of touring theatre companies. But the real alternative theatres could be said to have been the pubs and clubs and community centres up and down the country – the non-theatre places and the non-theatre audiences which most political theatre aimed to reach. In 1968 there were half a dozen 'fringe' theatre groups: by 1978 there were well over a hundred 'alternative' theatre companies, plus another fifty or more young people's theatre companies. In 1968, there were 34 arts centres (with theatre facilities); by 1978 there were over 140, plus a good 200 small-scale touring venues in London and the regions. In the sixties there were a handful of playwrights writing for the fringe; in 1978 there were a least 250 contemporary British playwrights, most of them working part- if not full-time in alternative theatre.[8] The statistics alone testified to the development of a new force to be reckoned with in British theatre; an alternative which developed new audiences, a new aesthetic, a new kind and concept of theatre.

David Edgar, in looking back over the decade in *Socialist Review*, wrote:

> 1978 is the tenth anniversary of all sorts of important things. It is also the tenth anniversary of the beginnings of a small, perhaps not very important, but nonetheless quite remarkable phenomenon: the growth of the socialist theatre movement in Britain.[9]

This book is the history of that remarkable phenomenon.

With very few exceptions, the material in this book has been based on interviews conducted specially for the purpose of the book. All views have been credited to those who expressed them. The 'contributors' were then given the opportunity to respond to the book in manuscript form: their comments have been incorporated into the completed book. For this is also their history.

My thanks therefore to the dozens of people interviewed for the purpose of this book and those who dug into their 'personal archives' – who were as anxious as I was to get the history accurate, to analyse their work and to address themselves to the issues of political theatre in Britain in the seventies. My thanks also to Douglas Hill and to Tony Harrison who encouraged me to write the book in the first place, to Stephen Burton who got me started when I was utterly daunted by the task, and to Nick Hern, drama editor at Eyre Methuen, for his continual encouragement and editorial expertise. My appreciation to my family, who have been infinitely patient and supportive, is impossible to acknowledge.

Martin Esslin, in his Preface to the 1961 edition of his seminal *The Theatre of the Absurd* wrote: 'what a critic wants to understand, he must at one time have deeply loved'. His comment applies equally to this critic's response to the political theatre movement in Britain – to one who similarly has 'derived some memorable experiences', who is 'convinced that as a trend it is important and significant, and has produced some of the finest dramatic achievements of our time'. But another of Martin Esslin's strictures also applies: '... if the concentration here on this one type of theatre gives the impression that its author is a partisan exclusively of its particular convention and cannot derive pleasure from any other type of theatre, this is due simply to the deliberate limitation of the book to one subject.'[10]

Catherine Itzin
September 1979

Introduction

'Works of art which lack artistic quality have no force, no matter how progressive they are politically. Chairman Mao

1968 – and before

1968 was a historic year which politicised a lot of people. Rarely can one year be singled out as an isolated turning point, but in the case of 1968 so many events coincided on a global scale that it clearly marked the end of an era in a historically unprecedented fashion, and the beginning of a period of equally unprecedented political consciousness and activism. People had 'never had it so good' (as Macmillan's election slogan had put it in 1959), and they wouldn't again.

1968 was the year of the Soviet, invasion of Czechoslovakia, the 'Prague Spring', the May Events in Paris (students joining forces with nine million striking workers to protest against the state), the Democratic Convention in Chicago (with tear gas and tanks in the streets), the peak of the Vietnam War (the Tet Offensive which put an end to the possibility of US 'victory'), anti-Vietnam demonstrations worldwide, the Vietnam Solidarity Campaign in full force in Britain with its Grosvenor Square demonstration of 30,000.

1968 was the year in which Martin Luther King and Robert Kennedy were assassinated, and the year of the attempted assassination of Rudi Dutschke. 1968 was the year that Richard Nixon was elected President of the United States; the year that the Chinese Cultural Revolution was at its peak. It was the year of anti-imperialist campaigns in Latin America.

1968 was the year after the war in Biafra and the Six Day War in Israel. It marked the beginning of Palestinian terrorist activities. It was the year after the fascist Colonels had seized power in the coup in Greece, the year after the murder of Che Guevara. It was the year after the Abortion Law Reform Act of 1967. It was the year of the crisis of capitalism reflected so dramatically in the devaluation of the pound in 1967.

1968 was the year that the Kenyan Asians were deprived of their rights as British citizens to enter the UK, following Enoch Powell's infamous 'rivers of blood' speech. It was the year that the Womens Liberation Movement found its voice: the year in which Germaine Greer's *Female Eunuch* and Kate Millett's *Sexual Politics* were published. It was the year in which economic sanctions were imposed on Rhodesia. It was the year that Shelter, the housing organisation, was set up, and Release started to help drug offenders. It was De Gaulle's last full year in office.

1968 was the year before British troops were sent into Northern Ireland 'to keep the peace', the year before the Londonderry March and Bloody Sunday. It was the year in which theatre censorship was abolished by Act of Parliament. And 1968 was the year of student revolt on an international scale. As well as Paris, there were riots in Warsaw, Belgrade, Berlin, Tokyo, Mexico City and Milan. It was the year of the student sit-ins in Britain, at Guildford and Hornsey Colleges of Art and at the LSE. 1968 was also – ironically – the United Nations' International Year of Human Rights.

For the theatre it was the radicalisation of the students which was most significant. For this was the period when the war babies came of age – including the products of the 1944 Education Act which had opened the doors of higher education to the working class. Student numbers in higher education increased dramatically in the fifties and sixties, and the proportion from working-class backgrounds increased to about 25 per cent.[1] Students became a socially identifiable group, and came to have an unusually important role, particularly in the area of ideology. Having inherited the earth – all the affluence and advantages that society had to offer – they discovered their disinheritance: the end of the big boom and its halcyon world-view, the end of the relative (if illusory) social stability which had characterised post-war capitalism.

Eric Hobsbawm, the Marxist historian, assessed the post-war period from an economic perspective:

> In the capitalist world there had never been a period of expansion and prosperity to compare with the fifties and sixties. All the developed industrial countries shared in it, even Britain whose capitalist economy was notoriously unable to overcome its problems ... if ever capitalism

looked as though it worked, it was in these decades. For, apart from dramatic technological progress and large profits, they brought strikingly impressive improvements in the standards of living of most people, due partly to rising wages and high employment, partly to great improvements in social security ... That there was plenty of room for improvement did not alter the evident fact that in material terms the lives of most ordinary people in the capitalist countries were undergoing a remarkable transformation for the better ... Capitalism and its ideologists therefore looked upon the world with considerable complacency.[2]

But in 1968 the materialist myth exploded for the middle-class young as much as for the working-class young, who literally *did* have it good compared to their parents and previous generations. Young people could see clearly, often for the first time, the contradictions between what they had been educated to expect and the reality of the world around them; they saw that their very standards of living were at the direct expense of the sub-standards of the imperialised third of the world.

1968 therefore marked the coming to consciousness – to political consciousness – of the war-baby generation, to an awareness of environmental plundering and pollution, to cold-war imperialism, to conspicuous consumption in the first and second worlds and to the struggles of the third world. The response was disillusionment, despair, pessimism – and anger. The significant thing was that this response – the rebellion – did not remain random, but became a movement of the political left, appealing (however confusedly) to Marx as a symbol of the revolutionary transformation of society. All of this came to be reflected in the theatre.

1968 not only politicised a new generation, it had strong political influences on important writers of the previous generation – Arden, Bond, Wesker, Mercer, Griffiths – whose work had been political to varying degrees in its subject matter or orientation. All these men were born within six years of each other and, in 1968, were all in their mid to late thirties. John Arden, already a major writer in 1968, 'a household name', as Roland Muldoon of CAST described him, with *Serjeant Musgrave's Dance* on exam syllabuses, was politicised by the Vietnam war, by India and by Ireland, and made a transition from committed pacifism to revolutionary socialism. With Margaretta D'Arcy he started writing a series of Irish plays which were virtually unseen in the British theatre in the seventies. They regarded themselves as political playwrights whose plays were censored for political reasons. With hindsight it was possible to see revolutionary politics latent even in Arden's pre-1968 plays.

A political perspective also explained the similarly paradoxical position of Edward Bond, who, for a major twentieth-century playwright, was also scandalously under-produced in Britain, and whose early plays aroused a violently hostile critical reaction, though they, too, very quickly came to be acknowledged as 'classics'. In retrospect Bond's plays could clearly be seen to be profoundly political (that is, written from a socialist perspective, albeit intuitive rather than intellectual): he himself came to acknowledge this. Though Bond's early plays were aesthetically accessible and of incontestable artistic quality, they were threatening, alienating and politically unacceptable. Hence the hostility. Arden's and D'Arcy's plays in the seventies were similarly threatening, alienating and politically unacceptable. Hence the subtle, but effective, censorship. Both Arden and D'Arcy and Edward Bond became closely involved in the politics of the theatre in the seventies, particularly in the Theatre Writers Union and its attempts to change the production system which so materially affected their work.

Arnold Wesker's response was almost the reverse. One of the very few avowedly socialist writers of the sixties, he retreated from the political arena at precisely the time the movement he had sought (in Centre 42) began to emerge. Yet, he too, in the seventies, was virtually unproduced: yet another 'classic' studied safely from academic syllabuses, just as Ibsen was studied. And, ironically, as far as the mainstream of contemporary theatre was concerned, Wesker could have been as dead as Ibsen.

David Mercer found himself in a similar situation: 'Three years ago,' he said in 1977, 'I married an Israeli, and my wife's brother came from Tel Aviv for the wedding. On the plane he fell into conversation with a bright young Englishman, and my name came up as the brother-in-law to be. "Ah, yes," said the bright young Englishman, "I've heard of him. Is he still alive?"'[3] In 1968 Mercer too had been writing plays from a Marxist perspective for several years and had been politically active with CND and the Socialist Labour League (later to become the Workers Revolutionary Party), with which he later parted company.

And Trevor Giffiths, though he did not start writing for the theatre until 1970, had also been active in CND and had written political journalism for 'New Left' publications throughout the sixties. 1968 did not politicise him as it did Howard Brenton and David Hare, for example, but it made him aware of political urgencies and prompted a change from journalism to the theatre. For many in the newer generation he became their Marxist mentor.

Just as there had been political or politically-inclined playwrights before 1968, there had also been precedents in the inter- and post-war periods for the development and proliferation of political theatre companies. There had been Unity Theatre, growing out of the Workers Theatre Movement of the thirties. There had been Joan Littlewood's Theatre Workshop at the Theatre Royal Stratford, in East London. And there had been Arnold Wesker's Centre 42 project. Each of these, in fact, represented aspirations reflected – and much more fully realised – by the alternative theatre movement of the seventies. Thus the work of CAST, The General Will, the early Red Ladder, Broadside Mobile Workers Theatre and North West Spanner had its ideological and stylistic roots in the work of Unity. Centre 42's ambitions to provide theatre for working-class people was achieved to a greater or lesser extent by companies like John McGrath's 7:84 Theatre Company, by Belt and Braces, Foco Novo and Monstrous Regiment. And Joan Littlewood's dream of fun palaces for the people – her concept of popular community theatre – was the goal of such diverse projects as The Combination in Deptford and Ed Berman's Inter-Action.

There were also less direct influences from previous historical periods of popular theatre, in particular from Russia and Germany. From post-revolutionary Russia, there was the Proletkult movement which aimed to politicise the masses; the Blue Blouses which emerged after the first wave of agitprop and during the comparative stability of the New Economic Policy; the use of posters for propaganda and the Theatre of Revolutionary Satire which animated them theatrically; the mass performance of *The Taking of the Winter Palace* in 1920; the work of Mayakovsky and Meyerhold. The radical theatre in Weimar Germany offered particularly suggestive parallels between that period and Britain in the seventies with the similar economic conditions contributing to a similar growth in political theatre. There was for example, the DADA desire to 'create gun in hand', to use art as a weapon; the use of expressionism to reflect the realities that the prevalent naturalistic mode tended to obscure or romanticise. There was the work of Piscator and his Proletarian theatre; the growth of the Volksbühne, the workers' audience organisation; Toller's political activism (for which he was imprisoned) and his political plays. This period in Germany produced a utilitarian worker-directed doctrine of art which also became prevalent in political theatre in Britain in the seventies.[4] Last, but not least, there was the hovering spirit of Brecht, perhaps the single greatest influence on the work of British writers and theatre companies alike, greatly reinforced by the visits of his Berliner Ensemble to Britain in 1956 and 1965.

There were more direct influences on political theatre in Britain in the occasional visits from (and some visits to) such foreign companies as the Living Theatre, La Mama, Bread and Puppet, the San Francisco Mime Troupe ('we try in our humble way to destroy the United States'), Luis Valdez's El Teatro Campesino, Joseph Chaikin's Open Theatre, Jerome Savary's Grand Magic Circus, Ariane Mnouchkine's Théâtre du Soleil, Grotowski's Theatre Laboratory.

But perhaps the most important immediate historical heritage of 1968 was the history of the Labour movement after the Second World War and its failure to institute socialism. The optimism after the war was immense and the expectations of the Labour government of 1945 were great – in anticipation of the nationalisation of industry and the creation of the welfare state. Clive Barker, who worked with Joan Littlewood and with Centre 42 and was of the Arden/Bond generation himself, remembered the euphoria on the occasion of the nationalisation of British Rail: 'Three of us took a train journey that ran over midnight, so after twelve we could say, "It's ours. It's ours."' And also of the nationalisation of the steel industry. 'But then,' said Barker, 'our families, working in steel, would come back and say, "It's no different, the same people are still in charge and it's less efficient than it was before."'[5] There was a great disillusionment – particularly amongst that first generation to be educated out of the working class – with the tokenism of Labour governments in nationalising industry and setting up the welfare state.

There was optimism again, particularly in the theatre, at the time of the putative 'revolution of fifty-six'. But by 1959 it had become clear that that impulse had been crushed – 'swallowed wholesale', as Barker said with some bitterness. The social system operated in the theatre system: 'We realised we couldn't change it.' And there was the progressive deterioration over the thirteen years of Conservative government from 1951. By 1963 spirits were at a low ebb in the Labour movement.

With the Labour government of 1964, there was some hope for social change. Within twelve months, however, it became clear that Labour was not going to alter anything; and this realisation motivated the first political theatre group, CAST, into alternative left politics and agitprop theatre. It was that vacuum of disillusionment that the events of 1968 began to fill. There was still, in 1968, some feeling of the possibility of reforming bourgeois capitalism, but the Conservative government of 1970, and the Labour government of 1974, finally crushed those hopes on the left, and fuelled the fire of political theatre.

This was the period of the proliferation of theatre companies and the heyday of agitprop. The working class was awakening and struggling. After 1972 – which David Edgar described as the period of 'class retreat' – there was again a change. It was a time – in a political climate – when the fervour could have been expected to flag. But while there were changes in strategies and structures, it became a new period of unprecedented growth in the theatre. Throughout, the left and its theatre were faced with the lack of a clear Marxist alternative to the existing political parties, and with the constant question of how to relate the theatre to political reality. The history of political theatre from 1968 to 1978 was the story of how that question was confronted by theatre workers.

Here are their activities, their analyses and some of their answers.

1968

In 1968, Jim Haynes – the expatriate American 'libertarian anarchist' who had started his counter-cultural activities in a bookshop-cum-theatre in Edinburgh in the mid-sixties – opened the Drury Lane Arts Lab, a warehouse at the top of Drury Lane converted into a variety of spaces for exhibitions, eating, drinking, theatre performances, music and cinema. In the one short year of its existence, it had an enormous impact, capturing the spirit of the counter-culture, presenting the first of a new generation of writers, actors and directors who were rejecting the structures of conventional theatre institutions. Portable Theatre, Freehold, Pip Simmons and the People Show either started at the Drury Lane Arts Lab, or played there regularly. The spirit of the Drury Lane Arts Lab lingered through the seventies, spawning dozens of imitations all over the country. By the end of the seventies there were over 140 arts centres throughout England, Scotland and Wales which owed something to Jim Haynes and his vision of an alternative culture.

Edinburgh in the sixties, and on into the seventies, was an important area of fertilisation for alternative theatre – in the annual Edinburgh Festival with its showcasing and coming together of British and international fringe theatre, and in particular with the Traverse Theatre opened in January 1963 under the direction of Jim Haynes and later Max Stafford-Clark. Haynes went on to invent and promulgate the Arts Lab, while Stafford-Clark was eventually (in 1974) to be co-founder with William Gaskill and David Hare of Joint Stock Theatre Group and (in 1979) to take over as

Artistic Director of the Royal Court Theatre. Many writers too saw their first work staged by the tiny Traverse before finding larger audiences often as a result of transfers to the studio theatres in the provinces being set up largely in imitation of the Traverse itself and to the new 'fringe' venues in London.

One such was the Open Space, the first (in 1968) of several important London venues. It was the brainchild of actress and administrator Thelma Holt and another expatriate American director and critic, Charles Marowitz, who had previously worked with Peter Brook on the RSC LAMDA Theatre of Cruelty season and who, indeed, had been involved with Haynes in 1966 in mounting a London Traverse season at the Jeannetta Cochrane Theatre. Their objective was to create an outlet for the best of new writing from England and America, and to provide a base for a permanent experimental company. Over the decade, they were more successful in the former aim than the latter, primarily for financial reasons, as the Open Space like other fringe ventures remained under-subsidised. For a brief period Marowitz did work with a semi-permanent company, proving his arguments for better funding by producing his best work, particularly his Shakespeare adaptations.

The other brave new venture in 1968 was lunchtime theatre, pioneered from 1966 by playwright David Halliwell (author of *Little Malcolm and His Struggle Against the Eunuchs*) and his shoe-string production company Quipu, operating at various times until 1973 at the New Arts Theatre, LAMDA (where it presented Halliwell's *K. D. Dufford Hears K. D. Dufford Ask K. D. Dufford How K. D. Dufford'll Make K. D. Dufford*), from a cellar in Soho, the Mercury Theatre in Notting Hill and finally from the Little Theatre in Garrick Yard off St Martin's Lane. Quipu was one of the first theatre companies to function as a collective of theatre writers 'committed to the establishment of a new kind of production organisation in which the means of production are owned, controlled, and developed by the artists whose work is being produced'.[1] It espoused what it described as a 'revolutionary' form of theatre – multiviewpoint drama, and as an illustration of the theory, Halliwell used the story of 'dog bites man'. Halliwell: 'In the multiviewpoint play you show the incident from the point of view of the man, from the point of view of the dog and then from the point of view of the bite.'[2] Though Halliwell pursued the theory in some of his plays in the early seventies, it proved to be a dead-end for him and for Quipu.

It was also in 1968 that a new arts magazine – *Time Out* – began publication. It grew out of the same soil as such counter-culture publications as IT (*International Times*) and *Black Dwarf*, but very quickly became a large-scale viable commercial venture. Its contributions to the development of alternative theatre – in providing free listings of productions and regular, reliable, sympathetic reviews of an area of theatre virtually ignored by the establishment press – was immeasurable.

Yet another expatriate American, Ed Berman, spear-headed lunchtime theatre in 1968, hand-in-hand with the community theatre that eventually became the Inter-Action network of community arts and theatre activities. Berman's lunchtime theatre migrated from Bayswater through Soho to a permanent central London venue, the Almost Free Theatre which opened in 1972. The development of Berman's Inter-Action is described in detail below as one of the most successful examples of an important area of new work in British theatre in the seventies.

As is CAST (the Cartoon Archetypical Slogan Theatre of Roland and Claire Muldoon), from 1965 the first avowedly socialist theatre company of the sixties, setting precedents of style, politics and new audiences amongst the working class – precedents subsequently followed in some form by most of the political theatre companies of the seventies. One of these was AgitProp Street players, later to become Red Ladder, originating from the AgitProp Information Service which provided posters and propaganda for the counter-culture of the late sixties, and developing into one of the most sophisticated and highly subsidised Marxist companies in the seventies.

It was CAST who provided one of the many catalysing influences on the work of John Arden and Margaretta D'Arcy in the process of their conversion from conventional theatre to alternative theatre – in their historic collaboration on *Harold Muggins Is a Martyr* at Unity Theatre in 1968. Whilst the following chronicles of the emergence of new theatre companies in 1968 illustrate the sources of new energy and ideas – the seedbeds of socially committed and socialist theatre – the essay on the work of John Arden and Margaretta D'Arcy shows how the attitudes of the previous generation altered in response to political events and an increase of political consciousness, how they joined forces as part of the political theatre movement of the seventies.

'The greatest privilege of my life was one Sunday morning, sitting in bed reading a review by that guy who used to do The Sunday Times *reviews ... that famous one ... Hobson, who was saying why does Arden deal with such guttersnipes and shitbags ... how can such a great name besmirch himself ... you know?'*[1] Roland Muldoon, March 1978

CAST (Cartoon Archetypical Slogan Theatre)

CAST was the first and for a long time the only avowedly socialist theatre company of the sixties. It was – and was still at the end of the seventies – one of the most important, not only for its content, but also its unique style and the context in which it performed. CAST was started in 1965 – that year of disillusionment following the Labour victory in the 1964 General Election – by Roland and Claire Muldoon. 'Just by historical accident', said Roland Muldoon, always a master of the throw-away and under-stated aside.

CAST's origins were at Unity Theatre, 'run then by the CP and doing silly plays like *Everything in the Garden*', said Muldoon. He and Claire ran a technical course at Unity in the evenings and had visions of this 'socialist theatre in the middle of Camden Town as a centre of dissension'. But by that time the Communist Party had turned away from revolutionary politics into mainstream British politics with its 'British Road to Socialism' policy. It wanted to be more respectable and Unity followed suit. So the Muldoons were disappointed. Roland Muldoon: 'We weren't in the CP, but we were coming round to Marxism. We were young and we were part of an enormous resistance to established politics – CND, Ban The Bomb, Anti-Apartheid, that sort of thing. We wanted to bring *this* into Unity. We were expelled for our efforts.'

By 1965, thoroughly disillusioned with the new Labour government and realising that there was nothing left-wing about it at all, the Muldoons resolved to form a workers' theatre group. The question was how? They found themselves 'sitting in a hired pub room in Camden Town, dreaming of changing the world, and theatre along with it ... It slowly began to dawn on us that the rooms in which we held our exploratory exercises were, on other nights, where our potential audiences sat.'[2] Looking back, Muldoon said:

We were the first of the contemporary batch of theatre groups to orientate itself towards the Labour movement. With twelve million people voting Labour, twenty-two million people going to work, with *x* million belonging to trade unions, it is, to put it simply, a big target .. It is clear to us that there are potential audiences throughout the country hungry for the service of the theatre, theatre that is prepared to gear itself to the functions of, for want of a better word, the community ... We are invited to union area AGM's, to towns and pubs, to where nothing has ever happened before, to political debates, workplaces, youth clubs and to the venues we like best of all – working-class socials.[3]

In retrospect, Muldoon could identify four definitive periods in political theatre and how CAST had related to them. 'In 1964 there was nothing; in 1965 there was nothing – except us. In 1966 there was something. By 1967 there was a counter-culture and by 1968 there was the whole arts lab scene. It happened quickly, almost overnight. That was the first period of political theatre – the period of protest, into which we were trying to insert a dialectical analysis.' That ended about 1969. The second period was the early seventies, after the Tories got in again and Arts Council subsidy started to extend to fringe companies. 'Then,' said Muldoon, 'there was a great move towards the working class by theatre companies, a period when the working class was becoming interested in straight class politics.' The third period followed the 'social contract' during which 'the I.M.F. won a major victory and forced the Labour government to halt the rise in the standard of living of the working class'. In this period CAST coupled the collapse of social democratic reformism to the rise of grass-roots fascism. The fourth period, Muldoon predicted, would be the arrival of a Tory government committed to class warfare.

Ironically CAST did not receive any Arts Council subsidy until its eleventh year, 1976, at the end of the third period. Muldoon: 'Then, in true showbiz style, the Arts Council gave us a grant.'[4] The grant and the changing political climate had had an effect:

We are changing our attitudes back to the beginning. We're not talking about what was happening in the seventies, we're talking again about confusion between fascism and social democracy and disillusionment. Political groups who are interested now in how wages alone are exploited must wonder what they are going to say to their audiences. They should be thinking about alienation and what has led to the rise of the National Front, the seeming collapse of the credibility of socialist ideology as a challenge to the capitalist state. We think we should be producing quick-hit fifteen-minute/half-hour plays. Like back to the old days. Get in, get out. This is a change from the past few years, when we and other groups were doing one to two hour plays, about this or that issue of concern. But that doesn't echo the audience's alienation any more. So we're back again to what the genre collectors call agitprop.

Or, rather, agit-*pop*, which was how Muldoon described CAST's distinctive style. CAST found its first audiences in folk clubs. Muldoon: 'Although often run by a Communist Party member, they attracted a wide audience. These clubs became our target and our springboard ... We were allowed on in the interval. We soon learned that we had to work fast, cut fast, to get at least a laugh a minute, if we were to stop the bastards going for a beer in the middle of it. This became the pattern of our work.'[5] CAST's style developed in the music hall tradition. Muldoon:

> The most important thing CAST did in the history of political theatre was turn to the audience. At the time, we actually invented looking straight in the audience's face and telling them what we were talking about. We called it 'presentationism' – sort of here we are, entertainers, but theatre as well. It's like a three-card trick. Once you get them watching, the magic starts. You start telling them a story, cut fast, distract them from what they thought was going on, catch them with a glass of beer in their hand, so they stay and watch. Now we're not *so* fast because people are prepared to sit and wait for a theatre group to come on. We have a style and a philosophy of the style – invented in that pub in Camden Town. Peter Brook used to come and say, 'Where did you get that style from?' As if I owed him something! And I told him our influences were working-class entertainers – and they are. Chuck Berry and Little Richard for instance – they were there – they were really present on stage and they influenced our acting style more than any avant garde experiment. Theatre then was all about sitting down and standing up and walking out of french windows. We were the first rock'n'roll theatre group. Other groups eventually took their historical references from the Russian Revolution and the agitprop of Germany, but we took ours from pop culture. We were a group with a gang ideology. All that collectivism came later.

The CAST style was distinctive, and so was the central character who figured in almost all of their shows – Muggins. Muggins was inspired in part by the Good Soldier Schweyk, in part by an old music hall song. 'Muggins,' said Muldoon, 'is the English archetype of the bloke who does everything and gets no reward. Charlie Chaplin, if you like. An Everyman. Except in each show he or she has a different Christian name – Harold Muggins, Hilda Muggins, Horatio Muggins, Maud Muggins. There's a part of everyone in

Muggins, and a Muggins in part of everyone. Muggins represents the working class – the people who are mugged!'

CAST's first show was *John D. Muggins is Dead*, dating back to 1965, before the RSC/Peter Brook *US*. With his usual modesty, Muldoon described it as 'the most important play of the time'. It was about the war in Vietnam, but from a dialectical perspective which was unusual at that early date. Muldoon:

> Instead of just saying that the bomb should stop and there should be peace in the world, we said that America was conditioning its youth through a process that we were all being culture vultures about – Elvis Presley, hippies, flower power, rock'n'roll. We showed that in the end John D. Muggins is taken out to South East Asia, full of his culture, full of an idea of freedom – just a victim of this bullshit. And he goes out to Asia and he dies. For what reason did he die, we asked? At that time that was quite sensational! Because folk clubs were into saying – we're really about peace. Though there was a groundswell of people even then who were much more initiated. We hit between the official ideological line, which was peace, and the idea that imperialism is created by capitalist society, the ultimate expression of which is to murder people in Vietnam, including our own people.

CAST's second show, which went into their repertoire in 1966, was *Mr Oligarchy's Circus*. Muldoon: 'We said capitalism was a circus, the ruling class was the circus master and the Labour Party was its bedfellow. It was a very funny play, very popular, playing at colleges to the radical students' movement in 1968. Red Saunders (later with Rock Against Racism) was with the group then, and he was very strong as Mr Oligarchy. But it also lost its meaning after a few years, because it was a bit naive perhaps, anti-Labour government, and hitting at everything.'

About this time CAST got together one of their most popular shows – *The Trials of Horatio Muggins*. This was a direct response to the radical student movement. Horatio was an ordinary worker who was tried by the revolutionary left – the extreme red-flag-waving people. He was tried for being petty-bourgeois, for being sold on colour telly and washing machines and for not caring about the world. Muldoon:

> At the end, though, he turned the trial around and said, 'You treat me as if I don't understand capitalism, yet I've been eating Walls' sausages all my life . . . you must talk to me in a language I can understand.' Horatio was saying – you've told me what's wrong but you haven't told me what I can do about it, how to deal with it. At the end of the trial he lectured his judges – the ultra-left – on the need for the

working class to strike and organise itself. But he couldn't believe in ideologies coming down from above – from students and intellectuals – just because they'd got turned on by it. He gave the students a lecture in a comic way about their own political absurdity. Audiences laughed at both sides and felt uncomfortable in the middle.

Muldoon explained:

In those days there wasn't even an organised revolutionary left, really, so there was quite a lot of open debate. Up to 1968/69 it seemed that all the left was doing was leading people to the US Embassy. We got fed up with this so we aimed our work at the working class ourselves. It was open debate to see which groups would develop into a substantial political force. So we listened to the arguments and got turned on by Marxist philosophy. The group we identified with was IS – International Socialists. The IMG – International Marxist Group, the only other alternative at that time, seemed to be into everything else but the working class. We used to joke at the time that they were into 'balding men's lib' – anything but the working class changing things. All the ideological debates at that time were about the Russians being state capitalists. That really got to us, because once you realised that Russia wasn't a socialist society you *could* talk about socialism to the working class of this country and agree with them about Stalinism which they feared. The IMG were saying Russia was a degenerated workers' state: we didn't know what that meant. We'd gone through the CP and Unity and the trades unions and seen the consequences of Stalinism. All through Vietnam the CP called for peace, but it seemed clear to us that the Vietnamese had to win. We could see that a new left party was going to be formed and that we could comment with our theatre on the relationship between that party and the class. That's what political theatre could be about, yet be free of dictation and the need to defend state capitalist oppression.

By this time we'd somehow got a reputation of being so red no one would touch us. We were self-educated working class: left school at fifteen, now twenty-one, twenty-two. We'd been bohemian for a couple of years, escaping our class origins. When we went to Unity we were beginning consciously to look for an expression of dissension. We had trouble with the counter-culture hippies. We played *John D. Muggins Is Dead* at the UFO Club in Tottenham Court Road, which was run by the *International Times* (IT) and where the Pink Floyd used to play. And they said, 'You're terrible, you're talking about killing and Vietnam and the real thing is love.' We just said, 'Go screw your arse,' you know. We did do a film in 1967 – a sort of protest film, an anti-Vietnam film made with the Vietnam Solidarity Campaign. It had a lot of people in it – Adrian Mitchell reading his poetry, Frankie Armstrong singing, Tariq Ali, Obi Egbuna, the anti-University folk. We filmed in the streets, at demos, outside the American Embassy and at a big pro-Viet

Cong benefit at the old YMCA in Tottenham Court Road where we
did *John D. Muggins*. It was very funny. John Arden came out and
read a poem on Ireland. It went on forever. Half-way through he said,
'Ooops, I skipped three pages.' He got the biggest laugh of the night.
Everybody was falling about because nobody had even noticed. But
they don't eat shit, the Ardens. They don't let anybody do it to them.

Not even CAST who later collaborated with the Ardens on a play
at Unity. It was shortly after this – in 1970 – that CAST did *Muggins'
Awakening*, which Muldoon described as their 'most advanced' show
stylistically. Ideologically it was a 'mind blow', but their IS contacts
'found it too way out'. It was about the nightmare again, of a world
that didn't make sense. Muldoon: 'It was a smashing play, high style.
It also took the piss out of the new wave of theatre, like burning
the butterflies in *US*. In the middle, we would light matches and
take a bow and the audience would clap as they did at the Royal
Shakespeare Company. We'd tell them that the world was much
worse than that crap, and how bad it was – going through Vietnam
and imperialism. Audiences used to sit and go "wow". By that time
they'd had the rock groups – the Beatles, the Who – and were quite
sophisticated. But the IS felt quite horrified because it wasn't enough
of a class analysis. About this time we began to worry about whether
we were just getting off on our own trip.'

Auntie Maud Was A Happening Thing came next. 'Quite Funny,'
said Muldoon, 'but not a great success. Auntie Maud was a bloke
really, representing capitalism, dying on a bed of his own making.
But everyone was willing him to live and to lead, even though he
was dead. Nobody could find anything else, so he kept having to
get off his deathbed and lead, for lack of any alternative.'

In 1972 there was increasing dissension within the group and
it started to split up. Those that left CAST created Kartoon Klowns,
and Claire and Roland Muldoon re-formed their company. The first
show by the newly constituted CAST was *Come In Hilda Muggins*
in 1973, a response to the big new issue of women's liberation.
Muldoon:

We showed a TV programme like *This Is Your Life* in which they
were telling Hilda all about her life. The telly were going to do
something fascinatingly different; instead of a celebrity, they were going
to take an ordinary person off the street and portray her life. But Hilda
didn't know what the fuck was going on – with everyone interpreting
her life for her. In the end she just said: 'Look, I work in a factory.
I'm fed up with the whole lot.' We got a lot of flack from the women's

movement who said stupid things like 'how can you have a play with four men and one woman!' We worried about it then, but could never come up with answers that pleased them. But now, if they persist with their daft criticisms we tell them to fuck off. It was about women in relation to capitalist economics, pointing out that working women – as well as men – should be about the fight for equal pay and unionisation in addition to their other needs. This was the beginning of Hilda's strength as a working-class woman. We actually had some controversial things to say at a time when feminism was divorced from socialism. Trouble is, it still too often is, and the confusion continues.

Sam the Man came next, in 1974, and stayed in the repertoire until 1977. Muldoon described it as a 'very successful play for touring and playing to working-class audiences'. It was about a Labour MP, dyed red: Bevan said of him 'his blood runs red with the cause of his class'. The play followed his career from the 1945 Labour government to the present, a predecessor of Trevor Griffiths' TV series *Bill Brand*. Muldoon:

> In the end the poor fellow was likeable, but ridiculous. We showed him as a nice old fool and really caught the audience out. They'd always voted Labour and believed in a Labour left, yet they were laughing at him. There was a poignancy: he was appealing to them as a real live human being, yet his politics were meaningless in terms of the class. The play was presenting the dilemma the left is in – there's a real vacuum in terms of working-class politics, which no one, as yet, is filling.

CAST got their Arts Council grant on the strength of *Sam the Man*. And that threw them into something of a quandary. The grant enabled them to go full-time for the first time in eleven years, which meant the end of doing two jobs, one during the day and theatre at night – what Muldoon described as 'living the contradictions'. But it made them slightly anxious about 'official interference' especially as they were about to embark on a play about Northern Ireland. Muldoon:

> But we thought fuck that – the Arts Council – and went ahead in 1977 with *The Other Way Around* which basically said the British government were the terrorists in Northern Ireland. We were worried about the Prevention of Terrorism Act and the bombs going off because we lived in Central London and became paranoiac and feared that the State would be spying on us. The next show was called *Cuts*. That was still 1977. The play started then, and ended in 1984 with everyone being cut by the Labour Party. All the services had gone and the working class had failed to resist. We were saying that if we allowed

it all to go on in the usual bland way, there would be mass unemployment and rampant racialism by 1984. It was a very successful show except that its predictions became truer every day. It thought, however, that Labour would win the 1979 election.

Then came *Goodbye Union Jack* (still 1977 with CAST feeling they had to show super-productivity to their new employer, the Arts Council). Muldoon: 'This was a Calendar of the Social Contract, and its victory, with nobody knowing what it was – going on to the rise of the National Front in the vacuum of Labour politics, covering Grunwicks, Lewisham, up to Christmas 1977. It was like a time bomb – tick-tick-tick-tick – ending with the question of what happens tomorrow. A calendar of political malaise.'

Still feeling – perhaps unnecessarily – paranoiac, the eyes of Big Brother Arts Council looking over their shoulder, CAST started 1978 by working on an adventurous big play called *Overdose* – about a surfeit of politics and disillusionment. Muldoon: 'It was an investigation into failed ideology, not saying the left had failed, but pointing out that they certainly hadn't succeeded. It was going to end in 1983 with a big battle against the fascists. But we scrapped it because it was negative.'

In response to how they read the climate of opinion, CAST returned to their hard-hit, half-hour format with *Confessions of a Socialist*[6] – about the archetypal working man (Harry Muggins this time), a Universal Gottlieb Junction Joint machiner who gets fed up, packs it all in, and then misses the Revolution in Britain while package-holidaying in Spain. By the end, Harry wakes up and discovers it was all a dream – and he's not quite sure whether it was a good one or a bad one. Muldoon: 'With *Confessions* we'd just about come full circle – back to *John D. Muggins Is Dead* in length, in style and content. Because we were talking about the nightmare world again and saying we must get harder.'

The show CAST were working on then – for 1979 – was to be their most serious so far, an Anti-Nazi League play called *What Happens Next*? Muldoon: 'That's a big question, you know what I mean?'

What would happen next for CAST and for political theatre generally was also a big question as far as Muldoon was concerned. Subsidy was crucial. Muldoon: 'In days of inflation, cuts and labour-saving investment drives, fuelled as it is by blatant capitalist policies emanating from the government, it remains essential that labour-intensive theatre be underwritten by increased funding.'[7]

Some people on the left were arguing that the subsidy boom of the seventies was damaging to political theatre, turning commitment and activism ('nothing to lose') into a job of work with hierarchies and expectations not unlike those of the commercial production system.[8] Muldoon disagreed: subsidy gave groups like Red Ladder and 7:84 the opportunity to do 'political' plays they might not otherwise have had, and for CAST to do 'political theatre' full-time. A contradiction it might be: taking money from precisely the state that the left would, in revolutionary circumstances, do away with, but a contradiction that had to be lived with. Muldoon:

> The trouble with subsidy, like everything the state does: it doesn't *really* know what's going on, the twists and turns of public debate. So some theatre becomes like an extension of the National Health Service bureaucracy. And then there's the issue of productivity: you're taking public money, so you're under an obligation to produce a product. There is pressure on groups to be more productive in terms of quantity than is particularly healthy in terms of quality. This tends to make groups lose touch. Take the firemen's strike in 1977, a dramatic event when the firemen were challenged by the Social Contract and defeated in just a month. But what could a theatre company do about it between Christmas and January? What happens is they write more and more abstractly, move away from the real concrete issues upon which an exciting relevant theatre should comment. And there are, of course, problems within the left – it's actually an ideological battle-field. And that's good for theatre, the Arts Council and the audience. Debate about contemporary issues is the real role for theatre.

As for CAST's function and the future: 'I believe we are again going in a direction where theatre has never been before. That is as a service and not as a bottle of medicine on a high shelf that promises to do you good if you can stretch up and reach it.'[9] And: 'We're a middle-aged group now, so we're in a position to talk about the last twenty years of alienation and what it means for the future. I think there is a new demand developing in the Labour movement. Unions have had the virtuous socialist theatre groups, now they're pissed off and they want entertainment. CAST will be there, giving them *political entertainment*. We're going to burn our bridges. We're not going to break our arse for the Arts Council, but we will for the working class.'

CAST was involved in one of the classic, legendary events in political theatre in 1968 when they collaborated with John Arden and Margaretta D'Arcy on the play *Harold Muggins Is a Martyr*, produced at Unity Theatre and involving many people who were later to become important in the political theatre movement. It was a historic occasion, too, because it was one of the things that marked a turning point in John Arden's career as a dramatist, coming during the period of his developing political consciousness. According to Muldoon, it was Arden who made the effort and contacted CAST. Muldoon:

> Arden invited us to his house in Muswell Hill, and we went up there thinking he must be fucking rich, because ... like we'd heard about him. He was almost a household name. Not as big as Wesker or Osborne, but my mum knew who he was. And we went to see him with all humility, though we were really crazy then, you know, hard to talk to. We were resistant to big deal offers and all the flash Liberals getting into the political theatre movement. We thought Arden would be part of the same scene. But then as we walked down the road in Muswell Hill we thought, well, this isn't really a rich area. And then there was a 'ban the bomb' sign on his house. He opened the door and there was no carpet on the floor and you had to draw up a house-brick to sit down. It was quite surprising really, to see this great play-wright living like that. And Arden said he didn't want his stuff on TV and that he was really into resistance and he said: 'I'd like to write a play for you.' Now half the group didn't want to know, but I thought it was a good idea, especially if it went on at Unity, because I thought we might be able to recapture the Unity spirit if we put on a successful production there. So we went ahead.
>
> Arden brought John Fox from the Welfare State down to build funny things around the theatre, and we went in and put a red flag up. The Management Committee at Unity took a decision that it would offend the neighbourhood and pulled it down. That was typical. Unity didn't went to know really, so we had to import people and *that* started the problems.
>
> Arden wrote the script. He liked the Muggins character so he used it, but made him a petty bourgeois, a shopkeeper, and wrote about the rise of fascism. I thought his target was unusual. Horatio Muggins had been working class; Harold was middle class. This fascinated me.

Harold Muggins Is a Martyr was, according to Albert Hunt in his book on Arden, Arden's 'most consciously propagandist play to date, about the employees of a broken-down old café which is taken over and modernised by a set of gangsters; they rebel against both their boss Harold Muggins, and the gangsters who are running him.'[10] It was written in what was to become D'Arcy/Arden's political theatre style in later plays, particularly *The Non-Stop Connolly Show*, but at this stage, it was fairly crude. Arden's text posed lots of problems for CAST. Muldoon: 'Between you and me, when we got down to doing this sodding play, I couldn't move anything. I mean his scanning lines, his perfect English was impossible. I mean we made up our own lines in CAST. So Raymond Levine, who was in the play, had to come out and he had five pages and he would just cut it down to four lines because that's the way we would do it.'

The play also proved too long for CAST:

> In the end we produced our very first two and a half hour spectacle, it went on forever ... and ever and ever. John and Margaretta were in it. On the first night, the Ardens were pronouncing their own words perfectly. I had a part in it – Buzzard the solicitor, I think it was – but I never learned my lines. For my entrance, I lined them all up at the back of the stage, because that was the only way as a director I could get in and block. So I walked in. I had an enormous great joint, and my lines written on pieces of paper, you know, and I just walked in and the whole audience broke down in laughter. Because I'd made the only CAST gesture of the whole evening. I staggered across, looked straight at the front row of the audience, held them and read the lines. There was a great clap and John just looked at me seething, as if I'd set the whole kaboodle up to get the only laugh of the evening. He regarded the text as sacred.

There were, according to Muldoon, 'internal rows about nudity'. Muldoon: 'Arden said, we'll have a naked woman and confront the audience with her. So I said, "No, shit man, we'll have a naked woman at the back with light bulbs going up and down on her tits, throw it away, you know." As we believed it was a throwaway point that was being made. And he said, "No, no we'll make a big point of nudity." So we said, "But we come from a different generation than you, John." And then the shit hit the fan. And he said, "You're more arrogant than Sir Laurence." I think the girl that was nude ended up on the Central Committee of the Workers Revolutionary Party.'

Albert Hunt, in his book on Arden, gave a rather different account of this scene. 'Ironically, the most successful scene has no direct connection with the political message, it's a strip scene. One of the gangsters who is transforming the Muggins' café introduces a stripper. With great excitement Muggins asks her to strip in front of him. She does so, beautifully but coldly, showing him, and the audience, an attractive body. But when she's completely naked, Muggins simply says, disappointed, "Is that all?" '[11] Hunt found that scene successful, but the play as a whole, less successful. Muldoon said it was a success after the first night, and after the train strike taking place then had ended: 'The audiences came and they used to debate all night.'

But the first night was a disaster. Muldoon:

> It was fucking atrocious. It went on and on and it was falling apart. The first night was the carriage trade and the critics – Peter Brook's gang was there and Wolf Mankowitz. There were the fans of CAST and the fans of Arden thinking this was going to be the greatest mix in history – forget sliced bread. 'Cos it was a cast in a million. But by this time Arden was being so fucking awkward and Margaretta so ridiculous that our lot was hiding from everyone. We were out the back getting stoned, you know. Didn't care a fuck. Said to ourselves, 'Ah shit, as soon as this is over, we'll go back to our audiences.'

John Arden remembered the play as 'perhaps no great shakes' and felt that critics had 'small idea what it was we were up to – but the occasion of its performance did give rise to a remarkable conference, really, symposium of many left-wing artistic groups and individuals who, maybe for the first time were made aware of each other and their respective work: and who were enabled in many cases to establish joint action and permanent cultural/political contacts.'[12]

Muldoon:

> The greatest privilege of my life was the next morning, Sunday, sitting in bed reading a review by that guy who used to do the *Sunday Times* reviews ... that famous one ... Hobson, who said why does Arden deal with such guttersnipes and shitbags ... how can such a great name besmirch himself, you know? We nearly hit the big time, you know, but we didn't want to. Apparently it was quite a turning point for the Ardens, but we haven't worked together since. We said, never again.[13]

'It is unfortunate that the jury should have to read this turgid piece of prose.' Judge Melford Stevenson in the High Court at *The Ballygombeen Bequest* trial, November 1977

John Arden and Margaretta D'Arcy

John Arden was always a political playwright in the broadest sense of the word. In the fifties and early sixties he described himself as a pacifist: '... I was a militant war-resister and an activist of the Committee of 100, perpetrating civil disobedience at every flourish of my coffee cup.'[1] He was closely involved with the CND movement and was a regular contributor to *Peace News*. In 1959 in defending *Serjeant Musgrave's Dance* against critical hostility (Harold Hobson called it 'another dreadful ordeal'[2]), Arden outlined his pacifist political outlook:

> This is not a nihilistic play ... Nor does it advocate bloody revolution. I have endeavoured to write about the violence that is so evident in the world and to do so through a story that is partly one of wish-fulfilment ... Complete pacifism is a very hard doctrine: and if this play appears to advocate it with perhaps some timidity, it is probably because I am naturally a timid man – and also because I know that if I am hit, I very easily hit back: and I do not care to preach too confidently what I am not sure I can practise.[3]

There was, even then, a definite note of ambivalence in Arden's pacifist stance, in retrospect raising the question as to whether there was not an unrealised sense that pacifism might not be an adequate – or indeed ultimately practicable – political response.

Certainly by the late sixties Arden had radically altered his political outlook. He had become disillusioned with the ineffectuality of policies of non-violence; he was sympathetic to, if not positively advocating, violent revolutionary activity to achieve a socialist society. He had become a revolutionary socialist. In defending himself in 1977 against accusations of a 'deteriorating aesthetic,' he described the difference between 'then and now', before and after his 'politicisation':

It occurred to me ... that a 'genuine Arden work' in fact meant 'a play like *Serjeant Musgrave's Dance*, which does not come to any positive conclusion – whereas non-genuine Arden would be 'Arden at last affirming from his own hard experience the need for revolution and a socialistic society: and moreover convinced that his artistic independence and integrity will be strengthened rather than compromised by so *doctrinaire* a stance ...' Twelve years ago I looked on at people's struggles, and wrote about them as an onlooker. Without consciously intending it, I have become a participant.[4]

There were reasons – including experiences in the USA in 1967 and in India in 1969, not to mention Ireland – for Arden's radical change in attitude. And though to many bewildered observers it may have seemed a Jekyll and Hyde transformation at the time, it was in retrospect the logical – arguably inevitable – conclusion to his political concerns and commitments. As Albert Hunt pointed out in his excellent study of Arden's plays up to 1972, Arden had always been 'a revolutionary' in the sense of rejecting authority, and 'this revolutionary attitude is embodied in "the style and type of the entertainment" offered in his plays.'[5]

Arden's first political awakening was to the politics of the production system, and to the realisation that political *content* was only a part of political drama and the politics of the theatre.

... by 1968 it had become apparent that the regular theatre for which I had written most of my plays was no longer an adequate medium for ... entertaining and invigorating audiences ... The so-called *revolution* at the Royal Court and Theatre Workshop in the late fifties had been largely a revolution of *content* ... the structure of theatre-management had scarcely altered a jot ... Nevertheless, even after my visit to New York and all the innovations I found there, my objection to 'regular theatre' remained primarily aesthetic. Plays presented according to normal practice were lacking in essential impact: there must surely be some far more 'electrical' method of putting the stuff across ... That an attempt to achieve this was bound of its very nature to involve serious political difficulties within the social set up of the theatrical profession itself was not at first apparent. At this time my only concept of *political* drama was one of *plays written upon political subjects*: and I was concerned only to improve the conditions under which such work could be set afoot ...[6]

'Improvement of working conditions' after 1968 took the form of direct confrontation with conventional theatre managements, and of political action and participation. Before that Arden's efforts took

the form of trying alternatives outside of mainstream theatre –
'initiatives in what is called "community theatre"'.[7]

It was at this time and in this area that John Arden first began
collaborating with his wife Margaretta D'Arcy, a collaboration that
was, by the seventies, also to embrace the subject of Ireland, a
collaboration, as Arden pointed out, 'between playwrights of very
different national backgrounds':

> I am English and a product of English public schools and univer-
> sity – plus three years experience in Scotland as a conscript and,
> later, a student at an art college. My theatrical experience began with
> student work as an amateur actor and writer, followed by the sub-
> mission of plays to the BBC radio and the Royal Court in the
> fifties. D'Arcy is Irish, and began her career in Dublin in the small
> experimental theatres that flourished there in the same period, where
> there was a much keener sense of the political implications of the
> drama than could be found in this country. She then came to England
> and worked as an actress in London club theatres and at the Horn-
> church Rep, which was the first of such regional companies to be
> funded from local authority finance. She had, therefore, from the start
> a degree of involvement in what is now known as 'community theatre'.
> We met in 1955, shortly after I had left Edinburgh: and my earliest
> published plays were thus written under the immediate influences of (a)
> Scotland and (b) Ireland – a joint impulse which has never in fact
> worn off. In particular, we have been constantly involved in political
> and community theatre in Ireland since 1971.[8]

In 1960, Arden collaborated with Margaretta D'Arcy on *The
Business of Good Government*, a nativity play created for performance at Christmas in a village church in Brent Knoll, Somerset. There was also the Kirkbymoorside Community Entertainment
in 1963:

> Margaretta D'Arcy set this up in our house in Yorkshire by means
> of an advertisement which I published in *Encore*. This was a free-
> ranging series of plays, films, concerts, poetry readings, children's
> shows, etc., based on broadly libertarian anarchist artistic views, and
> which brought together a lot of people who have since gone in many
> varied directions. Its politics were implicit rather than overt, and very
> much of the unstructured sixties.[9]

Then there was *Ars Longa, Vita Brevis*, based on children's games
and improvisation, produced by Peter Brook in his Theatre of
Cruelty season at LAMDA in 1963 and later at the Kirkbymoorside
Festival in Yorkshire in 1964. There was *The Royal Pardon* originating from 'a series of bedtime stories told to our own children

(aged 2–6)' and presented in 1966 to older children at the Beaford Arts Centre Festival in Devon. Insofar as John Arden and Margaretta D'Arcy were drawn in these instances to non-theatre audiences in non-theatre venues during the early sixties, they were laying foundations for the 'alternative' (touring and community) theatre movement that mushroomed in Britain between 1968 and 1978. But they were avoiding the establishment theatre.

Their 'community' theatre activities culminated in *The War Carnival* which Arden described as 'something of a turning point in my career as a playwright',[10] which he and Margaretta D'Arcy presented in collaboration with students at New York University in 1967. After the fact, Arden wrote about the project in the form of a parody of 'a right-wing reviewer for, shall we say, *Time* magazine ... not because we did not regard our project there as a serious one, but because the whole hysterical experience seemed at the time beyond rational analysis'.[11] In the event, it was an anarchic and aggressive anti-Vietnam play which owed much to the 'happenings' of the sixties – with Arden (and D'Arcy) participating, pretending to be a CIA agent and actually desecrating an American flag.

> Arden ... said it was better to burn a flag ... than to burn flesh ... With a few brief words asking people who did not want to kill not to join the Army, and people who did not want a war not to pay any taxes, Arden brought the show to an end. What did it all mean? Was Arden really a CIA agent? If so, he was not a very efficient one ... To sum up: despite all the Ardens could do, the war in Vietnam continues.[12]

This was a radically different Arden than the one who in 1965 had prefaced *Left-Handed Liberty* (about the signing of Magna Carta) with the relatively 'liberal' suggestion that liberty required that:

> a) We know what sort of liberty we are fighting for:
> b) Our methods of fighting are not such as to render that liberty invalid before we even attain it:
> c) We understand that we are in more danger of losing it once we have attained it, than if we had never had it; which is an Irishism, but clear enough for all that.[13]

On that note (as Albert Hunt put it) Arden had 'disappeared from the London theatre scene for three years'[14] to return radically politicised in 1968, writing and performing *Harold Muggins Is a Martyr* with CAST at Unity Theatre and the controversial production of *The Hero Rises Up* at the Roundhouse – the first of a series of confrontations with establishment theatre managements. During the period of self-imposed exile, Arden had changed political direction – from pacifism to political activism.

To understand the change, it is helpful to be aware of the ways in which Arden's work before 1968 was political – i.e. in precisely the way he later described it – as 'plays written upon political subjects'. In fact, all of Arden's early plays were quite blatantly *about* politics and political matters, often sparked off by political events, historical and contemporary. His first play, for example, *The Waters of Babylon* (produced at the Royal Court as a one-performance Sunday night production in 1957 and 'generally greeted with extreme puzzlement if not outright hostility'[15]), was a parable of local political corruption placed firmly in the context of twentieth-century European imperialism (in the character of its Polish émigré anti-hero Krank). It involved a terrorist sub-plot to assassinate Bulganin and Krushchev, the bomb further 'sub-plot-verted' for the use of the IRA, and a Premium Bond swindle. Arden showed that in an unprincipled – or rather a capitalist/imperialist-principled – society, Krank could not afford to have even humanist principles, and survive. With *The Workhouse Donkey* at Chichester in 1963, Arden further developed these themes of corruption in local government, to the extent of using the same character from *The Waters of Babylon* – Charlie Butterthwaite, the cynical, manipulating 'Napoleon of Local Government'.

Live Like Pigs (Royal Court 1958) and *The Happy Haven*, written with Margaretta D'Arcy in 1959, were on the surface simply 'social problem' plays, written in a style which audiences found alienating. But even at that stage, when Arden's political consciousness was more intuitive than intellectualised, the problems were framed by a socialist rather than a liberal perspective: in both plays he undertook to expose the contradictions of post-war British society.

Arden's basically dialectical approach became increasingly clear (certainly in retrospect though surprisingly not to many critics at the time) in his early masterpiece *Serjeant Musgrave's Dance* (Royal Court 1959). The play was, as Arden explained, sparked off by an incident in Cyprus:

> A soldier's wife was shot in the streets by terrorists, and according to newspaper reports ... some soldiers ran wild at night and people were killed in the rounding-up. The atrocity which sparks off Musgrave's revolt ... is roughly similar.[16]

And though the play was set in an unspecified historical period, it was about the results of an imperialist war waged by a capitalist society, and clear connections were drawn between capitalist economics and war. *Armstrong's Last Goodnight* (1965) – though again a history play set in sixteenth-century Scotland when the precarious peace between England and Scotland was threatened by border outlaws – was also sparked off by a contemporary political event: the Congo war. Arden described it as a deliberate 'moral' analogy of the Congo situation, influenced by Conor Cruise O'Brien's book *To Katanga and Back:* indeed the play was dedicated to O'Brien.

These were the political terms of reference of Arden's early plays. And they were so explicit that it is hard to understand how the plays could ever have been taken as anything other than profoundly political. But they were.

J. W. Lambert, in his 1961 introduction to the first Penguin edition of *Live Like Pigs*, concluded that Arden 'takes no sides'. And John Russell Taylor in *Anger and After* in 1962 had decided that the audience's problem with Arden's plays was not knowing where he stood: 'Arden permits himself in his treatment of the characters and situations in his plays to be less influenced by moral preconceptions than any other writer in the British theatre today ... his attitude to his creations is quite uncommitted!'[17]

Looking back, it is almost hilarious to read these comments, and even at the time, Arden found this sort of response bewildering. In 1964 he was defending (yet again) *Armstrong's Last Goodnight* in *Encore*:

> I find the whole sequence of events in the play so alarming and hateful (and at the same time so typical of political activity at any period) that I have – perhaps rashly – taken for granted a similar feeling among the audience. If such a feeling does exist ... then an over-emphasis upon it in the course of the play becomes redundant and self-defeating.[18]

Arden assumed – naively perhaps – that his audience shared his socialist world-view. He was wrong and he was misunderstood to be apolitical, at least, if not also amoral. With the benefit of hindsight, it is arguable (as it is with Edward Bond) that the initial hostility and lack of comprehension was a response (however subconscious) to the radical and disturbing political implications of the plays, and that the criticism levelled against Arden – that his style or aesthetic was alienating – was a way (again subconscious) of avoiding the political issues. Arden, at least, came to argue this.

Arden, also, eventually came to realise the extent to which he was intuitively before his time, almost prophetically so:

> ... years after my plays have been written and performed, events have as it were come full circle, I find my imaginative figments turning out as established fact, by no means entirely to my satisfaction. *Serjeant Musgrave's Dance* (1959) dealt with a massacre of civilians during a British Army colonial 'peace-keeping' operation at the same time as a bitter colliery strike in England. In January 1972 thirteen people were shot dead by the Paras in Derry, while industrial trouble raged in the coalfields on a level unknown since the 1920s. While this was happening, I was at work with D'Arcy on an early draft of *The Non-Stop Connolly Show*: in a sense the whole story of Connolly was a kind of inside out version of my invented Black Jack Musgrave ... *The Royal Pardon* (written with D'Arcy in 1966) shows a theatre company which makes a mess of a play about King Arthur and Merlin: their show is saved by a stage-hand and an actress, who are treated like dogs by the manager, are vindictively hounded by an officer of the law, and are eventually left to pursue their own theatrical destinies while the company complacently receives the honour of appointment to the Royal Household with munificent subsidy.[19]

Arden went on in the same essay to suggest that this was directly analagous to the situation he and D'Arcy found themselves in with the Royal Shakespeare Company over *The Island of the Mighty*. He referred also to his dedication of *Armstrong's Last Goodnight* to Conor Cruise O'Brien and to O'Brien's later exposure of the CIA's infiltration of cultural and educational establishments in the USA. He pointed out that O'Brien, as an Irish politician, 'supported the retention of British armed forces in Northern Ireland'; that part of the work of these forces was the setting up of 'a singular activity known as Psyops'; and that, 'if the Psyops project is as closely-related to CIA technique as it appears to be, then surely it is not a symptom of acute paranoia to believe that the drama ... has been melted down for observation, and, if necessary, remote control'.

Prophecy apart, the seeds of Arden's political development were well and truly sown in his early plays. The question is what happened to precipitate his politicisation. For Arden, as for many other theatre workers, the 'year of the pig' was a turning point:

> In 1968 many things had come to a head. There was the revolt of the students and workers in France, with all the consequent excitement

exported abroad from it. There was the frenzy of police brutality at the Chicago Democratic Convention. There was the Russian invasion of Czechoslovakia. There was the massacre in Mexico at the time of the Olympic Games. There was the prohibition by Stormont Unionism of a perfectly reasonable Civil Rights March in Derry, the incorrect accusation that Northern Irish Civil Rights was a front for the IRA, the savage attack upon the marchers who had the nerve to defy the ban, and the inexorable slide of the largely forgotten Irish problem into the maelstrom of blood and bitterness which to this day swirls wider and wider.[20]

This was the public arena. In the private, there was Arden's and D'Arcy's experience with *The War Carnival* at NYU, their work with CAST at Unity and *The Hero Rises Up* – all of which involved challenging the production system. In 1969, there was their visit to India which had a profound affect on them both. Among other things, they had gone to see the Chhau Dancers of Purulia and witnessed at first hand a 'whole scene ... of cultural exploitation following close upon the heels of material ditto'.[21] Their experience in India – including imprisonment – gave them a new perspective on western cultural values and also on Third World revolution: they were clearly drawn to 'that Indian peasant revolution that has never yet arrived, but which will inexorably have to come'.[22] Indeed, Arden said on his return that, whatever he wrote in future, he would view through the eyes of an Indian revolutionary. In 1969, British troops were sent to Ireland to 'keep the peace', marking the beginning of over ten years of urban warfare: for Arden and D'Arcy it was just the kind of colonial war that had sent Black Jack Musgrave mad. The main theme of their lives and work in the seventies was concerned with Ireland – with disastrous results professionally.

From 1968 the history of John Arden as dramatist – or rather John Arden and Margaretta D'Arcy as co-dramatists, for they collaborated on most of the major works in the seventies – was not so much what they wrote, but what happened to what they wrote. It was a history of unstaged plays, production problems, critical hostility and downright neglect. 'John Arden is one of the greatest dramatists in the English language for several centuries,' wrote Albert Hunt.[23] But his plays were virtually unproduced in the seventies. 'He is denied the conditions he needs for his work,' said Hunt.[24] 'We have not worked in the British theatre since 1972,' said Arden. 'The British theatre is not interested. It has not invited us to work for five years.'[25]

He had a theory as to why:

> The great difficulty is that dramatists will rarely be told: 'Your play is *subversive*: we are imposing a political restriction upon its performance:' an aesthetic or bureaucratic reason will rather be advanced. The play is too long; the cast is too large; the project does not qualify for a grant because of some unfortunate technicality, perhaps the author's normal residence is outside the UK ... and so on. In my case it has been incontrovertibly passed on to me (though never put down on paper in so many words) that any work of mine done in collaboration with D'Arcy (which in effect means all my Irish material) is altogether out of line with the requirements of more than one subsidised theatre ...[26]

To advance such a conspiracy theory of censorship might seem absurd to anyone except Arden and D'Arcy. But to deny the *effective* censorship of their plays was equally absurd. For the events in their working lives since 1968 were a chronicle of *effective* if not deliberate censorship: and the results were the same in either case.

The first troublesome and ill-boding occasion ...

> was the production of *The Hero Rises Up* (1968) at the Institute of Contemporary Arts [finally produced at the Roundhouse], when D'Arcy and myself discovered the limitations of such bodies as the midwives of free experiment ... We were genuinely – if naively – flabbergasted by the sudden and fearful rigidity of the ICA officials: had the day at last arrived when gentlemanly accommodation of artistic and administrative differences in the theatre would be no longer possible? And, if so, what did this bode for our work in the future?[27]

The answer: not much good. A similar situation – that is, a conflict with an establishment theatre management – arose with *The Island of the Mighty* at the RSC in 1972, culminating in the playwrights going on strike and picketing the Aldwych. The issue in this case was the director's interpretation of the play, and the authors' contractual rights to attend rehearsals and to do necessary work on the text. Denied their rights, the authors decided to go on strike. Arden and D'Arcy saw the conflict as one of industrial dispute and they got the official backing of the Society of Irish Playwrights and the sympathy of NATTKE members to their picket line. They felt that Equity let them down, however, in not officially supporting their strike, and perhaps most significant, the RSC treated the matter in personal rather than political terms:

The RSC had put out a series of justifications and explanations of their part in the argument, but they never recognised the right of the playwrights to take the trade union action; they never discussed the dispute in terms of a trade dispute but preferred instead to treat it as a matter purely of 'artistic' controversy involving temperamental incompatibilities and other personal issues. They also used a 'divide-and-rule' technique, implying that whereas John Arden was a sincere though sadly misled writer of talent, his partner Margaretta D'Arcy was no more than a 'political activitist'.[28]

In the end, Arden and D'Arcy disowned the production entirely (and the Eyre Methuen text of the play was published without the normal cast list of the first production). The occasion recalled with some irony a prophetic statement made by Arden in *Peace News* nearly a decade earlier after the Chichester production of *The Workhouse Donkey* in 1963. (In that instance there were no confrontations, but Arden was conscious that Chichester was not the most suitable theatre for a play described as a 'celebration of anarchy' and envisaged as an 'entertainment of six or seven or thirteen hours' allowing the 'audience to come and go throughout the performance', in an atmosphere with 'some of the characteristics of a fairground or amusement park'.[29]) Arden:

> You get somebody like Lord Chandos on the National Theatre board and the mind boggles. I wouldn't like to think that the theatre in the next few years was going to be run between the Aldwych and the National rather like the world is run between Moscow and Washington ...[30]

Yet by the time of the Aldwych dispute, Arden's facetiously described fantasy had more or less become the reality of major subsidised theatre.

Little did he know in 1963 to what extent he would become a victim of the theatrical cold war. It was after the Aldwych dispute that the Ardens ceased to be 'invited to work in the British theatre'.[31] They had acquired a 'reputation' for being difficult: and this because they tried as workers to exert some control over the means of production – control which they had a contractual right to exert. At that time the concept of 'writer as worker' was virtually unheard of. At that time too the Ardens recognised the need for an organisation to protect their rights. Shortly after this, from entirely independent initiatives, the Theatre Writers Group (later Union) started and flourished almost overnight into a force to be reckoned with in the British theatre. The Ardens became active members of the TWU. And by 1979, the idea of playwrights on picket, of playwrights demanding control over their working conditions – from wages to casting – thanks to the efforts of the TWU (aided by such action as Arden and D'Arcy took) – was no longer regarded as ludicrous.

Arden's and D'Arcy's problems with the theatre could have been dismissed as personal rather than 'political' but for the issue of Ireland, their Irish plays and the fate of *The Ballygombeen Bequest* and *The Non-Stop Connolly Show* in particular.[32] The *Connolly* plays – 'a dramatic cycle of continuous struggle in six parts and 26 hours' – evolved over a considerable period of time. At an early stage, the BBC was asked to commission the play and refused. Arden was told that if he had already written a masterpiece, the BBC would probably have had to produce it. But he hadn't (yet) and it didn't. During the process of researching and writing *Connolly*, Arden and D'Arcy were invited to work with students (in 1973) at the University of California at Davis. They decided to work on the American section of *Connolly* in the face, as it turned out, of considerable opposition.[33]

The Non-Stop Connolly Show was eventually produced once in its continual entirety over the Easter weekend in 1975 at Liberty Hall in Dublin – where, according to Eamonn Smullen, an official of Sinn Fein, the Workers Party, 'the plays were enthusiastically received by a large Dublin audience in the headquarters of Ireland's largest union'[34] (the TGWU, which, incidentally, had sponsored and helped to produce the show). Fourteen hours of *The Non-Stop Connolly Show* were later produced for a limited period of consecutive one-hour lunchtimes at the Almost Free Theatre in London in 1976. That was the beginning and the end of the production history of D'Arcy/Arden's second masterpiece. Albert Hunt, belatedly reviewing the *Connolly* plays in *New Society* in 1979 described it as 'the major theatrical development in Britain in the 1970s.[35] Certainly this epic play was an absolute and unequivocal repudiation of the claims that the quality of Arden's writing had deteriorated and of those who used that as an excuse for neglecting the work of Arden and D'Arcy.

Had the *Connolly* play been censored? There was 'analagous' evidence that such was indeed the case. The reputable and respectable TV director Kenneth Griffith produced for ATV a documentary on the Irish Republican Michael Collins which was banned outright and locked in the ATV vaults: 'I'm not even allowed to see it myself,' said Griffith.[36] The film was based entirely on history, on statistics and facts, and recorded dialogue: nothing was invented. The film traced the life of Collins from birth to death, showing why he became what he became – a formidable patriot and activist until his death in 1922. From those facts emerged a *positive* view of Irish Republicanism – one that converted Griffith from neutral disinterest to partisanship. Because of the treatment and because of the Irish subject matter, it was banned. It was perhaps not unreasonable to assume a similar response to *The Non-Stop Connolly Show*.

The case of *The Ballygombeen Bequest* (produced briefly in a teachers' training college in Belfast, then Edinburgh and London by the 7:84 Theatre Company in 1972 before being stopped by a writ for libel and slander) was different: but the results were the same. The story of the play concerned an absentee English landlord who attempts to evict a tenant family from his inherited estate in Ireland. The play was – in extending the action to the North, and ending with the torture and murder of the son by the British Army – a parable of British imperialism in Ireland. At the Edinburgh Festival, the 7:84 Theatre Company distributed to the audience with the programmes a duplicated sheet giving the name and address and telephone number of an absentee English landlord who was in the process of evicting a tenant family from his property in Ireland. The audience were called upon to protest. This gesture towards political activism turned the show into a piece of unprecedented agitprop particularly as the final court hearing in the eviction case was still to take place. It was the man named in the programme who had been feuding with the Ardens who issued the writ in a civil action for libel and slander. The case was *sub judice* and the play went out of circulation from 1973 to 1977 when the case was heard in the High Court before Judge Melford Stevenson. The play was a comedy: the court hearing was a farce.

The prosecution's case rested on the specific point that the landlord dramatised in the play was shown to have got his tenant drunk so that he would sign over the tenancy. The defence claimed that the play had to be taken as a whole, that it had to be taken as a fictional allegory within which was contained fair comment. Arden's and D'Arcy's defence rested largely on the history of British imperialism in Ireland:

> We determined from the start to 'fight the case politically', ... We felt that our defence to the suit – based upon our 'objective and scrupulous analysis of the political realities' behind the apparently genial relationship of the landowning sporting English neo-squireens in the tourist areas of Ireland with their dole-drawing, small-farming, boat-servicing Irish ghillies – would easily outweigh any suggestion that we had been only concerned to hold up one individual to obloquy

and contempt for reasons of personal malice. To this end we mustered a sunburst of excellent witnesses from Ireland – historians, sociologists, politicians, journalists: and we anticipated a flow of rhetoric from the witness-box that would reveal to the astonished English jury the full horror of the Elizabethan/Cromwellian/Williamite/Anglo-Irish settlements, the Treaty of 1922, Partition, the EEC, and the insidious influence of the native Irish *comprador bourgeoisie* – known locally as the gombeen men. Of course nothing like this was to happen or could happen.[37]

The Judge's response was that he was not interested in having Irish history in the English courts.[38] Of the play itself, the Judge said that it 'was unfortunate that the jury would have to read this turgid piece of prose'. When the defence replied: 'Milord, these are famous British playwrights,' the Judge said: 'I've never heard of them. I have no pretensions to being called a man of culture!' He didn't think 'we'd do a disservice to the theatre if this case were never heard of again'.[39] In the end, the jury was discharged, the case adjourned and finally settled out of court with Arden and D'Arcy still denying libel and slander, apologising, pleading impecunity, and agreeing to make changes to the play according to the order of the court.

Because of court action, *The Ballygombeen Bequest* was totally silenced. Albert Hunt had pointed out: 'it's the first of the Ardens' plays to take up a clear-cut Marxist position',[40] and it was the first to deal with current events in Northern Ireland from this position. There remained a lingering question as to possible connections between the Ardens' politics and the fate of that excellent play. D'Arcy/Arden's new play on a similar subject – *The Little Gray Home in the West* – was still unproduced in 1979 so the chronicle of censorship continued.

Their experiences left Arden and D'Arcy more than a little embittered. D'Arcy did not want to be included in a book on British theatre. D'Arcy: 'I am Irish. I am not a part of the British theatre. I am a foreign writer. I am Irish writing about the Irish about which the British don't understand or care.' Arden: 'We are classified as British because the British refuse to see Ireland as separate. That classification is a symptom of British imperialism.' D'Arcy: 'Ireland is a foreign country, colonised by the British who are now waging an imperialist war there. The beginning of the Third World War is taking place in Ireland. The threat is a socialist Ireland – another Cuba.' Arden took a copy of Webster's *The White Devil* from his book shelves and started reading out anti-Irish lines from the play.

Arden: 'The English have adopted an attitude analogous to anti-semitism in their dealings with the Irish which goes back a long way; there is a long history of imperialism.' D'Arcy: 'If I were a Polish writer and my plays were done in London, I would be regarded as a foreign writer produced in Britain. As an Irish writer with a play produced in London [this was shortly after D'Arcy's *A Pinprick of History* at the Almost Free lunchtime], I am regarded as a British writer!'[41] What had started sounding like pique began to take point for anyone who believes in a separate self-determining Ireland as D'Arcy and Arden do. From their point of view, inclusion in such a book as *Stages in the Revolution* quite literally constituted a form of betrayal.

Lack of a political platform for their plays led the Ardens to direct political action – sometimes through the Theatre Writers Union – and to civil disobedience. In December 1978, Margaretta D'Arcy was in Armagh Prison charged with a breach of the peace under the Northern Ireland Act. Her crime: writing the words 'H Block' on the wall of the Ulster Museum during a poetry reading.[42] In her defence statement D'Arcy wrote: 'I am accused of provoking a breach of the peace. This is not good sense. The peace in Northern Ireland is already most savagely broken. What I was trying to do was to provoke a breach of the silence about the reasons for the overall public breach of the peace. I believe that the arts are being deliberately used by the State to reinforce that silence.'[43]

D'Arcy's 'writing on the wall' was a deliberate attempt to draw attention to the 'criminalisation' of republican and loyalist prisoners – and the anomaly whereby some 'political prisoners' had political status while others were classed as criminals. It was also a protest against 'the pretence of normal life' – against academics and arts patrons in particular, in their ivory towers, 'apparently untroubled by the troubles'. D'Arcy's demonstration was firmly placed in a fine tradition of civil disobedience: for her efforts she herself was 'criminalised.'

Her defence read, in part, as a self-review of the 'drama' she instigated:

I wrote on the wall about H Block. I hoped that this would be the beginning of a communal artistic happening . . . I was pleased to discover that a number of people in the room seemed to understand what I was doing and stood up for me against those who said I should stop. But then I was taken out of the room by the attendants. I deliberately made a technical assault on these men in order to demonstrate, without actually doing them any harm, how suppression of free speech will lead to violence. I would have preferred the members of the public to have asked them to leave me alone . . . But as it was I was compelled to carry my little improvised play to the end. The other characters in it (the museum staff) brought the plot to its conclusion by sending for the police. By trying to create a very small and imperfect work of art showing how much more important works of art had been censored because they referred to military violence, police repression, erosion of civil rights, etc., I myself found myself repressed by the state upon criminal charges.[44]

The Theatre Writers Union took up her case with a resolution 'supporting her right to introduce urgent political issues into artistic debate and calling on the government to recognise the political nature of the conflict in Northern Ireland and to abandon its inconsistent policy of treating republican and loyalist prisoners as ordinary civil criminals'. D'Arcy was fined and released.

The question was – with their plays denied production and themselves effectively denied the right to work – whether John Arden and Margaretta D'Arcy had much choice given their political commitment except to perform their own dramas off-stage in the public political arena?

*'You've shown me my life. I've been nothing but a cabbage –
you've shown it to me.'* A 50-year-old engineering worker
after a performance of Red Ladder's *The Big Con.*

AgitProp Street Players/Red Ladder

In the spring of 1968 CAST called a meeting at Unity Theatre,
of people who were 'both political and also into culture',[1] and
proposed that an organisation be set up to 'mediate between cultural
groups' and to act as a 'booking agency' for groups such as CAST.
As John Hoyland, who with the feminist Sheila Rowbotham and
others was involved in left politics in the late sixties, said: 'There
was a gap between the left and cultural work which needed to be
filled. There was a dissatisfaction with the straight left at that time,
as being unimaginative and puritanical, and a dissatisfaction with
underground culture as being socially irrelevant and separate from
political realities.' Out of that meeting AgitProp was formed for
'the application of the imagination to politics and the application
of politics to the imagination'.[2]

People had been fired by the May Events in Paris and mobilised
by the war in Vietnam. Hoyland: 'They had started looking around
for something that would be more cultural, more imaginative, more
rooted in the smaller details of people's lives – and more applicable
to Britain.'[3] Before the formation of AgitProp there had been ad
hoc 'guerilla cultural activities' such as 'poster alteration' in the
London tubes – what Chris Rawlence, a founder member of Red
Ladder, described as 'situationist' cultural events.

> What they were doing was silk-screening sections of posters, but
> changing the message so that an advertisement for a film became –
> with a bit stuck over it – an attack against the Vietnam War. A group
> of about thirty people would go around – highly co-ordinated – to
> all the tube stations in London with these little bits of poster and some
> glue.[4]

So a Harrods ad which read 'We close late every night' would be
altered to read 'We clothe every child in napalm'.

The AgitProp Information Service that was set up out of the Unity meeting was seminal – particularly to a whole strand of theatre work that was to develop over the next ten years. One of its first projects was to set up an Index of 'anybody doing any kind of cultural work – architecture or printing or poster-making or puppetry and to make the service available to the left (political groups and students)'. According to an early brochure, AgitProp aimed 'to provide a comprehensive information and communications service for all those who are working towards a revolutionary transformation of our society'.[5] Very quickly the services expanded. In addition to the Index there was an Entertainment Booking Agency, a Lawyers' Group, a Publicity Group, a Music Group, a Special Effects Group (for making banners and placards). There were publications: *Red Notes*, a *Directory of Organisations* ('a left what, who and where'), *Directory of Left Publications and Bookshops*. There was a library of left publications, educational packages, print workshop, poster workshop. There were conferences: Workers' Control Conference, Conference of Socialists in Higher Education, National Convention of the Left – and a Black Dwarf Dance! And there was a street theatre group.

AgitProp Street Players actually developed from the Festival held in Trafalgar Square on 20 July 1968. At that time Hornsey and Guildford Colleges of Art were under occupation by the students and asked the embryonic AgitProp if they could help put on a play for the Trafalgar Square Festival. What evolved was *The Little Artist*: 'with half a dozen Lichtenstein-type drawings which a narrator stood in front of – about the plight of the poor art student and the oppressive powers that be'.[6] John Hoyland wrote the script:

> There was an artist, very individualistic, who lived in a town being threatened by this big dragon called Capitalism who was terribly cruel. Eventually he gets all the people mobilised, a revolutionary force that destroys the dragon. The idea came from Cuba and China – the massive dos in stadiums with two or three thousand kids holding up thousands of placards to make a tableau. We got a good artist to do some drawings on graph paper which we then transferred in proportion to placards which unfolded to make a picture eight foot high by twenty feet long. There were five of them.[7]

AgitProp Street Players then developed over the next few months doing plays for GLC (Greater London Council) tenants on rent problems in the East End, Hackney and Tower Hamlets, where the slogan was 'Not a Penny on the Rents'. According to Chris Rawlence:

There was a big response — anti-response — to Horace Cutler's imposition of 75 per cent rent increases over a period of three years. And thousands of tenants got involved. So both in response to a demand from the tenants themselves — which was important — and to a need for people to be able to use their own skills and crafts in a political way, about half a dozen of us got together and made the simplest of little sketches, a seven-minute thing saying basically: shall we pay the rents, no we won't. There were seven in all.[8]

It was part of the ideology of AgitProp than anyone could and should learn to do it. And one of the people — an old tenant of 68 who got involved in the Poster Workshop — asked for a play for the tenants' campaign. So there was a direct link between the Poster Workshop part of AgitProp and the tenants. The first sketch was performed at an Action Committee meeting in the autumn of 1968. Delegates from different Tenants Associations liked it and the group collected 14 bookings that first night. It snowballed and they sometimes did three meetings a night. Kathleen McCreery, who joined AgitProp early in 1969 and was involved later with Red Ladder, and then with Broadside Mobile Workers Theatre, explained:

The sketches had to be short, twelve to fifteen minutes was the maximum since they had to be fitted into the tenants' meeting — first restriction. With so little time to say anything, they had to be simple in the extreme: we could only put over a few ideas, clearly. Subtlety and development of characters was out. They had to be topical and flexible since the situation of the tenants was changing constantly. The content consisted of staying just one step ahead of the tenants themselves, predicting what the Housing Minister Greenwood or the Arch-villain Cutler might do next, warning the tenants not to fall for it: so it was strictly agitational. The criterion was: did it help the struggle or not? The function was morale-boosting, unifying, but also to contribute to a tactical debate because there were different forms of action the tenants could take at each stage. Later, as the sketches became more sophisticated, we put the struggle of the tenants in a broader framework, implying that the current struggle was one battle in a much bigger war against the capitalist system.[9]

One of the tenants' plays was *The Rose-Tinted Spectacles*, written in a music hall style. There were two stock characters, Joe and Lil, the archetypal tenants who appeared in all the plays. Lil was played by Chris Rawlence in drag, tall with blonde curly wig, fag hanging from the lower lip, hairy legs and boots showing from under a pink negligee. Joe was a little bloke. They were a comic pair. Kathleen McCreery:

The women in the audience absolutely loved him. There was always a row of women in the front killing themselves. They laughed partly because the whole thing was so gross and far-fetched and silly, partly because the form of music hall and drag was part of the tenants' cultural heritage. Lil was presented as a strong, dominant woman, as the activist in the rents campaign: and the women in our audience were themselves in the forefront of the struggle. In that sense they 'identified' with Lil – and he made them laugh.[10]

Joe was timid and thick: Lil was militant and not about to be taken in by the wiles of slimy Horace Cutler or urbane Greenwood. The present from Cutler was a pair of rose-coloured specs, through which they would see that, if they paid, everything would be all right.

Another of the successful tenants' plays used the image of the Garden of Eden. In it Joe and Lil received a notice through the letterbox, saying the rent increase was going to be cancelled. They thought the struggle was over, when Horace Cutler entered in a dream as the serpent, tempting them with the apple symbolising 'pay the rent and it'll be all right'. This was at a time when the GLC were using all sorts of devices to persuade people to pay the increases. The play included a strip, with pink underwear revealed, the obligatory balloons and fig leaves. When the balloon burst, Joe and Lil awoke to realise the struggle was still on. It was at this time that the group started to use the famous Red Ladder, as a visual device to attract attention – a cheap and portable way to elevate themselves outdoors – and as a useful metaphor of the class structure.

By 1969 the group had moved on to a play about squatters, not so successful: according to Chris Rawlence 'it was too grossly analytical, using two ladders and money bags to show how the money went – on interest, to the council; the length of the housing queue, why some people had to squat'. It was about housing problems and showed the relationship between council tenants and squatters and played to both. The *Squatters Play* also related to other AgitProp activities, like the campaign against Centre Point, the central London office block built by Harry Hyams and still standing virtually empty in 1979. The rallying cry of the campaign was 'Cathy Come to Centre Point, It's Empty' (after the impact of Jeremy Sandford's TV documentary on the homeless – *Cathy Come Home*) and 'Capitalism Equals Empty Houses and Homeless People'.

A turning point for AgitProp Street Players was a play they did for the Ford Strike at Dagenham in the spring of 1969. Aesthetically it was pretty weak, except for the one-line that gave it its title: *Stuff Your Penal Up Your Bonus*. In a dispute over wages and wild-cat strikes, management offered a holiday bonus scheme linked to productivity and good conduct, but a penal clause – the loss of the holiday bonus – for those involved in unofficial stoppages. This was also the time Barbara Castle was trying to push through 'In Place of Strife', the Labour forerunner to the Tory Industrial Relations Act. From an AgitProp Newsletter:

> The Ford strike prompted AgitProp to galvanise itself into a week of activity which was something of a vindication of our thinking about political communication and demonstrated how we would like to be able to operate all the time. In a few hours we worked out a fairly effective street play which we took out to Dagenham and performed three days running. We also produced placards announcing the title of the play; a leaflet with, on one side, an excellent drawing of a wild cat being lured into the 'Penal Clauses Cage'; and a series of four stickers supporting the strike. In addition, the poster workshop produced a large number of posters advertising strike meetings. It all could have been done better, but the fact that it was done at all earned us good will and gave us some valuable experience as well as providing the Ford militants with a useful gesture of solidarity.[11]

Chris Rawlence reckoned it had an impact because they had bothered to go and stand in the rain and support the strike, because there wasn't a feeling of 'They're going to take advantage of us and stuff a leaflet down our throats or get us to join something'.

That experience – and the relationships that developed with dockers and East End workers during the rent strike – decided the group to direct itself towards the trades union movement. As John Hoyland put it:

> The general feeling of the Red Ladder people at that time was that they did not come out of the theatre tradition; they did not see themselves as theatre workers for a long time. They saw themselves as doing political propaganda in a particular form. The main impetus was political rather than theatrical.[12]

There had been the 'terrific excitement about revolutionary politics – people got very caught up with it and became politicised over night – all they talked about was revolution and how to get it'. But there was concern about the lack of connection with the English working class. There had been an editorial in *Black Dwarf* at the time of the big October Vietnam Demo in '68 which concluded that when the demo was over the task should be to create revolutionary policies for England. In the Ford strike, there had been the seeds of that connection. And by 1969, the group felt they could make a play about industrial struggle, the history of industrial relations over the past ten years.

So they did a 'Productivity Play' – *The Big Con* – with the intention of finding trades union audiences for it. Kathleen McCreery: 'We began to see that perhaps we could really perform for industrial workers, that we could actually make a working-class theatre. We decided that the question of productivity bargaining was the key issue facing the British working class and that we would make a play about that.' In the late sixties productivity bargaining was a relatively new phenomenon. Managements wanted to get rid of the hundred-year-old practice of piece work, with its attendant wage drift and restrictive practices and replace it by a system where they had more control over work pace and shop-floor organisation – payment by the hour, known as 'measured day work'. In this process the carrot of a higher hourly rate for greater productivity concealed the reality of harder work.

The Big Con had the stock characters – Joe the militant young worker, Harry the older staunch Labourite, Britannia the boss and the trades union official Slicker (an elision of 'arse licker'). In this play AgitProp decided to deal with the question of ideology and to develop the inner life of the working-class characters (they weren't so concerned about the ruling-class characters), to show people going through a learning process. It was a move away from the classical agitprop of the early plays: 'this process did not mean that we fell into individual psychologising or kitchen-sink realism, because the characters were larger than life, representative of more than just themselves'. The two ruling-class characters transformed themselves into the various facets of the state – the media, capital, the work/study bloke with the clock glasses – so that the links between these different organs could be clearly seen. The basic class structure was depicted with Britannia on top of the ladder, Wilson or Heath puppets on either hand, the boss on the step in front, Slicker on a lower step, then the workers on the floor. The rat race became a stylised competition in which the boss, having been born with a silver spoon, doesn't even have to try, while Wilson urges the workers to remember the Dunkirk spirit because things aren't going too well for Britain. This led to a stylised rendering of the famous Dunkirk slaughter, the class structures reproduced on the battle lines. The dead rose up as Britannia sang 'We'll meet again ...' Suddenly the singing would be interrupted and the familiar rhythm of the production lines started again. Kathleen McCreery:

We actually found workers in our audience singing along with 'We'll meet again', and really enjoying it. All of a sudden, smack would come the noises of the production line and you could see the expressions on their faces as they realised 'I've been conned'.[13]

At the beginning of the play, the less militant Harry had a dream about doing the boss in, donning the bowler hat and taking his place. By the end of the play, he realised that it was necessary to dismantle the whole structure; not to take on the attributes of the ruling class. The group had previously used placards to provide missing information: here they used them to comment on what was happening – 'Never before have so many worked so hard for so few'.

The Big Con was first performed at the Institute for Workers' Control in Nottingham in September 1970, out of which eventually came dozens of bookings: from the AUEW engineering section, the *Shop Stewards Quarterly* in Hertford, extra-mural studies for shop stewards in Southampton, a TASS weekend school. The play became very popular. Rawlence: 'It was the first time since the thirties that stuff like that had been seen in the context of trades unions. And I think it was probably better than a lot of that stuff during the thirties.' Kathleen McCreery recalled an engineering worker about 50 years old, getting up and saying 'You've shown me my life. I've been nothing but a cabbage – you've shown it to me.'

After the 'Productivity Play' came *The Cake Play* – a piece of 'classic agitational propaganda' which used the strong central image of the 'national cake'.

Three workers baked the cake and in return they received a slice, which they handed back to the big boss on top of the ladder from whom they received wages to buy their slice. They didn't get enough cake/wages, so they pulled out the knife – the strike knife. At which point the Boss invoked the powers that be – the Tories – who bring in an axe to get the knife. So the Industrial Relations Act and its history was played out against the symbolic cake.[14]

The Cake Play was first performed in January 1971 and stayed in the repertoire until 1974 – as long as the Industrial Relations Act was in effect, with the second half constantly changing to keep up with current events. The most spectacular performance of *The Cake Play* was at the Hyde Park March and Demonstration against the Industrial Relations Bill in February 1971:

There were 170,000 people in Hyde Park with banners: 'Agitate, Educate, Organise', 'Labour is the Source of All Wealth', 'Unity is Strength'. We performed it eight times, going between the rows while the people were lined up, and it took 3 hours to march off. So 5000, 6000, 7000 people must have seen it in the space of a couple of hours. It was phenomenal.[15]

This was a time of high political consciousness amongst the working class. Rawlence: 'The play drew its energy from the energy of its audience and vice versa. It was a real dialectical relationship between play and audience.' Another phenomenal performance took place outside Pentonville Prison where the five TGWU shop stewards gaoled for defying the Industrial Relations Act – the Pentonville Five – were imprisoned in 1972.

> We had predicted years before we'd made the play that somebody was going to be put inside because it was one of the provisions of the Bill that somebody could be gaoled. When we arrived at Pentonville we asked the shop steward – 'What about the police, are there any troubles about us performing?' And he said, 'Don't worry, we've got them under control!' And the police actually blocked off the entire Pentonville Road to allow us to perform. We'd been invited by the dockers, and the police were concerned to avoid any trouble as the place was packed with thousands of angry workers. There was an unofficial general strike on the cards.[16]

After *The Cake Play* came an 'Unemployment Play' – 'straight economy, a potted *Capital*, it didn't work, it was crude and boring'.[17] And then the 'Technology Play', *Happy Robots*, which originated in collaboration with members of TASS and the AUEW.

> It was about the relationship between the shop floor and the drawing office, about amalgamation, which was going through in the AUEW. The play was about those relationships and the introduction of NC machines, i.e. computerised borers and lathes on to the shop floor. It was about one man's decision whether to go along with management's desire to computerise. He decided to ignore the inevitable redundancies downstairs, until he discovered himself out of a job as well. It ended with 'Will they still need me, will they still feed me when I'm 44?'[18]

Ken Gill, then Deputy General Secretary of the AUEW's Technical and Supervisory Section, was full of praise for Red Ladder's work with them: 'The group has been extremely useful in provoking discussion on the main issues facing the Labour movement today, such as the Common Market, unemployment, productivity bargaining, the Industrial Relations Act and trades union involvement in politics. The plays are also valuable educational tools, presenting abstract ideas like inflation in striking visual terms that everyone can understand. As delegates at our annual conference unanimously concluded, "That play teaches more than a dozen lectures".'

It was during this period that the identity of the group gelled, the name was changed to Red Ladder and they applied for and received – in 1973 – their first Arts Council grant of £4000 (which by 1978/79 had risen to £43,000). The group also developed a political consciousness and theory of theatre, though they were never aligned to any political group or party. Hoyland: 'Red Ladder had the good sense to realise that if they were identified with a particular organisation they would lose the confidence of working-class audiences. So the agonising over which organisation to join was short-lived.' And there was no sector of the British left whose theory or practice they agreed with. But they thrashed through political theories as a group and attempted to put theory into practice in working methods:

> The level of political discussion within Red Ladder at that time was incredibly high. They would read Lenin and Marx and other theorists every week and have a discussion about it. The political discussion was also about how to organise the group. For many years they were an absolute model of democracy . . . They had weekly meetings, a whole afternoon to discuss the group, to ensure that everybody had an equal role, that all work was rotated, including the Chairman of the Day . . . I remember going on tour with them and an argument developing in the lorry about whether there should be a run-through before the show. At a certain point it became clear that they couldn't sort it out informally and somebody said, 'Who's Chairman of the Day?' Whoever it was said, 'I am.' So they said, 'All remarks through the chairman.' This was in the lorry! There was no other group that was so thorough at collective work.[19]

They also used a collective work process which was particularly integral to the creating of one of their major plays, the one that brought them into the public eye – *A Woman's Work is Never Done* or *Strike While the Iron Is Hot*. That was the period of the Working Women's Charter and the play bridged the gap between trades union politics and the increasingly influential women's movement.

> It was very much influenced by Brecht's *The Mother*. It had an episodic structure and it took a central character through an enjoyable learning process. The question of equal pay and parity was graphically illustrated by the man's pint of beer and the woman's half-pint; capitalism was an umbrella over-shadowing everything. What you saw was a working-class woman on the threshold of becoming a revolutionary.[20]

In performance, the process of developing political – and *sexual* political – consciousness was portrayed humorously. Thus in an early scene the wife Helen nags her feet-up, telly-watching husband Dave about her boring life as a housewife and is contemptuous of his union meetings. Later, when Helen herself has gone out to work and got the sack for taking a week off to have an abortion, she joins the union and becomes an active militant in the cause of equal pay. So the tables have turned on the domestic front, and Dave is doing the ironing, child-minding and running the crèche at Helen's union meetings.

With *A Woman's Work* the Red Ladder style had begun to change, moving away from classic agitprop and towards a new kind of realism:

> Agitprop that may have been sophisticated in 1972 had, by 1974, become a strained hectoring to all but deaf ears. The political climate had changed. The mass confrontations of the past four years were over. The trades union leadership was not prepared to unite in opposition to a re-elected Labour government even though it was pursuing moderate Tory policies. Although important struggles were to occur in the next few years, the overall picture of class struggle was one of downturn.[21]

The Red Ladder style responded to this political climate.

In 1974 while Red Ladder were doing their 'Women's Play', the group split. One part went on to form Broadside Mobile Workers Theatre – initially to produce 'bespoke' theatre, tailor-made plays for tailor-made situations – servicing the immediate requests of working-class audiences and the trades union movement. And they had no doubt of the demand in that area, with such comments from a rank and file member at Pilkington's as: 'We, the rank-and-file workers of St Helens, have seen, through the plays of Red Ladder Theatre, the reality that lies behind our "Democracy", the reality of the employing classes' constant exploitation of us, the working people. It is us against the bosses and there are no halfway measures! Red Ladder put it so clearly that it is vital that all workers see these plays.' Thus Broadside continued to develop plays along the earlier agitprop lines and later expanded the form and its content. Kathleen McCreery:

> We went on to develop a multi-faceted, multi-pronged approach, the result of demands from the movement and also our own analysis of what was needed. We eventually came to use continuous characters who develop throughout the entire play, realistic scenes (in the Brechtian sense), dealing with complex issues not tied up in slogans.[22]

Red ladder went in a different direction – North to Leeds. Rawlence: 'What we wanted to do in Yorkshire was to establish a cultural presence for socialist theatre within the region.'

In their first three years at Leeds, from 1976 to 1979, Red Ladder produced three plays and three cabaret club shows. Much o⸍ their time was spent in establishing themselves in Yorkshire. They started with a ten-year strategy to open up sixty or seventy venues for socialist theatre, to develop a regular, growing and broadly based working-class audience. By working through the trades unions, tenants' and community associations, local authorities, schools and arts associations, the aimed to establish a popular cultural-political presence in which Red Ladder would be experienced as part of Yorkshire life.

Their first project was a club show, performed to working men's clubs and pubs where thousands would gather every weekend, where they could replace the usual racist, sexist content with socialist content:

> We made many mistakes. Our initial anxiety, treading carefully with such non-political audiences, led us into the trap of pandering over-much to our assumptions about what they could accept. But in the context of 'Saturday night out', the balance between politics and entertainment is hard to gauge. A left-wing critic in London, seeing the show, declared that the red was wearing off the ladder; in an Otley working men's club we were paid off at half time – 'Commie rubbish'. (Thankfully our only such disaster.)²³

The first major play was *Taking Our Time*, a history play about the textile industry and the rise of Chartism in the 1840's based on the Plug Riots in Halifax in 1842. On a straight political level the play aimed to make a comparison between then and now, an economic crisis which governments and employers sought to solve at the expense of the working class.

But as the title implies it was more than a historical narrative about Chartism. A major theme was the smashing of a popular culture, the values and way of life of the handloom weaving communities of the West Riding that millowners, state and church had to destroy. For the new mills required a well-regulated work force subject to the discipline of the capitalist clock. The mechanical method of factory production had to supplant the domestic rhythms of the handloom and the spinning wheel. Skilled craftspeople who had controlled their leisure time and the rhythms of the working day became factory 'hands'. The working class was born. In the play we described this conflict through two related plots: the struggle between a Methodist preacher and Tom, a travelling tinker-clown; and the experience of one weaving family facing unemployment and starvation at the transition.[24]

A Woman's Work had made Red Ladder take sexual politics very seriously. This they extended in *Taking Our Time*, aptly in that working-class women prior to 1850 played a prominent and militant role. And the group saw the importance of not romanticising life before the Industrial Revolution. In this respect they diverged from the agitprop style of their early days and subsequently of Broadside.

> The problem: how to maintain the critical awareness of an audience without 'correct-lining' them to sleep; how to maintain emotional interest without lulling them into a stupor of heart-rending identity.[25]

The aim was to get the socialist ideas flowing out of the story and the people, moving beyond agitprop into a different kind of realism.

Nerves of Steel, ready at the end of 1978, was set in the present-day steel industry, researched in Sheffield and Scunthorpe, about the deterioration and breakdown of a relationship between a man and a woman – *his* relationship to work, to overtime, to a campaign to prevent closures in the steel industry, set against *her* demands for a different sort of life. It took further the question of the relationship of feminism and sexual politics to the industrial struggle. It related very closely to South Yorkshire experiences. *Taking Our Time* had reached an audience of ten thousand in West Yorkshire: the task for Red Ladder with *Nerves of Steel*, then with *Power Mad* in 1979, a play about nuclear power, was to extend that audience.

'... the most dynamic phenomenon on the British community arts scene ... the most exciting community arts group in Europe ...' Council of Europe Report on Inter-Action, 1978

Ed Berman and Inter-Action

(Ambiance Lunch Hour Theatre Club, The Other Company, The Almost Free Theatre, Dogg's Troupe, OATS, Fun Art Bus, Father Christmas Union, Community Cameos, City Farm, BARC – British American Repertory Company)

Ed Berman, founder of Inter-Action, was the 'impresario' of alternative theatre and community work in the seventies. An expatriate American, he started in the mid-sixties as a playwright, shared the distinction with David Halliwell's Quipu of launching the first permanent lunchtime theatre in 1968, and by 1978 had created a veritable empire of community arts and professional theatre activities. Over the decade, having used dozens of different venues and squats, Inter-Action moved, in 1977, into a purpose-built building (flexible and expandable) in Kentish Town – the nerve centre for far-flung activities as varied as horse-riding lessons, self-help gardening clubs, summer sports camp, skateboarding, a city farm, education work with video, architectural advice and of course theatre – from community (Dogg's Troupe) to international (The British American Repertory Company). Servicing all of this was the community resource centre, including printing, video, recording, photography, silk-screening, music, electrical and textile work, xerox and community transport.

Berman regarded the whole venture as profoundly 'political', but not in the strictly socialist sense of Red Ladder:

I am suspicious of statements on politics which are not borne out by actions. I believe that structure and personal action are more important than what you say. It doesn't really matter to me what statements you make. If you don't live it or put it into practice in the structure of your work or personal life, then the statement is just bourgeois titillation and self-deception. And that's really where the dividing line has come between me and most of the so-called political theatre which I think is usually posing. If not, they often postulate things which are either impossible to achieve or impossible to live by, by people who have never tried to do either. I think it's action that's needed, and structural changes. I think that can happen in the theatre, but it has to be thought about. Acting is no substitute for action.[1]

Berman used the words 'social enterprises' to describe his politics. Berman: 'It's clear to me that if you accept the *structure* as "political" as well as the intellectual and the verbal, then we are as "political" as they come. "Political" is not a code word for "Marxist".'

Structure was the key to Inter-Action from its beginnings – in practice a co-operative within a charitable framework, with a communal living arrangement for the workers. As was the aim of doing theatre and community work, and inter-weaving the two.

Berman: 'I never saw why the same techniques that are used to create illusion couldn't be used to create reality. In 1967 I wanted to do experimental theatre that was of genuine use to the community, not in an intellectual sense, but in a structural and physical sense.' So there was always a deliberate two-pronged attack – of theatre experiments ('a policy of only doing new plays, and plays that are structurally different') and experiments using communication techniques and structural changes within the community. From the beginning, too, Berman 'had a very clear idea to set up a living cooperative, and of working as cooperatively as possible within the constraints of a charity'.

Berman came to England in 1962 as a Rhodes scholar: 'I wanted to leave America because I didn't like its dominant ethos, its overwhelming consumerism. I like it here because at least at that time I thought things were very different. They're becoming less different now because of the ever-increasing domination of American culture on other countries.' Berman's venture into lunchtime theatre in 1968 coincided with the beginning of his community work:

> What happened was I had started to do a lot of work in community theatre in Notting Hill with the Inter-Action Game Method on play sites, the Method being a training technique that works with actors as well as non-actors to get them to create something together very quickly. It's based on children's games and not on verbal or intellectual ability. We worked in various parts of North Kensington, on the early Carnivals and on housing action. We were using theatre and communication skills as an instrument in the community.

Within three short months in 1968 Inter-Action had got off the ground. Berman: 'We had two theatre companies and two community activities involving about 16 people, though none of them could pay and we were all living on the dole or off friends.' They tried to get a space in Notting Hill which proved to be difficult. At the same time they were working in Camden and Kentish Town, in a shop-front opposite the Roundhouse in Chalk Farm. 'Within three months we had The Other Company touring and the lunch-hour theatre starting at the Little Theatre in St Martin's Lane, then moving to the Ambiance restaurant. We also ran youth club and playground activities that summer and were running Inter-Action Games Sessions in various institutions.' There was the beginnings of the Dogg's Troupe 'doing things on play sites as well as running play schemes, with some street theatre for children'. And there was the 'itinerant' lunchtime theatre: 'We went from the Ambiance to the Green Banana in Soho. In those days, lunchtime theatre was new, and restaurant owners jumped at it to save their trade. Eventually you could figure out that any restaurant that would have you would be having money troubles. After the Green Banana we went to the ICA for a season of Black Power plays; then we were homeless for a brief period before we got ensconced in the Almost Free [a small theatre near Piccadilly Circus] in 1972. We put on an average of ten plays per year for eleven years.'[2]

Roland Rees directed many of Inter-Action's early lunchtime plays, including *The Electronic Nigger* by Ed Bullins, an American Black Power playwright. Rees: 'Berman got Bullins over for that play and really ran him as far as publicity went. At that time lunchtime theatre was a real novelty.' The production conditions at the Ambiance were perhaps typical of lunchtime theatre: 'We used to rehearse in an atmosphere that was still steamed up from the previous evening. We would gather in front of the steel drums at 11am and the guy who ran the Ambiance, from Trinidad, I think, used to sleep in the toilets and would wander out in a turban with his girl friend in the middle of rehearsals. Extraordinarily difficult circumstances. We were all mad.'[3]

Many of the seasons of lunchtime plays – from the Black Power Season at the ICA in 1970 to the Rights and Campaigns Season (plays on Jewish issues) at the Almost Free in 1978 – were structured on themes, with the intention of spawning new theatre groups.

> Looking back it was a very seminal approach to the fostering of self-expression for theatre groups from different areas of the libertarian movement – Black theatre, Black Power theatre, Women's theatre, Gay theatre, Jewish theatre. It was planned in advance, built

around the concept that the theatre is a structure which can intercede in reality. I think there's no better proof of the success of this approach than those companies we've encouraged to set up. We simply provided a structural framework and a season to cut their teeth on.

The Black Theatre of Brixton, The Womens Theatre Group and Gay Sweatshop were spawned from Inter-Action lunchtime seasons.

The same structural approaches were applied to the working methods of Inter-Action which Berman felt were 'more representative of the workers than any business in the country'.

> Every division in Inter-Action has an elected representative on the Central Committee that makes all finance and policy decisions, although ultimately these can be overturned on appeal to the trustees. The living situation is a proper housing cooperative (without co-ownership at present). From the beginning we were trying to combine a cooperative work and life style, which we've achieved, with the necessary compromises with the legalities that exist.

Berman was always the Artistic Director of Inter-Action productions and as such chose the plays. Beyond that he said he had no control. The staff of the theatre operated independently and collectively in their decision-making. All the jobs were shared and inter-changeable on a rota basis. Having set up the various projects, Berman gradually pulled out of each area of the organisation. Berman: 'I've moved away from each area to a greater or lesser distance depending on its strength to run itself. The success depends on experienced people running something that has a past and a future to it, as opposed to a now and only a now type of thinking.'

In addition to communal living, the structure included equal pay and a pension fund:

> We had a long-term view as early as 1968 when we decided as a matter of policy that we would have a pension fund, create a situation where people could come in, work for many years, have families, take sabbaticals. In 1968 we planned a sabbatical leave system which is now operational: you get two months in the fourth year, up to one year off out of seven, paid. That was all part of the original plan of a working community.

By 1972, Inter-Action was in a position to provide an advisory service based on the 'cooperative' experiences, for new groups wishing to work in a similar fashion: 'We help about 1200 groups a year with advice, mostly community groups with a small percentage of arts groups. There are always two types – one which is fostered out of rebellion and takes up an antagonistic, anti-establishment stance. It doesn't want to win, just to fight and when it wins or comes close to winning, it will quit. We avoid these groups. Then there's the type of group that would like to achieve something on a long-term basis and doesn't know how to get started. We advise them on such things as registration, charitable status, fund-raising, structure, financial planning, personal problems and how to manipulate bureaucracies. Sometimes a group just needs a part of this service, but we never do simply fund-raising because no group's problem is ever just money.'

Inter-Action's projects ranged from starting a Father Xmas Union to 'trying to get planning permission for Buckingham Palace'. Berman:

I set up an official trades union for Father Christmases, as a Friendly Society (however unfriendly to some). Every year we have done one or two major events, like taking on an institution or an establishment body in a larky way. But it's always made its mark. We got arrested for being a real trades union – the Father Xmas Union – for picketing Selfridges for using non-unionised labour. It was an extraordinary embarrassment for the police because their children wouldn't speak to them as they'd arrested Father Christmas.

Inter-Action worked on the principle of 'intervention into reality' and on 'mediation'. Berman: 'You do an event, a theatre event, like the Father Xmas picket, which reaches say a hundred people in its primary life, but it attracts the media: so you mediate your message to millions. It has to be carefully planned, but it's another form of inserting yourself into reality.' The same principles applied in the Buckingham Palace escapade:

We were taking advantage of the same thing that property developers take advantage of – that you don't have to own a piece of property to get planning permission. You just get planning permission, buy the land cheaply, then go ahead and build an expensive office block, without telling the owners. I just used that information. I didn't own Buckingham Palace at the time; in fact, I still don't. But I applied for planning permission to develop a youth hostel. They eventually found an obscure law that the Queen's property is not subject to the same planning laws as the rest of us. But they panicked for a while until they found this law because it was the only way they could get out of giving me planning permission. And it got us the publicity I wanted at a time when we were fighting to save Piccadilly from the planners and the property developers. We made the point very nicely that perhaps there ought to be some curtailment of the planning laws.

Berman attacked the British Army one year for demonstrating the use of real weapons to children in a department store. He sent a cable to Lord Carrington, then the Defence Minister, saying 'remove your troops from my sanctuaries or I shall attack, signed Super Santa' (Berman's title in the Father Xmas Union). He sent a copy to all the media, who rang Carrington, then negotiating with Dom Mintoff in Malta. Berman: 'He was put out, to say the least, with all those phone calls: "I'm negotiating the future of the western world and you bother me with this mad man?" But he'd had war declared on him. The event embodied my concept of "real" theatre.'

More seriously there was The Other Company (TOC) which started embryonically in 1968 and went on until the untimely death of its director Naftali Yavin in 1972. TOC used the basic Inter-Action Game Methods as a training technique and to work on experimental plays. The company worked productively with James Saunders and produced *Games After Liverpool* in 1971 – 'more a prescription than a play on paper, a series of statements for the director and actors to work with'. TOC also produced *Sagittarius* and *Virgo* by Ed Berman (Ed. B.) in 1968 and in 1971 Peter Handke's *Offending the Audience*, followed in 1972 by Handke's *Self-Accusation* and *Prophecy*. The Fun Art Bus was, in the early seventies, a TOC project which continued after TOC was disbanded.

There was the City Farm project which evolved out of an environmental play called *The Last Straw* about a group of farmers who were tired of planners running motorways through their farms and decided to come to the city to teach the city slickers a lesson by bulldozing a farm into the middle of the city. Berman: 'It was a droll idea and worked well as a Christmas play and as family entertainment. At the end of each performance we would step out of character and invite people to come and see a real farm in the middle of the city in six months' time. And then we proceeded as a theatre company to build this farm. We couldn't see the difference between building an environmental farm inside a building or a real one outside: you needed the same materials and the same structure – the animals, buildings, fences, a financial structure, care of the animals, an educational programme, an audience. Again we were able to carry theatre into reality.' From that first pilot scheme, by

1978, thirty other 'city farms' had been created around the country with help from Inter-Action, with another fifteen on the way.

There was the Dogg's Troupe and OATS (Old Age Theatre Society). The Dogg's Troupe emerged from the 1968 street theatre and started operating formally from 1969 performing plays for children. Berman: 'The plays are all of social significance, though they may seem on the surface just simple comedies. The social significance lies in the fact that they're participatory – with participation on the part of the children and follow-up work with them in their own communities.' Berman called it the 'Lone Ranger' technique – of bringing adults in to learn to do similar things with their own children, to learn to run their own play schemes. This was another aspect of Inter-Action's structural policy. Berman: 'To me the participation is "political" – that you allow your script to be changed by the people involved. That's what politics is all about – giving people the opportunity to change something, with the extension into "reality" of the follow-up.' The Dogg's Troupe averaged 580 performances a year – 'a very high productivity level'. Berman: 'Location is also political. *Where* you do something, and for, or with whom is probably more important than what you say.'

The Dogg's Troupe's policy was only to go to places where they were invited, doing less 'guerilla theatre' after the Father Christmas Union came into being. The follow-up involved linking up with a community or with youth workers, having discussions before and after and providing equipment for further work – video or radio, costumes. The Dogg's Troupe operated as a permanent company for the whole year, and split into five units in the summer, each directed by one of the performers. So in this area alone Inter-Action had five companies on the road between 1974 and 1978. The Fun Art Bus was one of those units. OATS was an off-shoot of the Dogg's Troupe: it operated with three old people and three young performers for a year, but disbanded on the death of one of the eldest.

The West End transfer of Tom Stoppard's *Dirty Linen* (commissioned for Berman's American Centenary Season at the Almost Free) provided the opportunity to create a new West End contract, another example of the way in which Berman attempted to change whatever system he found himself in:

> The *Dirty Linen* transfer gave me the opportunity to set up a West End contract which gave everyone a share of the profits, including the box office lady. And there were things like every actor was entitled to two nights off a month for other theatre or TV or film work,

which keeps them refreshed and gives the under-studies a chance to go on stage. This is an extremely happy company of a higher calibre than you would normally find in a play in its fourth year.

The same type of principles were embodied in BARC – the British American Repertory Company – launched in 1979:

> We've just got permission from both Equities – in the US and the UK – to set up a company with equal numbers of Americans and British and spending an equal amount of time in both countries. Everyone will be paid the same and there will be profit-sharing should any of the plays transfer. The company will do newly commissioned work on issues. It really combines many aspects of Inter-Action's work in the seventies and should function as a model that anybody can copy. Or as an opening for others to develop their own ways of overcoming the Equity problems.

The new centre in Kentish Town which opened in 1977 was an important development 'but still a means to an end'. Until then Inter-Action had moved around in a variety of short-life housing: 'we'd been pushed out of five buildings until we finally built this one. Each time we made a deal with the GLC or Camden Council.' Inter-Action also used fifty-six different derelict houses from 1970 for its workers. Eventually Inter-Action renovated eight houses owned by the Housing Trust. The new building was 'temporary, a way of avoiding having to move again, only a framework' – but with fourteen different units of work. Berman: 'All the walls move. It has an expandable structure and one end's been left blank for expansion.' There was a bar, coffee bar and a community area. In 1978 there were 30 different Inter-Action activity groups a week for adults and children – with a notice board listing what people could join. To run the organisation there were 60 people working centrally, plus another 40 hired for specific projects.

Berman's plans included considerable future expansion – 'obtaining one or more theatres in the West End to act as a transfer house for fringe companies on contractual terms fairer than those offered by commercial houses. It's a logical way to grow, given a certain set of principles. We can prove that a house is commercially viable by paying everybody equally, fairly profit-sharingly and by requiring that money be paid back to the Arts Council if the play was originally subsidised.'

In 1978, a Skateboard Park had been completed which would 'have more users than anything else anyone has done in this neighbourhood in a hundred years – a sad comment in some ways, happy in others'. The City Farm and a new riding school were being rebuilt. Inter-Action was developing educational work on ecological problems for children with a new mobile theatre – the Animobile. And there were the Community Cameos, a community theatre venture started to mark Inter-Action's 10th anniversary – 'William Shakespeare and Edward Lear alive and well and living in the community'.

Despite his impressive empire (which earned him almost as many envious enemies as admirers) and his grandiose visions (the envy derived in part from the success with which he realised these), Berman felt that a perspective was required about the actual political impact and the real effects on social change. These, he felt, were modest. The City Farms, for example, in thirty different neighbourhoods might have three and a half million children visiting in a year. 'But that's infinitesimal, significant for the kids, but small in the total scheme of things. If you really want to change something you have to do it en masse. There's no political philosophy in the world that hasn't dealt with the masses.'

At the same time, Berman felt his achievements were not negligible by comparison with 'conventional' political theatre for which he had some contempt. Berman: 'Political theatre that stands up and spews out doctrine is of minimal use to most people. It usually speaks to a committed or semi-committed audience. I wonder if political theatre has ever changed anyone's opinion on anything or whether it has just corroborated and consolidated. A lot of people who do political theatre think they're saying something new and important and changing people's minds, but that's a charade. Political theatre does have a function of course – a flagship function, of consolidating and galvanising in terms of campaigns. That *is* important, but it should not be misunderstood to be other than it is.' Inter-Action might not have been as 'flamboyantly political as those who stand on their hind legs and bellow about the role they have to play'. But Berman thought it was more 'realistic' about its work. 'We are modestly effective in a small area of 10,000 housing units in West Kentish Town and Gospel Oak. And in other neighbourhoods in over twenty countries. But there are tens of thousands of Kentish Towns in the UK and hundreds and thousands of them in Europe and millions of them in the world, so how significant is it really?'

1969

Some of the most important developments in British theatre in the late sixties took place outside London. Of these, the work of Albert Hunt with students at Bradford College of Art was missed by most of the wider public because of its regional and educational context. But from the staging of the Russian Revolution in the streets of Bradford in 1967 through the innovative pastiche of *John Ford's Cuban Missile Crisis* in 1970, it had perhaps the strongest influence on the future work of political theatre companies in the seventies. As did the work of the Welfare State (which started in 1968 and eventually based itself in Lancashire) and the Pip Simmons Theatre Group (which grew out of the Drury Lane Arts Lab). While these groups were not socialist in the same sense as later companies, they experimented with visual presentation, and the content of their work was very much anti-establishment in its orientation. These – along with Portable Theatre, the nursery slope of the Brenton/ Hare/Wilson generation of playwrights – were the early touring companies. There was considerable contact, collaboration and cross-reference amongst the *people* involved in the late sixties (e.g. Welfare State worked with Albert Hunt and CAST, the Ardens worked with them all), such that the growth of political theatre was often a matter of rich cross-fertilisation.

1969 saw the opening in London of new venues which were to prove important to the presentation of new work in the seventies. There was the Oval House, for many years a South London youth centre, which expanded its terms of reference to take in touring theatre companies and later to provide a venue for the meetings of the many new alternative theatre organisations. There was the Soho Poly, a lunchtime theatre started in Soho (next to Better Books) in 1968 by Fred Proud and Verity Bargate and which then became established in a tiny cellar in Riding House Street behind the BBC as one of the most important venues for new plays, presenting an average of twenty per year over a period of ten years.

And in 1969 the Royal Court acknowledged new developments in alternative theatre by opening the Theatre Upstairs on its top floor, more than doubling its main stage output. As the writers' theatre from the fifties under the artistic direction of George Devine, and home of the 'revolution' that produced John Osborne's *Look Back in Anger*, the English Stage Company at the Royal Court theatre had been, by 1968, the single most significant force in new writing in post-war British theatre. Ann Jellicoe, a Royal Court writer, summarised its impact:

> Before 1956 no commercial management bothered about new plays; the list of new writers was complete with T. S. Eliot, Christopher Fry and John Whiting. The Royal Court changed that ... Two years after opening in 1956 the English Stage Company had found fourteen new playwrights. By 1966 there were forty. Today [1976] it must be nearly a hundred.[1]

One of the main contributions to new writing was the famous Theatre Writers' Group organised between 1958 and 1960 by George Devine and William Gaskill, including such members as John Arden, Edward Bond, Ann Jellicoe, Keith Johnstone and Arnold Wesker. Under the artistic direction of William Gaskill from 1965 to 1975 the Royal Court gained a new lease of life, and with the new post of Writer-in-Residence (held at different times by Howard Brenton, Christopher Hampton, N. F. Simpson, David Halliwell, Caryl Churchill, Mary O'Malley, Alan Drury and Leigh Jackson) it provided the opportunity for promising playwrights to produce some of their best work.

The Royal Court was the theatre that took the leap and produced the plays of Edward Bond when the critical climate was particularly hostile to the playwright who was to become one of Britain's major writers. As John Arden made a transition in the late sixties significant to his work and also to the period as a whole, so did Edward Bond. The essay devoted to him highlights two important aspects of Bond's work and its relation to the political theatre movement of the seventies: the socialist politics inherent in his early plays and the subsequent development of a conscious socialist ideology and aesthetic in his work through the seventies, analysing his political philosophy in relation to his plays. In so doing, it articulates the ideas current in the arena of political theatre during the seventies.

'That's not well,' cried Fonda/Kennedy, 'What do you think this is, one of your god-damned movies?' from *John Ford's Cuban Missile Crisis*, 1970

Albert Hunt and the Bradford College of Art Theatre Group

At eleven o'clock in the morning on 2 November 1967, a dozen students suddenly appeared on the steps of the Queen Victoria monument in the centre of Bradford. They were all dressed in black – black jeans, black sweaters, black polythene capes tied round their necks, and they all wore red armbands. They climbed up the steps, turned round, and began to read aloud in unison from the thoughts of Chairman Mao. A policeman at the foot of the steps tried to pretend nothing was happening. At roughly the same time, two miles or so from the city centre, a procession of more than a hundred students, led by a dance band, came swinging through the gates of the park in which the city's main art gallery, the Cartwright Memorial Hall, is set. These students, too, were dressed in black, but with white armbands. The girls had boots and long skirts that swung round their ankles, and they carried wooden home-made rifles. Behind them in the procession, were four huge, twelve-foot puppets, made out of cardboard boxes painted black. The students carried slogans on banners: 'Support Your Government', 'Down with Red Agitators', 'No Peace with Aggressors'. In the city bus station, a bus arrived from Barnsley. About twenty-five students, in black with white armbands, got off the bus and looked around. A van drove up, crudely camouflaged. Out of it leapt a student with a red armband. He picked out the four prettiest girls, told them to get in the van, and drove away. Inside the van, the girls had their white armbands exchanged for red. Outside a bread shop in the city centre, a queue of two dozen students formed. They wore red armbands and carried the slogan 'Peace, Land, Bread'. Each student bought one teacake. Then they took their teacakes across the town to a disused post office that had been left to crumble in the middle of blocks of high-rise council flats. In the shop window were placards telling people they could take anything they liked from the shop, for free, and could leave anything they liked except money. A wordless poster showed Lenin reaching out over the Italianate city hall and the mills of Bradford.[1]

That was the beginning of *The Russian Revolution* presented in the streets of Bradford by Albert Hunt and his Bradford College of Art students. It was undoubtedly the largest-scale piece of street theatre produced in Britain in the sixties or seventies – an event which encapsulated the imaginative possibilities of political theatre and which set a precedent for the following decade. The idea was simply to turn Bradford into St Petersburg and to recreate the October Revolution in the form of a dramatic game. Its impact was immeasurable.

It was, however, only one of the many inventive and formative creations of Albert Hunt and his students. There had been the *Vietnam War Game*, a week-long event during which ten students spent a week doing research and reading and then 'chose the parts they were going to play in the game. A wealthy textile student from Malaya, who was violently anti-communist, insisted on playing the current Saigon leader, Marshal Ky. An apprentice jeweller, a Polish emigré, who was also violently anti-communist, became President Johnson. An active member of the Young Conservatives cast himself as the Soviet Union; two bright girl dress-designers made up the American delegation; two first-year boys played China and North Vietnam respectively; and a Buddhist and an NLF representative (a girl who never spoke for three days) completed the group.' The brief for the game described 'a rapidly developing crisis situation. The United States had bombed areas close to the Chinese frontier, and there were rumours of a threatened blockade of Haiphong'. When the situation was devised in 1966 it was regarded as inconceivable, but eventually became part of the Nixon/ Kissinger peace policy in 1972. Hunt described the project:

> The game reached a climax of mutual deception. It was virtually won by the girl playing the NLF ... Since the Saigon representative had refused to sit at the same negotiating table as the NLF, she'd suggested two tables, with Saigon at one, and the NLF at the other, and everybody else at both. (This suggestion pre-dated by about two years the agonising discussions about tables during the Paris negotiations.) Now, as the Russians and Americans announced, with their final move, an agreement to call off the blockade, she produced a trump card. She'd been negotiating quietly with the Buddhists, and had agreed, temporarily, to work with them on paralysing Saigon with a general strike. The boy playing Ky resigned in angry protest because the umpires allowed the move. He said the NLF would never have any influence in Saigon. Two months later, the Tet offensive began. All the people playing the great powers claimed to have won.[2]

Like all of Hunt's work, the *Vietnam War Game* was a method of using theatre to educate, integrated into the radical concept of alternative education outlined in his book *Hopes for Great Happenings*.[3] Perhaps best known of Hunt's creations was *John Ford's Cuban Missile Crisis* which in 1970, presented the Cuban Missile Crisis as a John Ford movie. Hunt:

> We wanted also ... to use this form of popular entertainment to put forward for consideration ideas – political, social, even philosophical – that concerned us. We wanted to question accepted ideas about normality, accepted attitudes towards both historical and contemporary events. And we wanted to question the accepted attitudes, not only of our 'enemies', the political right, but of our 'friends' on the left. We wanted, in fact, constantly to re-examine our own attitudes. When we were dealing with the Second World War, we tried to suggest that the issues were not as simple as popular history made them out to be ... that the picture of Churchill as the great war leader was not the whole truth, and that the parallel between Eichmann and Harris was too close for comfort. When we looked at the Cuban Missile Crisis, we tried, not only to put the actions of the Kennedy brothers in a less heroic and more realistic light, but also to question some of the myths that had grown up and around Guevara.[4]

John Ford's Cuban Missile Crisis was commissioned by left-wing students from Bradford University as part of the Lenin Centenary Celebrations in April 1970. Hunt:

> We had the idea from the start of telling the story as if it were a Western: Dean Rusk had himself used the language of a Western at the height of the crisis ('We was eyeball to eyeball, and I think the other fellow just blinked'). And Norman Mailer, in *The Presidential Papers*, had seen Kennedy as a film hero. 'Of necessity', he wrote about Kennedy's nomination for President, 'the myth would emerge once more, because America's politics would now be also America's favourite movie, America's first soap opera, America's best seller'.[5]

Hunt's approach to several scenes in that show illustrated his influential style. He'd written an episode which outlined US intervention in Cuba since the beginning of the century. But it was all verbal and it was necessary to work out a more dramatic documentary style of presentation and one which related to the Western idiom. They came up with the idea of a cattle rustling scene, using flat, two-dimensional, but very realistic looking cows which 'sat on the stage and stared out at the audience'. And they invented a scene in which the US became a cowboy trying to protect a girl (Cuba) from a Mexican cattle rustler. Hunt: 'The rustler was branding the cattle with an S, so the cowboy turned the S into a dollar sign – and took the cattle to his own side of the stage. All the information was kept in the scene – but it was transformed into metaphor.' And there was the sequence at the height of the crisis when Kennedy moved to confront Krushchev, whose ships were approaching the line. Hunt: 'Ford intervened with his usual catchphrase, "That's well, print it". "That's not well", cried Fonda/ Kennedy. "What do you think this is, one of your goddamned movies? We're gonna see this thing through." History had overtaken the myth. The dramatic action was that of the sheriff threatening to blow somebody's brains out: the "real" results would have been world catastrophe.'

The work of Albert Hunt and the Bradford students was amongst the first of a kind of political theatre that was to be developed by many groups, from The General Will to 7:84, from North West Spanner to the Womens Theatre Group. It was also amongst the best of the decade, despite Hunt's use of inexperienced student actors.

'It is possible, I think, in the West now, still to make a concrete alternative.' John Fox, 1976

Welfare State

Welfare State was founded in 1968 by John and Sue Fox, then based at Bradford College of Art with Albert Hunt, with whom they collaborated on some early events. Welfare State were often considered a fringe theatre group though they described their work as 'performance/sculpture, time/painting'. Their work was certainly theatrical, but spectacle rather than theatre in any conventional sense. Their performances were not plays, but epic poems, visual and aural, though virtually without words. They dealt in ritual, myth and magic. *The Runway*, for example (from 1973), was concerned with the ritual of man's evolution – Everyman's journey through history, culture, life and space in 25 cantos: r-evolution with the emphasis on evolution. Many incidents were presented simultaneously, though separate and seemingly unconnected. Thus, simulating a fairground ambience, an end-of-pier comedian repeated the same joke, garbled microphonically, while a rat catcher pressed rats like leaves in an ancient tome, while an apprentice spaceman soldered his fingers together. Everyman entered to a mound of sand, on which were enacted primitive rituals: sand castles became symbolic abodes; a circle of wooden spikes was encircled by a ring of candles (fire), this encircled by blocks of ice as the Ice Age encroached on the early shelters of civilisation. Everyman was seduced into a metal drum, a contraption suggestive of a space ship, where he was shaved by a demon barber using a fluorescent tube ignited with a soldering iron. A sex-goddess was wheeled in to the tunes of Bessie Smith while another woman gouged the eyes from her child and ate her bread/baby.

Welfare State were described variously as dream-weavers, purveyors of images, sculptors of visual poetry, civic magicians and engineers of the imagination. They described their work as:

... devising handmade ceremonies, namings, memorial services, performances, processions and dances, constructing sideshows, environments and landscape sculptures and arranging workshops and teaching courses for any sympathetic space, situation or season.[1]

An early manifesto stated that the company 'believes that imagination, original art and spontaneous creative energy are being systematically destroyed by the current educational processes, materialism and bureaucratic decision-making of western large-scale industrial society'. Welfare State therefore undertook any useful project 'which aims to counteract such culture of death'. With each show, the work was new, craft-based and hand-made, and often the creative process was demonstrated as part of the event. Welfare State preferred situations which provided the opportunity to work with a grass-roots group and to do long-term follow-up.

John and Sue Fox were involved in the staging of *The Russian Revolution in the Streets of Bradford* with Albert Hunt and with Hunt's mental health show *Move Over Jehovah*; and they worked with John Arden and Margaretta D'Arcy on *Harold Muggins Is a Martyr* at Unity and *The Hero Rises Up* at the Roundhouse. Their earliest shows – *St. Valentine's Firestorm* and *The Tide is OK for the 30th* – were done as ad hoc events in 1968 and led to the formation of the early Welfare State. In 1969 they created *The Cabinet of Dr. Calighari* which was very successful and recorded on a John Peel LP. During 1970 Welfare State directed themselves towards street theatre, drawing on work done by students at Bradford College of Art. The first of these was subsidised by the Yorkshire Arts Association and created the core of the initial group.

It was only in 1972 that Welfare State formed into a solid core of eight people based in a commune in Leeds. There was an anti-intellectual, anti-establishment bias in the group from the beginning. John Fox:

Most of the people in the group ... had a fine arts background of one kind or another, either as lecturers or students in art colleges. They tend to be very non-university, non-verbal, very much about making images. And certainly with no theatrical experience at all ... I used to feel very inadequate because I didn't have all the right words of criticism at my fingertips. But then I realised I was completely brainwashed not only by direct grant grammar school, but also by an Oxbridge education which removed so much of one's sensual feelings ... I feel personally that I've got back to when I was ten years old and could react simply and directly before I was fucked up by twenty years' schooling and conditioning ...[2]

Fox described himself in 1972 as 'very political, left in a sort of non-verbalised way. We know instinctively that people are repressed in our society and are against it. It represents quite a threat to the existing order of things for twenty or thirty people playing musical instruments and wearing fantastic costumes to suddenly appear and march through the streets in an apparently anarchic fashion.'[3] During the seventies, Welfare State became one of the most sophisticated 'performance arts' groups and one of the most highly subsidised of alternative theatre companies.

Welfare State always deliberately sought out new audiences:

> We play to very varied audiences. On a beach, on a bank holiday, in a Royal Park, in a University or a Working Men's Club. A student audience is somewhat self-conscious: they are not sure about Art ... but a street audience is very spontaneous. If they don't like you they walk away or throw things. When Maskar, our fire eater and Magician, eats razor blades and walks on swords, he gets the same gasps and applause whether we are working in a fairground, a dance hall, a circus marquee or a university refectory. Similarly our street plays have worked in very formal schools, art galleries and museums and also borstals, housing estates, mental hospitals, youth clubs and discotheques.[4]

Welfare State regarded themselves as purveyors of popular theatre in its most primitive and traditional forms:

> Our theatre can be enjoyed by everybody on one level or another. When we use devices culled from the mummers and music hall and fairground and pantomime, it is not out of sentiment, or to make nostalgic resurrections ... but rather because such traditional popular forms are very good theatre. In fact we do a lot of reading and research into traditional and pagan rituals and legends: we've built up an extensive card file for reference ... An escapologist is a good example of popular theatre. You know what is going to happen ... yet it might not. It is entertaining and skilful and tense and vaguely symbolic of everyman escaping his predicament.[5]

The use of legend by the Welfare State was illustrated by the recurrence in their work of the hero figure, Lancelot Quail, who in 1972 went on a month-long Arts Council subsidised pilgrimage from Glastonbury to St Michael's Mount:

> The procession of brightly decorated vehicles which made the 150-mile journey included four caravans, a nine-ton truck housing a generator and office, a hearse, a converted bus, an ambulance, and an exhibition wagon towing a converted army rocket trailer with a circus tent. They followed in reverse a route of magical significance pre-

viously travelled by Phoenician tin traders, Joseph of Arimathea and King Arthur. It was not a Second Coming but a First Going Away. Welfare State could not see that there was anything left to come for, but there were good reasons to leave the barbaric and insensitive culture.[6]

In 1973 Lancelot Quail reappeared in the form of Icarus on the site of their new base in Burnley when they performed *Beauty and the Beast*, using their 'wasteland' environment to 'juxtapose the grotesqueness of the cold dark labyrinth which houses mental and physical cripples with the beauty of the Sun King's world of warmth and light inside the tent, and it is concerned with the attempts of the creatures in the labyrinth to escape their world and, like Icarus, fly to a better one.'[7]

Welfare State rejected conventional theatre:

> We have worked within theatres, but we find they are sadly bugged with many hang-ups. For example, take two theatres we have worked in: the Northcott Theatre, Exeter, had 38 staff for basic administration. It was a very unhappy scene because of career-jostling, hierarchies, and role-playing. A microcosm of capitalist society nursing a jaded culture. Petty rivalries almost prevented us getting the show on at all. At the Gardner Centre [in Sussex University] we had a much happier time personally, because most of the staff were very helpful, but there, in a circular auditorium with potentially one of the most flexible arenas in the UK, we were obliged to keep the seats in fixed rows and accept a lighting rig geared to proscenium theatre and pre-plotting shows in advance. Basically we are happy to work anywhere ... unfortunately once you step into a theatre, you tend to be in a certain cultural bracket ... The contact with the audience is more direct in the street. The audience don't feel there is a barrier and often come up to talk after a performance.[8]

Like groups such as Red Ladder, Welfare State were often aware of the need for and, at the same time, the contradictions of state subsidy:

> It is possible, I think, in the West now, still to make a concrete alternative. The paradox is that we receive government money ... in the Arts Council there are young officers who are very concerned that the kind of research that we are doing should go ahead. They realise that something is wrong with the country, with the system, with the theatre. Therefore they are prepared to put money into research ... And yet the paradox is that if we are successful then the system as it stands will no longer be tenable.[9]

Fox described Welfare State's work as 'a commando or pathfinder

mission' working 'on different rules from the main battalion ...
The shows are about change, the movement from one situation to
another. They are not in any sense agitprop stories. They are designed to have their own logic in terms of their own poetry. However, they do, I believe, have some kind of relevance to wider social
problems.'[10] Welfare State's missionary work included many religious elements inspired by the fact that 'we live in a society
that has very little spiritual belief in anything ... It is a question
of how far we, as "theatre people", can relate to or discover alternative spiritual values.'[11]

John Fox held strong views about political theatre generally, and
regarded much of what was done by 'groups with social aims as
baby-minding to keep children off the streets, but it has nothing
to do with art or theatre or poetry. Much of political theatre is
patronising to the working class because it comes from a university intellectual position ... the audience doesn't have to be told the
landlord is a bastard, they already know it. We are attacked by
both the right and the left. The right says we are anarchists and
the left says we should be reaching the workers. But if we are
about any kind of political statement, it is about being very strong
and free individuals ... You cannot forever suppress human
energy.'[12]

'Since I can't think that Mr Simmons is anti-semitic, there must be some purpose ...' New Statesman, 1975

Pip Simmons Theatre Group

The Pip Simmons Theatre Group was formed out of the Arts Lab in Drury Lane run by Jim Haynes, and operated until 1973 when it disbanded, re-forming in 1974. Peter Ansorge in his book *Disrupting the Spectacle* described the group: 'A typical evening in the company of the Pip Simmons Group combined the energy of a football match or pop concert with a decisive attack on mainstream liberal values. The shows were steeped in cynicism, excitement, despair and good music.'[1] In style, the company was more closely aligned with Welfare State and The People Show than with socialist theatre companies.

Superman (1969) was inspired by American culture, based on a real comic in which Superman became involved in the Civil Rights Movement. In the Pip Simmons show Superman was the star of TV talk shows, delivering theories about juvenile delinquents, negro rights and pop music. The show was done in a cartoon-style with one-dimensional characters, and the sort of dialogue found in comic-book bubbles. Ansorge described the show as 'the blueprint for cartoon shows'.

Do It! (1971) was based on the book by Jerry Rubin of the same title, about the student attack on the Chicago Democratic Convention in 1968. The first part dealt with the storming of the Convention, the second part with the trial of Rubin and the other Yippies. Ansorge described it as follows:

The first half was an attempt to recreate the 1968 riots in the auditorium ... The students in *Do It!* were clearly the products of comfortable middle-class homes, who seemed equally obsessed by rock music and the more aggressive notions of the US Peace Movement ... *Do It!* was part of the violent landscape of the late 1960s ... At one point during *Do It!* the Yippies threw faeces into the faces of the Pentagon guards and then proceeded to run hysterically through the audience demanding support for their actions. Simmons once described to me the reaction during a performance at Southampton University. 'We were asking "If you'd been a guard at the Pentagon what would you have done?" We divided audiences in this way. At Southampton it took about five minutes for the audience to get the message. Then one of the actors screamed "Come on! You can't all be pigs!" and about thirty people joined the actors running through the audience. It was like a madhouse.'[2]

The George Jackson Black and White Minstrel Show (1973) was based on the minstrel shows that were popular in the American South during the nineteenth century, in which whites blacked themselves up to mock negroes. Again Ansorge described the show:

> It was assumed that the audience were also long-standing slave owners. After almost three quarters of an hour of sneering racialism the atmosphere in the auditorium could have been cut with a knife. The audience were deliberately lured into the snares of racial thinking. Towards the end of the first half a slave auction was held. The minstrels ran through the audience begging to be bought. The purpose was to evoke a direct response from the audience. The interval was spent with some of the audience, having had the slaves they had bought chained to their wrists, trying to find a point of contact with their new acquisitions. I watched several people in the audience ask their slaves to buy them drinks; a few gave them their freedom. They had accepted the false vocabulary of a master-slave relationship.[3]

In the second half, the star of the show, George Jackson, ended tied in a sack. Ansorge:

> A spotlight focused upon the red sack in which Jackson was struggling to escape – the sack was raised upwards on a pulley. The sack throbbed, vibrated with activity until suddenly, a hand emerged to signal to the audience. It was the fist of the Black Panther salute. Immediately shots were fired at the sack and inside the body stretched in its death spasm. The show was over.[4]

Ansorge commented on the ambiguity of Pip Simmons's attitude towards his material, and the frequent attempts to provoke a direct response from audiences. Nowhere was this more apparent than in *An Die Musik* (1975), based on the sad irony of Jews in a concentration camp being forced to play beautiful music for the cultural pleasure of the Nazis who were degrading and murdering them. The play opened with a prologue – or operatic interlude – of grotesquely caricatured Jews at table (which provoked Benedict Nightingale in the *New Statesman* to remark that 'Since I can't think that Mr Simmons is anti-semitic, there must be some purpose . . .'). Then the audience watched the camp prisoners perform three pieces of music (the Schubert of the title, a Liszt, and Beethoven's 'Hymn to Joy') at the whip-command of a sadistic SS officer who brutalised and humiliated them – beating them, making them beat each other, beating the rhythms of the music on a woman's bare breasts, and finally gassing them while they played away. In this case the ambiguity was alienating and much too open to misinterpretation: for example, that the material was anti-semitic instead of – as it was no doubt intended – critical of anti-semitism. Certainly it recalled the Jew who paid a lot of money for a crudely anti-semitic engraving in the Portobello Market to prevent it from falling into the hands of someone who might enjoy it.

In their later work – *Dracula* (1974), *The Tempest* (1977) and *Woyzeck* (1977), the Pip Simmons Theatre Group became less overtly political in their subject matter, further developing their own distinctive, very visual and surrealistic performance style.[5] And they performed less frequently in Britain, more often abroad where they had a large cultish following amongst devotees of avant-garde theatre.

'We do not need a plan of the future, we need a method of change.' Edward Bond, Preface to *Lear*, 1973

Edward Bond

When Edward Bond's *Saved* was sent to the Lord Chamberlain in 1964, whole scenes were censored. It was subsequently produced at the Royal Court in 1965 as a 'private' club production, but was nevertheless successfully prosecuted and the theatre fined in 1966. And the play provoked hysterically hostile reactions like B. A. Young's in *The Financial Times*, who found the play 'poisonously objectionable'.[1] The main cause of the controversy was the now famous scene of the stoning to death of a baby in a South London park. It was this isolated act of violence in a subdued naturalistic landscape that offended, alienated and outraged.

Out of all proportion, suggested Bond in his own self-defence in the first published edition of *Saved*. He described the stoning as a typical English understatement and said: 'Compared to the "strategic" bombing of German towns it is a negligible atrocity, compared to the cultural and emotional deprivation of most of our children, its consequences are insignificant.' Violence such as the stoning, he said (and the hara-kiri of *Narrow Road to the Deep North*, the cannibalism of *Early Morning*, the punctured ear drums, rape and murder in *Lear*), was the necessary and inevitable consequence of an unjust society. He argued that the social injustices were quantitatively more violent and morally reprehensible than the individual acts of retaliative violence they unleashed. And he eventually concluded that his early plays had provoked such critical hostility because they were so fundamentally 'political' – in recording and reflecting the realities of society (i.e. capitalist society) truthfully. Bond: 'At the moment, in our society as it is, the truth is more terrible than the caricature of it.'[2]

Bond developed in the ten years from 1968 to 1978 from being intuitively political (as he described it) to being consciously political (or politically conscious); from talking about social comment to talking about socialism; from talking about morality to talking about Marxism; from being socially committed to being committed to a socialist society. During the decade Bond arrived at a theoretical and ideological framework (argued through his Prefaces and other prose) which made sense of the experience he had perceived (particularly during the war and his working-class childhood) and portrayed in his plays.

The Pope's Wedding (1962) preceded *Saved* and dealt with the meaninglessness of life for young East Anglians that drove one of them, Scopey, to 'try to get inside the skin' of the old hermit who seemed to have a secret understanding of some kind of meaning. It was a 'violent' attempt at the impossible (as the title suggested) motivated by a social environment that offered worse than nothing.

An adaptation in 1967 of Chekhov's *The Three Sisters* was followed in 1968 by *Early Morning*, banned outright by the censor (before such censorship was abolished later that year by Act of Parliament). It was a radical departure from the 'stylised naturalism' of *Saved* into a surrealist, expressionist mode which Bond described as 'the imagery of emotions – a journey through the "subjective head" of people in the real world of *Saved*'. Set consecutively in a Victorian milieu where Queen Victoria and Florence Nightingale are lesbian lovers, the princes George and Arthur are Siamese twins, and Disraeli is plotting rebellion; outside a Kilburn cinema where queue jumpers are killed; and in a heaven where the dead 'live' by cannibalising each other, the play presented a satiric view of a corrupt society.

Narrow Road to the Deep North, also produced in 1968 (ironically, given the controversy by this time surrounding Bond, commissioned by the Canon of Coventry Cathedral) and regarded by many as one of Bond's best plays, was a less anarchic, much more Brechtianly dialectical and 'historically distanced' piece than *Early Morning*, but no less savage in its condemnation of an unjust society. In it, Bond continued to develop earlier and what would become 'recurrent' themes, finding for them a new poetic clarity.

There was the quest for truth and understanding (the poet Basho off to the far North in search of enlightenment); religion, repressed sexuality and insanity as escapes from intolerable injustice; babies abandoned by parents out of economic necessity; cultural deprivation; the violence of fascistic dictatorship; the 'dialectics of dying'. (For Bond death is often difficult and violent, the dead often forced to live again as ghosts, then to die again with difficulty – one of his most powerful poetic images.)

In *Lear* (1971), certainly, his next full-length play, Bond married

these themes into an epic vision. Lear's quest leads him from building the walls of injustice, through an enlightening madness to
attempting, at least, however unsuccessfully, to scale and destroy the
symbolic wall. But not before he suffers miserably at the hands of
his daughters, whom he himself raised and conditioned to use
violence. Not before he 'murders innocence' in the gravedigger's boy
who befriended him with brotherly love. Not before he watches part
of the 'revolutionary' alternative follow in the same ruthless footsteps
of the 'ruling class' they wished to overthrow and replace. Bond
described the play as a two-fold attack: 'one on Stalinism, as seen
as a danger to western revolution . . . and on bourgeois culture as
expressed in Shakespeare's *Lear*':

> Lear had the wall built. He knows one old blind man can't pull it down,
> he doesn't even seek that sort of 'success'. But he knows there is not
> much time left to him. Soon he will die or be killed. So he uses his
> last day to make a gesture to the young people he knows and all those
> who come after him. In mounting the wall it is as if he were mounting
> a barricade. His gesture is: make revolution, whatever its cost it is less
> than the cost of the alternative. If you like he christens himself with
> revolution on the day he dies. Being so old, and having gone through
> so much, he is beyond questions of pessimism and optimism . . . and he
> has only one thing left: knowledge and so he acts.[3]

The Sea (1973), a deliberate departure from the 'tragic' to the
'comic' (if such a generic label can be used of any of Bond's work),
was followed by two plays based on historical personages: *Bingo*,
about Shakespeare, and *The Fool*, about the Norfolk poet John Clare.
In both, Bond was concerned with the relation of the artist to society
and the function of the artist, but also, by extension, with everyman
('I think the contradictions in Shakespeare's life are similar to the
contradictions in us'). Shakespeare was portrayed as caught between
preaching humanitarianism and libertarianism as a playwright and
practising the opposite by siding with the landowners on the issue of
the Enclosures, turning his back on the poor. And Bond showed
Clare, confronted with the contradiction of starving while being
courted by the upper classes, retreating finally into the lunatic land-
scapes of his own mind. Bond: 'Clare was driven into madness by
the ruling class, who made it impossible for him to produce culture
in direct relationship with his society.'[4]

In addition to his ten full-length plays and several adaptations (after
the Chekhov, Bond adapted Wedekind's *Spring Awakening* for the
National Theatre in 1974, obviously attracted by its emphasis on the
*de*structive as opposed to the *in*structive elements of education), Bond

wrote five short plays for what could be described as agitprop political purposes: *Black Mass* (1970) for the Anti-Apartheid Movement to commemorate the Sharpeville Massacre; *Passion* (1971) for a Campaign for Nuclear Disarmament mass meeting at Alexandra Palace; *Stone* (1976) for Gay Sweatshop, the alternative theatre company that campaigned for homosexual liberation; and *Grandma Faust* and *The Swing* (1976, under the umbrella title *A-A-America!*) for Inter-Action's American Bi-centennial season.

The Bundle (written after *The Woman* – Bond's first direct venture into the sexual politics which are inseparable from either capitalist or socialist politics – but produced before, in 1977) clearly marked a turning point for Bond. In it, with full political consciousness, he employed an innovative method of 'dramatising not the story, but the analysis'. *The Bundle* was also Bond's most politically important play in not only showing society as it is, but in suggesting a solution. Bond: 'We mustn't only write problem plays, we must write answer plays ... The answers aren't always light, easy or even straightforward, but the purpose – a socialist society – is clear.' In *The Bundle*, the bundle by the river at the beginning is an abandoned baby: at the end, the bundle is rifles. Bond's answer in *The Bundle*: armed insurrection.

In retrospect, Bond can be seen to have been a 'socialist' writing socialist plays long before these were common or in any fashion accommodated, indeed, before he himself recognised the full radical implications of his work. He came to acknowledge this: 'I would say that I always had a political attitude, but that I did not have any vocabulary or ideas to express it. I was aware of the injustice and in that sense had a class attitude to it, but I wasn't aware of it conceptually. I had no conceptual language with which to enlighten myself or others.[5] So for Bond, the period 1968–1978 was a process of political self-education. From 'instinctive' to 'intellectual' socialism, his political thought developed not only through his plays, but also his Prefaces and public statements. The Prefaces were always written after the plays had been produced: 'I have got to make it work with some sense on the stage before I feel happy talking about it in a Preface, or prose. Then the Prefaces are the structures of the plays, really, the premises on which the plays are based, the things the plays assume.' In this respect the Prefaces provide a good guide to Bond's conceptual development (as well as a structural explication of the plays themselves), and to his process of politicisation. In 1978 Bond himself could see the difference between *Saved* and *The Bundle* in terms of his political consciousness:

I had a sense of outrage and I was quite clear about where the real guilt lay and where it did not. I didn't think the kids who murdered the baby were guilty. I thought they were themselves victims and I was clear about the moral relationship. But I don't think I could have analysed it. If you look at the Preface you can see that I couldn't.[6]

Over the decade, Bond discovered the concepts to explain what he had been writing about from the beginning: that capitalist society is violent. Eventually he came to envisage a non-violent socialist society, and finally to look at the methods of achieving that society, even if that involved necessary 'justifiable' violence itself.

Despite the critical hostility to *Saved*, Bond defended the play as being 'almost irresponsibly optimistic':

Clutching at straws is the only realistic thing to do. The alternative, apart from the self-indulgence of pessimism, is a fatuous optimism based on superficiality of both feeling and observation.[7]

He blamed the environment for what happened to the characters: their pent-up fury (and 'the lack of any social sense, and sense of human community, which is a consequence of the self-interest ethic of capitalism'[8]) at the conditions under which they were forced to live was the chief cause of the corruption and violence. He blamed the morality of society – a morality based on religion, and which created moral illiteracy and moral bankruptcy. He called for moral scepticism and analysis, not faith. Said Bond in retrospect:

I began with a load of undigested material. I had grown up in a war situation. That presented a problematic state of affairs which I tried to portray in *Saved* – just to put down what it was really like, to describe the problem. I didn't say why it is so, is it necessary for societies to be like that and if it isn't, how do you change them? It would never have occurred to me earlier in my life to vote Tory, it would have been unthinkable. That's simply class background, but I have had to learn the concepts to define that in terms of my own class experience. It's been a matter of finding the truth of my unconscious class experience rather than learning a theory.[9]

He described a discussion after *Saved* and being shocked because the people taking part, though sympathetic to the play, seemed oblivious of their responsibility for what was in it:

There was a probation officer, a couple of middle-class critics ... some of the very people I was saying were responsible for this situation, sitting down and making judgements, just as the Queen's housekeeper tried to ban the play.[10]

In his next Preface – to *Lear* in 1972 – Bond elaborated on the reasons for violence and the reasons for writing about it:

> I write about violence as naturally as Jane Austen wrote about manners. Violence shapes and obsesses our society, and if we do not stop being violent we have no future. People who do not want writers to write about violence want to stop them writing about us and our time. It would be immoral not to write about violence.[11]

Animals, he said, were aggressive when their territory or status was threatened. Likewise with human beings, who in adverse conditions behaved unnaturally, whose behaviour deteriorated. Human beings, he said, behaved aggressively when deprived of physical and emotional needs: with constant deprivation, there was constant aggression. 'Why, in the first place, do we live in urban, crowded regimented groups, working like machines (mostly for the benefit of other men) and with no real control of our lives? ... People who are controlled by others in this way soon lose the ability to act for themselves, even if their leaders do not make it dangerous for them to do so.' Aggression, Bond concluded, had been institutionalised – 'moralised, and morality has become a form of violence'.[12] At this stage he blamed the social structure.

Bond then defined 'social morality' as a weapon to maintain the social structure and its injustices. 'The institutions of morality and order are always more destructive than crime.' The problem, he said, was that people 'have no real political or economic control over their lives'. And he concluded: 'There is no way out for our sort of society: an unjust society must be violent.' The answer: to live justly. 'We do not need a plan for the future, we need a *method* of change.'[13]

In the Preface to *Bingo* in 1974 (a play about understanding what is wrong but, because of the historical period, being able to do nothing about it – the plight of Shakespeare), Bond had become much more conscious of the economic basis of injustice and the extent to which 'economics' determined the structure of society.

> We live in a closed society where you need money to live ... We have no natural rights, only rights granted and protected by money. Money provides food, shelter, security, education, entertainment, the ground we walk on, the air we breathe, the bed we lie in. People come to think of these things as products of money, not of the earth or human relationships , and finally as the way of getting more money to get more things. Money has its own laws and conventions, and when you live by money you must live by these. To get money you must behave like money. I don't mean only that money creates certain attitudes or traits in people, it *forces* certain behaviour on them.[14]

In the end, human values were replaced by money values – the aim not to satisfy real basic needs, but artificial needs. Again it was the social order at fault:

> Most established social orders are not means of defending justice, but of defending social injustice. That's why . . . law-and-order societies are morally responsible for the terrorism and crime they provoke.[15]

Bond concluded that 'you can only change your life by changing society'. Factories were not bad in themselves, but what they made and how they were organised were. People had to be able to choose how they wanted to live and work, 'to choose a new purpose for society, a new culture'. The essential thing was that people should be responsible for their society. They would then act responsibly.

With hindsight, it is clear that Bond was making a consistent concerted critique of capitalist society, without as he has said, having the conceptual tools at that point to describe what he was experiencing, observing and thinking. In the Preface to *The Fool* in 1976, there was, for the first time, an overtly Marxist analysis. The Preface actually opened under the heading of 'Capitalism':

> There is a discrepancy between what we have to do to keep our society running and what we're told we ought to do to be humam. Our economy depends on exploitation and aggression.[16]

There were, said Bond, deep and destructive ironies in capitalist society:

> We need anti-social behaviour to keep society running, but this behaviour destroys society. The worker must 'know his place' in the factory, but be an insatiable egotist outside it. The good citizen must be schizophrenic. And capitalism is incompatible with law and order. Ideally, capitalism would like to take a commodity out of one can – a tin – and put it into another can – a person. And although capitalism feeds on technocracy it is itself devoured by it, because technocracy destroys the acquiescing basis of society throughout the entire world – and while it grows rich on the poor it teaches them that the customer is always right . . . Capitalism cannot satisfy the acquisitiveness it creates to maintain itself.[17]

The capitalist solutions to these problems were fascism – 'the rational form of capitalism' – and affluence, 'where nothing is valued for itself, but only for its consumption or possession'.

Bond discussed technology and the lack of culture – or rather the capitalist misuses of technology and the need for a new culture. The latter was imperative because it – human culture – was, in fact, the equivalent of human nature – both of which were socially conditioned. Capitalism created a schizophrenic society using force and morality to restrain change. The new enlightenment, the new culture was necessary, but 'we can't achieve that till we change our political and social base'. Bond defined culture as:

> ... the rational creation of human nature, the implementation of rationality in all human activity, economic, political, social, public and private. A culture must unite technology, science, and political and economic organisation, and relate them to our environment in such a way that we can continue our lives and broaden them socially and humanely. It must show us how we can live and how we ought to live so that there is a future for us.[18]

In short, culture was what a person 'is and what will become of him'. The species, said Bond, only had a future 'as a self-conscious collective'. In the process of social change, art played an important role in the solution of social problems. Art informed people and 'in the context of culture what we know becomes the ground for action'. Art helped to create meaning and purpose in an apparently irrational world. 'Art is the human being claiming a rational relationship with the world.'

In the Preface to the first volume of his *Collected Plays*, Bond's political analysis was becoming more precise. He was discussing the same themes as in the Preface to *Saved*, but now firmly from a Marxist perspective. He described violence as a political device, the modern equivalent of the doctrine of original sin — God as a device of class rule:

> Capitalism has had to drag its hell up out of the ground and set it in our midst. If men are necessarily violent, they will always endanger one another, so there must be a strong authority that will use violence to control violence. This authority is the ruling class. It maintains its existence by using violence and being able to organise it politically.[19]

Bond continued to discuss human nature as a product of social relationships: 'We create our subjective selves through our objective social relations, and our self-consciousness is not primarily the fruit of private introspection, but of social interaction.'[20] Bond had, however, taken a great step forward in realising that the violence created by capitalism could, in fact, be used against capitalism: 'Class society must be violent, but it must also create the frustration, stimulation, aggression and — if necessary — physical violence that are the means by which it can change into a classless society.'[21] And then Bond came to some truly radical conclusions:

> We have to understand that not only is capitalism destructive in war

and peace, but that it is *as* destructive in peace as in war. Its peacetime destructiveness is caused not so much by naked force as by its false culture ... Culture is the way we live ... it takes a lot of violence to keep a capitalist peace, and ... under capitalism war can never lead to peace. Using violence to create socialism out of capitalism would not mean introducing violence into the peaceful politics of a world of law and order ...[22]

In *The Bundle* (1978) Bond demonstrated this thesis in persuasive dramatic terms: that violence was not only a condition of capitalist society but a necessary pre-condition of attaining a socialist society. The play was Marxist in its content, its treatment and its message. As before, Bond used the parable of a historical setting and he sub-titled *The Bundle* the 'new *Narrow Road to the Deep North*'. The play begins with the poet Basho embarking on his journey in search of 'enlightenment'. To this end, he abandons an already abandoned baby, which is 'saved' by a ferryman for its future usefulness as a worker. The baby – the 'bundle' – grows up to become Wang, the leader of the people's revolt, after rejecting the offer of a secure place in the social order and choosing to put himself outside the law. Bond removed any suggestion of romanticism from his revolutionary line by showing Wang in his turn abandoning a baby, by risking and ruining the lives of his mother and father.

> The ferryman takes the child because as a humanist he can't abandon it. He knows that taking the child will hasten his wife's death. He tries to justify taking it (he is in the position where to have loving or humane feelings is dangerous and a shocking self-indulgence) by saying the child will become a good worker. Later, Wang's and the ferryman's situation is reversed. The ferryman and his wife are abandoned to the water. This time Wang is blackmailed by his humane feelings (as earlier the ferryman had been): at a similar cost. So finally when Wang finds the baby by the water he says: no. One is not enough. I must save more. I will not be seduced into one gesture of kindness when this will divert me from my total purpose.[23]

Basho does not find enlightenment: he becomes a judge, an instrument of the landowner's 'social morality' for maintaining the status quo.

Every scene in the play is structured to illustrate the contradictions. Wang as a young man is stranded by the flood with his step-parents and villagers, on the high ground of a graveyard. (The river was Bond's symbol of industrialism.) All but they have something to barter with the landowner's men for their lives. Wang has a choice between drowning and selling himself into slavery. He abhors the idea of becoming a slave, but his instinct for survival finally forces him to submit. His agonised shout of 'Buy me!' echoes as the epitome of capitalist exploitation. Wang robs from the rich to give to the poor: not food or money, but guns – the tools of violence necessary to replace capitalism with socialism.

Bond's Preface to *The Bundle* continued to analyse the function of social institutions and social morality as weapons of the ruling class:

Social institutions control law, education, civic force (police and armed forces), scientific research and so on – all the machinery and knowledge we need to live together and create a common life. But the control is deeper. It permeates the ordinary use of language, mores, customs, common assumptions and unquestioned ideas. Together these things – institutions and their social reflections – make up a tacitly accepted view of life, a consciousness of the world which is also in large part a self-consciousness.[24]

Bond now came to emphasise another aspect of culture, seeing it not only as something created by social institutions and imposed on their members, but as the way in which 'working people brought social institutions, economic and political organisation, into line with their experience and needs as workers and consumers'. He had come to equate moral self-consciousness with socialist consciousness: 'self-consciousness is created in the process of understanding the world and our own behaviour'. And in this respect, art and theatre were very important – in helping to create self-consciousness especially by placing ordinary experience into larger concepts and interpretations, and then showing how these concepts are reflected in ordinary experience. Audiences could be 'made to see aspects of the situation or character which the socially prescribed response blots out . . . They will judge . . . We shall give them tools of historical hindsight and access to what is usually hidden, distorted or blurred. This can result in a development of understanding, an improved interpretation of the world, and so in a development of self-knowledge and self-consciousness.'

The theatre, said Bond, can't by itself change the world, but 'theatre can co-operate with all those who are in any way involved in rationally changing society and evolving a new consciousness. It may initiate the change in some people.'[25] Theatre could analyse what is recorded and reproduced and stimulate analysis in the audience. It could show characters not just as individuals, but as class functions: 'We have to show the mask under the face, not the mask on it.' In the end self-consciousness – however acquired – could develop into political consciousness. Bond suggested that in open class war, theatre would have a different function, but given society as it is, 'the theatre could tell the truth and provide human beings with a new image of themselves'.

Originally Bond simply had a sense of class outrage which prompted *The Pope's Wedding* and *Saved*: 'Outrage at what was done and how life was wasted, but that was an emotional attitude, which I've had to learn how to pin down – you can't go on writing unless you start thinking and questioning your experience.'[26] He was increasingly able to articulate ideas: he had lacked a 'view of history and an understanding of people in other countries'. For Bond, writing itself was a method of learning:

> It's not enough to say something is a political truth. You have got to be able to relate that to the experiences of people in their lives and if you cannot do that you have not understood the truth accurately.

Before he acquired a political consciousness, Bond felt he 'put a lot of energy into fighting the symptoms of that class situation rather than the causes of it'. The ultimate realisation was that:

> ... a class society inevitably produces an irrational consciousness in people until they come to that moment where the economic foundations of that particular society are so out of key with the structure of that society that it no longer holds together and so real oppositions can be created.

Bond felt that the theatre had important functions. One was indirect and not unlike a scientific discovery:

> When a scientific discovery is made, it isn't automatically available to everybody, but it's a scientific truth. It can function like the polio vaccine or the Pill, gradually over a period of time radically, materially changing the nature of society.

And in this sense, over a period of ten or fifteen years, Bond felt that the theatre had changed the cultural life of the country. Theatre could also be used to 'disturb society in such a way that the institutions of society lose their grip', to struggle against the measures which the ruling class used for repression. Perhaps most important, theatre could provide people with an image of a socialist society and an image of themselves in that society:

> We have to create an image of what a socialist mind is, so that people can say, oh yes, that is possible for us ... We've got to be able to create a socialist image of what society is about ... because theatre does change the way people are seeing and the way people interpret themselves and the way they understand themselves, and the way they *should* think of themselves. It goes very deep, and can't always be measured instantly.

In a revolutionary situation, Bond felt theatre had a different, more direct function – 'the image in art would be much more closely related to what was happening in the street, and that situation would be changing radically'. Before a situation of revolutionary conflict, theatre functioned to work out the problems of culture, 'saying what it is to be a member of one's society, what the obligations and possibilities are, how human beings really are related to one another, how they can only exist in solidarity'. That image, said Bond, was 'something socialist art can change'.

Bond elaborated on his views on the use of violence in a revolutionary situation:

> One has to acknowledge violence. It's not that one would want to use violence, but that violence is used to maintain societies. It would not be a matter of introducing violence, for it is already there. Ideally, I would like to see societies changed without violence, but if there were a revolutionary situation and people wanted to change their society, it is obvious that this would be resisted. It's not that one would choose to be insurrectionary, but that insurrection would be thrust on one ... I think that armed revolution is justifiable if it is politically effective.

Bond increasingly regarded technology as a potentially important tool for revolutionary change:

> Technology is a very valuable thing which is greatly misused. It's not being used for rational purposes at all. It is being used to create surplus for wasteful consumption. Just as early capitalism ruthlessly exploited the working class, late capitalism is ruthlessly exploiting technology in order to create waste. So it is important to separate technology itself from its use as a product of capitalist economy. You can't abolish technology any more than you could abolish the plough. Indeed, given technology political change becomes more imperative, and, as it destroys the economic base of the old social super-structures, it even makes change more likely or probable.

Bond intended to show this in *The Bundle* – 'to demonstrate that the economic activity by which they all live – the water (symbol of industrialism) – actually controlled their cultural life and their social life, and in order to change this they have to capture the river (or industry) which is the economic stratum of their society'. It was important for Bond to transfer that idea to western society, to equate it with the characters in *Saved* – 'unless the economic foundations of their life become their own responsibility'. The idea of people controlling their own lives, and thereby being responsible for them, was a key element in Bond's socialism. 'If they work in a factory, then the factory has to be in a real sense theirs and they'll have to be responsible for their street and their school.' Members of the Theatre Writers Union (in which Bond was very active) taking responsibility for working out their own contract was another illustration of people taking responsibility, controlling their lives. It was in this context that Bond felt 'that technology was not an enemy of socialism, but creates the opportunity for socialism and solves many of the practical problems of socialism'.

The idea of responsibility ultimately defined for Bond the nature of socialism:

> Socialism is where people who do the work are responsible for the cultural institutions because what they learn by their practical activity they teach and inscribe in the mores and laws of their society. When those two things come together you have socialism.

Integral to this concept was the idea of work as part of culture: 'the way people actually earn their living is what tells them what the nature of the world is really about'. At the same time, said Bond, culture combined enormous statements about the nature of truth and the universe and statements about what was the correct tie to wear, or how to get on a bus. It was important to realise that the way we live our lives was not something destined or fated, but an invention of society. And while art was a product of culture, it often stood outside and functioned critically. It, too, could tell people about the nature of the world, and was therefore potentially revolutionary.

That Bond used the Theatre Writers Union as an example of socialism in practice was no accident, and it was significant. He had been closely involved in the TWU from its very beginnings:

> I don't think the Union would have existed in 1968. Had it existed I would have joined it. Because what you've got as a writer is something of social value. It's an asset to the community, it's useful and ought to be used. I think that a society which doesn't use that talent is impoverishing itself. Therefore the needs of the writer should be cared for and their interests looked after. Then they are free to do what they want to do and not what entrepreneurs tell them to do. If they are organised rather than isolated individuals, they can begin to have an effect on the organisation of the theatre. Writing is work, cultural work and the TWU acknowledges this.

Thus, in a very real sense, the Theatre Writers Union was an ideological and practical extension of Bond's own socialist philosophy. By 1978, Bond had arrived at a clear view of his functions as a socialist playwright: 'It is not enough, certainly, just to show what is wrong. One has to try to show why things go wrong and how they should be corrected. I think that is what I'm going to spend my time writing about now.'

1970

At the turn of the decade, new venues continued to open and old ones to adapt to the new developments in the theatre. In 1970, the Kings Head, another important lunchtime venue (though soon expanding into evening performances as well), was started by Dan and Joan Crawford in a pub in Islington. Its greatest success was in providing a novel and satisfying ambience for theatre – the backroom of the pub with food provided before the shows – and in discovering several long-running and successful shows. The first of these were novelist William Trevor's lunchtime plays *Going Home*, *A Night with Mrs. da Tanka*, *Marriages* and *A Perfect Relationship*, plays which attracted critics like Harold Hobson of *The Sunday Times* and which helped to introduce the idea of fringe theatre to an 'establishment' audience. A highpoint for the Kings Head was the production in 1974 of Robert Patrick's *Kennedy's Children* (a retrospective of the United States in the sixties, the assassination of Kennedy and the Vietnam war) which eventually transferred to the West End, as did Stewart Parker's *Spokesong* (about the troubles in Northern Ireland) in 1977.

During this period the Hampstead Theatre Club played a role similar to that of the Open Space in premiering new writers. It was a fringe theatre on the edge of the establishment with regular transfers to the West End, with an 'apolitical' policy, but producing occasionally radical new plays. It opened in 1960 with Harold Pinter's *The Room* and *The Dumb Waiter* and in the early sixties, under the artistic direction of James Roose-Evans, produced a combination of boulevard and avant-garde plays. In the history of political theatre, it was particularly important for its production of John McGrath's *Events While Guarding the Bofors Gun* in 1966, and thereafter had a much more 'political' cast to its repertoire, with plays by Giles Cooper, Wole Soyinka, Athol Fugard, John Bowen, Heinar Kipphardt, Michael Hastings, Barry Bermange, LeRoi Jones, Peter Terson and Clive Exton. In 1970 Hampstead produced David Hare's *Slag*.

By 1970 the theory of political theatre was becoming as important as its practice. And Bond and Arden were not the only figures of the previous generation of playwrights to respond to the emergence of the political theatre movement. There was David Mercer, one of the few Marxist playwrights of the sixties, and Arnold Wesker, the self-styled socialist of the post-1956 'revolution'. Unlike Bond and Arden, they did not become closely involved in the developments of the seventies, but their ideas were important to an understanding of the political aspects of the new work. In 1970 both were separately involved in heated exchanges about their political views, and in the following essays, Mercer – from an end-of-decade perspective – explains the politics of his plays and defends his own aloof and sceptical political stance; and Arnold Wesker – in the context of a lengthy and heated correspondence with John McGrath in 1970 – raises the crucial questions which faced practitioners of political theatre: Wesker accounting for his apathy in relation to the new movement, McGrath formulating the theories which he was to put into practice when founding the 7:84 Theatre Company in 1971.

'Perhaps on the appointed day at the appointed time, they will simply take me out and hang me.' David Mercer (letter to Catherine Itzin, August 1978)

David Mercer

In the spring of 1970 D. A. N. Jones, then drama critic for *The Listener*, took David Mercer to task for being a 'bad' Marxist, if a Marxist at all; 'perhaps Mercer has made a mistake about himself',[1] wrote Jones in a patronising, knuckle-rapping tone. Mercer was, in fact, an easy target for this kind of attack, for he was one of the first of the few self-declared Marxist playwrights of the sixties, at a time when others of his generation (he was born in 1928 in Yorkshire and his coevals included Osborne and Pinter) were more concerned with success than with socialism.

But Mercer's Marxism was almost a historical inevitability, the result of his own particular dialectical development. He had grown up in a working-class environment, son of a railway worker ('completely pro-union ... thought the Labour party was right for the working man'[2]) and a dominating puritanical mother ('The typical threat in my family was that if I was a bad boy my mother would have me scrubbed and in my best suit ready at quarter to nine in the morning to go to the orphanage'). At the same time, his parents 'were upper-working class, highly respectable – and very ambitious for their children'.

In his teens (after leaving school at fourteen, working as a lab technician doing post-mortems and in the Royal Navy doing VD tests on sailors) Mercer 'made a few contacts which began to lead me in the direction of realising the huge cultural world and the huge stratified social world which existed and to give me some kind of perspective on it and an ambition in it'. And then, of his time as a mature student ('I think I was totally retarded – emotionally, intellectually, in every conceivable way') at university, Mercer said, 'I began to make the connection between political philosophy in terms of Marxism and the circumstances under which I'd been born and brought up.' Through this process of 'political self-education' (reading Marx, Lenin, Trotsky, Freud, Adler, Jung, Orwell, Koestler, Weissberg, Wittgenstein, Sartre – at random) Mercer arrived at a 'crude Marxism' – 'the feeling that Marxism-Leninism was the basis for a coherent political philosophy'. But this was the period of the Cold War (1949–1953), so Mercer's newly acquired political consciousness involved 'a horrified awareness of what had happened to the Bolshevik Revolution, and what Stalinism meant'.

CND (The Campaign for Nuclear Disarmament) provided Mercer with his opportunity for political activism, following a bitter reaction to the Communist Party's lip-service reaction to the Korean War. But his relation to CND was also ambivalent: 'to concentrate on the issue of nuclear weapons was an undialectical thing to do. I perhaps still hadn't properly understood the dialectical approach to history and so I was a bit impressionistic in my politics, the communist-without-a-party idea. I couldn't see any development of communism to which I could give my allegiance.'

Mercer's political world-view was further 'complicated' by a nervous breakdown in 1957 (which took him to the doors of the Tavistock Clinic where the British Institute of Psycho-analysis pronounced him 'a suitable case for treatment') and by his subsequent interest in R. D. Laing's 'political psychiatry'. Laing had written: 'One gets the impression that many diagnostic assessments of mental illness are as much political, social and moral as they are clinical' and that 'the diagnosis schizophrenia is a political act'.[3] Mercer's 'crude Marxism' thus came to include a concept of madness as a 'psychological revolution', an upsetting of the psychological order analagous to a Marxist-Leninist concept of the upsetting of the social order, or as Mercer said, 'attempts by individuals to reclaim for sanity whole areas of human experience whose validity is rigorously denied by society'.[4]

With this idiosyncratic theoretical armoury, with a passionate ideological commitment derived from it, and with a concept and practice of playwriting as an unconscious or at least sub-conscious process of discovery ('I really don't understand what conscious intention in writing is, at any level' and 'I regard the process of writing itself as an instrument of inquiry'[5]), Mercer proceeded to produce an impressive body of work which explored themes of Marxism and madness. 'I was,' said Mercer, 'looking for a synthesis between the problems of the individual in society and the problems of the society that produces the individuals.'

Mercer's two television trilogies[6] *The Generations* (including *Where the Difference Begins* 1961, *A Climate of Fear* 1962 and *The*

Birth of a Private Man 1963) and *On the Eve of Publication* 1968, with *The Cellar and the Almond Tree* 1970 and *Emma's Time* 1970[7] were fundamentally concerned with the conflict arising from the contradictions between the private man (madness) and the public man (Marxism); between the de-classed individual (the new bourgeoisie) isolated by education and then by inclination from working-class roots, and the politically committed Marxist, in an uneasy, ill-defined relationship with the class struggle, trying to grapple with the moral dilemma of the human condition.

Where the Difference Begins (Mercer's first play, 'released' by psycho-analysis) was unashamedly autobiographical. The central figure was his working-class father, who on the death of his wife realises he has also lost his sons by education into the middle class, and thus comes to question change, progress and his socialist values. Mercer later regarded this portrait of his father as 'vastly idealised' and 'did him' as he was in *After Haggerty* as 'really a reactionary working-class racist bigot' who 'still thinks he's Labour'. It was left to the second generation in *A Climate of Fear* to question the values of their newly-bourgeois parents, by acquiring a political conscious-ness in the context of the CND movement which commits them to direct action. Mercer's views, unambiguous at this stage, were expressed through the mother's decision to turn her back on her middle-class marriage and to join her children in the Movement – with a commitment that saw her departing from a demonstration in a Black Maria. By *The Birth of a Private Man*, Mercer was developing his anti-hero's disillusionment with the Marxist causes to which he had been committed, his concomitant mental breakdown, through to his death, shot-down simultaneously from East and West while scaling the Berlin Wall. In another early television play, *A Suitable Case for Treatment* (1962) the hero, Morgan, was the classic example of the Mercer personal/political dilemma – educated out of his working class and alienated from revolutionary politics by events in Eastern Europe, escaping into madness. 'I think that if you are intellectually and emotionally committed to a particular ideology, as I was and am to theoretical communism,' said Mercer, 'and yet find no way of becoming active in the world which is consistent with your beliefs, this does create just the kind of split that is dramatised in *A Suitable Case for Treatment*.'

The second trilogy showed Mercer not only superlatively sophis-ticated in the use of television techniques, but pursuing his 'enquiry' into the relation between the individual and society with greater political sophistication, more 'self' consciousness and now, too, with some cynicism. The hero of *On the Eve of Publication* is Robert Kelvin, a successful, heavy-drinking, dying novelist – a crypto-Mercer. It was a Proustian play: about time, the past, memories (of the Labour movement, the Soviet Union, storming the Winter Palace, Czechoslovakia and Kelvin's Communist friend Sladek). The tone was essentially despairing. The 'literal' connection of the play with *The Cellar and the Almond Tree* was slight (Sladek became the central figure), but thematically it was very powerful. The two plays implicitly juxtaposed the posturing Western intellectual (Kelvin/Mercer) with the 'Real-politik' of Eastern European socialism and then called even that into ironic question. The almond tree symbolised the aristocratic past in Czechoslovakia (portrayed with some nostalgia) and the cellar a post-revolutionary torture chamber. The play ended with a congratulatory after-dinner toast of 'comrades: the Soviet Union' followed by a flashback to a Gestapo interrogation in the cellar, with the discomforting suggestion that people (capitalists, Nazis, communists) come and go and little really changes. Significantly, the play was written after the Soviet invasion of Prague in August of 1968. The end of *Emma's Time* was similarly ironic, but less cynical: the late Kelvin's mistress of the title collaborates with friend Sladek to write 'a true history of the Czech Communist Party' dedicated to the dead Kelvin.

After Haggerty (1970), Mercer's first major and most successful stage play, summarised his recurrent preoccupations perhaps too baldly – indeed Mercer described it and the Kelvin trilogy as 'summing-up plays'. The 'Mercer figure' is now a left-wing theatre critic, Bernard Link; his father, now the 'reactionary, racist bigot'; and an American woman whose husband, Haggerty ('It's incredible the number of people who came out of that play not catching on to the fact that Haggerty's black'[8]), dies in the front line of an African guerilla war of liberation, while Link lectures on drama in the midst of international crisis, western society crumbling around him. The dialectics of Mercer's own political development had led him from the Berlin Wall of *A Private Man* to the brick wall of *Haggerty* – to political impotence.

This, and the opening of *Flint* hard on the heels of *After Haggerty*, was the context in which D.A.N. Jones launched his attack and attempted to 'unmarx Mercer'. For Mercer had dared to point out failures of Marxist politicians in Eastern Europe; dared to associate 'the Soviet world not with waving cornfields and ballet in the evenings but with prisons, torture, censorship, military repression and falsified history'[9]; dared to doubt, to despair even, of developing a 'socialist consciousness' in the wake of the ghastly Soviet example. So Jones hurled a barrage of questions at Mercer, calling him, if not a 'running dog of capital, traitor to the working class', then a misguided Marxist, a good, grey, decent liberal – a bourgeois defector:

> What happened to the class conflict, determined by the relationships of productive forces? Why is this Marxist so concerned with the psychological problems of declassed individualists? Why does the proletariat appear in his work not as a positive force but as a collection of pitiable bores and dignified ninnies? Why are the self-styled Marxists in his plays always disenchanted and embittered? Why does he write about the bourgeoisie for the bourgeoisie? Why has he never joined a Marxist organisation?[10]

Mercer's response the following week in *The Listener* was more in sorrow than anger, more despairing than defensive:

> The answers are that the psychological problems of declassed individualists are revealing about matters of class conflict and alienation; that it would take a Stalinist to be an enchanted and unembittered Marxist; that I do not write for the bourgeoisie – but a bourgeois culture owns the means of production without which my plays cannot be seen; that I have never joined a Marxist organisation because I have not encountered one in my lifetime which I could give my allegiance to without abdicating my critical intelligence.[11]

Nearly a decade later, however, on the occasion of the opening of *Cousin Vladimir* (1978) – which Mercer described as 'at least an invitation to people to be more scrupulous in the way they think about this development in East-West relations [the phenomenon of dissidence] and to reconsider the kind of society in which Soviet dissidence plays the role it does in relation to who and what we are, and where we're at'[12] – Mercer answered the questions at length, in the process addressing himself to the key issues of political theatre.[13]

Mercer said that he stood accused that his 'work in no way reflects the nature of the class struggle, the general dialectical play of the forces in society, or the depiction and resolution of the classical model of Marxism in dramatic terms'. Mercer apologised for not 'performing to order, not because I am a corrupted and/or unrecalcitrant citizen of a bourgeois democracy (though objectively I may be either or both of these without it affecting the truth or falsity of my abstract convictions); but rather due to a crucial divergence of opinion between myself and my critics about (1) the nature of the creative process itself; and (2) the whole question of whether it makes sense (vis-à-vis truth) for the artist to be placed under any kind of obligation to perform in a certain way and according to certain axioms and precepts at all'.

As for the work process itself, Mercer reiterated that it was 'spontaneous, intuitive and undirected' until it was rewritten and 'modified by conscious operations'. He continued: 'The play may or may not then *turn out to be* (to contain or imply) a view of human relations and social phenomena consistent with a particular ideological point of view. But a Marxist model – or indeed any kind of philosophical or ethical model – taking precedence at the commencement of the play would in my opinion render the whole exercise pointless. I regard the process of writing itself as an instrument of inquiry.'

Mercer did not intend to suggest that this process, 'unconscious in its origins', absolved him from responsibility, but he said:

> I do regard it as a tiresome tendency of the left to feel entitled to arraign the writer as if before an ideological court, awarding plus or minus grades according to whether he reinforces or subverts in his work their own *a priori* view of the true nature of political and social relations, not to mention the nature of material reality itself. In other words, the left has a casuistical way of substituting a set of ideological criteria for *criticism* – and thus political evaluations are amazingly transformed into value judgments. This kind of dishonesty has a long history in the Soviet Union (yes, we know that's *Stalinism*) and its ugly consequences – the corruption and degradation of both art and artists – are plain for all to see.
>
> But Stalinism has no monopoly of the means of strangulation. Despite the lip service paid to 'the freedom of the artist' by (in my experience *all*) The Marxist-Leninist organisations in the western democracies, it is perfectly clear that these comrades would be singing a different song once they had the brutal priorities of a successful social revolution thrust upon them. This last would be a predicament one could comprehend, but one which it would be dangerous to compound with much sympathy. This – at all levels of social and cultural endeavour, including science – is the path from Kronstadt through the Moscow trials and post-war assertion of Soviet hegemony, to Prague in the spring of '68. Mayakovsky's suicide was hardly an act of the revolutionary equivalent of romantic despair – more a recognition that the imperious demands of 'objective reality' as understood by gangster/Leninists and naive utopian Marxists alike (many unfortunates having failed to make a proper distinction between 'philosophical' and 'moral' idealism) . . . that these demands would overwhelm any fastidiousness in the hearts of

harassed Bolsheviks about who was in the way of the revolution and who was not.

The fact that this nicely conforms with the bourgeois-liberal-western view of the Bolshevik Revolution in no way detracts from its truth; nor does it absolve communists from the obligation to explain convincingly how they would avert this apparently ubiquitous development as it presents itself on the historical evidence. I have yet to encounter the Marxist/Leninist/Trotskyist/Maoist or any other style of faction which does not claim to have 'learned the lessons of Stalinism' and promise a revolutionary perspective sanitised of the 'mistakes and errors' of post-revolutionary Soviet society. Any comrade with a sense of justice or even a mere crude lust for power would be insane not to propagate this claim. I simply do not believe them. I believe that the best of them believe themselves, and that is as far as I will go.

In short: not only did Mercer's Marxist critics not have a monopoly of truly communist principles, they had a history of 'bad' practice which they could not satisfactorily account for. And none of them had found the *truly* socialist solution for western society, a fact which Mercer obviously felt tarnished their credentials as critics if not as Marxists.

To D. A. N. Jones's charge of over-emphasis on Eastern Europe and the bourgeoisie, Mercer replied:

If in many of my plays I have concentrated on the predicament of the artist and the intellectual in Russia, Central and Eastern Europe (at the same time running my nit-comb through the Anglo-Saxon educated middle class), I suppose it is because it is there, in the socialised countries where revolutionary hopes have so tragically foundered, that one must look for the how and the why of the grotesque distortions and moral outrages that seem to go hand in hand with the exercise of dogmatic revolutionary power.

So far as this country is concerned, I think it would in any case be more pretentious for me to write about the working class – with whom I have had no direct or other than superficial contact for twenty-five years – than to (as D. A. N. Jones puts it) 'write about the bourgeoisie for the bourgeoisie'. And I must confess I have never understood what kind of ideological crime is involved in writing about the bourgeoisie. I would say that in general they haven't come out of it very well. I'd have thought there's an excellent case (and an important place in drama) for knowing who and what they are, what they are up to. But I reject the criticism, because anyway I reject its (usually unacknowledged) premise: that there are subjects which are the legitimate preoccupation of a writer, and those which are not.

This, felt Mercer, explained why the self-styled Marxists in his plays were often so disenchanted and embittered. But he said:

At least I think most of my chaps flagellate only themselves, and have no wish to run out into the street snapping the ideological handcuffs on sinners who stumble across their paths. Whether the phenomenon of such characters is worthy of serious interest ... well, the audience – as Lenin said of the Tsarist army, in another context – will vote with its feet.

To Jones's question – 'Why does the proletariat appear in his work but as a collection of pitiable bores and dignified ninnies?' – Mercer replied:

I haven't introduced a 'proletarian' into my work since I embedded a fairly accurate portrait of my own father in a play called *After Haggerty* in 1970. Dad himself would be a bit sniffy about precisely what's meant by this Jones feller and his lofty imposition of glib categories. When I was a child in the thirties, my father was an unlettered and ill-informed 'Keir Hardie socialist'. He was this by instinct, by his unformulated but very real awareness of the class situation then prevailing – and by the brutal daily evidence of what it is to be a worker (in his case a locomotive fireman) in a society where work, bread and the pitiable amenities of such a material life as he could aspire to were the arbitrary fief of a small, totally powerful and intransigent ruling class.

I abhor what the next forty years in this country made of people like my father – that's to say, the uneducated but lively 'grand old men' of a magnificent Labour movement in this country: consistently courageous throughout its history, noble in its clumsy vision of a better world, progenitor of the real trades union power we see today – and as individuals, ultimately made redundant in their most cherished beliefs by developments in post-war capitalism of daunting complexity; outraged by the increasing tide of evidence about the hell created in their cherished Soviet Union; and finally and insidiously incorporated into the myths of class-mobility and consumer consumption which began to take hold after the fall of Attlee's government in 1952.

I do not think I presented this man as either a 'bore' or a 'ninnie' in *After Haggerty* – but as a man humiliated and uncomprehendingly wounded by the tide of events around him which left him washed up on his small anachronistic rock, prime fodder, due to his estrangement and bitterness, for the reactionary atmosphere and neo-fascistic myths so artfully disseminated in the seventies – from Mrs Thatcher on the left, so to speak, to the National Front on the right.

Even the children of such men as my father were stolen from them (1944 Education Act), to become, when they were fortunate enough to acquire and complete a higher education, either absorbed into the very middle class which had been the villain of the piece to worker-socialists; or the confused and (ideologically speaking) rootlessly rebellious 'declassed individualists' (see Jones) of whom perhaps Jimmy Porter was the theatrical prototype.

Jones had asked why Mercer never joined a Marxist organisation. Mercer replied:

> In my student days thirty years ago I could never understand why anyone could still be a pro-Soviet communist at all. Perhaps I was in a sense lucky in that I grew up with the damning and (I believed and still do) irrefutable evidence against Stalin in particular and the course of the Bolshevik Revolution in general. It was simply out of the question to give one's allegiance to any extant Marxist organisation whatsoever. But yes, it is actually possible to retain a Marxist orientation without either joining a party or swallowing the mind-boggling intellectual dishonesty which seems to overtake people once they have set themselves up as the torchbearers of this or that version of the received wisdom.

Not one, clearly, for agitprop over-simplification or a behind-the-barricades brand of revolutionary socialism, Mercer embraced his adopted middle class (even when it kept its arms judgementally folded) – and tried to maintain a questioning moral and ideological integrity. The result: rejection from the left, misunderstanding and mistrust from the middle. At the same time, Mercer did not have the dubious privilege accorded to his contemporaries, of being courted and comfortably accommodated by the middle class and the mainstream, perhaps precisely because his work and his entire world orientation were so overtly political, critical and uncompromising. He wrote about middle-class intellectuals (and suffered ostracism from the left – from the like of D. A. N. Jones), but always with a tongue-in-cheek, lashing wit, a déclassé distance and a rigorously analytical eye for fatal flaw. And always too with a vision of socialist Utopia, while maintaining a (healthy) scepticism about the ways and means of realising a socialist society.

Addressing himself to the future and the function of the artist in society, Mercer outlined the problems:

> One huge difficulty that presents itself immediately is that in no way does the working class of any of the western democracies in the seventies display the characteristics of a revolutionary or potentially revolutionary force. The uneasy resilience of late capitalism, the substitutive effect of the 'Welfare State' and mixed economies – unemployment and economic recession notwithstanding – are here stubbornly to infuriate us. The power of the communications media over citizens of East and West alike is something unparallelled in the

history of human society. The concentration of physical power and the means of psychological manipulation in the hands of the state and/or big business, is unprecedented.

I believe we have come to a point in the West when the parliamentary form of social democracy is our best hope for sustaining a sufficient degree of freedom in which we can thoroughly overhaul our political philosophy. I think we need to defend the social democratic system for as long as may be necessary (against both our revolutionary comrades on the fanatic left and our right-wing enemies on the fascist right) to arrive at an understanding of how we may achieve its dissolution in a just and humane fashion – and with the consent of a majority of our citizens.

I would say that in the end the artist stands closer to 'the people' (and by this I mean not a class or classes, but whatsoever humanly characterises a society) than the political intellectual; and if the stern commissars of the New Man can live without morality, then the sooner they can be redeemed from this awful misconception by any means at our disposal including the stubborn anarchy of individual vision – the better off we shall be.

Sartre is perhaps the sole candidate in the last fifty years for having attempted both a synthesis and a reconciliation of 'the dialectic' with an existential or phenomenological enterprise which at least takes into account the bald ethics of choice. It would be tragic if we became complicit in any kind of society which denied men and women the total freedom of enquiry necessary to pursue this at once daunting and exhilarating task – through science, philosophy art or any other discipline.

Mercer defended the individual's 'freedom of enquiry' against both capitalist and communist repression, in the process (and in the practice of his art and craft) laying himself open to criticism from both camps, but particularly to allegations of anti-Marxism. Yet *Cousin Vladimir* was a repudiation at least of the latter. Having presented in the play a grim picture of democratic western society, warts and all (symbolised by a gang of hard-core alcoholics), and an equally grim communist eastern society (with its brainwashing and repression), Mercer allows his two Russian dissidents *to choose*. And they choose to return to Russia. Mercer explained: 'I haven't abandoned my intellectual or moral sympathy and belief in a Marxist critique or the dialetical method, but I do not think the human species is any longer fit for a humane Marxist revolution – in either the east or the west. But in the long-term view, the chances are better in the Soviet countries.' And such was the implicit message of *Cousin Vladimir*.

It was ironic that such a rigorously analytical and politically critical playwright should have been virtually hounded off the stage during the period – the seventies – in which political theatre flourished in a fashion he could not have envisaged when he started writing in isolation in the early sixties. In self-defence Mercer felt compelled to 'unmarx the Marxists':

These *faux logiciens* of the left remind me of nothing so much as the man condemned to death for murder in a little anecdote dear to the heart of linguistic philosophers. The condemned man manages to prove that, by the very logic of his guardians, it will be impossible for them consistently to implement his execution. None the less, on the appointed day at the appointed time, what *actually* happens is that they take him out and hang him. I think a rigorous course in linguistic philosophy might work wonders for Marxists of any persuasion. Perhaps on the appointed day at the appointed time, they will simply take me out and hang me.

In the last analysis, however, for all his political conviction, Mercer was ambivalent, if not sceptical, about the function of political theatre: 'I believe firmly that effective ideology is a matter of concrete political work among people who are going to bring about social change: it's a class question. That's one side of me. The other part is the feller who writes these plays which just take society as it is: and about that I feel rather helpless.'[14]

'It is interesting and not altogether surprising that Wesker's bourgeois-cultural elitist ideas have found a warm welcome within the "arts" machinery of the Labour Party establishment. He could, indeed, be the laureate of Wilsonian politics.'
John McGrath, *Black Dwarf*, June 1970

Arnold Wesker

In the early sixties, at the time of John Arden's *The Workhouse Donkey* at Chichester, Arnold Wesker described Arden as a 'wishy-washy liberal'. Arden replied in *Peace News* in 1963:

> What I call a wishy-washy liberal attitude is an attitude that presents both points of view to a certain extent, but doesn't really believe in either. I think that in most of the controversial questions I handle in my plays, I do in fact have quite definitely a strong view on one side or the other. But I don't regard it as the business of a dramatist to try and tell the audience to accept these views.[1]

In retrospect there is a certain irony in Wesker's description of Arden, for, if anything, time proved Arden to be the politically-committed activist and playwright and Wesker the sort of confused and prevaricating liberal that Arden described.

At that time, though, Wesker was a vocal, self-declared, self-styled socialist – son of the working class and veteran campaigner for causes such as the Committee of 100 and Centre 42. He was regarded almost as a prophet, diagnosing social ills and evangelising a socialist future. And he was writing plays on political subjects. But after a meteoric rise to a position of stature as political spokesperson for a generation (it sometimes seemed for the nation), he found himself (by the end of the sixties) increasingly isolated and disillusioned. Centre 42 had failed culturally. His plays were failing critically and commercially.[2]

The seventies proved an even greater set-back for Wesker. And he found himself alienated not only from the right, but from the left – and from the theatre itself. In *Tribune* in 1978 Wesker said: 'My personal diary is a record of catastrophe.'[3] And so – from the fraught and hostilely received production of *The Friends* at the Roundhouse in 1970 to the disastrous production of *The Merchant* in New York in 1977 – it had been.[4] At that time none of his major plays of the seventies – *The Journalists*, *The Wedding Feast*, *The Merchant* – had received major British productions. By 1978, Wesker was 'world-weary' and 'overwhelmed with a sense of isolation and impotence'.[5] He felt his energy for public, political life had been expended: 'I could never again put myself on a platform to make a speech.'[6] He had abandoned socialism: 'I think that I am, and probably always have been, an old-fashioned humanist.'[7]

Wesker analysed his situation as one of personal failure. The rejection of his plays 'confirms, I suppose, that I don't fit anywhere at the moment – in the English theatre'. And: 'Perhaps I shouldn't be talking about this, but it seems as if the personality of the man has got in the way of the work. For reasons which I really don't think I understand, I do seem to arouse hostilities and irritations.'[8] His experiences left him bruised and bewildered. Curiously though, Wesker never appeared to analyse the situation as one of political failure – a failure that was almost inevitable given the political circumstances in Britain in the seventies, the system itself, and Wesker's always equivocal socialism. Yet a 'political' perspective went a long way towards explaining Wesker's dilemma and shedding light on the fundamental problems facing socialist writers.

Hindsight certainly illuminated the conflict in Wesker's early plays between enlightened humanism – utopian socialism in the William Morris tradition – and revolutionary socialism as a cause to be struggled for. In the end for Wesker, humanism won out. John McGrath identified the problem in 1970, when Wesker was still defining his stance as socialist and still defending it, albeit diffidently.

Reviewing *The Friends* in *Black Dwarf* in 1970, McGrath concluded that Wesker should not confuse anybody, including himself, into thinking that he was a socialist or that the play – 'ideologically bankrupt' – was related to any possible form of socialist theatre. *The Friends*, wrote McGrath, was bourgeois in form and bourgeois in effect: 'to reassure the middle classes that humanity is all one, we are all mortal and the differences between us are not really so important'.[9] What angered McGrath (and the tone of the review was very aggressive, as Wesker quite rightly pointed out) was Wesker's treatment of the British working class, reflected in the formulation: 'How can we respect and look for guidance to the virtues of the proletariat, when the British working class is so corrupt and backward?'[10] And the lack of any 'Marxist – let alone Leninist – thought in his approach'. McGrath dismissed Wesker's socialism as 'a tremulous flirtation with "progressive" ideas'.[11]

According to McGrath, *The Friends* was indicative of Wesker's lip-service socialism ('the portrait of Lenin on the wall remains little more than a decoration'), but by no means an isolated instance. *The Wesker Trilogy* (heralded in the wake of the 'revolution' of 1956 as a monument to the working class), wrote McGrath, 'made a minimal, possibly irrelevant, demand for articulacy and the values of a good liberal education to be brought to the working class. It displays a lamentable ignorance of the strengths and values of the working class itself.' Hence Wesker's 'bemused inaction' and his disappointment and bitterness about 'any thought of revolutionary social action'.[12]

Wesker's Centre 42 campaign, like his early plays, 'prefigured the ideological bankruptcy' – conceived as it was from a 'bourgeois concept of culture' and based on a false assessment and analysis of the working class. Thus the crusade to bring 'culture' *to* the working class was based on a concept of culture as product to be sold by 'superior' artists to 'inferior' workers for their betterment: i.e. cultural imperialism. The kindest of McGrath's conclusions about Wesker's politics at this time was that he was unable to accommodate 'romantic, nineteenth-century pre-Marxist utopian socialism to the twentieth-century capitalist rat-race'.

If McGrath's review seemed unnecessarily hostile, it nevertheless raised the crucial issues of political theatre – the questions of aesthetics and audiences and the function of the political playwright as artist and activist. These were, in fact, the issues that confronted politically-inclined theatre workers in the seventies. From Wesker, who did very much regard himself as deeply socially committed – a socialist if not a Marxist-Leninist – McGrath's attack provoked a response which developed into a lengthy, analytical correspondence between them. In it they addressed themselves to such issues as the class nature of culture ('or the dark relationship between theatre and socialism, between bourgeois culture, working-class culture and revolutionary culture'[13]), the revolutionary potential of the British working class, Labour Party reformism, the legacy of Stalinism and the nature of socialism. There was, not surprisingly, a degree of personal antagonism.

Wesker was hurt. In 'old style Stalinist decree-making' fashion, McGrath had 'passed judgement', using 'unworthy, childish, simplistic labelling' and 'stale, jaded Stalinist jargon'. Worse, McGrath had indulged in 'spit-and-run fringe left-wing polemics'. He'd written irresponsibly, having only seen the play once, and he'd got his facts wrong – e.g. Esther in *The Friends* had died of leukemia not cancer! But, wrote Wesker:

... most damning of your attitude to me and my work is that it is shared by 'Peter Simple' in the *Daily Telegraph* together with a host of other snide right-wing journalists.[14]

The irony was that Wesker had suffered at the hands of the right-wing critics, and a not insignificant part of his career had involved taking them on in defence of his plays.[13] Here he saw himself being attacked by his own side – the left, and was understandably bewildered. Why, he asked, could not McGrath speak in a 'friendly, comradely' fashion? Basically, however, Wesker accused McGrath of being a counter-revolutionary, suffering from bourgeois guilts and repeating ancient ruling-class arguments 'that the workers are best left happy and undisturbed'. Then Wesker went on to offer his own definition of revolution:

> *I've* always spoken about what the working man *could* be and felt anger that he's abused for what he *is*; and in doing this it was necessary to tell him what he is as I know him from experience. He's *my* class and my background and therefore what I say I say from love and a concern for wasted lives. You might want him to remain only a happy 'pint-drinker' but I say you are patronising and insulting to do so. He is capable of infinitely more and within him is a spirit which I want to see as other than the sour, doctrinaire and uncharitable spirit such as emanates from your article. That's what my revolution is about.[16]

McGrath attempted in his next letter to analyse the English tradition of idealism which he felt was 'responsible for holding back many sensitive, intelligent people [including Wesker] from revolutionary socialism' and how this led (often subconsciously) to reformism. McGrath isolated three sources of idealism. The first was the fear 'that the price of revolution was Stalinism'. This fear arose from the historical circumstances they had grown up in – the same Stalinist circumstances which alienated David Mercer from an active form of committed Marxism. If Stalinism were the inevitable price, said McGrath, then neither would he pay it. But historical circumstances had changed: there had been alternative revolutionary situations in China, in Cuba, in North Vietnam – even in Korea – and in France in 1968. And the situation in England was different again:

> In this country, the time is ripe for revolutionary socialism to make itself known as a real alternative to the failed 'pragmatism' of the Labour leadership.

McGrath agreed that fear of Stalinism should breed caution (but not contempt for socialism): he did not feel it needed to paralyse the left. He thought Wesker's reaction had been evasive:

> Surely we must be as honest and ruthless with each other as we can be, as direct, aggressive and vigorous as possible, to mark out our positions, to define our values, to awaken the contradictions, to heighten the ideological temperature, to confront each other's consciousness boldly.

The second source of the 'idealism' which prevented direct action, said McGrath, was the English intellectual tradition which opted for 'debating society reasonableness' and which had 'kept most English writers politically back in the eighteenth century'. The characteristics of this tradition – reticence, understatement, obliqueness, politeness, flippancy – were the direct result of the rise of industrial capitalism and the nineteenth-century bourgeois family; were 'the social arms of parliamentarianism – a method of making sure that nothing serious is ever argued articulately and in depth'. The effect: 'to block the development of socialist theory in this country', the socialist theory that 'must be a guide to action, to change'.

The third source of idealism, argued McGrath, was reformism – the issue 'central to the dilemma of so many people who "believe" in a socialist revolution, but somehow can't act on that belief'. (*The Friends*, thought McGrath, was impressively accurate in expressing this precise confusion and sense of powerlessness.) Wesker was rendered impotent by the contradiction. McGrath:

> For you *seem* to be a 'reformist': yet you consistently claim to be a 'socialist'. You *seem* happy for the 'parliamentary process' to continue indefinitely; yet you are always talking about 'revolution'. Your cultural ideas presuppose the status quo: but you know that for them to succeed, we need a completely new kind of society. You say the working class is 'your' class, and you want the working man to be 'what he *can* be': but you draw the line at organising the working class to seize power, which you who say you are a socialist know is the only way for the working man *really* to be 'what he *can* be'.

McGrath used a letter of Wesker's which was published in *The Times* in June 1970 to illustrate not so much his reformist tendencies (which as Wesker pointed out, were not a crime – yet!) as his misunderstanding of the meaning of socialism. Thus Wesker talked about workers' participation in industrial management, but failed to ask: 'how can 3000 workers get control?' Wesker referred to the demise of the stock market, but failed to take into account that 'the machine can only be destroyed by the organised principled efforts of the international working class'. Wesker talked about educating the electorate on 'the complexities of the political machine', but never mentioned 'the need to *overthrow* that political machine, the most devious of all the capitalist system's devices for self-preservation'. In short Wesker's socialism stopped short of 'the necessity for the overthrow of the capitalist system by the working class, and the building of a socialist society, thus clearing the way for the many, many revolutions which are to come'. Wesker's was a classical expression of the phenomenon of idealism.

Wesker, according to McGrath, failed to see the necessary implications of socialism, or if he saw them was unable to follow them. Similarly, McGrath felt, Wesker 'fails to see any other kind of culture than middle-class culture'. McGrath:

> As one who has claimed so frequently to be a socialist, you will no doubt agree that the accepted cultural values of a society tend to relate directly to the values of the class in that society which is in economic control. In other words, the accepted cultural values of *our* society relate directly to the values of the upper echelons of the bourgeoisie.

As for working-class culture – television, movies, and pop music – 'it is a weapon in the hands of the bourgeosie'. The questions confronting the writer were therefore:

> Are we going to create a *revolutionary* culture, whose task is to *transform* working-class culture, as it now exists, and to work with the political movement to create a revolutionary consciousness amongst the people? Or are we going to sit on our arses and moan about the backwardness of the people?

The implication was that McGrath would create a revolutionary culture while Wesker sat on his arse.

The reason, said McGrath, that he didn't adopt a more friendly or comradely tone was because TV compères were friendly and Jim Callaghan was comradely: 'In the name of friendliness and comradeliness, realities are submerged and the whole confidence trick of capitalism sold to the people.'

Wesker did *not* accept McGrath's criticisms sitting on his arse, and he absolutely disagreed with McGrath's analysis of culture – as bourgeois, as a tool of the ruling class. Culture was more complicated than that implied, said Wesker:

> What is revolutionary art? Art whose forms are different from anything we've seen before? ... or using bourgeois art forms to say revolutionary

things? ... I've never encountered working-class art ... I don't
subscribe to the affected notions that music hall was art, or that pop
music is art ...

And in defence of what McGrath was calling 'bourgeois art', Wesker
quoted from Lukács to underline the fact that Marx himself had
not found it necessary to dismiss the cultural achievements of the
past. Culture was not just theatre or music or art, but a nation's
total way of life: 'its patterns of social, legal and economic relationships'. Hardly any of which were controlled by the working class – or
at least not effectively so. Wesker then explained that working-class
culture could be stimulated precisely *because* of ruling-class control,
arising out of repression and opposition, and 'that the ruling class
can produce, from its own ranks, people who survive its crippling
effects'. Wesker was 'no more satisfied with it [*The Friends*] than
I am with the life I lead', and he was 'not happy with the
parliamentary process in so far as I'm frustrated by the miniscule
influence I have on that process'. He invoked the vision of socialism
held by Sarah Kahn in *Chicken Soup with Barley*:

> You think it doesn't hurt me – the news about Hungary? You think
> I know what happened and what didn't happen? Do any of us know?
> How do I know who to trust now – God, who are our friends now?
> But all my life I've fought. With your father and the rotten system
> that couldn't help him. All my life I worked with a Party that meant
> glory and freedom and brotherhood. You want me to give it up now?
> You want me to move to Hendon and forget who I am? If the electrician
> who comes to mend my fuse blows it instead, so I should stop having
> electricity? I should cut off my light? Socialism is my light, can you
> understand that? A way of life ... I've got to have light. I'm a simple
> person, Ronnie, and I've got to have light and love ...[17]

Wesker showed Sarah's vision – the light of socialism (in full
awareness of the Stalinist betrayal) – but the problem, as Wesker
acknowledged, was what to do with what you believe. And this was
where he and McGrath parted company. Wesker:

> We are not in a revolutionary situation in this country, however unfair
> is the distribution of wealth ... you have to face the fact about the
> nature of art and education that their impacts are not immediate. Their
> effects accumulate over a period of time. Having accepted this the next
> question is: can our situation afford us to wait? And though the answer
> is neither exciting nor romantic, it must be – yes. There is injustice
> in Britain, but no oppression – we cannot borrow 'other people's
> urgency'. Neither you nor I are a Marx or a Guevara – we're not even

Leila Khalids. There's no dire circumstance to force us into the excitement of taking to arms, secret plottings or threats of violence. We might wish we were such people and that the situation was so straightforward. It is not and we are not and there is in the dishonesty of pretending otherwise an inbuilt bomb to explode our hopes, frustrate our energy, disappoint our friends and consign us pathetically to the growing up of left-wing factions while those controlling power more subtly than we have cared to analyse it look on and thank God for our callow fervour.

Given the non-revolutionary situation, Wesker asked himself how he could contribute to the long-term creation of socialism, how to put *his* vision of socialism into practice: the answer had been with the Committee of 100, with his plays – and with Centre 42.

Despite its short life and its failure – fully acknowledged by Wesker – Centre 42 had not been just a grand vision, but a concrete attempt by Wesker to put his political and cultural beliefs into practice. And to the extent that he pursued that progressive venture to its end, Wesker could not be accused of rhetoric without action.

The concept grew out of Wesker's desire to address himself to 'the bus driver, the housewife, the miner and the Teddy Boy' to the 'Mr Smith' who 'died, not having had a glimpse of anything that might have told him what it [life] was all about, not having understood much'. It grew out of his feeling that 'education is not merely scant and inadequate, but is bankrupt of any values'. It grew out of a desire to 'undermine people's existing values and impose our own upon them'. It was a concept of a 'movement' that would let 'England know that its community was alive and kicking and critical and eager'. In response to the 'general malaise' Wesker urged artists to 'pick up our poems, our plays and films, tuck them under our arms and go out to the public and do battle with them'.[18] And despite its failure, Centre 42 was a very real forerunner – in theory and practice – of the alternative theatre movement (of small-scale touring and community arts projects) which grew up much more organically at the end of the sixties and flourished in the seventies.

The idea of going to the trades union movement in 1960 was original, audacious and indicative of the project's connections with the genuine grass roots Labour movement. And the fact that the unions took up the concept at national level – though they never put their money where their mouth was – was reflected in the Resolution 42 of the 1960 Trades Union Congress which gave Centre 42 its name:

Congress recognises the importance of the arts in the life of the community especially now when many unions are securing a shorter working week and greater leisure for their members. It notes that the trade union movement has participated to only a small extent in the direct promotion of plays, films, music, literature and other forms of expression including those of value to its beliefs and principles. Congress considers that much more could be done and accordingly requests the General Council to conduct a special examination and to make proposals to a future Congress to ensure a greater participation by the trades union movement in all cultural activities.[19]

In the autumn of 1962, Centre 42 organised a series of festivals for Wellingborough, Nottingham, Leicester, Birmingham, Bristol and Hayes (Middlesex). Each was mounted at the invitation of the local trades council. The Nottingham Festival had the support of 56 separate unions from the Basford & District Bleachers' Association to the large National Union of Miners. Each one-week festival included art exhibitions (local and children's art as well as 'highbrow' art), theatre (Bernard Kops' *Enter Solly Gold*, Stravinsky's *The Soldier's Tale*, Wesker's *The Nottingham Captain*, Charles Parker's 'radio/theatre' ballad *The Maker and the Tool*), plus folk, jazz and poetry concerts.

Though John McGrath criticised Centre 42 on grounds of 'cultural imperialism' (and there was similar comment at the time), the main criticism in 1962 was simply bad organisation. Centre 42 had bitten off more than it could chew. Director Geoffrey Reeves, who was closely involved in Centre 42, catalogued these problems in *Encore*, emphasising the *experimental* nature of the venture:

The purpose of Centre 42 is to hot up the climate: we are working for the changes that will take place in ten or twenty years. We are fighting at the moment not for standards of work so much as the opportunity to work.[20]

And the extent to which Centre 42 succeeded in this purpose has often been overlooked.

Ten years later, the changes *had* taken place. The statistics spoke for themselves. In 1968 there were half a dozen 'fringe' theatre groups: by 1978 there were well over a hundred alternative theatre companies (either touring on a national basis or based in specific communities), plus another fifty or more young people's theatre companies. In 1968 there were 34 arts centres: by 1978 there were over 140, plus a good 200 small-scale touring venues in London and the regions. In the sixties there were a handful of practising playwrights in the fringe or political arena: in 1978 there were at least 250 British playwrights, who worked part, if not full, time in alternative theatre. Centre 42 had come true, independent of its originators and on a scale they could not really have envisaged. And interestingly, many of the theatre companies (particularly the avowedly socialist ones) made effective use of the trades unions at a grass roots level in precisely the way the TUC had envisaged with its Resolution, and as the Centre 42 festivals had attempted. The one irony was that Arnold Wesker never became involved in the movement once it actually started.

To criticisms of cultural imperialism ('hectoring folk singers thrusting a supposedly superior form of culture in their faces'[21]) Wesker replied in the 1961/62 Annual Report of Centre 42, and later in a lecture in 1966:

> You would like to appear the guardian of the people's right to pursue whatever they care to pursue in that state of 'non-grace'. But all you are doing is justifying the bother you do not care to take to ensure that every man enjoys the knowledge you enjoy. In the past men defended material wealth for the few with the same arguments – 'leave them in their back-to-backs, they would only put coals in the bath-tub' – and they were as dishonest when applied to money and property as they are when you now apply them to art.

As to the reasons for Centre 42's failure, lack of money was obviously one:

> Forty-two failed to raise money from the Labour movement and the Arts Council – with Jennie Lee at its head ... Victor Feather's words to me in 1965 were 'I've been instructed by the General Council of the TUC to tell you that you need feel no obligation (or responsibility) to them and that they feel none towards you or Centre Forty-two.' Jennie Lee's words to Forty-two in 1968 were: 'Arnold must realise that what he wanted to do is now superseded by the work that I've been doing and he must reduce the scope of his aims accordingly.'

There were those who regarded Centre 42's need for and failure to raise funds as symbolic of its bourgeois conception. But the alternative theatre movement as it eventually developed could not have grown to its size and scope at the end of the seventies without just that subsidy – which was eventually forthcoming. Geoffrey Reeves concluded:

> If you are prepared to run a revolution then somewhere you must chance your arm. If it is merely an attempt to make what we know as good art available ... for anyone who wants it, then all we are doing is propagating Tory party policy into fact. Freedom of choice, etc. The

point is, surely, that we must make a stand in the work we do. You cannot differentiate between the nature of the work (what goes on the stage) and the circumstances under which it is performed. If we are going for a social revolution, then it must be *social*. No one is compelled to go and see what we do: but we must make it vital, exciting, so that people want to come. This implies not merely charitably offering our taste to them, but making a real effort to see into *their* lives, into *their* roots, so that we produce something compulsive for both of us. Something popular.[22]

John McGrath would no doubt have responded that the error was in conceiving of a *social* revolution without, or as separate from, a *socialist* revolution. That, in fact, it *was* only good art being made available; that Centre 42 *was* perpetuating bourgeois culture, not creating a new revolutionary art form, or even a working-class art form. That Centre 42 *did* take a stand, but it was a social reformist and not a *socialist* stand, and that it was therefore plastering over the cracks of capitalism. At the same time, there were radical ideas in Centre 42: that what is performed is inseparable from where it is performed and for whom – hence performance to non-theatre audiences in non-theatre places. And the awareness of the need for new forms. All of which were to become basic tenets of the eventual alternative theatre movement.

As far as Wesker's plays were concerned it was inevitable to conclude – with Wesker – that he was always an old-fashioned humanist (while bearing in mind that that is a critical comment and not a capital crime!). And that such attacking, antagonistic attitudes as McGrath's – indeed as also of *Encore*'s, which in 1963 was calling Wesker the 'kind of projection for those disaffiliated and liberal idealists all over England whom Jimmy Porter first brought to self-awareness'[23] just at the time Wesker was calling Arden a wishy-washy liberal – these attitudes were perhaps a response to Wesker's pretentions to a political position which he blatantly did not fully embrace. *The Kitchen* and *The Trilogy* were probably Wesker's first and last overtly socialist plays, Sarah Kahn's impassioned plea for socialism (quoted earlier) probably his last positive statement in favour of socialism. The Marxist critic Jeremy Hawthorn, writing in the magazine *Mainstream* in 1965, concluded by saying: 'Wesker needs to go back to Sarah and start again from her.' McGrath would no doubt have agreed.

Certainly Wesker's plays after 1968 dealt either with basically humanist issues – *The Friends* and *The Old Ones* – or with 'political' subjects in isolation from the overall political system, with less and less political insight – at least with less political analysis. Thus *The Journalists* presented the moral dilemmas of journalists on a major national newspaper (researched at *The Sunday Times*) in a pseudo-documentary style without ever relating the moral and party political issues to the economic fact that this was the capitalist press and that this fact alone defined and determined the moral issues. *The Wedding Feast* (adapted from a short story by Dostoyevsky) presented industrial conflict on largely individualist lines. Louis Litvinov might be the rich owner of a shoe factory, but he was a nice guy at heart, kind and (paternalistically) generous. The workers' aggression, too, was presented as a personal issue: and one was asked to sympathise with the 'great divide' between them, while the important economic bases of the class barriers were ignored. *The Merchant* was most blatant in minimising or ignoring the political issues ironically, since Wesker's clever re-interpretation of Shakespeare was rooted in the economic basis of anti-semitism in Shylock's bond:

> ... because of the need for all dealings with Jews to be contractual, it is in fact Antonio who insists on the bond, in order to save Shylock from breaking the law, respect for which was so crucial to the Jewish community's existence in Venice.[24]

Shylock's race depends on abiding by the law of the land: abiding by the law of the land means destroying a friend. But there was little analysis of the law of the land! Wesker had apparently removed himself from the political arena.

Wesker's argument was that though capitalism was clearly corrupt, socialism might be equally so:

> My position, I think, is that I *know* there is a conflict within a capitalist society: but I *suspect* there is this other conflict within socialist society ... it's natural to look for the contradictions of capitalism because it has been around a long time: but suppose socialism has its contradictions too?[25]

For David Mercer, Eastern Europe was a barometer, a source of socialist inspiration, a bulwark against the Soviet failure. For Arnold Wesker Eastern Europe had the opposite effect: it had been a source of his disillusionment with socialism:

> There is something about the nature of state control which is anti-social, anti-human and I am disturbed by it ... You see, while I'd like to think that I've lost none of my capacity for outrage against inequality and injustice, yet I suppose I am increasingly worried about con-

tributing towards the creation of a state of society which considers it is doing me a favour in giving me my liberty ... More than anything I'm disturbed by what appears to me the emergence of socialism in the east as a system which often cynically confers and takes away individual liberty and feels it has the right to do so.[26]

In an interview in *Tribune* in 1978, Wesker developed this line of argument and returned to the old themes of culture and education, trying to relate the two:

He [Wesker] had just seen the television film of the Prague Spring and had just been to a football match with his son. Both experiences had overwhelmed him with a sense of isolation and impotence. He saw totalitarian forces at work in the invasion of Czechoslovakia; he saw totalitarian forces at work when America smashed the Chilean government of Allende. Did he see totalitarian forces – or their potential – in the crowd of young West Ham supporters? ... He saw a fundamentally resentful labour force in the east; he saw the same 'force' in the west. He recalled meeting with East German town councillors on the occasion of a production of *The Wedding Feast*. It was a 'cold' confrontation. There were well-intentioned speeches by the well-meaning officials about the working class which suggested to him a 'socialist' view of the working class as a herd of wild animals, to be contained, well-fed, pacified. He thought he detected a fear of the working class. Could intellectuals in the west, he wondered, be concerned with the working class more out of fear than feeling?[27]

Wesker was even further convinced in 1978 – as he had been in his *Encore* article in 1958, 'Let Battle Commence' – that the source of anti-social and anti-socialist problems was a lack of culture. He quoted (in the *Tribune* interview) from John Elsom's book on *The History of the National Theatre* referring to Matthew Arnold's concept of culture:

Without a 'culture' ... men were exposed to all kinds of fanaticism, superstition and hypocrisies – simply because they had no context in which to consider them rationally, no language, no touchstones of sanity, no trained instincts for beauty or moral aspiration.[28]

Wesker saw a lack of context, a lack of culture in Czechoslovakia, in the East German town councillors, in the local comprehensive where his daughter was attacked for her middle-classness, in the football crowd. This was the source of his fear, his sense of powerlessness.

He was anxious not to imply that his own personal sense of isolation necessarily characterised the state of the world. Some people would always have energy, however Sisyphus-like. There would always be new generations. But he felt he had made his contribution.

He read from his epitaph for his mother's funeral: 'And in what lay (her) strength? It was a strength of a particularly Jewish character, a strength comprised of an ancient, healthy fear that human madmen are knocking at the gate, lurking everywhere ready to pounce, and so one must be on guard, be careful; together with a sense of humour that mocked that fear and brushed it away with a third quality; a powerful belief that the madmen must be countered and that there were honourable and good people enough to do it.'

The circumstances in Britain in the seventies demanded a stance which catalysed a movement: Wesker did not take a stance and isolated himself from that movement. When asked in 1978 where he stood relative to the barricades he answered simply and honestly, 'I don't know.' Yet the madmen were knocking at the gate, and the knocking at the gates of the eighties was getting louder. Wesker's strength in the struggle against them would not have been insignificant.

1971

It was in the context of the political issues debated by Bond, Mercer, Wesker and McGrath that the 7:84 Theatre Company was formed in 1971, as a Marxist group aiming to take socialist theatre to working-class audiences. 7:84 was one of the most striking examples of an attempt to put theory into practice and to relate political theatre to political realities. There was a special signficance to the company in that John McGrath had established himself in conventional theatre and television and seemed set for a successful career, which he abandoned in response to his new political consciousness and socialist commitment. The work of 7:84 was amongst the most important in political theatre in the seventies.

1971 saw the start, too, of Hull Truck, rather more oriented to the counter-culture of the sixties than the socialist politics of the seventies, but important in developing the techniques of improvisation, and producing a distinctive new kind of theatre with a political bias to its content.

The seventies were to mark the beginning of many new organisations in response to the needs of the new theatre and the demands it made. There would be the Association of Lunchtime Theatres in 1972, The Association of Community Theatre (TACT) in 1973, the Independent Theatre Council (ITC) in 1974 and the Theatre Writers Union (TWU) in 1975. And there were to be changes in Equity from 1972. In 1971, however, the campaign for a British Theatre Institute was launched in the editorial pages of *Theatre Quarterly* (the new theatre magazine which started in 1970, following in the footsteps of *Encore* from the fifties) – pressing the need for an institute for the theatre analagous to the British Film Institute, whose function would be primarily archival in 'preserving the theatre's past . . . systematically working on the gathering together and cataloguing of contemporary material'.[1] Though the BTI did not achieve its original grandiose aims, it spawned, in the process of its campaign in 1972, the British Theatre Museum, waiting in 1979 to be housed in Covent Garden, and in 1976 the Drama and Theatre Education Council (DATEC), an umbrella organisation for educational theatre interests. And in 1978 it had spawned an embryonic British Centre of the International Theatre Institute.

John McGrath and 7:84 Theatre Company

In his correspondence with Arnold Wesker in June 1970, John McGrath declared that 'in this country, the time is ripe for revolutionary socialism to make itself known as a real alternative to the failed "pragmatism" of the Labour leadership'.[1] He suggested that 'we have to oppose bourgeois theatre by creating a truly revolutionary theatre, in order to help bring about a change in society and in our own art'. For McGrath, using the existing media was one means to this end:

> The forms of television are potentially art forms. In the hands of David Mercer, the TV play has a certain stature. Peter Watkins has produced television films, which, to say the least, cannot be dismissed. The series, much abused, has the same potential as the Victorian weekly magazine held for Dickens. Similarly, the pop song today has, if anything, rather more potential than the Tudor lyric as Wyatt found it. In the cinema, the comedy, the adventure story, the drama, the epic are all forms which may not yet have revealed their full powers. Do we walk away from all this because *Coronation Street* is not *Barchester Towers*, because Mick Jagger isn't Beethoven, because *The Dirty Dozen* isn't Chekhov? Or do we reject involvement with these forms because they are functions of squalid capitalist enterprise?[2]

McGrath's short answer was no. He had himself worked in television at the beginning of his career: 'I decided it was stupid trying to write for a Royal Court audience, or for a West End audience. It seemed to me perfectly obvious that all the people I knew and cared about at that time were watching television, so I thought, well, fuck it, I'll go and write for television, and try to use the popular medium in my own way, and contribute through that to people's lives.[3] This involved writing for *Z Cars* in its early days: 'What we wanted to do was to use a Highway Patrol format, but to use the cops as a key or a way of getting into a whole society ... to use a popular form and try and bang into it some reality.'[4] At that time in the sixties McGrath found it possible to achieve something in television 'because that was a time of liberal influence, not the time of organised reaction which we now have'.

McGrath had an early success in the 'bourgeois theatre' with his play *Events While Guarding the Bofors Gun* at the Hampstead Theatre Club in 1966, based on his own army experience, and about 'cold war' military life in Germany, where British soldiers are involved in the absurd and futile exercise of guarding an obsolete weapon. In the play McGrath was concerned with the 'root-consciousness of the oppressed who are driven to futile, alienated work'.[5] McGrath then worked for a time in films in Hollywood. But:

> I finally came to the conclusion that the mass media, at the moment, are so penetrated by the ruling-class ideology, that to try to dedicate your whole life – as distinct from occasional forays and skirmishes – to fighting within them is going to drive you mad.[6]

This was the period leading up to the formation of 7:84 Theatre Company in 1971, a period of rejection of establishment values and the realisation that 'there has to be a struggle, there has to be a political organisation, there has to be a very hard, bitter, disciplined fight against the powerful forces of capitalism'. The events of 1968 in Paris were extremely important to McGrath:

> I went over and spent some time there, until they started exporting foreigners. And the importance of the thinking around that whole time, the excitement of that whole complex set of attitudes to life which that para-revolutionary situation threw up was incredible – the thinking about ordinary life, the freshness of the approach, the urgency and the beauty of the ideas was amazing. But what didn't happen was the organisation. For a lot of reasons. A lot connected with the French Communist Party, a lot connected with the fact that the rest of the left was split and disorganised, and with the fact that a lot of the student leadership was middle class and not dedicated to social revolution, and with the power of De Gaulle and his wiliness as a politician. And there, in the middle of all that, you have the absolute contradiction.[7]

McGrath's answer to the contradictions as expressed in his own life was to set up a theatre company 'in opposition to bourgeois theatre – a truly revolutionary theatre'. This was 7:84 Theatre Company.

The setting up of 7:84 overlapped with a period between 1970 and 1972 when McGrath was working at the Everyman Theatre, Liverpool, 'work as important', said McGrath, 'as that later with 7:84, not least because the Everyman had – as a result of the policy and the hard work of Peter James and then Alan Dossor – forged strong links with a working-class audience and its traditions'. It was with the Everyman that McGrath wrote the original version of *Fish in the Sea* and *Soft or a Girl?* (later adapted to the East End and produced at the Half Moon Theatre). McGrath:

> *Soft or a Girl?* was written for a popular working-class theatre – the Everyman. It was a socialist play with a socialist theme. It was a great success, playing to packed houses, 80 per cent working-class. It put the Everyman on the map as a working-class theatre.[8]

McGrath had also worked at Sussex University on a play about Winstanley and The Diggers, and in Edinburgh in 1970 with Richard Eyre on *Random Happenings in the Hebrides*. 7:84 was eventually the result of various attempts to get a 'different kind of touring theatre off the ground'.

7:84's first production was McGrath's *Trees in the Wind* which played at the Edinburgh Festival and then on the fringe circuit which had been created by Portable Theatre and Pip Simmons. The title of the play came from a quotation by Chairman Mao – 'Wind will not cease even if Trees want to rest' – and was about three women each of whom embodied a mass of contradictions. Carlyle is an ex-actress who is studying Marxism–Leninism within the People's Revolutionary Party of which she is membership secretary. She reads about the Chinese revolution and the achievements of Mao, but finds herself unable to deal with the problems in her own society. Belle, a psychiatric social worker who's just been jilted by her boyfriend for a Republican Senator's daughter, knows that she is merely patching over the cracks in the system, but feels impotent to change it. Aurelia chronicles the atrocities of war, torture, pollution and the oppression of women: she has withdrawn from direct action to formulate theories on why the world is bad – for her grandchildren. Into their middle-class world arrives working-class Joe who highlights the contradictions in the lives of the women and forces them to confront both their realities and their fantasies – and his own. The play builds to a final indictment of capitalism and class society.

In 1971 there were productions of two short Trevor Griffiths' plays – *Apricots* and *Thermidor*, followed by a revival of Griffiths' *Occupations* in 1972. There was McGrath's *Plugged into History* in 1972 and *Underneath*, about two people who both claim they build bridges. McGrath:

> One is a designer with a very elitist attitude, who designs an experimental type of bridge which is very likely to collapse. And his attitude

is, that if progress is going to be made, it's going to have to be at the expense of a few hundred lives, maybe – though he's a very kind, gentle, wonderful man, who does make progress in the construction business. The other is a man who actually works on the bridges, and gets killed on one. The link between the two is the man's son, who grows from being a kind of upper-class drop-out, and works with the man who is killed on the bridge, sees him killed and goes through a politicisation as a result. It's about a conflict of ideology ... and about the value of human life.[9]

Also in 1972, 7:84 produced two plays by John Arden and Margaretta D'Arcy – *The Ballygombeen Bequest*, which was soon stopped by a Court injunction, and a new version of *Sergeant Musgrave's Dance* – *Serjeant Musgrave Dances On*, in which Musgrave became a para-sergeant coming back from Derry after Bloody Sunday.

1973 was a decisive year for 7:84. The company experimented with a cooperative structure and *modus operandi*, but unsuccessfully, and there was a split which formed the new group Belt and Braces. A new 7:84 Company was set up in Scotland to work separately from 7:84 England. That year 7:84 England produced Adrian Mitchell's *Man Friday* and a joint production with Belt and Braces of *The Ragged Trousered Philanthropists*. 7:84 Scotland started with its great success *The Cheviot, The Stag and the Black, Black Oil* written by McGrath. This play was set in the highlands of Scotland – Euro-tourist paradise, haunt of grouse, deer and millionaire sports-men, and also the home of a unique people with a language, culture and a way of life all their own. The play told the story of the people from the time they were cleared from their homes to make way for sheep in the first half of the nineteenth century to the present. It showed the clearances as more than just the ruthless greed of a few men, but as an inevitable part of a process that was still going on in the operations of the oil giants and the multi-national corporations.

McGrath later described how, when he was researching *The Cheviot, The Stag and the Black, Black Oil*, it proved impossible to discover who owned what land. No land census had been taken in Scotland since 1871. The Scottish landowners' federation ran a register, but would not disclose the acreage of any individual owners. McGrath:

> I was told about a retired forester, called John McEwan, who was then aged 86, living in the heart of Perthshire, who detested the landlords so much that he had photocopied hundreds of ordnance survey maps at his own expense, stuck them together and gone round the boundaries marked on them with a machine which calculated the acreage. He

intended to publish this information, but hadn't finished his work on it. Two members of the company, one night after rehearsal, drove up to see him. He gave them a thorough political grilling and eventually decided they were all right, and they came back with one of his pillow-cases stuffed with maps, sheets of acreages and ownerships. Now, armed with this we could not only publish the most important facts in the programme, but also tell them to the audience at a certain point in the show, and add local information for the area we happened to be in. The effect was truly electric; the best guarded secrets of the Lairds were revealed publicly to people who sometimes lived on their estates and didn't know how big they were.[10]

The play was important in that it was seen and liked by the very Scottish highland audiences it was about, and that it experimented with the popular theatre forms with which McGrath was to continue to work. Structurally it was based on the Scottish *ceilidh*, a form dating from the nineteenth century, a means of 'reinforcing the Gaelic culture and of a political getting together'. *The Cheviot* proved so successful that it was adapted and broadcast on BBC-TV.

During 1974, 7:84 England temporarily closed down and 7:84 Scotland produced two new McGrath plays – *Boom*, about North Sea oil, and *The Game's a Bogey* – contrasting the life of John MacLean, the great Scottish socialist of sixty years ago, with life in present-day Glasgow. Again the play used song, pantomime, ribald parody and comic sketches to tell the story.

1975 was a productive year both for the English and the Scottish companies, and included several plays by McGrath which have been generally regarded as amongst his best. There was *Little Red Hen*, set in Scotland in 1975 during a period of great political activity, when hopes were high and the revivalist fervour of the Scottish Nationalist Party (SNP) was at a peak. The play paralleled a similar period in Scotland fifty years before during the heady days of 'Red Clyde' when a socialist Scotland seemed possible. In the play the young 'hen', a crusading SNP worker, is stopped in her tracks by her granny, the old 'hen', who recreates the past before her eyes as a reminder of what went wrong. She then shows the young 'hen' what she thinks the SNP is all about and demands to know how they are going to succeed where Maxton, Wheatley, Gallacher and Maclean had failed.

There was *Fish in the Sea*, originally written for the Everyman in 1971 and set in Liverpool in the 1970s, the title taken from Chairman Mao's analogy of the Party as the head and body of a fish, the people as the water through which it moves. The play was about the Maconochie family whose lives are disrupted by the occupation of the factory where Mr Maconochie works – a determined, patient, organised working-class action against the ruthless rationalisation of a multi-national corporation; and by the arrival of a Glaswegian anarchist who recognises in one of the daughters a kindred spirit. McGrath:

> The main elements I wanted to set in some form of dialectical motion were the need for militant organisation by the working class; the anarchistic anti-organisational violence of the frustrated working-class individual in search of self-fulfilment here and now; the backwardness of some elements of working-class living; attitudes to women, to socialist theory, the sexual oppression, poetry, myth, etc.; the connections between this backwardness and Christianity; the shallow optimism of the demagogic left, self-appointed leaders of the working class and the intimate realities of growing up and living in a working-class home in Merseyside. To me, these were the main elements of working-class Liverpool, and the conflicts between them are at the centre of the play.[11]

There was *Yobbo Nowt*, about a working-class woman who awakens to political consciousness and activism. Marie is a nobody (the meaning of the title), 33, with two kids and a husband who stays out – a working-class woman cocooned inside her own enforced domesticity. One day she stops to have a think – nothing very special – but it ends up with her throwing her husband out. She is launched into the world for the first time and she confronts what life in present-day England has to offer her and to demand from her. According to McGrath, she 'learns the world reality as she fights to get her share'.

And there was *Soft or a Girl?* – a modern-day Romeo and Juliet story. The sexist title was the refrain of a father to his son whenever the lad came a cropper on the battlefields of the class system: 'What are you? Soft? Or a girl?' In the Half Moon version, the play opened on a Wapping roof top during the war where working-class Mr Hurley and middle-class Mr Martin meet in temporary classless matiness, artificiallly induced by the war effort for national unity. Camaraderie is short-lived, though, for they are blown into 1975 and forced to watch from their historical crow's-nest the 'free' society of the future they were fighting to save. Mr Hurley's boy meets Mr Martin's girl. Their unsuccessful attempts to come together make it clear that class society has not died. As the action continues, the 'deceased' Hurley and Martin descend to play themselves as if they had lived on and the play ends with a disastrous meeting of the two wartime comrades in the Hurley's council flat – disastrous because they indulge in the hypocrisy of hospitality when they should, implied McGrath, be behind the barricades. It takes the courageous young lady to expose everyone. 'You are owned by them,' she says to the Hurleys, referring to the Martins, 'so how can you have them indoors, and drink with them and make polite small talk? No wonder nothing changes.'

In 1976, 7:84 Scotland produced McGrath's *Out of Our Heads*, relating the problem of alcoholism to the wider political issues. 7:84 England did *Relegated* by Shane Connaughton, *Our Land, Our Lives* by Steve Gooch and McGrath's *The Rat Trap*. In 1977, 7:84 Scotland produced *Trembling Giant*, (originally written for the English company) a polemical, political pantomime arguing the case for an independent Scotland.[12]

While 7:84 Scotland was making the giant tremble, 7:84 England was producing David Edgar's *Wreckers* and charting *The Life and Times of Joe of England* about a bright young lad from the North who comes, like Dick Whittington, to make his fortune in the South. But he discovers a corrupt system, realises the true nature of capitalist society and succumbs to it. In 1978, 7:84 Scotland produced *His Master's Voice* by Dave Anderson, an indictment of the media, the capitalist system and the Labour party in that order, using a punk kid involved in the record business. And 7:84 England were producing Margaretta D'Arcy's and John Arden's *Vandaleur's Folly*.

The fact that John McGrath rejected his promising career in the establishment theatre and media and committed his full resources to starting 7:84 in 1971 was a sign of the times in the theatre, significant in indicating the strengths of socialist commitment to socialist theatre. McGrath's rejection of the establishment was categorical. In 1975, when asked what he would do if Peter Hall commissioned a play from him, he answered: 'I would run about twenty-five miles. The point really is that the National Theatre and the Aldwych have got the facilities for very exciting work, with the workshops and everything else. But it's that "everything else" that would make me run ... I'd rather have a bad night at Bootle. You get more from it if somebody's going to come up at the end and say, do you know what's happening in Bootle? You see they're being amalgamated with Southport, and Southport is a big Tory strong-hold, so the people of Bootle are being ripped off ...' For McGrath the National Theatre was a political statement:

In its structure and its productions, it embodies a set of values and assumptions that are demonstrably those of the ruling class: even when it attempts 'left-wing' plays – it gobbles them up into its high-cultural meritocratic maw.[13]

And 7:84 was also a political statement:

The theatre has always been a public statement of how individuals relate to each other and to their own destinies – and this is profoundly political: it cannot be escaped. Our politics are different, of course, from those of the National, the RSC, the West End. We look at people ... from a socialist perspective ... we are Marxist.[14]

In 1978, with eight years of practice behind him, McGrath was in a position to analyse the theory of his revolutionary theatre, its role and its relation to society. He began by defining the kind of political theatre embodied by 7:84 Theatre Company:

... theatre of political change, that is fairly conscious of its aims ... theatre that exists somewhere within the shadow or at least the penumbra of the ideas of Marx and the Marxists ...; theatre that has as its base a recognition of capitalism as an economic system which produces classes, but sees the betterment of life for all people in the abolition of classes and capitalism; that sees that this can happen only through the rise to state power of the current under-class, the working class, and through a democratisation – economic as well as political – of society and of the decision-making process; theatre that sees the establishment of socialism not as the creation of a Utopia or the end of the dialectic of history, but as another step towards the realisation of the full potential of every individual human life during the short time that every individual has to live ... a socialist theatre.[15]

This socialist theatre McGrath distinguished from other kinds of political theatre e.g. anarchist theatre ('when it is conscious of anything at all, sees struggle for state power as a self-defeating aim') or social democratic theatre ('sees the betterment of the working class as a process of gradual gains within a basically capitalist framework').

McGrath isolated three main areas of activity in political theatre:

... first, the struggle within the institutions of theatre against the hegemony of the bourgeois ideology within those institutions; secondly, the making of a theatre that is interventionist on a political level, usually outside those institutions; and thirdly, and most importantly, the creation of a counter-culture based on the working class, which will grow in richness and confidence until it eventually displaces the dominant bourgeois culture of late capitalism.

McGrath emphasised that theatre was not just plays, but 'a means of production with bosses, workers and unemployed, with structured relationships and varied contradictions: it is through its structures as much as through its product, that theatre expresses the dominant bourgeois ideology'. It was necessary to take account of three different sectors of the theatre – commercial or West End, the major subsidised (NT, RSC, reps) and the fringe or touring theatre. The commercial theatre, said McGrath:

> ... in structure ... resembles a nineteenth-century small capitalist enterprise with investors, called angels, a manager, employees on the lowest possible wages and a product which it hopes to market for a profit ... The central contradiction is the old one between the social or group effort means of production and the private ownership of those means ... The ideology contained within the product of this system is usually residual in the extreme. Indeed nostalgia is one of its main preoccupations.

McGrath regarded the major subsidised theatre as financially and ideologically dominant in the seventies:

> The correspondence between the changed economic structure of British capitalism now using a servile state machine to prop itself up and the economic structure of these theatres propped up by millions of pounds of public money is immediately apparent ... As power structures these theatres reflect the nationalised industries, i.e. they are capitalist structures but without the need to make profit ... Sometimes they have a spurious air of democracy, even worker representation on their boards, and to enhance their reputation sometimes even tackle bold subjects like the Russian Revolution, safe in the hands of Robert Bolt.

For McGrath, it was the 'emergent' or fringe theatre that offered 'the possibility of a highly principled creative, Marxist cultural intervention – enriching the Labour movement, making its ultimate victory worthwhile'.

An analysis of late capitalism was the backdrop to McGrath's ideas about the theory and practice of political theatre. McGrath:

> The state becomes the central political problem for a Marxist, together with the party or the means of overthrowing that state and replacing it with a socialist state.

He then asked the crucial question: what can a laugh or a song or a dance or even a penetrating socialist drama do to contribute to overthrowing the state? The answer – something: by challenging ruling-class hegemony as Trevor Griffiths, David Edgar, John Arden and Margaretta D'Arcy, Edward Bond, Howard Brenton,

David Hare had done. Something, by presenting 'work with a socialist content of high standard' as many theatres had done. All this had a function, said McGrath, as did polemical interventionism and agitational theatre – created in support of a strike or a struggle, fund-raising, for or against a piece of legislation, sexism, racism, fascism, multi-nationals, the role of the British army in Northern Ireland. McGrath: 'Theatre is a graphic way of presenting other people's experience. Even of re-presenting our own experience of history to ourselves!' But the real revolutionary theatre was that which created a counter-culture, and that was the aim of 7:84.

For that kind of theatre, says McGrath, aesthetics *per se* are the least important issue. He summed up aesthetics in three short sentences: 'It works if the audience get it with the same sense of wonder and rightness and relevance that you as a group got it with. If the instinctive reaction is not jarred by any incongruous worries, and if the subterranean connections are made and the scene itself is gripping ... That's the end of aesthetics.' McGrath did not reject bourgeois art. 'For the record, bourgeois theatre has created great valuable works which should be performed and treasured. This does not mean one therefore approves of capitalism any more than an appreciation of Sophocles implies approval of slavery.' Nor did McGrath accept that everything working-class was *ipso facto* good or above criticism.

7:84 was an example of McGrath's theory in practice: 'the creation of a counter-theatre, an emergent truly oppositional theatre, based on the working class, which would grow in richness and in confidence until it eventually displaces the dominance of bourgeois theatre in late capitalism'.

But by the end of the seventies McGrath was confronted with a fundamental problem in his political theatre – both in theory and practice. In 1970 he had thought the time was ripe for revolutionary socialism, with the implication that Britain was or was becoming pre-revolutionary, that there was the potential for a revolution. By the end of the seventies nothing in this vein had materialised. It was questionable, therefore, how long it was possible to persist in doing this kind of theatre when the external political circumstances showed no indication of responding or changing in a socialist direction. The climate was clearly more receptive in the early seventies, less so after the Social Contract. In the absence of revolutionary socialism or a movement towards it in the society at large, the representation of socialist theatre – and the work of 7:84 – was running the risk of becoming repetitive, operating in a vacuum, speaking to a void.

'This is you, this is us, this is our lives, this is how we live them, do we like it very much?' Mike Bradwell, 1978

Hull Truck

Hull Truck was founded in 1971 by Mike Bradwell because it 'was fairly obvious no one would give me a job doing what I wanted to do – i.e. improvised plays'. 'Bradwell had worked with Mike Leigh, the other 'impresario of improvisation' and with Ken Campbell. He wanted 'to write by directing' – effectively applying cinematic *auteur* techniques to the theatre. He'd been influenced by the American writer Mike Weller. Bradwell: 'His plays are basically all about young Americans of the Woodstock generation, realistically told. Stories about things that have happened to people of this generation, working out their lives through various hip philosophies and the dope culture. Nobody was doing it properly. So the first idea was to construct plays through improvisations about people of our age group. At that time they were younger than now – they were about 19 to 23 in 1971.'[2] Bradwell wanted to use music to reach the *Rolling Stone/Melody Maker* market and to reflect the lives of that generation. Bradwell: 'Stylistically the actual construction of plays has been very Chekhovian. Chekhov and Bo Diddley have been the two great influences on my career.'

Bradwell knew that no one would employ him to do this, so he decided to employ himself. He advertised in *Time Out* for actors, offered them 'half a peanut to work from Hull', decided £500 would kick it off, wrote to some rich and famous people for money, got a couple of tenners which he used to write to more rich and famous people. And then decided to do it himself, starting with Hull Truck's first show *Children of the Lost Planet* in 1971, 'about a group of people living in a large house in Hull, trying to live communally and failing miserably'.

Apart from the van breaking down and having to hitch that tour with props in back-packs, it worked. And Hull Truck went on to produce their next show *The Last of the Great Love Goddesses*. This was commissioned by a youth conference and set in a technical college canteen. It was about a boy who fancied a girl on a secretarial course and finally plucked up the courage to talk to her. He invited her to a party where his best mate got off with her. Bradwell: 'A sad little love story.'

Then came *The Weekend After Next*:

> It was about two kids of about nineteen who had fallen desperately in love before they left school and home for the first time and gone to live in different towns at different colleges. Though they had been wildly in love with each other in the summer, by Christmas the relationship had been totally fucked up by the fact they were both learning things with different people.

Hull Truck performed the play at the Royal Court Theatre Upstairs for an improvised plays season in 1973. It was a critical failure, but it got them an Arts Council grant for a non-existent play with a bogus plot. Bradwell explained to the Arts Council that because of Hull Truck's improvisatory techniques the title and the plot might change. It became *The Knowledge*:

> The central character was a young school teacher. She had just left teacher's training college, was in her first teaching job; she was a keen sort of middle-class liberal school teacher. Suddenly out of her past turned up this bloke she once had a relationship with at school. He had got more money than sense and had become a rich hippy. He got involved with a girl called Maggie, who was an out-and-out acid casualty. He also got involved with a bloke called Dooley who was an out-and-out rock 'n' roll casualty. It was about the interaction of those particular characters. It is easy to describe them stereotypically, but they weren't, they were real and specific. They seemed like stereotypes, because they were true.

The Knowledge was Hull Truck's first critical success, under controversial circumstances. Before playing it in Manchester the company warned the venue that the people in the play said 'fuck', smoked dope and talked about sex (which people in Hull Truck's shows tended to do). So Manchester billed it as a 'hippy whodunnit' and the show was censoriously cancelled after the first night. But there was a rave review in the *Guardian*, so they were away, with a commission to do a BBC-TV play called *The Writing on the Wall* about a girl lecturer in Art History at a polytechnic who lived with a painter, who was encouraging a young student to write poetry.

Then came *Oh What!*, about

> a squaddy who had just come back from a tour of duty in Belfast,

on leave at home. He spent the whole time getting pissed in the pub and meeting people who gave him a bad time because he was a squaddy. He met a bloke he'd been at school with, who was a bit of a wet and wanted to play in a space rock band. He met an International Socialist lecturer in Liberal Studies from the polytechnic, who got drunk and insulted him. And a working-class lad who was straight down the line CP. That was one area of relationships. The other was two sisters whose father was a lecturer in sociology at the university. One of the sisters had become an agrarian freak living off the land in the country with a photographer who buggered off although she was pregnant by him. And her sister who wrote for *Cosmopolitan*, who was a bit of a liberated lady in London. It was all about the interactions of these relationships.

Oh What! was described variously as a 'responsible critique of a flailing generation', 'a parody of the counter-culture' and a 'Marxian analysis on the need for radical social change'. And it put Hull Truck very much in the public eye.

Bridget's House[3] was, in 1976, the last of the series of improvised plays with the original core company of performers. As usual, the show's strengths were in the characters and the inter-relationships. The house in question was tenanted by a motley collection of misfits, let by a self-described social parasite who had inherited her status along with the property from her ex-husband. Her ex-marriage had also left her with a legacy of loneliness, sexual frustration, biting sarcasm and cynical stoicism. Very little happened, but the play included a lot of brilliantly barbed character assassination, some very funny, caustic social comment and at least six recordable songs – music being very much a part of Hull Truck's shows. *The Times*' response was that 'Hull Truck is a very special company which should be seen ... their savage mockery is never without affection and we can learn something about ourselves from the clarity with which they present their characters'. Bradwell described *Bridget's House* as 'a death-of-the-sixties play, the last play where we got hippiness out of our system, it was like Gorky's *Lower Depths* with jokes and it went to the National', playing in the Young Vic.

In 1978 a new company came together to produce *Bed of Roses*, 'very much about the nature of marriage and love and religion'. Bradwell was sceptical about conventional political theatre. Occasionally accused of not being 'political' – like 'What are you doing to bring about the Socialist International?' – Bradwell argued that he was more interested in the dialectics of social people than the invective of party political platforms: 'I am interested in the politics of relationships between people. I don't like plays about who to vote for.' Bradwell thought his plays worked politically on a personal level:

> Messages are not written on the wall; messages are hopefully within every play we have done. You can pick out aspects of yourself and your mates in the characters we portray on the stage and re-investigate what you are doing to other people and what other people are doing to you and see the pain and misery caused, and try to see why they cause all that pain and find some understanding. Messages are not 'storm the barricades'; the messages are 'this is you, this is us, this is our lives, this is how we live them, do we like it very much?'

Hull Truck's greatest success was its method of working. The plays were devised by the company in conjunction with Mike Bradwell, as director, and were punctuated with music and songs which complemented and commented on the action. Bradwell usually worked with each actor in isolation, discussing the kind of character he wanted and helping the actor to work out minutely detailed background information. After research and background studies had been completed, the actor moved to interior monologues. This allowed the actor to find the character before meeting the unpredictable demands of another character, and it created a source for the inner thoughts and fantasies which were central to the creative process. Gradually Bradwell brought the characters together in various situations and combinations. Relationships and antagonisms were explored and a dramatic line began to evolve. The transition from improvisation to a highly selective organised play was achieved by a careful process of finding which things to develop and which to discard, eventually distilling the essence of the improvisations into tightly constructed and dramatically paced scenes. When it came to performance, nothing was ever written down, but each scene was as carefully rehearsed as it would have been had it come from a script. Bradwell described the process in practice:

> If you want to know about vicars you go out and meet some vicars and go to church and theological college and find out what the exams are and what you've got to know. And how you dress and what sort of gags vicars tell. And build a complete and very detailed background study. If you've got a couple of characters who are going out on a date, then the actors actually do it in character – go to the pictures and the Chinese in character. Do it over a long period of time and get it exactly right. I set up the improvisations we do, keeping an eye open for possible areas of conflict. I then go away and work out a scenario based on the story, using the improvised scenes. Then we rehearse it as we rehearse any play. We add the music at that stage.

Hull Truck proved that improvisation – so often the avant-garde euphemism for amateurism – could be first-class professional entertainment.

1972

By 1972 'fringe' theatre – and particularly lunchtime theatre – had become firmly established in the landscape of London theatre. The Soho Poly had opened in 1968, the Kings Head in 1970. In 1972 the peripatetic Ambiance Lunch Hour Theatre section of Inter-Action was permanently housed in the Almost Free Theatre in Soho. Quipu was operating from the Little Theatre in Garrick Yard. The Half Moon Theatre had found its premises in a deconsecrated synagogue in Aldgate. And in April 1972 the Bush Theatre opened in an upstairs room of an Ind Coope pub on one corner of Shepherds Bush Green with a policy of producing new plays by living playwrights, British premieres of foreign plays and performances by visiting companies. It very quickly established a distinct identity and by the end of the seventies had become one of the most important fringe venues. There were a number of other venues and theatre companies by this time, too – Basement Theatre, Act Inn, Recreation Ground, Wakefield Tricycle Theatre Company and the Open Space – doing regular lunchtime theatre as well as evening shows.

In 1972 all of these fringe ventures found themselves facing common problems with Equity (unionisation) and with the Arts Council of Great Britain (subsidy). Equity was concerned with the welfare of its actor members and, as its then assistant secretary Vincent Burke wrote in *Time Out*: 'To ensure both that the actors involved are not being exploited and that the existence and possible growth of fringe and lunchtime theatre does not constitute a threat to the established theatre and aggravate the unemployment situation for actors as a whole.'¹ The Arts Council simply wasn't finding enough cash to meet the growing requirements of fringe theatre. So in the autumn of 1972, the Association of Lunchtime Theatres (ALT) was formed out of a large meeting of over forty fringe theatre workers held at the offices of *Time Out* (who spearheaded the campaign) with the aims: 'to promote lunchtime theatre, to present principally new and neglected plays and playwrights, to provide alternative venues for actors, directors and designers, and to encourage audiences by making theatre more accessible'. ALT also wanted 'to establish a code of practice for lunchtime theatre, to provide facilities for mutual help and information and to provide the means for the representation of lunchtime theatre in their dealings with official bodies'.²

The ALT was the first of several organisations (later TACT, ITC and TWU) to launch campaigns aimed at persuading the Arts Council to increase its subsidy in the area of fringe and alternative theatre. And subsidy became a major issue in the seventies. There was no doubt that political theatre (or indeed the various other areas of alternative theatre) could not have developed as it did without the benefits of subsidy. And through the seventies the Arts Council did increase its subsidy to this area of theatre – rarely without pressure, however, and invariably with criticism of the whole apparatus of government subsidy to the arts, and specifically of the policy and structure of the Arts Council. The subsidy debate took place on many levels – within the organisations representing theatre workers, within the Arts Council itself, and within the political parties and national organisations concerned with government involvement in the arts, indeed within the government itself. The issues were important: they included artistic and administrative policies at national, regional and local levels; decentralisation of arts funding; democratisation of the Arts Council and its process of decision-making; definitions of art and its evaluation; and, of course, questions about how the 'subsidy cake' was divided and by whom. The essay on subsidy which follows summarises the issues and describes the various campaigns for reform which finally forced the Arts Council to acknowledge that arts subsidy was a political issue.

Amongst the new fringe theatre companies was Foco Novo, started in 1972 by Roland Rees, David Aukin and Bernard Pomerance. Rees had been directing on the fringe since 1968, particularly with Ed Berman's Ambiance Lunch Hour Theatre Club. He had always been interested in producing new playwrights and was instrumental in introducing American playwrights (Mike Weller,

Rochelle Owens, Leonard Melfi, Israel Horovitz) into the English repertoire. And he often promoted the work of black authors and actors – Mustapha Matura, for example. It was his desire to produce new plays by new writers that prompted him to set up Foco Novo. David Aukin had been 'managing' Freehold and The People Show (and, later, Joint Stock) and took the initiative in setting up Foco Novo because of his interest in the work of Rees and Pomerance. Bernard Pomerance was the American playwright whose play, *Foco Novo*, eventually gave the company its name.

The play *Foco Novo* was the company's first production, and was based on the same events as the Costa-Gavras film *State of Seige*, about the American CIA agent Dan Vitrioni, who was kidnapped by Uruguayan urban guerillas, the Tupermaros. Rees:

> We presented *Foco Novo* in a garage in Kentish Town, putting the audience in the back of the garage and presenting it both inside and in the lane leading up to it, and in the streets and on the roof. Because it was about police searches, and also the agent being kidnapped in a garage. We used a 'live' car with its headlights shining into the audience. We used very little other light. Just the summer twilight and as it got darker, we used the lamps of the car while the 'police' searched the roofs. The audience could hear feet stamping on corrugated iron over their heads.[3]

Rees pointed out that Foco Novo had never been able to work in such an environmental fashion again because it was subsidised to tour to more or less conventional venues. After its initial production, Foco Novo Theatre Company was formed and by the end of the seventies had developed into one of the major touring companies.

There were productions in 1975 and 1976 of *Arthur Horner* and *The Nine Days and Saltley Gates*.[4] Also in 1976, there was the adaptation by Adrian Mitchell of John Berger's book *A Seventh Man*, about migrant labour in Europe and specifically the plight of Turkish workers in Germany. In 1977 there was Bernard Pomerance's *The Elephant Man*, the story of a Victorian sideshow freak, John Merrick, and of Frederick Treves, the doctor who rescued him from ridicule and abuse. (This play was eventually performed on Broadway in 1979 and became an award-winning success.) In 1978 there was C. P. Taylor's *Withdrawal Symptoms*, about a middle-class girl in the process of being 'wound down' from heroin addiction in a half-way hostel. And there was *On the Out* by Tunde Ikoli, a young black writer, dealing with the criminal subculture that tempts the unemployed young. There was Colin Mortimer's *Free Fall*, about another middle-class girl who gets sucked in by the machinations of a fanatical religious sect. Early in 1979, Foco Novo produced David Zane Mairowitz's *Landscape of Exile*, about Frederick Engels and the origins of the Labour Party between Marx's death and Engels' death. Most of the plays produced by Foco Novo were concerned with 'social problems' of one sort or another, but not from a strong socialist perspective.

A striking characteristic of the political theatre movement in the seventies was the extent to which the flourishing of new writing coincided with the growth of alternative theatre companies and was often, in fact, consequent upon it. Most of the important new writers started their work with companies and continued to work with them after establishing their reputations, motivated often by political commitment in the broadest sense – to non-theatre audiences and non-theatre venues. Thus Howard Brenton and David Hare started with Portable Theatre in 1968 playing at the Combination in Brighton, and later in the seventies Hare wrote *Fanshen* and Brenton *Epsom Downs* for Joint Stock Theatre Group. Caryl Churchill worked regularly with Joint Stock and Monstrous Regiment, and Edward Bond wrote for Inter-Action and Gay Sweatshop. And so forth. The development of David Edgar as a playwright perhaps epitomised this inter-relationship between writers and companies. The essay which follows chronicles his career – from the early years with The General Will in Bradford to his collaboration with Monstrous Regiment in 1979 – illustrating one strand in the pattern of political theatre.

'I'm a child of my time ... there is now a movement on the move.' David Edgar, 1978[1]

David Edgar and The General Will

Both as a playwright and political activist David Edgar epitomised the growth of political theatre in Britain in the seventies. Politicised by the events of 1968, he graduated in drama at Manchester University and took up political journalism in Bradford, writing plays in his spare time. As these were increasingly successful, he abandoned journalism for full-time political playwriting. He worked his apprenticeship with The General Will in the early seventies, producing classical agitprop. Having perfected that form, Edgar went on – in 1973 – to experiment with various forms for political theatre, culminating with the production in 1976 of his anti-fascist play *Destiny* by the Royal Shakespeare Company at their small theatre in Stratford, then on the Aldwych main stage in 1977 and finally on television in 1978 – an event regarded by many as one emphatic vindication of the political theatre movement. By 1978 Edgar had a firm footing in the establishment – major subsidised theatre and television – but continued to write for political theatre companies (7:84 and Pirate Jenny, for example) and continued, too, with his extra-curricular political activities. Edgar's career from 1968 to 1978 was a microcosm of the political theatre movement in theory and practice.

In terms of his political orientation, Edgar described himself as 'a child of my time' – specifically that 'vague 1968-ish axis' and the 'failure of the 1964 Labour government'. His background was 'a combination of the New Left and the counter-culture'. The intellectual component was Marcuse, but the counter-culture provided the sexual and life-style influences. Edgar: 'I was on the political end of the counter-culture, strongly influenced by the IS [International Socialists] with whom I have always had a close relationship.' Though 1968 was crucial, Edgar continued a process of political self-education that went on throughout the seventies. His writing career started at the same time as the Conservative government of 1970 – when he worked with director Chris Parr, then at Bradford University, while Albert Hunt was at Bradford College of Art. His early plays included *Two Kinds of Angel*, *A Truer Shade of Blue*, *Still Life: Man in Bed*, *Acid* and a full-length play on Rosa Luxemburg called *Bloody Rosa* produced by Bradford University and shown at the Edinburgh Festival. Then came his first play for The General Will in 1971 called *The National Interest*, a documentary about the first year of the Conservative government. That was the beginning of The General Will: 'It arose out of the university, but very quickly ceased to have any relationship with it.' Edgar said there was a 'healthy creative tension' between the work of Albert Hunt and Chris Parr, though they collaborated only once:

> We were jointly asked to create an opening ceremony for the National Student Drama Festival at Bradford University. Earlier that year, Harold Wilson, Chancellor of the University, had given the then Prime Minister Heath an honorary degree. The idea was to reproduce that event exactly, to open the Drama Festival. I wrote the 'script', as I'd been there, Albert played the organ, Chris played a Security Guard, and we ended up giving honorary degrees to everyone who came to the Festival.

In 1972 Edgar left journalism for the theatre when he started working extensively with The General Will, one of the early, seminal political theatre companies. With them he wrote *The National Interest*, *The Rupert Show*, *State of Emergency*, *Rent, or Caught in the Act* and *The Dunkirk Spirit*. The first two he wrote himself (though they were then 'quite bloodily re-written with the company'), the rest on a system of 'day-to-day discussion and/or improvisation' with the company: 'I would then go away and write the scene, bring it back, look into it and discuss that. So I was writing a scene a day.' They would decide on a subject, read about it, build the plot – 'put together the basic outline, so we knew roughly what each scene was going to do, then it was a matter of deciding how to do it'. Edgar described what he and General Will did as 'pure un-adulterated agitprop – we did not deviate from that at all, we were classic'.

> We were presenting our views of the world in memorable images. I think we thought we were presenting a political image, in fact we were presenting an economic one. That was what distinguished General Will – the sophistication with which it treated economic history. To the end of going to people who were involved in their struggles or who were committed to those struggles even if they weren't directly involved,

and putting contemporary history in a Marxist context. And because it was an era of primarily economic struggle, our major purpose was to present a Marxist economic perspective of what was going on – of the crisis of capitalism, why it was in crisis, of the economic tactics of the ruling class to solve that crisis, and the response of the working class.

The National Interest, the first of the Edgar/General Will collaborations, was a series of sketches about events under the first year of Tory government, done in a cartoon style. It started off as a play about the Industrial Relations Act, and expanded. They dramatised the actual Industrial Relations Act by portraying the Tory government as Chicago gangsters, raiding the workers inside their factories with lines like 'Now, you come round here Bugsy with your Clause 101'. And they used the image of the dreaded dole beast in a sequence about rising unemployment: the beast was a hideous creature who high-jumped over unemployment figures against a month-by-month Olympic commentary. There was a clause in the 'IRA' which said that supporting an unofficial strike was known as 'unfair industrial practice' and was an offence under the 'IRA'. So they got the audience to sing a song in support of an unofficial strike and then arrested them. Edgar described it as a 'fairly obvious combination of the agitprop tradition with a cartoon style, with one or two quite nice theatrical effects'. *The Rupert Show* in 1972 attempted to transfer that style to the issue of pornography and sexual politics. It was dramatised as a church service, the songs were hymns and the sketches the 'lesson', 'sermon', 'credo', etc. At the end, riot police raided the hippies saying 'free your head' and then hit them over the head. Edgar: 'Quite a good image.'

Rent, or Caught in the Act (1972) Edgar described as 'a classic example of the bedrock way political theatre can work'. It was a simple, unsophisticated show which explained what the Housing Finance Act was all about. It was devised for and played to tenants' groups, giving them the information in the Act in an entertaining way. Edgar: 'I mean, how many working people have time to sit down and read an Act of Parliament? Providing information is an important function of political theatre. It can also create a rich and total and three-dimensional political vision that ultimately can change people's minds.'[2] The task with *Rent* was to take a group of people through the various situations in which the Act would affect them. They felt this was impossible to do naturalistically, so they decided on the form of Victorian melodrama, with music hall acts. Edgar: 'Not because it was a popular cultural form, but because it was funny, and because it was a very good odyssey form.' Thus there was a family called the Hard-Done-Bys – Joshua, Lydia, Honest Tom and Lydia's fiancé – who were thrown out of their ancestral home. There was a lawyer called Devious of the firm Devious Devious and Downright Dishonest and some villains called Paynorm, Hiveoff and Sir Jasper Pricestroke. Edgar: 'We put them through private landlords, public landlords, a squatting scene and then into a high-rise flat in Camden. Honest Tom became the borough councillor and sold out. And Lydia's long-lost brother returned at the end to become a tenants' activist. It was quite funny.'

State of Emergency was a chronicle play on the year of 1972 showing the major events of that twelve months, each done as an image. So there was a scene about the Upper Clyde, a sequence about the miners' strike of 1972 and one on the docks dispute. Edgar: 'It was Living Newspaper basically, with much less cartoon imagery, a stronger developing style. A lot of it was yesterday's headlines and therefore, because we didn't have any historical perspective, historically significant things like the miners' strike got swamped by quite small incidents. But there were some good scenes. There were two ridiculously over-articulate working-to-rule railwaymen, standing on the platform explaining the difficulties of moving off. There was a graphic sequence about the dock strike explaining the complicated issue of containerisation, using cardboard boxes. There was a scene about a guy who refused to join the AUEW on religious grounds who came with his cross and got attacked. And we did Sir John Donaldson, Chairman of the Industrial Relations Court, as a schoolmaster.'

The Dunkirk Spirit, which toured until the 1974 General Election, was a full-length epic on post-war Britain starting with the end of the war in 1945, but opening with Chamberlain's declaration of war on Germany. It then followed two sailors returning from the war, chronologically through the Labour government and on to the seventies. Edgar: 'We tried, instead of using a whole series of little images, to find very big block images for each period. So for the fifties we took shipbuilding which was booming then. For the Labour government of 1964–1970 we used the image of bright technocrats. We looked at the various anti-working-class methods of that government, satirised the white-heat technological revolution, men in white coats. Then for the period after devaluation we did a scene on productivity deals as an *It's a Knock-Out* game. We did the theory of surplus value by blowing into balloons – it was quite good, with about twenty balloons bursting in the scene. Then we did a highly-structured scene about international money, to get the international perspective which involved a game of three-cornered brag between America, Germany and Britain. They all had gold and were buying chips: the cards became various happenings. And it did actually explain what was going on.'

Though the General Will started in the same vague and unconsidered way as most groups at that time, they aimed broadly for a working-class audience.

> We began to realise that our shows had to do two things – to be entertaining in commenting on events the audience would know about, and to provide a context in which to view events – a political, theoretical context. And because of these factors, the plays worked best with what the jargon calls 'advanced workers' – at things like TASS weekend schools, shop stewards, Labour Party and IS socials. They worked badly with fairly apolitical workers. The nadir of the whole experience was a NUPE gig in Bangor, playing to striking workers, and they couldn't relate to it at all.

General Will started by playing to student and arts centre audiences, and ended by playing to miners' welfare centres and workers. David Edgar left the group when there was a division of opinion about what kind of material should be played to what kind of audiences. Edgar: 'My feeling was that we should remain very slick and almost arrogant in our relationship with the audience. The group's feeling was that there should be much more room for a relationship with the audience in the sense of popular culture. Which I disagreed with because I was fearful that it would become vague and unspecific and imprecise.' About a year after Edgar left the group in 1974, it changed its nature radically and became a community theatre company with a 'gay' emphasis.

Edgar then embarked on a variety of experiments – 'ways of doing political theatre in theatre buildings'. He tried to use an allegory form in *Death Story* in 1972, which was a reworking of Romeo and Juliet set in Northern Ireland. There was *Excuses, Excuses* about a working-class arsonist in Yorkshire which involved a play within a play, characters who were actors performing a documentary drama. Then he developed a line of parody in *Tedderella*, a panto about Ted Heath and the Common Market, and in *Dick Deterred*, a parody in which the Watergate story was told in the form of Shakespeare's *Richard III*. Edgar: 'I thought these were very good and was very pleased with them. But the limits of the form were very clear. It came down to showing off how clever you could be. Which was pleasurable, but as a serious political form they really didn't work.

They didn't even work on the cartoon level of providing images that people retain.' Edgar then tried a 'social realist' approach in *Baby Love* which was based on an actual case of baby-snatching.

1973 was a key year for Edgar, the beginning of several years of experimenting with different forms. He tried working with a documentary form in *The Case of the Workers' Plane*, a play about the aerospace industry and the building of Concorde in Bristol, and *Events Following the Closure of a Motorcycle Factory* (1976) a documentary on the destruction of the motorbike industry in Britain. There was *Operation Iskra* which was an attempt to use the thriller form:

> It was the first play I had written about hardline politics – urban terrorism and counter-insurgency – in contemporary England not using agitprop. It was the first time I tried to talk about politics using realistic techniques.

There was the first draft of *Destiny*, and an experiment with a medieval epic about the Black Death called *O Fair Jerusalem*. From the successes and failures of his many experiments in this period (and he is one of the most prolific writers of his generation), Edgar started to analyse seriously the form and function of political theatre:

> For the first time I consciously thought that what we need to do is to create a style for the presentation of public life. Going right back to why do people go to the theatre: because they are curious, because they want to see other people, because they want to extend their experience into those areas where they cannot extend it by direct experience. Which meant a number of things: people might enjoy plays about China because they would tell them something they didn't know. Or if we want to know what it was like living in the fifteenth century we can't experience that either, so we go to plays to tell us what it was like. In the same way, we want to see things that are very directly related to us, but which it is very difficult to experience anyone else experiencing. I mean one cannot get inside anyone else's love affair, and we only lose our virginity once, so it's quite important to see other people doing it. In the same way with families, we are fascinated by the way other people behave in families – again it is something we can't observe directly. That seems to be the reason for the stranglehold of domestic subjects; people want to know about it because it extends their experience, or it provides useful information with which they can better their lives. Now it seems to me that public life has become increasingly difficult and complex, obscure and influential. Great public events now influence our lives much more directly and demonstrably. And one of the most important things going on in this country in the last ten years has been wage negotiations. I wanted to create a theatre

that could tell about this key, vital factor in our national life. What I wanted to do was create a theatre of public life.

Edgar wanted this theatre of public life to be as complex, rich and as ambiguous as the bourgeois theatre had traditionally been. So he started looking at the dynamics of political activity – and particularly at meetings. Edgar: 'Most people have at some stage attended a meeting; meetings are the stuff of public life. The meeting scene is as essential to the sort of theatre I'm talking about as the bedroom scene is to domestic drama. The relationship between chairman and speaker, between secretary and treasurer is as central to what I am trying to do as the love interest to domestic drama.' Thus in *Destiny* there was the meeting to inaugurate a branch of Edgar's semi-fictional Nation Forward Party. Edgar:

> In spite of the fact that this was a meeting to which very few of that audience would go – I hope – clearly they would relate to it, recognising elements of meetings – the incompetence of the chairman, the embarrassment of the collection to pay for the room, the long awful silences. They would recognise the way in which meetings operate in the same way as they would recognise the dynamics of love play, of seduction, the fumbling nature of sexual contact. And in that way would recognise the actual machinery by which decisions are made – the way in which rhetoric operates, the way in which the very form of a meeting determines the content of decisions. I want to force people to think in the theatre like they think when they watch current affairs programmes on television or read the newspapers.

Creating a theatre of public life or finding ways of expressing ideas in an accessible form Edgar regarded as not an easy task.

> I think revolutionary ideas are hard. I mean Marx's *Capital* is extra-ordinarily badly written, but even if it were well written, the ideas Marx expresses are difficult ideas. So you have two alternatives. You can make things ridiculously simple and partisan – in the sense of getting people to support socialism in the same way as they support Leeds United, on a straight tribal basis, which seems to me not in itself a bad thing, but futile and dangerous because it won't actually lead to the building of socialism. Or you have to struggle to find a way of presenting extremely complex, difficult, precise ideas. I mean we all know that the Bolshevik Revolution happened because in 1903 there had been an obscure debate in an upstairs room in a Highgate pub about the membership rules of the Bolshevik Party. And that is why the Russian Revolution happened. On a very precise level. The ideas are both difficult and precise. If you make them simple and vague you are not in fact expressing the ideas. So the struggle is to find ways of expressing complicated ideas in an accessible form.

During the period of transition in 1973–1974 Edgar abandoned the agitprop form he had perfected:

> I became a social realist. I think the only radical alternative to social realism, which is agitprop, was no longer suitable. Agitprop was a response to the times – an increase in working-class consciousness and militancy between 1970 and 1974. It was also a response to changes in history or an awareness of what the real history had been. Which may never revert. Though it's possible, if we get a Thatcher government, that agitprop may take on a vital role again. But the historical conditions of 1970–74 were unique in post-war history – suddenly after thirty years the working-class movement awoke with such speed and strode back onto the stage of history, like a broom sweeping people in its path. I don't think it will happen again for many years. That is not to say the working class won't again become very militant, because we now know they can do it. It is back on the historical agenda, as is the crisis of capitalism, and it will remain on the agenda. But the surprise, the joy, enthusiasm, mistakes of that period are in a sense very specific. And that was the soil in which agitprop grew.

For subjects like women, race and fascism – the crucial subjects of the day from the mid-seventies – Edgar felt agitprop was no longer suitable, 'because they are the areas in which the subtle combination of the personal and political, the emotional and the intellectual, takes place. They are fused subjects and the great inadequacy of agitprop is in inculcating consciousness'.

Destiny actually combined elements of agitprop and social realism, and Edgar described its structure as agitprop: 'The way I wrote it was that I said I wanted to make this point in this act, these points in this scene, other points in the overall order. I then constructed a plot to fit that. And that is a technique of agitprop writing.' At the same time, in making it a play about public life, Edgar was careful to provide no information about the sex lives, marital status or individual psychology of the characters 'in order to force people to look at the public aspects of people's behaviour'.

Destiny was epic in structure, in that it started in India in 1947 at the beginning of the end of the British Empire: the characters then appeared in the present-day industrial Midlands where fascism is beginning to flourish in the form of the 'Nation Forward Party'. An unofficial strike of Asians at a local factory coincides with a by-election in which there is an alarming change in polling patterns in favour of the Nation Forward Party. And Edgar showed that it is ordinary working people who are responsible. The play particularly followed the life of a small shopkeeper who, when he loses his shop, inclines increasingly towards the fascist party, and then becomes its candidate in the local election, only to discover at the end, that it was the highly placed friends of that party who had been responsible for the loss of his shop in the first place. There were powerful scenes in the play: the meeting in the pub to celebrate Hitler's birthday; violence on the picket line and the confrontation of two former friends, one of whom had joined the Nation Forward Party, the other going the way of the left; the news received by the former Indian army officer of the death of his son in Northern Ireland, and how this fuelled his energies for the fascist party; the elections themselves in which the Labour candidate is threatened with violence; and the final horrific invocation of Hitler.

Edgar at first considered setting the play in the thirties, or in a future fascist Britain, 'but I soon realised that the only way to alert people was to do a play based on real fascist parties operating in Britain now . . . I was determined from the start to show how the British middle class was just as susceptible to fascism, potentially, as the German middle class had been in the 1930s.'[3] The play was based on detailed research into the extreme right. Edgar read about thirty books on contemporary and historical fascism and interviewed about as many people, including a number of Asian and trades union leaders. Though the play was fiction, all but one of the incidents in it had actually happened:

> To give an example of how the play works: There are Hitler birthday parties held regularly and, as coincidence would have it, Enoch Powell delivered his 'rivers of blood' speech on Hitler's birthday. Now I don't know if there was a Hitler birthday party in 1968 which heard the news of that speech, but it's a fair bet, and I've written a scene on that supposition. Another example: there is a strike by Asian workers at a foundry in the play. Now here the actual progress of the strike is based on what happened at Mansfield Hosiery and Imperial Typewriters, while the atmosphere is based much more on the different conditions of the West Midlands foundry industry and the struggles they've had there.[4]

Edgar wanted, in *Destiny*, to get inside the skin of fascists. Edgar:

> There are a number of things about fascism which people now, thank God, do understand. They understand that it won't go away if you ignore it; they understand the kind of soil in which it flourishes. What I think they don't understand is why large numbers of ordinary people, often people heavily involved with the Labour movement, become attracted to an ideology which is self-evidently obscene. I wanted to create characters that the audience could relate to and in a way that

they could confront in themselves. It is facile to say that all the members of the National Front or the National Party wander about in jackboots, siegheiling all the time, that they are self-evidently ghastly horrible people. It is not only facile, it is counter-productive to create monsters (though there are some monsters in those parties). I wanted to create believable people. Some of them are pleasant; some of them are unpleasant. All of them make terrible political, psychological and emotional mistakes. That's what the play is about.[5]

Edgar's aim with the play was 'to put the frighteners on the conventional play-going audience – people who might be attracted in the direction of fascism'. He also hoped the play, which he thought contained a 'fairly controversial political line', would contain some political insights for the Labour movement. Edgar: 'If *Destiny* has a virtue, it is that it is true. And that is always upsetting.'[6]

Destiny took a long time – from 1973 to 1977 – to reach a large public stage and to have the impact its material warranted. At the time of the Aldwych production, 7:84 Theatre Company were touring another David Edgar play, *Wreckers*, which managed effectively to link the 1972 docks dispute with the internecine struggles within the Labour party in Newham Northeast, in East London in 1976. The play contained a ballad refrain: 'Where were you in seventy-two?' referring to the 1972 dock strike, during which five dockers were gaoled by the National Industrial Relations Court. In the play Midland Cold Storage was the apparent enemy but was eventually shown to be simply the local link in a chain leading to the House of Lords, which, in fact, emasculated the 1976 Dock Labour Bill. Edgar showed that behind the front of an Ulster Bank, Midland Cold Storage was owned by Lord Vestey who also owned (in addition to 100 companies in the UK and in countries abroad, including the worst of the fascist dictatorships) land in Australia, which bred Vestey cattle, slaughtered in Vestey slaughterhouses, transported in Vestey lorries, shipped in Vestey ships to Vestey cold storage depots and thence to Vestey shops. 'A Vesteyed interest' quipped Edgar. In the play the East End workers discovered the inter-connections between industry and politics, and became sufficiently politicised to be able to fight the battle in the East End constituency trying to oust a right-wing Labour MP. *Wreckers* was typical of David Edgar's desire to use the theatre to provide information in an entertaining fashion.

As was *Our Own People* which was toured by Pirate Jenny at the time that *Destiny* was receiving its television showing. Using a documentary approach, Edgar wrote the play in the form of a 'Com-

mittee of Inquiry into a dispute between employees of the Darley
Park Mills Company "Beckley" and their employers'. The work was
weaving, the workers Asians claiming discrimination. In the first
act, representatives of the strike committee, the National Union of
Weavers, the owner, and the Community Relations Commission
presented the 'facts' to the chairperson, the Baroness (impartial, of
course) Cockburn. The Asians claimed that their women on the day-
shift were treated rudely by the overlookers, that the white woman
shop steward was unsympathetic, that their men were forced on to
permanent night-shift and that all Asians were barred from
promotion. By the time all of the evidence was presented, Edgar
had created the impression that the whole situation was simply the
result of 'progress', unfortunate, but inevitable. In the second act,
however, he went behind the scenes to expose the racism, sexism
and fascism at the root of the dispute. He showed the shop steward
to have been seduced by the National Front, and spewing out the most
unmitigatedly vile racial hatred despite friendly overtures from an
Asian co-worker. The boss and the union were proved to have done
a dirty deal (described as a gentleman's agreement) to bar Asian
promotion to the new weaving machines. And some of the Asians
were shown to have crossed the picket line, not out of bad faith,
but because they were illegal immigrants and subject to blackmail.
Like *Destiny*, the play was a fiction combining facts from several
real-life situations. It illustrated what Edgar believed were the
possibilities of theatre: 'It can, at the same time, present a political
analysis and the real problems of living people; it can at once present
the facts of a situation in an entertaining way and link those facts
to the real aspirations and fears of flesh and blood characters.'[7]

Political plays were the beginning but not the end of Edgar's
political work: 'To do nothing except preach from television or
theatrical soapboxes is to undermine every word that's written.' It
was also necessary to be actively involved politically. So Edgar wrote
political plays for a living and was also 'actively involved in actual
politics – two trades unions, the anti-fascist movement, journalism
for radical publications'. In other words Edgar accepted that theatre
itself would not change the world. But neither did he underestimate
its importance. Edgar: 'You know the old joke about the man who
was sentenced to 999 years and said to the judge, "I can't possibly
serve all that" and the judge said, "Well do as much as you can."
Well, one does as much as one can.' Edgar:

You can speak to a working-class audience in touring theatre, in very small numbers. You'll spend most of your time speaking to radically inclined middle-class people, which seems to me to be an *under*estimated activity, by the way. If you work in television you speak to a mass audience, but not en masse, and you are faced with both overt censorship and the censorship of the form itself. If your plays are performed in the major subsidised theatre, you will speak widest through the things that the play inspires, in the media for example. And consciousness will be raised, which is important. But ultimately consciousness is raised by activity in struggle, and not by propaganda. By the interface of propaganda and struggle, the interface of theory and practice. That is what raises consciousness in a Marxist sense. In the theatre you have only half of that process, but that perspective does have an influence.

Edgar regarded the penetration of subsidised theatre as important: 'the ability to be able to speak from one's own neck of the woods, to shout through one's own megaphone, has led to some significant advances.' And Edgar felt it was important to work simultaneously in all areas – television, major subsidised theatre and small-scale touring.

Edgar also felt it was false and counter-productive to expect plays to have a one-to-one relationship with politics, that that was not comparing like with like. Edgar: 'To ask how many barricades did this play build is ludicrously to restrict the medium, and the potential of the medium. It is to take a medium that has the capacity to show collectively to people the heights and the depths of human achievement, human failure, human joy and human pain and, in fact, reject all those possibilities. You cannot expect a creative artist to do that any more than you can expect the man who designed Chartres Cathedral to build council houses.'

Edgar didn't think there would be a 'sell-out' from his generation of writers. 'My feeling is that there is now a movement on the move, as opposed to just a spontaneous response.' He pointed out that in 1967 there was one independent socialist theatre group in Britain (CAST) and that in 1978 there were at least eighteen full-time subsidised socialist theatre groups in addition to perhaps as many unsubsidised groups who propagated revolutionary socialist ideas. He pointed out that of the eight new plays produced by the Royal Shakespeare Company in 1977/78 five had been written by socialist revolutionaries; that socialist writers had significantly penetrated the medium of television. While socialist theatre had not built up a mass working-class audience, it had created substantial support among the socialist movement – members of revolutionary parties, non-aligned supporters of various Marxist organisations, causes and campaigns.

Edgar felt that 'the realisation that socialist playwrights cannot themselves change the world may yet help them to discover ways of contributing in no small measure to the work of those who can'.[8]

Subsidy

Alternative theatre – and particularly political theatre – could not have developed on the scale it did in the seventies without subsidy. This was, from the beginning, one of the fundamental ironies – that theatre companies whose stated aim and *raison d'être* was to do away with the capitalist state and its institutions (including the Arts Council of Great Britain) and replace it with a socialist society could only work to achieve those ends with financial assistance from the hated state. This, however, was a minor tension compared to the major conflicts which occurred in the area of subsidy as a whole.

There was conflict, for example, on the purely materialist level of who got how much money. Whilst alternative theatre was munificently funded in the seventies by comparison to the virtual non-subsidy of the sixties, it was cripplingly under-subsidised in relation to what it wanted to do and in relation to the amount of subsidy that went to establishment theatre (the major subsidised London companies and regional theatres). There was, therefore, a large body of opinion critical of how the Arts Council cake was cut.

Who cut the cake – who made the decisions – was also an issue, calling into question the structure of the Arts Council and its *modus operandi*. Thus there were moves at many levels (from the grass roots to the government department responsible for arts subsidy) to democratise the structure of the Arts Council and the selection of the Council and its advisory panels.

Questions were asked about how (in secret or in public), where (centrally or regionally) and on what evaluative basis decisions were taken. And there was the question – for whom? For whom the arts? For whom arts subsidy? Dealing with these questions inevitably raised the issue of arts and ideology, of arts policy in the widest political sense. From a socialist perspective – that of the socialist theatre workers – the Arts Council was an elitist organisation, composed of elitist individuals perpetuating an elitist status quo: subsidy was a political issue.

The Arts Council was constituted in 1946 out of the wartime Council for the Encouragement of Music and the Arts (CEMA) under the Chairmanship of Lord Keynes. It started with a Treasury grant for all the arts of £175,000; by 1967/68 subsidy to the theatre alone totalled £1,705,609. There had been a boom in arts subsidy in the mid-sixties, after the Labour government of 1964, when Jennie Lee was Minister for the Arts. She inaugurated what subsequently became known as the 'bricks and mortar' policy, which built the new regional theatres and their studios.

In 1967 the Arts Council was re-constituted by Royal Charter from Her Majesty the Queen, as, ostensibly, a politically independent subsidising body. The chartered objects of the Arts Council were:

a) to develop and improve the knowledge, understanding and practice of the arts

b) to increase the accessibility of the arts to the public throughout Great Britain, and

c) to advise and co-operate with Departments of Our Government, local authorities and other bodies on any matters concerned whether directly or indirectly with the foregoing objects.[1]

The Charter further stipulated that the Chairman and eighteen members of the Council would be appointed by the Secretary of State for Education; that the Council could appoint committees and panels 'to advise and assist them in the exercise of ... their functions'; that the Council could appoint Chairmen of the panels and that the Council could 'regulate the procedure of any committee or panel'; that the Council would appoint a Secretary General and 'such other officers ... as the Council may determine'. Thus was it royally decreed, and thus, effectively did the Arts Council operate.

It was precisely this structure – reflecting the privileges, elitism and inequities within society at large – that was the subject of criticism:

There is not enough money spent on the arts in this country. But God forbid any increase should go into the hands of the Arts Council to administer ... The Council is supposed to be the responsible executive body. And yet on the Drama Panel you know nothing more than their names and have no idea how they carry out their responsibility in the decision-making process. There must be some means of holding them responsible. The Minister for the Arts is not answerable to Parliament for anything the Arts Council does; it can't be questioned in the House. There's no way in which the policy of the Arts Council can be directly challenged by an elected body. It is answerable only to itself. It is an absolutely appalling anti-democratic situation.[2]

Those were the views of Malcolm Griffiths, an alternative theatre director, teacher, founder of ITC, and from 1971 to 1976 a member of various Arts Council panels. In an article in *Theatre Quarterly* in 1977, he attacked the Arts Council on many fronts: its lack of policy, its ideology, its anti-democratic structure, its administrative ineptitude and the ways in which it acted as a force of censorship and repression in the arts. The ultimate indictment related to the inevitable ideology of a royally chartered, appointed body administering taxpayers' money:

The Arts Council is there to perpetuate the monopoly of an elite, essentially the ruling classes, over the national resources, the people's money ... The Arts Council doesn't take any account of the changes that have happened and will continue to happen within our society and within our arts ... The Arts Council quite clearly is against any attempt to make it and its decisions and the class in whose interests it supports the arts, accountable to the people who actually provide the money.[3]

And this, basically, was the view endorsed by Hugh Jenkins, Minister for the Arts from 1974–1976 who wrote in his book *The Culture Gap: An Experience of Government and the Arts* in 1979 that 'I know of no one who carries weight in Parliament who wishes to bring the Arts Council under political control in the sense of subjecting its artistic decisions to questioning in the House of Commons.' But the fact was that the Arts Council was 'technically irresponsible (i.e. not responsible to anyone), answerable for its decisions only to itself'.[4] Jenkins' view was that 'the Council is a group assembled by a series of chances, a collection of random choices made by a very tiny ingrown electorate advised by the Council's own bureaucracy and finally approved by a Secretary of State or Prime Minister who knows little about the people concerned and naturally opts for what he is told is safe, which means the arts establishment'.[5]

It was in this context that Hugh Jenkins, as Minister for the Arts, attempted to reform the Arts Council – to democratise it. He pointed to the fundamental absurdity of the Royal Charter – 'the curious proposition that to retain its independence *from* government it was necessary for it to be appointed by the government'.[6] He felt that a 'wholly appointed government arts patronage agency had no convincing defence' against criticism. He wished to 'make the Council more responsive and responsible to the constituencies of arts practitioners and their organisations all over the country including the regional arts associations'. Jenkins:

> I think we ought to get rid of the Lady Bountiful image of the Arts Council, handing down small or large munificences from on high and we ought to try to move in a direction in which artists feel they have a say in the distribution of state support and help.[7]

Behind Jenkins' proposals for democratisation was what might have seemed the formidable support of the Labour Party's 1974 General Election Manifesto – 'to make the Arts Council more democratic and representative of workers in the arts and entertainment'. And there had been parliamentary precedents in the 1949 Select Committee on Estimates which, with evidence from Equity and the Theatre Managers' Association (TMA), had recommended measures to bring the Arts Council in closer contact with the theatre profession and trades unions. Twenty years later, in 1968, another Estimates Committee had recommended that the Council become a more representative body. But as Jenkins said: 'Once again, the Arts Council thumbed its nose at Parliament and pursued its increasingly exclusive course.'

In practice, Jenkins proposed a new structure which would reverse the flow of power:

> The governing body would not be appointed by the Minister, nor would it appoint its own advisory panels. Instead, the Council would be elected by the Panels which would be made up of persons chosen by trades unions and managerial bodies in the arts and entertainment ($\frac{1}{3}$), Ministerial appointees ($\frac{1}{3}$), and persons elected by a Conference of local authority arts and entertainment committees ($\frac{1}{3}$).[8]

Instead of power stemming from the government through the Arts Council down to recipients, the 'elected representatives of the consumers, with the relevant bodies in the arts, would collectively determine the distribution of government aid according to principles which would be expected to emerge at a National Conference. The Council would allocate budgets to the separate panels and would itself be funded by the Minister, whose power would be conditioned by a compulsory rate.'[9] Jenkins' proposals were based on the assumption that national devolution would come about in the foreseeable future, followed by a regional government in England. He proposed abrogating the Royal Charter and replacing it with a piece of legislation which depended on the creation of a new government department 'of the Arts, Communications, Entertainment and Sport (ACES) with a Cabinet Minister and one or two juniors: transfer to this department all responsibilities for the arts' ...[10] There would then be, within the new Ministry, an Arts Council, Sports Council, Communications Council (including TV radio, press) and a Museums Council. The proposals were radical and they were not implemented.

Jenkins' proposals did, however, provide a fair reflection of the views of the Labour Party and the TUC, both of whom (along with the Liberal Party[11] and the Conservatives) studied the subject of arts patronage in some detail and prepared proposals for reform. In 1974, the Labour Party published *The Arts: A Discussion Document for the Labour Movement*,[12] and in 1975 *The Arts and the People: Labour's Policy Towards the Arts*.[13] In 1976 the TUC published a consultative document *The TUC Working Party Report on the Arts* whose brief had been 'to consider and make recommendations on ways in which trades unionists and their families may be enriched by, support and contribute to the Arts'.[14] This report was also radical in its recommendations, of particular interest in coming from the trades union movement and being concerned with the availability of the arts to the workers and working class.

But there were crucial questions which Labour policy ignored and which were of vital concern to political theatre workers – which arts and which people? There was the fear that without answers, all of the fine-sounding reforms, bulwarked by equally fine-sounding socialist sentiments – a new Ministry for the Arts, local authority legislation and a democratised Arts Council – would simply be exercises in structural shell-making.

In all of the discussion there was still an implicit assumption of art as object, as something to be consumed, the major concern being how to make the product more widely available as distinct from accessible. The Labour Party did not, as the TUC had done, address itself to art as an experience of which most of the population was deprived, to art as a conveyor of cultural and political values, to art as a force for social (or socialist) change as much as a force to reinforce the status quo. It did not identify which people: or where these people were. People in school, for example? Labour policy said that arts appreciation should be developed in schools through increased funding, but in a period of stringent education cuts that was a principle unlikely to be put into practice. People in prison? People in hospital? People at home? With 51 per cent of the population women, many working at home, that was an untapped audience.

People at their work places? Or just people at leisure in existing places of leisure? Deciding which people where was a priority in defining any arts policy, the end to which a democratised structure was but a means. The Labour principles were fine, but, as political theatre workers knew from experience, the practice left more than a little to be desired.

One of the major arts policy documents of the seventies was the Calouste Gulbenkian financed Redcliffe-Maud Report of 1976 which came down strongly in favour of devolution: local authorities were 'the chief arts patrons of the long-term future'.[15] The assumption behind devolution was that artistic decisions – and policy – should not be decided centrally, on a national basis, but regionally on a local basis – and that a large proportion of subsidy should come from local government. Devolving responsibility for arts patronage to Regional Arts Associations was central to Hugh Jenkins' proposals for democratising the Arts Council; and, as well as being the major recommendation of the Redcliffe-Maud Report, it was official Arts Council policy. It was part and parcel of the national movement to devolve political responsibility to Scotland and Wales (which was anticipated throughout the seventies). The Regional Arts Associations (fifteen in 1978) which had grown up spontaneously and organically, seemed the logical patrons of the arts on a local level, in conjunction with local authorities: but this form of arts patronage was, on examination, as fraught with potential problems as the devolution of national political control. As Roy Shaw, Secretary General of the Arts Council, pointed out on the occasion of Manchester County Council's attempt to cut the North West Arts Association grant to North West Spanner: 'If devolution puts clients at the mercy of political pressures, we shall have to reconsider the whole question.'[16] North West Spanner's case illustrated the pitfalls of petty-political local authority influences. So did the cutting of Avon Touring Company's grant in 1978 by Avon County Council's Leisure Committee, and the problems which Theatremobile faced when they tried to present a play exposing the dangers of asbestosis in a local industry.

In 1979 devolution was going ahead as planned, with an awareness of the problems of bureaucracy and political censorship, but with no alternatives and no safeguards. The alternative theatre movement's view, however, was that devolution was 'a recipe for anarchy and rampant individualism which could only benefit the conservative and reactionary currents increasingly flowing in our society'.[17]

Whilst the patterns of patronage were debated at all levels of

government, those at the receiving end – particularly the alternative
end of the receiving end – struggled on the proverbial shoe-strings
and suffered. Charles Marowitz, director of the Open Space, argued
that 'the establishment merely tolerates alternative theatre: the aid
given to the experimenter is little more than hush money'. With
some bitterness he asked:

> As the Open Space slithers into its eleventh year, reeling from the
> worst financial crisis in its history, its GLC grant entirely withdrawn,
> its Arts Council subsidy only marginally increased one asks oneself,
> is it really worth it?[18]

And he concluded that 'the establishment powers that govern such
matters do not really want healthy small-scale alternative theatre in
England. They would be quite content with the National, the RSC,
Covent Garden and perhaps half a dozen other "okay" producing
organisations with respectable credentials ... their tolerance takes
the form of self-congratulatory gestures in regard to organisations
which they would just as soon see disappear.'[19] Sadly, Marowitz's
views were supported by statistics.

In 1973, the fringe was receiving only 4 per cent of the total
allocation for drama, which was then £3.2 million. This had more
than doubled in 1977/78 tp £16 million. In 1973/74 the fringe
received £250,000: sixty companies had to share an amount equal
to only half the grant to the National Theatre (i.e. £500,000). In
1977/78 between them the National Theatre and the RSC had £4.2
million – all the rest of drama £6 million. Of that £6 million, £4.75
million went to theatre buildings; touring (thirty-three companies)
received only £872,000. New projects (58) received £229,251. By
1978 support for community arts had become official Arts Council
policy, following a two-year pilot study, and community arts was
receiving three quarters of a million pounds. The figures spoke for
themselves: the fringe remained seriously under-subsidised, particularly in the light of the evident significance of its work through
the seventies. And the amounts of subsidy that went to alternative
theatre as compared with the establishment theatre was dispropor-
tionate. It was also doubtful if the increases would have come about
without constant pressure from such groups as ITC, TACT and
TWU. And by the time the allocation for 1978/79 was announced
in March 1979, there was another campaign underway – 'a mass
picket of the Arts Council to protest at inadequate funding for
alternative and small-scale theatre – in particular the poor allocation
for New Applications and Projects, to demand an increase and to

call on the committee to refuse to distribute the money until there is one'.[20] The struggle for funds continued.

For alternative theatre, this inequity in subsidy was a political issue and though the Arts Council repeatedly denied that there was anything political in art ('Truer to say that much art tends to be critical') or in arts subsidy ('. . . the only time the present writer has heard politics discussed at the Arts Council was when the Drama Panel held a seminar . . . on Theatre and Politics . . .')[21], the Secretary General's Annual Reports repeatedly revealed a great ideological divide.

In Roy Shaw's inaugural Report as Secretary General of the Arts Council in 1975/76, he made the unfortunate distinction between 'roses for the few' (high art for the elite) and 'dandelions for the many' (art of questionable quality for the masses). He outlined a new policy of 'preserving and improving traditional centres of excellence', but said 'we must also spread the excellence as widely as possible (through touring, for example) and we must additionally cultivate the arts among the large proportion of the population which they have hitherto not reached'.[22] To the forty-seven alternative companies subsidised by the Arts Council at the time (and the as-many-again who were not subsidised), this was a back-handed statement of policy – with the implication that popular art was not as good or as valuable as high art. The Annual Report for 1976/77 was also riddled with aesthetic class distinctions which contradicted the Arts Council's apolitical claims. Shaw still distinguished between 'high art' ('often complex and demanding') and 'less demanding' popular art – with the clear implication that the former was better than the latter. He acknowledged the need and demand for popular art, but regarded it simply as a stepping stone to something bigger and better. 'By all means let us develop arts at a less demanding popular level: but to dismiss as elitist the subsidising of the great works of the past or the often "difficult" works of contemporary artists is to condemn the lock on the door to enrichment because you have failed to give people a key that fits it.'[23] The barrier to an appreciation of high art, said Shaw, was inadequate access to higher education.

The problem was that the educational inequities referred to by Shaw functioned as politically as the artistic inequities. This was splendidly illustrated by Arthur Koestler writing in *Tribune* in 1944 to working-class readers alienated by 'highbrow' book reviews, when he spelled out the political connections in no uncertain terms: 'Let us not be hypocritical about it. The wall [which separates those

who have read Proust or Kafka or Péguy from those who have not]
is there and the more we try to explain it away, the harder we bump
our heads against it. It's no good trying to jump over it: our task
is to abolish it. But that is a political not a literary task. It is, I
believe, the main and ultimate task of Socialism.'[24] In 1978, as
in 1944, people were still waiting for the key to highbrow art, and
they would probably still be waiting in another thirty years time.
In the meantime alternative theatre was trying to provide an alternative 'key' despite establishment opposition.

In 1974, David Edgar had summed up the impossible contradictions in the Arts Council's line of thinking: 'It seems to me that
the Arts Council cannot go on with this blanket idea of standards
... it does not occur to them that some reps, while being "good
of their kind" are producing very dreary work. There is a ... false
distinction between the programme that is produced and the
standards that are applied to it which is surely an impossible one
to maintain.'[25]

But in 1978 the Arts Council was still maintaining that position,
and defending it vigorously. And in the last analysis, the Arts
Council's levels of subsidy put a discriminate value on art – that
RSC Shakespeare was valued more highly and was regarded as
'better' than street theatre or community theatre. And in 1978 the
political theatre movement was still maintaining that these were
political issues. At the end of the decade, the Arts Council appeared
at last to have been awakened to this view. In a slightly ironic, but
also slightly alarmist tone, Roy Shaw wrote in *The Guardian* in 1978
that it was possible that 'in sponsoring community arts the Arts
Council have brought a Trojan horse into the citadel of the arts
– one which seeks to subvert this whole society and with it all
traditional values in the arts'.[26]

A fairer assessment might have been that the Trojan horse of
alternative theatre and community arts was, with socialist conviction,
intent on creating a more equitable society, equitable art and
equitable access to all art. While Shaw was worrying about 'sub-
version', most of the writers and workers within the political theatre
movement were worried about subsistence and concerned about past,
present and probable future repression from the Arts Council. Such
were the politics of theatre subsidy in the seventies.

1973

The formation of the Association of Lunchtime Theatre in 1972, together with further developments in fringe theatre prompted, in 1973, the formation of the London Association of Community Theatre Groups, later to become TACT (The Association of Community Theatres), from the beginning an avowedly political organisation, concerned with 'popular theatre'. TACT identified a movement originating from the student theatre experiments of the mid-sixties, the annual National Student Drama Festival, the arts lab movement and the work of community artists. It defined the role of its theatre as part of a large class struggle, as a means of 'understanding and experiencing class solidarity' and of changing concepts of culture. Together with the ITC (Independent Theatre Council), which it spawned in 1975, TACT was an active and important pressure group in the seventies, campaigning on behalf of the interests of political theatre workers.

The Half Moon Theatre in Whitechapel had opened in 1972, but came to prominence in 1973. The aim of its co-founder, actor Maurice Colbourne, was to create 'a rehearsal space/workshop with living accommodation' inspired by the alternative society of the sixties. But the potential of the place as a 'natural' theatre soon became apparent and they mounted Brecht's *In the Jungle of the Cities*. 'The initial idea was to gather a small ensemble of actors, evolve a production, tour it with financial support, then come back and play it in the space and test the water.'[1] When *Jungle of the Cities* opened, it played to good houses and from that first success the Half Moon went on to become one of the most important left-wing, politically conscious London venues and producing companies, under the direction of Pam Brighton in the early seventies and of Robert Walker in the late seventies.

One of the Half Moon's most successful early productions was Steve Gooch's adaptation of Brecht's *The Mother*, a production that was to influence many political theatre workers subsequently. The play itself was one of Brecht's *Lehrstücke* or 'learning plays' from the period 1927–1933 when he had abandoned the dominant expressionism of his earlier plays for consciously didactic drama – in this case, in his own words 'to teach the tactics of class warfare'. The central character, a widowed mother (universal figure of motherhood), became a prototype in the political theatre work of the seventies, her process of political self-education a model for many plays as diverse as John McGrath's *Little Red Hen* and *Yobbo Nowt*, Broadside Mobile Workers Theatre's agitprop plays and North West Spanner's worker-oriented shows.

In Brecht, the mother is illiterate and poor, watching with ignorance and trepidation as her son becomes involved with revolutionary workers in Russia. She does not at first see the point of distributing leaflets in the factory if this leads to imprisonment, greater poverty and misery. The play traces her education in revolutionary communist doctrine and her development into a leader and agitator in her own right. The mother learns to read the leaflets she distributes and she is lectured about the necessity of strikes. But the final change in her outlook is the result of bitter personal experience: her home destroyed by the police on suspicion of subversive activities, peaceful demonstrators slaughtered on the whim of the authorities, her own son's long imprisonment without trial. Would not anyone be politicised in such circumstances implies Brecht? And it was on that assumption that other work was modelled on the play: on the assumption that a central character who goes through a political education, with whom the audience identified, would lead an audience through a similar learning process.

The Half Moon also produced a number of other plays by Gooch during their particularly productive period of collaboration between 1972 and 1974.[2] In 1972 there was *Will Wat? If Not, What Will?*, about the peasant uprising of 1381, deliberately attempting to tell the side of the story ignored by the history books – that of the peasants rather than the ruling class. There was *Female Transport* in 1973, about the growing self- and class-consciousness of six working-class women convicts en route to exile in Australia in the early nineteenth century. And in 1974 there was *The Motor Show*, co-written with Paul Thompson.

The Motor Show was the first production of Community Theatre, a company set up in 1972 by a group of professional theatre workers (including Roland Rees of Foco Novo and Anne Engel of the Womens Theatre Group), who organised themselves on a collective basis to create theatre within a working-class community. They chose Dagenham and decided to do a show about the Ford Motor Company, one of the main employers in that area of London. Gooch and Thompson researched the show at the Ford works, talking to car workers on the assembly line and to shop stewards who were also instrumental in arranging performances and drawing the workers and their families to see the play. *The Motor Show* became a 24-scene epic spanning sixty years of struggle between Ford and the trades unions and its working-class members. It used songs and a fast succession of music hall, documentary and realistic scenes to show the history of the Ford empire from the Model T and the introduction of the production line, through the slump of the 1930s, to the industrial relations struggles of the early seventies. Having played in the community, the play transferred to the fringe where its agitprop style, combined with its social realism, became a model for many subsequent shows.

Community Theatre failed to root itself in Dagenham and its members went on to form other groups. Gooch went on to write *Strike 26* in 1975, about the General Strike, and in 1976 both *Made in Britain* (with Paul Thompson), about British Leyland, and *Our Land Our Lives* for 7:84 about young marrieds in a market town and the socio-economic issues of agribusiness. Then in 1978 the Royal Shakespeare Company produced Gooch's *The Women Pirates: Ann Bonney and Mary Read*, based on two notorious eighteenth-century women rebels. Gooch's approach (as in his other plays) was Brechtian, emphasising the economic situation which determined the individual careers of his two heroines, using songs and slogans to set the scene, to develop the narrative and to comment on the characters and society – to give a pirate's eye view of imperialism. Like most of Gooch's plays, *Women Pirates* used a historical setting and focused on sexual politics as well as socialist politics. Throughout the seventies Steve Gooch was one of the most active of the activists in the political theatre movement.

By 1973 political theatre companies and writers were beginning to make an impact outside their immediate environments, and the issues of their concern were beginning to seep into the establishment arena. Indicative of this was Christopher Hampton's *Savages* produced at the Royal Court in 1973 with Paul Scofield in the leading role of a British diplomat kidnapped by urban guerillas in Brazil. One function of the play was to provide information about Brazilian society – the statistics of starvation and genocide charted with figures on profits and exploitation and the facts of political dictatorship there. The play had been inspired by an article in *The Sunday Times* colour supplement which contained a paragraph describing the extermination of the Cintas Largas tribe in Brazil. Hampton then made an eventful and educative trip to Brazil to research the play. After his visit, Hampton concluded that 'though the Indians are an awful problem, it's not anything like as serious as what's happening in the country as a whole – which is truly dreadful'. He had started simply wanting to write a play about Indians, but came to understand that the Indians were only a part of a larger problem:

> ... the more I researched, the more I thought it was all really caused by the system – of which the Indians are just a symptom. The Indian problem is a result of the economic policies of capitalism – a simple statement, but true.[3]

That Hampton could come to such conclusions, from a previously apolitical stance, and write a successful mainstream theatre play (with a leading British actor) indicting capitalism in no uncertain terms was symptomatic of the increased general consciousness of the political climate and specifically of the work of more overtly political playwrights and theatre companies.

A further instance was the production in 1973 of Trevor Griffiths' *The Party* by the National Theatre at the Old Vic, a play about left politics in Britain by a Marxist playwright, and also starring a leading British actor, Laurence Olivier. Hampton's play had been a coincidental and circumstantial foray into politics: Griffiths', at the opposite extreme, was a part of a deliberate strategy to 'penetrate' bourgeois theatre with socialist ideas and ideology. And Griffiths' career – discussed in the following essay – was a concerted campaign towards that end.

'The future is clearly one of struggle, and absolute unremitting commitment to that struggle.' Trevor Griffiths, 1979[1]

Trevor Griffiths

In an interview in *The Leveller* in March 1979, Raymond Williams was asked what he thought about the left using the 'dominant means of mass communication in every possible way to its own advantage'. He replied:

> I would put it this way. We have to establish the fringe culture – there's no alternative to that – but if we don't also contest the central institutions then we are giving away too much. You run radical theatre groups wherever you can, but at the same time you really do think seriously about establishment theatre and about establishment broadcasting. You really get in there with proposals for more democratic structures, which a lot of those institutions want, and in any case are the necessary dimension of any serious challenge to the orthodox position.[2]

Williams' answer summed up the 'interventionist' position taken – with the major subsidised theatre and television – by Trevor Griffiths, one of the most important Marxist playwrights of the seventies. Griffiths himself said in an interview in *The Leveller* in 1976:

> 'Strategic penetrations' is a phrase I use a lot about the work of socialists and Marxists in bourgeois cultures ... I simply cannot understand socialist playwrights who do not devote most of their time to television. That they can write for the Royal Court and the National Theatre, and only that, seems to me a wilful self-delusion about the nature of theatre in a bourgeois culture now ... It's just thunderingly exciting to be able to talk to large numbers of people in the working class, and I can't understand why everybody doesn't want to do it.[3]

Griffiths regarded community theatre as important, but thought it was vital to penetrate the major subsidised theatre and the mass media.

Griffiths' *The Party* produced by the National Theatre at the Old

Vic in 1973 was a prime example of this approach. The subject matter of the play was overtly political. Set at the time of the May Events in Paris, the play functioned as a dramatic commentary on the present political situation in Britain. The main character, Joe Shawcross, is a successful television producer who is shown to be sexually and, by analogy, politically impotent. The main action of the play is a meeting he's called of political friends, to discuss the implications of the Paris uprising, its relation to socialism and how that might be achieved in Britain. His friends include an academic Marxist-Leninist revisionist, Andrew Ford; a Trotskyist working-class leader, John Tagg; a former communist writer, Malcolm Sloman, who is drinking himself to death because 'he can't bear the thought of himself successful in a society he longs to destroy'; and others representing student, black and women's liberation groups. In short, Griffiths peopled the stage with a cross-section of the left in Britain, brought them together in a 'party' to discuss the lack of a political party.

The first act was structured around two set-piece speeches from Ford, who presents a lengthy political analysis along the lines that Marx's nineteenth-century analysis of capitalism is obsolete; that Lenin revised Marx to the needs of the Russian Revolution, but that Lenin's analysis is irrelevant to the state of capitalism in twentieth-century Europe; that Russia and the socialist countries of Eastern Europe aberrated under Stalinism; that the European proletariat has been absorbed into adapted capitalist institutions; that multi-nationals have changed the face of capitalism; that the only real revolutionary forces left are the national liberation movements of the third world. Tagg replies to Ford's analysis with an attack on the elitist attitudes of intellectuals without contact with the class roots of socialism; with a rejection of the view that the working class has lost its revolutionary potential; with the claim that the European proletariat has been betrayed by the communist parties and their leadership, and the spectre of Stalinism; and with the assertion that the answer lies in replacing the corrupt anti-revolutionary leaderships with vital revolutionary ones, the result of patient organisation and disciplined effort. Sloman's view is that the revolution will come from the masses when the masses are ready. The ultimate message of the play was that revolutionary impulses – pending the real revolution of the masses – would inevitably be absorbed by the capitalist system. It was a pessimistic view, particularly for those on the left.

The play was motivated by Griffiths' impotence in the face of the great upheavals of 1968 – Paris, Detroit, Watts.

It started with the experience of the Friday night meetings at Tony Garnett's, where sixty or seventy people would cram into a room, with the whole sense, the aching need to ... to do more, to get it right, to be correct, to read the situation as a first step towards changing it utterly. And with it all the faint sense of, not silliness, but lack of candour that people proffered. For example, in relating their life roles to their abstracted revolutionary roles. The lack of connection between what they did day by day and what they did night by night.[4]

It was motivated, too, by a sense of responsibility to the left – 'to the history of the left thought and left action – socialist, communist, revolutionary – whatever'.[5] With *The Party* Griffiths was one of the first socialist playwrights to debate the problems of socialism from a large, public, establishment stage, with all the attendant risks to the left – the potential of abuse and misuse by the right-wing press, for example.

The place of performance of *The Party* was important to Griffiths. He had written a short time for the fringe. 7:84 Theatre Company had produced *Apricots* (a lyrical erotic interlude on the sexual politics of love in marriage) and *Thermidor* (a short, sharp analytical look at emergent Stalinism in the Soviet Union in the thirties, dramatised as an interrogation between a bureaucrat and a suspected 'dissident') in 1971; also in 1971 *Occupations* had been staged at the RSC's London 'fringe' venue, The Place; and in 1972 he had written *Sam Sam* (an autobiographical play about two working-class brothers, one educated into the middle class) for the Open Space. But, as Griffiths said, 'One of the reasons I wrote such a short time for the fringe is because I realised how impotent it was as a mouthpiece to the whole of society.'[6] In writing *The Party* for the National Theatre Griffiths was fulfilling one of the functions of the socialist playwright described by John McGrath as 'principled Marxist interventionism'.[7] In doing so, he faced obvious problems. McGrath:

> It is no doubt useful to the general movement of socialist ideas to have them aired prominently, to enter the 'national', or at least the metro-politan consciousness on a certain level of seriousness; and occasionally to draw into those theatres certain politically conscious members of the Labour movement, but good as those works may be, the whole process is not contributing to the creation of a new genuinely opposi-tional theatre ... In Trevor Griffiths' *The Party*, the character of an old Marxist revolutionary from Glasgow was taken over by Lord Olivier, and became a vehicle for a star to communicate with his admirers; a juicy part for the artistic director. The process, the building, the wages structure, the publicity machine, the free internal drinks' budget,

all these can turn opposition into novelty; but it would be short-sighted to deny the value of trying.[8]

Many people commented at the time on the contradiction of Lord Olivier playing a Trotskyist and *The Party* was consistently attacked by the left press as 'a piece of anti-socialist propaganda', and for its pessimism about the possibilities of socialism in Britain. These attacks left Griffiths bewildered:

> I get tons of shit lowered on the plays quite regularly by *Workers Press* or *Socialist Worker* or *Tribune* or whatever. And it's difficult to know why, because I feel myself to be the very opposite of a political opportunist. I feel myself to be patient, painstaking, obstinate and all those kinds of tortoise-like qualities, whereas I'm seen to be a fly-by-night, gypsy, uncommitted floater. What was it Corin Redgrave said? Oh yes, he described me as 'paddling in the shallows of revolutionary practice'.[9]

But Griffiths defended his position:

> One of the reasons I am deeply unpopular, and particularly with the groupings, is that I don't champion one group – IS, IMG, WRP or whatever.[10]

The Party, Griffiths felt, had demonstrated the need for, and also the lack of, any such viable party in Britain. That was the truth of the matter – an important truth to be aired and analysed – and if that alienated the left, then it was more symptomatic of the problems of the left than of problems with *The Party*. So Griffiths would continue to act in a principled Marxist interventionist fashion.

Griffiths' interventionist coup was his thirteen-part television series, *Bill Brand*, about a left-wing Labour MP. It was viewed by an audience of millions. The idea, according to Griffiths, was 'to try and set out an extended critique of parliamentary democracy in the form of a popular TV series'. The idea came to him on General Election night in 1974, waiting for the votes to be counted, with the anticipation amongst many of a Tory majority, and the final very narrow Labour victory. At that point Griffiths felt it was imperative to analyse the Labour movement and the Labour Party. Griffiths:

> What I was trying to say throughout the series was that the traditions of the Labour movement were inadequate to take the struggle further, and that we had to discover new traditions, or revive even older ones. And that we had to seek connective tissue between electoral party politics, which still has a mystifying mass appeal, and extra-parliamentary socialist activity.[11]

Again, Griffiths said he believed in mass parties, though he couldn't see even the germs of those parties in the present left groupings, and he wanted the series to convey this. Bill Brand himself was left of the Tribune group and the story involved a struggle for leadership within the Labour Party. Griffiths:

> I think the sharpest criticism of the whole series was of Tribune itself and its relative impotence, its nature as a pawn in the game. Brand was a composite of a whole lot of things that are still just tolerable inside the Labour Party: a kind of Marxism, a kind of democratism. I think the Labour Party is going to split in the early eighties in a very serious way. And when that happens it's important to know where those people on the far left of the party are going to go.[12]

Griffiths thought 'it would be possible to talk to the Labour movement and the Labour Party through the plays and say "it seems to me that these are the sorts of issues that are going to be raised, these are the personalities that are going to emerge, and these are the dangers that will ensue should a revisionist such as Roy Jenkins be placed in power".' In fact, the plays were prophetic about the Labour Party's swing to the right against the left, Tribunite element of the party.

It was important that these issues could be discussed through the mass medium of television. Griffiths: 'I chose to work in those modes because . . . I have to work with the popular imagination . . . I am not interested in talking to thirty-eight university graduates in a cellar in Soho.' Griffiths felt that with *Bill Brand* he was achieving what community theatre groups claimed to do – 'dealing with now, dealing with political life now, political commitment constructed out of people's lives'.[13] He was talking to people and making socialist ideas available on a mass scale. Griffiths: 'If for every *Sweeney* that went out a *Bill Brand* went out, there would be a real struggle for the popular imagination. The two things would be saying, "It's like this isn't it?" And people would be free to make liberating choices about where reality lies. Testing both against their own experience.'[14]

Whilst congratulating Griffiths on the achievements of *Bill Brand*, David Edgar, in an article in *Socialist Review*, pointed out some of the problems of 'strategic penetration' in television:

> The inherent problem with television as an agent of radical ideas is that its massive audience is not confronted en masse. It is confronted in the atomised, a-collective arena of the family living room, the place where people are at their least critical, their most conservative and reactionary (the dwelling-addressed postal vote will always get a more reactionary response than any other form of balloted decision).[15]

The problems were exacerbated, said Edgar, by format scheduling, which had the 'effect of dulling the audience's response to challenging material by placing it within a predictable and familiar framework of regular programme slots'. Then there was the drama serial form, 'which demands an empathetic and thereby uncritical identification with its central character or characters'. Edgar: 'The danger of a project like *Brand* is that, by the end of thirteen episodes, the audience is identifying with Brand exclusively as the pivot of the story (my hero right or wrong) and sympathising with his views and actions only insofar as that is necessary to the experience of following the story.' There was also 'the danger of psychologism': 'Griffiths in fact gave the audience ample opportunity to judge his central character's actions psychologically, by giving him a broken marriage and a feminist mistress.' And there was the 'wallpaper' problem: 'What people are conditioned to want is defined by the barrage of programmes surrounding *Brand* which use the *same* form to present an *opposite* view about human behaviour. On commercial television, the problems of "strategic penetration" are even more acute, as the experience itself is strategically penetrated back by raw capitalist propaganda at twenty-minute intervals.'

Despite the problems, Griffiths felt the battles ought to be fought on and for television 'because if we evacuate that ground, it is an instrument for fascist repression. I mean like hand-made. It's just there and ready and the signs are that it could be used very quickly and very efficiently.' He felt, too, that he had 'created a sort of alternative drama inside television':

> Our process was quite different. The rehearsal process was egalitarian, democratic, destructured, de-starred. We talked with each other, we wrestled with the text. We created such an extraordinary community kind of work within the organisation. People were politicised in the course of the series and by the end of it they were challenging management decisions about when the plays would go out and how they would be promoted.[16]

Bill Brand was the culmination for Griffiths of a considerable amount of writing for television, all of it political. There was *All Good Men*, a BBC Play for Today in 1973 about a retiring Labour MP of working-class origins who is about to receive a knighthood and to be interviewed about his socialist convictions. His belief in social change by gradual evolution working through the established system is violently opposed by his son and daughter, who accuse him of being out of touch with ordinary people and of failing actively to support the General Strike in 1926. That play had an audience of five million, broadcast during the miners' strike and thus made more politically topical. There had been a play for *The Fall of Eagles* series, a kind of *The Party* set in 1903, about the formation of the Bolshevik split, dealing with Martov and Lenin and the confrontation that developed between their particular ideological positions, presenting the twenty-three-year-old Trotsky as a brilliant opportunist. And there was an adaptation of Griffiths' stage play, *Occupations*, set during the Italian workers' occupation of factories in Turin in 1920 under the leadership of Gramsci, centring upon the character of Kabak, a representative from the Communist International in Moscow whose views on the potential revolutionary situation were in stark contrast to Gramsci's own. And there had been *Through the Night* in 1974, a play about a working-class woman with breast cancer confronting the bureaucracy of the National Health Service, showing the way in which individuals running institutions are trapped in an unsympathetic system.

Griffiths was older than the generation of Brenton, Hare and Edgar and was not politicised like them in 1968, but in the late fifties and early sixties at the time of CND and the Committee of 100. He was involved in the emergence of the British New Left: 'We're talking about Edward Thompson, Peter Worsley, John Rex, Stuart Hall, Alexander McIntyre, the *New Reasoner* and the *Universities Review* which became the *New Left Review*.' In 1960–1961 Griffiths was chairman of the Manchester Left Club and a year later acting editor of Labour's *Northern Voice*. He was strongly influenced by Raymond Williams' *The Long Revolution* in the early sixties: 'It liberated me.' Griffiths was thus primarily writing political journalism until 1968, which 'was about the time that I started to get some objective perspective on the events of the fifties and early sixties – '68 pointed out the urgency of the need for social change'.

He felt that a version of the future was carried in the past and that his 'early plays were to some extent an attempt to explore the dialectical conflict that exists in the past, to see what energy could be released from it for the future'.[17] In 1968 he regarded himself as a revolutionary Marxist who believed that through various means of organisation, it would be possible to create an insurrectionary moment and then to exploit it for revolutionary purposes. In 1978, influenced by Edward Thompson's *The Poverty of Theory*, he had come to regard himself as a revolutionary socialist faced with the problem of 'trying to work out ways in which revolutionary change can occur which don't depend on an insurrectionary moment'. Lenin provided a model of insurrection which was 'superbly adequate for

its own historical moment, but increasingly inapplicable thereafter'.
Thompson's book had demonstrated that being a revolutionary
Marxist could mean something else than debating the necessity and
means of insurrectionary revolution, that it could be more related
to 'the way in which society is likely to go', that there were
possibilities of socialist humanism. Griffiths said that he had always
'been very excited by the thought of violence', but that Thompson
had made him more rather than less cautious about 'how you relate
revolutionary energy which is violent energy to revolutionary
struggle'. He felt that in re-evaluating his revolutionary socialism,
he was becoming more politically aware of the possibilities of
achieving socialism in British society. Griffiths:

> Morally, capitalism was exhausted 50 to 100 years ago, certainly 50
> years ago. The way that people ought to organise their lives is not
> within capitalist structures . . . and that's why my plays are never about
> the battle between socialism and capitalism. I take that as being
> decisively won by socialism. What I'm really seeking is the way forward.
> How do we transform this husk of capitalist meaning into the reality
> of socialist enterprise? The socialist future? You ask the question in
> a world way, and you ask it in a particular social way.[18]

Griffiths led the way in assuming a socialist perspective in his
plays, in *presuming*, instead of setting out to persuade, that it was
theoretically valid: in doing so he opened the doors to other, younger
socialist writers, and was instrumental in capturing a corner for
socialist plays in the subsidised theatre.

Griffiths' plays, like those of Edward Bond, were self-confessedly
concerned with 'moral' issues. And like Mercer, Griffiths used the
theatre to discuss the moral and practical issues of the left, including
the less pleasant issues such as Stalinism:

> A lot of my work is about Stalinism because I think that is a major
> responsibility for the left. It has to answer the questions raised by its
> own history. It seems to be absurd for the revolutionary left to say
> we don't take any responsibility for Stalin, as absurd as the National
> Front saying we take no responsibility for Hitler. History has got to
> be answered.[19]

Griffiths described his work generally as 'committed to analysing
Marxism and to condemning Stalinism without discrediting socialism
in the eyes of the world', and in this sense his work could be seen
to be a search through theory for a useful form of action.

This was, for example, quite literally the content and structure
of *The Party*. It was the substance of *Occupations* – with its debates

between Kabak and Gramsci about the best course of action – with Kabak's pragmatism set against Gramsci's concern for his men and the need to risk them as the vanguard of a national insurrection. In the play, as in history, the revolutionary situation collapsed when the workers accepted a negotiated settlement. Just as Griffiths was committed to presenting the warts of socialist history, he was careful to present capitalism as more than a caricatured force of evil. Thus in *Occupations*:

> There is Valetta, who is on the board of Fiat and who has these extra-ordinarily far-sighted plans about social welfare, workers' holiday camps in the hills, a children's crèche, workers' houses, death grants and so on – all of it has come to pass, and all of it has been constructed by a much more virile capitalism than anybody could have imagined at the time at which Fiat was spelling this out. It's all documented. It seems to me pointless to present that man with horns and a tail and an irreducible, inescapable ugliness. Because that isn't the way capitalism presented itself to the working class, after the failure of the occupations in 1920. And I suspect it isn't the way capitalism presents itself now.[20]

In *Comedians*, Griffiths approached an analysis of capitalism through the unlikely, but very effective situation of a Manchester evening class in stand-up comedianship. The 'lecturer', a retired comedian, teaches his students that comedy should be complex and serious and should say something about society. The students are put to the test when their acts are adjudicated by a man who believes that comedy should be crude, cheap and commercial. As lucrative contracts await the winners of the competition their political commitment is challenged in a real, bread-and-butter fashion. Some of them sell out and conform to commercial capitalist expectations in their acts, but Gethin Price (in one of the single most powerful scenes in seventies theatre) performs a scathing, terrifying and very unfunny attack on bourgeois society. And he 'loses'. Griffiths:

> Those that succeed do so by ... the surrender of most principles worth having ... and the two who don't succeed retain what is most important about them, but return to their exploited work situation. But the man Price smashes the categories and says, No – I stand in no line, I refuse my consent. He is unremittingly hard and decisive, discovers himself and takes the first steps towards repossessing himself.[21]

The play was structured on contradictions: the evening 'class' itself and its purpose; class society; the dreams and ambitions of its members and their possibility of realisation; the function of comedy in a capitalist world. In the end it is Gethin Price with his revolutionary anger and violence who triumphs over the humanist gradualism of the teacher. Griffiths thought that *Comedians* asked more questions than it answered: it asked 'what do we do? I don't think the play answers that. I just think it says that there is a potential for doing something enormous and poses the question to an audience that is *willing* to answer it or *wants* to answer it in some way.'[22]

Griffiths in fact described all of his plays as 'interrogative statements' in a process of 'strategic penetration'. And he felt that the achievements of the past ten years had been very important. His plays, and those of Brenton and Hare and Edgar at the very least, acted as an affirmation of the choices made by people in 1968, of those who were radicalised by the political events then. And he thought it important to recognise the achievements, however far they failed to reach their goals in socialist terms. Griffiths: 'Who would have thought in 1956 that I or Brenton or Edgar or Hare would be having work – very committed work – on television. We must not only read it as repressive tolerance, we've got to see ourselves as agents in this struggle, because it is a struggle.'[23] At the same time he 'didn't expect any major sell-out such as we saw in the period 1956–1966'. This was partly because one of the achievements of socialist theatre had been to force the theatre and society to 'make essential accommodations to the fact that politics is here, and here to stay'.

He thought the future was likely to be bleak, involving a great deal of censorship and repression. Griffiths: 'The future is clearly one of struggle, and absolutely unremitting commitment to that struggle. This generation has learnt from the absorptions and assimilations of previous generations of radical writers.' Griffiths had spent the two years from 1976–1978 writing a film – for Warren Beatty – about the life of the American communist John Reed: 'I know that there are still going to be collisions and confrontations and there's going to be a steady erosion of things I want to say, and a final calamitous chopping-off at the market place. It's often not just that you're not achieving everything you wanted to achieve, but that you're actually being made to say something the opposite.' To resist such pressures was an important part of the struggle. Griffiths envisaged the possibility of direct censorship in the future: 'Anybody knows the different feel around now from four or five years ago. I think it's wrong to be alarmed by it. I think we should be stiffened by it, know that we're facing it and let it make us more realistic. There could be changes inside the theatre that will make it extremely difficult for us to get work. Of course, the argument would never be that we lacked talent, but that they were bored with these left-wing things.' In that eventuality, the struggle would not end, just become more difficult. Griffiths felt that the future of political theatre was very much at the mercy of political control. He referred to what had happened with North West Spanner and with Theatremobile: 'Increasingly there is going to be municipal and regional control and the Arts Council seems to me to be tightening up, getting its house in order.'[24] Griffiths thought that even he had something to learn from Gethin Price's integrity in *Comedians*: 'There are things that I will not do in my life, my professional life, and there are also things that I will do and justify politically. Everybody's got to find that balance, and that balance is constantly shifting. And you've got to remember that each new step is a step into the unknown. All you can do when taking that step is be prepared and think hard ahead.'[25]

'TACT opposes all forms of Fascism'. TACT Constitution
1978

The Association of Community Theatres (TACT)

TACT started (as the London Association of Community Theatre Groups) late in 1973. Unlike the Association of Lunchtime Theatre or the later Independent Theatre Council, TACT was from the start an umbrella organisation which recognised the political concerns of its constituent community theatre companies, and its draft constitution in 1974 described the ways in which 'community theatre was political'.

  i) its content attempts to deal with the everyday reality of ordinary people's lives, to reveal the causes for the suffering, bad housing, low wages they experience.
  ii) it performs in places where people gather to socialise, as part of larger events (carnivals, meetings, demonstrations, rallies, parties, etc) perhaps, rather than attempts to gather people, socialised into theatre-going, into the theatre.
  iii) it is often followed by a discussion in which the assertions of the theatre group, and the dominant ideology they challenge, are both measured against perceptions and experiences of the audiences, for their validity. A dialectical process unfolds, in which people's understanding of reality is sharpened ...
  iv) it attempts to develop a form and style which is hard-hitting, direct and involving. [1]

The role of community theatre was envisaged as part of the larger class struggle and as a means of changing dominant concepts of culture. By 1978, the embryonic politics were succinctly embodied in a new TACT Constitution:

TACT is the organisation of Community and Political Theatre companies, which aims to make an active contribution to the struggle of the majority of the population against exploitation and oppression – political, economic, cultural or on the grounds of race, sex or age. TACT opposes all forms of Fascism. [2]

In defining its purpose, TACT was anxious to make clear the specific contemporary historical circumstances which gave it context and also the historical perspective to which it related:

> The political turbulence of the past few years has thrown up some thirty or forty self-originated theatre groups who share the aim of performing their shows in Labour Clubs, Canteens, Tenant and Community Associations, schools, techs, shop floors, picket lines, Adventure Playgrounds, youth clubs, OAP evenings, pubs, etc. And the success that many of these groups are having – of packed working-class audiences – is not simply due to the fact that there is a live show on at the club instead of the theatre. The success is due more to what many of these groups are taking as the contents of their shows: the real events that shape and influence the experience of most people's lives – the plight of pensioners, redundancy, the lump, the oppression of women, the cost of living, anti-Trades Union legislation, racialism, oil and the Scottish people, etc. So it's not just any old entertainment, but an entertainment that aligns itself with the progressive interests of the audiences for whom it is intended.
>
> The Depression of the 1930s gave birth to the Workers Theatre Movement in Britain. This movement involved the emergence of well over a hundred small theatre groups who put on short agitational sketches – and in some cases longer plays – at Trades Union and Unemployed meetings. The Workers Theatre Movement was, largely, a movement of the working class, in that many of the performers were drawn from the ranks of the unemployed. As such they were not professional groups in the same sense that they had had a formal theatre training or that they aimed to make a living from the work. Rather, they were people who wanted to use their self-acquired performing skills in the struggle for socialism.[3]

From the beginning, TACT's aims were to become a national, not a London organisation; to campaign to obtain Equity cards and an Equity minimum wage; to press the Arts Council to grant-aid community theatre companies to a level to enable payment of the Equity minimum; to press the Regional Arts Associations (including the Greater London Arts Association) to negotiate with the Arts Council on behalf of community theatre for revenue grant aid; 'to press the Arts Council into putting money where its mouth is as regards "taking the arts to the broad mass of the people"'; and 'to seek co-operation amongst companies as regards sharing of scripts, research material and resources'. By 1979 TACT had succeeded in every one of its original aims, thereby contributing to a radical change in the landscape of British theatre.

In April 1974 the first National Conference was held, turning the

London Association of Community Theatre Groups into The Association of Community Theatre (TACT) on a national scale. By 1978 TACT had forty member companies including: Broadside Mobile Workers Theatre, Bread 'n' Butter, CAST, The Combination, Common Stock, Community Theatre, Counteract, Free Form, General Will, Half Moon, Interplay (Leeds), Mayday, North West Spanner, Puppet Tree, RAPP, Red Ladder, Recreation Ground, Sidewalk, West London Theatre Workshop, Belt and Braces, Combine, Live Theatre and 7:84. By 1978, the Arts Council of Great Britain's overall allocation for this area of theatre had increased from £250,000 (1973) to £1·1m. Companies such as Red Ladder were subsidised to the tune of £37,500. In 1976, the Arts Council officially acknowledged the principle of Equity minimum wages in its grant-aid allocation to alternative theatre companies, and the consequent increase of subsidy that this entailed. That this area of theatre was still grossly under-subsidised by comparison with other areas (e.g. major subsidised and regional theatre) was still a major issue with TACT, but pressure had produced significant results. By 1978 Equity had – after enormous struggle – agreed to unionise the fringe and had started to operate a fringe contract.

Last, but not least, TACT had succeeded in stimulating greater co-operation amongst companies. In 1978 they organised a central equipment resource for hire, loan or sale – everything from heavy-duty needles for stitching leather to vans and lights, plus a central register of contacts for bookings. And they had held two large weekend Performance Conferences, first in 1977 and then in 1978. These were in part to afford member groups the opportunity to see each other's work: being primarily community-based all over the country, groups were often ignorant of what their co-workers were doing. But more important, TACT members wanted to define with, and if necessary, for the Arts Council the kind of criteria that could be applied to evaluating their work. *Tribune* summarised the problem in January 1978:

> The point which the Arts Council must recognise is that community art is different in *kind*, not necessarily quality. At the moment the Arts Council subsidises one kind of theatre at the expense of another kind – RSC Shakespeare, say, at the expense of street theatre. This ignores the fact that there is good and bad Shakespeare, good and bad RSC Shakespeare and good and bad street theatre. This system of choices and its inequitable consequences are probably not motivated by explicit political bias, as a recent *Guardian* article suggested. It is the by-product of an *implicit* ideology. But the ultimate and irrefutable measure of

this value system is money. So in 1976/77 the National Theatre received £2.5 million, the RSC £1 million, the whole rest of drama £5.5 million and community arts a measly half million. Obviously RSC Shakespeare is valued more highly, is regarded as 'better' than street theatre. The real question is on what *qualitative* grounds the RSC's *Henry VI* cycle requires more money than the staging of the Russian Revolution in the streets of Bradford, to quote a classic example of community arts in this decade? And though the Arts Council claims to make assessments solely on artistic values, it has never been able to define its criteria for judgement – for the RSC, or the National, let alone street theatre or community arts. Perhaps precisely because the judgement has been of *kind* (with all its political/ideological connotations) and not of *quality*.[4]

TACT wanted to define criteria of quality for their *kind* of theatre.

Ten groups performed at the 1977 Conference. Not all of the work was good of its kind, but the Conference concluded that community participation, community response and community demand should determine the criteria of evaluation rather than a concept of 'abstract excellence' that was irrelevant and inappropriate to their kind of theatre. And the Conference unanimously passed a motion censuring the Arts Council:

> This Conference rejects the use of conventional aesthetic standards to assess the funding requirements of any community or small-scale touring company, believing that the structure and composition of assessment bodies necessarily preclude any judgement that is able to reflect either the priorities of such companies, or the concerns of their audiences.[5]

The Conference called for a meeting with the Arts Council – officers and panellists. The response from Richard Hoggart, Chairman of the Drama Panel, was not encouraging:

> Thank you for your note of 7 December and the enclosed resolution. I will ask for it to be issued with the papers for the next meeting of the Drama Panel, together with this reply. I shall not do so with much pleasure, since your resolution seems to me, I'm afraid, likely to give unnecessary aid and comfort to the opponents of community or small-scale touring theatre companies. Let me show why. Your resolution is about relevant standards of judgement for the kind of work TACT promotes. An important issue. But, for 'community theatre' and similar phrases in that resolution let us substitute (say) 'bingo', 'soft-porn films' or something similar. The resolution then makes just as good sense. Surely a resolution whose language and substance are so easily adapted to activities which, as I assume you would agree, are simply not worth the expenditure of any public money, clearly isn't very useful. In short, I suggest your resolution is intellectually and imaginatively confused

> I think of myself as a defender of the best aspirations of community
> arts against, e.g. such critics as Roy Fuller. But with resolutions such
> as this emanating from your corporate body you hardly need enemies,
> and you embarrass your friends.[6]

Despite the antagonistic tone of Hoggart's letter, TACT replied
tactfully:

> It was a motion that came out of a conference, approved unanimously
> by theatre workers from throughout the country, as far north as
> Newcastle, as far south as Cornwall. It should therefore be taken with
> real seriousness ... We could as easily do the same for the objects
> of the Arts Council as established in the Royal Charter. But the motion
> is not about soft-porn films, nor are the prescribed objects of the Arts
> Council 'to develop and improve the knowledge, understanding and
> practice of soft-porn films; to increase the accessibility of soft-porn
> films to the public throughout Great Britain; to co-operate with govern-
> ment departments, local authorities and other bodies to achieve these
> objects'. ... It would be disappointing to conclude that, by dismissing
> the motion as 'intellectually and imaginatively confused' you indicate
> that assessment of Arts Council policy – or dialogue on these issues
> – may not be possible.[7]

Hoggart became more tactful himself, perhaps realising the absurdity
of his arguments, and thanked TACT for the care with which they
had replied, though he felt they were 'still a long way from agreement,
or indeed from speaking a common language'.[8]

The Arts Council was obviously not anxious to discuss the issue
of assessment, but a meeting was finally held (with Secretary-General
Roy Shaw, Drama Panel Chairman Richard Hoggart and Drama
Director John Faulkner) on a much smaller scale than TACT had
hoped, the results of which were not promising. The TACT
delegation felt that they were 'treated in an extremely patronising
and insulting manner by the ACGB triumvirate'.[9]

Basically the issues were unresolved when in 1978 TACT held
another similar, but much larger conference, also concerned with
self-criticism and standards, but with a much stronger sense of
urgency because of cuts in subsidy – and threatened cuts – to TACT
companies. Those performing included Major Diversion, Counteract, Clapperclaw, Red Ladder, EAST Soapbox Theatre, Itinerant
Theatre, Broadside Mobile Workers Theatre, Beryl and the Perils,
The Combination, Word and Action, Covent Garden Community
Theatre, Stirabout, and Avon Touring. The official report on the
Conference (commissioned from *The Leveller* journalist Terry Ilott)
judged it 'a great success, not only helping to raise standards of

performance and political awareness, but also providing the opportunity for members of groups to have informal contacts, to exchange experience and information and to discuss common problems'.[10] But in 1979 TACT was still at loggerheads with the Arts Council on the issue of standards and assessment.

1974

In 1974 Robert Patrick's *Kennedy's Children* opened at the Kings Head where it drew packed houses for a year and then transferred to the West End – the first such fringe transfer, as the Kings Head was proudly to claim, though it was followed in 1976 by Tom Stoppard's *Dirty Linen* from the Almost Free. Patrick's play was such a success and attracted such a cult following because it so perfectly captured the moods and the movements of the sixties. It was another indication that the subject matter and concerns of political theatre were having an impact in a wider context.

At the same time, the new National Theatre on the South Bank (plagued by building delays and escalating costs) and the Royal Shakespeare Company were both facing serious financial problems. The National Theatre was requesting additional government funding, and the RSC was threatening closure and asking for an emergency supplement from the Arts Council. There was a caucus of opinion that questioned the amount of subsidy received by the major sub-sidised theatres compared to that received by fringe and community theatres, and levelled specific criticisms about how subsidy was spent. In November 1974 an attack was launched by RSC actress Helen Mirren in the pages of *The Guardian*:

> There has been much made of the quaking economics of the Royal Shakespeare Company and the National Theatre by the culturally-conscious press ... To myself and many colleagues of my generation who have been involved in work with the National and the RSC, the expenditure on costumes, sets and staging in general has been excessive,

> unnecessary and destructive to the art of the Theatre ... the realms
> of truth, emotion and imagination reached for in the acting of a great
> play have become more and more remote, often totally *un*reachable
> across an abyss of costume and technicalities ...[1]

There were specific criticisms and comparison of the £250,000 for
the set of the Roman plays at Stratford (never used again) with Buzz
Goodbody's *Lear* at The Place in London (in an RSC season) with
sets, costumes and overtime costed at a grand £150. Mirren's views
were widely shared.

In response to the climate of opinion, within the relatively short
space of four years, the RSC radically altered its policy and, significantly, expanded its activities. This involved the opening of two
studio theatres – The Other Place in Stratford in 1974 and the Warehouse in London in 1977 – both theatres committed to producing
new writers and new writing. And the RSC attracted the brightest
directors, performers and writers from the alternative theatre, with
the result that the repertoire of new plays in both theatres was
remarkably political. In addition to David Edgar's anti-fascist play
Destiny, the RSC produced Edgar's adaptation of *The Jail Diary
of Albie Sachs* (about the imprisonment of a radical South African
lawyer). And the RSC Warehouse specifically committed itself to
a campaign against apartheid in South Africa with the dramatised
readings of the inquest into the death of Steve Biko, *A Miserable
and Lonely Death*. The RSC effectively maximised its resources in
terms of quantity without sacrificing quality. It eschewed the kind
of conspicuous over-production Helen Mirren complained of and,
by the end of the seventies, had quite organically come to function
as the national theatre in everything but name. Just a few examples
of the writers produced by the RSC in 1974 indicates the extent
to which that single theatre was influenced by the emergence of
political theatre.

By 1974 playwright David Rudkin had begun to re-emerge with
more overtly political work than his earlier *Afore Night Come* (RSC
at the Arts 1962). In 1972 the Almost Free had produced *The Filth
Hunt*, about the activities of a self-appointed Pornography Commission who ultimately, under the leadership of the Devil, join
forces with their repressive allies, the pornographers themselves.
In 1973 the RSC presented his *Cries from Casement as His Bones
Are Brought to Dublin*, which narrated the life of the Irish rebel,
Sir Roger Casement, to his execution for treason. Rudkin described
the play as about 'the Ulsterman of British allegiance who through
exploration of his homosexual identity discovers his larger alienation

from the world, acts on his discovery by the only means that his historical situation affords, and pays the price that the world exacts'.² And in 1974 Rudkin's *Ashes* was presented at the Open Space. The play paralleled the impotency of a couple trying un-successfully to conceive a child with the individual's impotency in relation to the political struggles in Northern Ireland. Rudkin de-scribed his purpose in political terms: 'I believe the dramatist's function in a society to be to transmute the idiosyncrasies of per-sonal life experience into metaphors of public, political value to mankind.'³ Later, in 1977, the RSC produced Rudkin's *The Sons of Light*, a five-act work of epic vision and imaginative richness, a complex parable of power politics with an original psycho-sexual subtext which was ten years in the making and drew on sources as diverse as Thomas Hobbes, Plato, Freud, Martin Luther and Karl Marx. As with most of Rudkin's plays, however, the political elements were secondary to personal and psychological matters.

1974 also saw the RSC production of Tom Stoppard's *Travesties* – the first of several excursions by one of Britain's wittiest writers, into the literal arena, at least, of politics. The play capitalised on the historical coincidence of the presence in Zurich in 1917 of Tristan Tzara (the inspiration of Dadaism), James Joyce and Lenin, and provided an opportunity for Stoppard to debunk Marxism and to put (down) Leninism side by side with fascism as a form of totali-tarianism. In an interview in *Theatre Quarterly* at that time, Stoppard elaborated on his feelings about the failure of the Russian Revolution and all that 'sailed with her'. Stoppard:

> The repression which for better or worse turned out to be Leninism in action after 1917 was very much worse than anything which had gone on in Tsarist Russia. I mean, in purely mundane boring statistical terms, which sometimes can contain the essence of a situation, it is simply true that in the ten years after 1917 fifty times more people were done to death than in the fifty years before 1917.⁴

Stoppard therefore opted for 'human solidarity' rather than 'class solidarity' and pursued his mission to expose the repressions of Soviet communism in 1977 with *Every Good Boy Deserves Favour* – a seventy-minute study of Soviet dissidence featuring two prisoners in a Soviet psychiatric hospital, one a madman who conjures up an orchestra (conducted at the first performance by André Previn), the other a man tortured for being a friend of a friend of a dissident. In 1978 Stoppard's *Night and Day* dealt with internecine political strife – a guerilla war – in an easily identifiable African state, and with analogous internecine political strife within the world of journalism and its embattled unions. Again, Stoppard was concerned with freedom and freedom of speech – from a liberal or right-of-centre perspective. The *Plays & Players* review of *Travesties* congratulated Stoppard for taking an oppositional stance to the then current left-wing views, for 'hitting out at the materialistic view of the world and society which is the sacred cow of Bond, Planchon, Brecht, etc'.[5] In doing so, it sympathetically summed up Stoppard's relation to the political theatre movement of the seventies.

It was also in 1974 that the RSC – in the experimental season at The Place following Rudkin's *Cries from Casement* – produced Snoo Wilson's *The Beast*, based on the life of Aleister Crowley 'the wickedest man in the world'. Wilson, with Howard Brenton and David Hare, had started writing in the late sixties with Portable Theatre and, like Rudkin, developed his own distinctive style of anarchic ambiguity outside the political mainstream of his contemporaries, though he also, like Rudkin, occasionally dealt directly with political issues such as the troubles in Northern Ireland and apartheid in South Africa. Wilson regarded himself as a socialist writer ('I am a socialist ... I vote Labour, with misgivings ... that's being a socialist, isn't it?'[6]) but his plays often proved difficult for critics to confront and analyse, not least because of their complex plotting and seemingly impenetrable stylistic inventiveness.[7]

Snoo Wilson was also one of the collaborators on the group-written play *England's Ireland*, discussed in the following essay on Howard Brenton, one of the Portable writers who, with David Hare, was to establish himself most firmly in the new generation of political playwrights consciously attempting to educate and influence bourgeois audiences, and simultaneously attempting to realise a collective dream of a truly popular socialist theatre. And the following account of the emergence of Belt and Braces Roadshow from a split within 7:84 Theatre Company in 1973 indicates how the political debate inside the political theatre movement generated not only new ideas, but new theatre companies.

'My feelings at the moment? Feelings of revolutionary socialism' Howard Brenton, 1975[1]

Howard Brenton and Portable Theatre

In 1974 the National Theatre approached Howard Brenton wanting to commission a play. The new National Theatre building had not yet opened, but the NT suggested to Brenton that he write a play for the Cottesloe, the experimental studio theatre. He was, after all, a fringe playwright of considerable repute: *Magnificence* had been a critical success at the Royal Court in 1973; *Brassneck*, written in collaboration with David Hare, had been a popular success at the Nottingham Playhouse in 1973; and the 1974 Nottingham Playhouse production of *The Churchill Play* had been widely acclaimed.

Breton's first major decision was whether to accept the commission at all. He was one of the first of his generation to be invited into the establishment theatre, and he was faced with the question of how far that step might compromise the principles – artistic and political – that he had lived and worked by. He decided to accept the commission:

> It would be beautiful to have a play there. One might as well make use of its facilities. The best of English theatre is subsidised ... I want to write big formal plays of Shakespearean size ... You just can't write a play that describes social action with under ten actors. With fifteen you can describe whole countries, whole classes, centuries ...[2]

Brenton wanted 'to get into bigger theatres, because they are in a sense, more public. Until that happens, you really can't have any worth as a playwright ... I decided in 1973, when I was resident dramatist at the Royal Court, that I would get my plays on as big a stage as I could.'[3] The Cottesloe wasn't big enough or public enough (and quite possibly signified tokenism towards the fringe), so Brenton insisted that the NT commission his play for the main stage. They did, and he wrote *Weapons of Happiness* for the Lyttleton. Brenton's was the first new play to be produced in the National

Theatre. For a playwright who had started with the Combination in Brighton and with Portable Theatre in 1968, this was a big step – across a big divide.

At that time (1974), perhaps in part by way of rationalisation, Brenton was talking about the failures of the fringe:

> I think the fringe has failed. Its failure was that of the whole dream of an 'alternative culture' – the notion that within society as it exists you can grow another way of life, which, like a beneficent and desirable cancer, will in the end grow throughout the Western world, and change it. What happens is that the 'alternative society' gets hermetically sealed ... a ghetto-like mentality develops. It is surrounded, and, in the end, strangled to death. Utopian generosity becomes paranoia as the world closes in. Naive gentleness goes to the wall, and Manson's murderousness replaces it. The drift from the loving drug scene in Amsterdam in the late sixties to the speed and wretchedness five years later illustrates the process. The truth is that there is only one society – that you can't escape the world you live in. Reality is remorseless. No one can leave. If you're going to change the world, well, there's only one set of tools, and they're bloody and stained but realistic. I mean communist tools. Not pleasant. If only the gentle, dreamy, alternative society *had* worked.[4]

Ironically, only a year earlier, Brenton had been making fervent claims for the fringe as a weapon in a repressive society:

> It could be the one surviving democratic means of communication. That could well happen. If the police surveillance and interference became very heavy and the Arts Council was nobbled – and there are signs of that happening already, that kind of thing – then the back street activity, almost on the level of being an abortionist, an illegal doctoring service, could be one of the few surviving possible means of communication with people. And the fringe should never forget that. That's the underground philosophy and it may become very pertinent before we know where we are. Seeing the pressure on the BBC now – the burden they have to bear to get even my couple of TV plays through. Theatre people know almost nothing of this reign of terror. The poverty of means and the idea of underground theatre, which is habitually underground, shouldn't be forgotten.[5]

The implicit ambivalence of Brenton's attraction to fringe/alternative/underground theatre and also to the large public stage was a contradiction that threaded through his work. And paradoxically he was accurate in both of his seemingly irreconcilable assessments. He was aware of the need for and the advantages of both worlds and was at the end of the seventies, still struggling to reconcile the conflict. Most of the theatre writers and workers of Brenton's generation faced this dilemma.

It was anti-establishment anger which initially ignited Brenton and Portable Theatre in 1968:

> Part of the energy behind Portable was simply: the bastards won't do our plays, we'll do them ourselves. That was a good reason at the time, but there was nothing more behind it than that. It was against the bastards, it was boiling for a fight against the established values in the theatre.[6]

Ironically Portable was not political when it started: in retrospect it was regarded as one of the first political theatre companies. But the initial motivation was to find new audiences. Alternative theatre in early 1968 had hardly started. The Theatre Upstairs was only struggling into life in 1969, and apart from the Little Theatre in Garrick Yard, there were few venues. The fact that Portable was touring – playing in non-theatre places to non-theatregoers – pushed it in a 'political' direction, 'to thinking about political theatre'. Brenton:

> If you set up an antagonistic theatre touring to people who have never seen the theatre before, it transforms itself into political theatre. It has a political effect. And the anarchic, antagonistic theatre becomes increasingly one of political content. This is what happened to us. It reached its peak with *England's Ireland*.

Ironically again, when Portable became 'too political' – with its two group-written plays, *Lay-By* and *England's Ireland* – it came to an end. Brenton: 'The organisation went bankrupt over those two shows.'

Lay-By came out of a meeting at the Royal Court in 1971 organised by David Hare who simply said 'anyone who wants to write a play with me join me in the bar'. Brenton:

> We had great rolls of wallpaper, and big children's crayons and the seven of us crawled around on the floor scribbling a continuous text, and you looked down and saw the latest line, and there'd be an argument about the next line.[7]

The seven writers were Howard Brenton, David Hare, Trevor Griffiths, Brian Clark, Snoo Wilson, Hugh Stoddard and Stephen Poliakoff. The play was based on a newspaper article by Ludovic Kennedy about a wrongful conviction for rape; involving fellatio between a van driver and a girl hitch-hiker on a motorway lay-by. It included poses for a porn photographer, and the fellatio in the back of the van in the presence of the driver's mistress. a mother of five. The framework of the play was the questioning of the girl concerned by a lawyer. The play ended in a hospital mortuary where the girl was taken after attempting a knitting-needle abortion. Brenton:

> ... it raised a lot of – not so much issues, as the landscape of the people up the M1. And it seemed like this extraordinary suppurating artery going up England ... There was a lot of aggro in it. In a way, it could be read as a manifesto of that group, for that kind of theatre. At the end, when the two hospital attendants are washing the corpses of the three main characters, and pulping their bodies in a huge dustbin into jam, we tried to put every phoney humanist statement that you could hear in the theatre from our elder playwrights into that. It was a total piss-take – the end ... It was group warfare that created that show.[8]

There was a feeling of carnage about the 'lay-by' story which the writers captured in their play. And there was carnage in *England's Ireland*, though its scope was much wider and it was politically a much more aggressive play – jointly written by Howard Brenton, David Hare, Tony Bicât, Brian Clark, David Edgar, Francis Fuchs and Snoo Wilson during one week in 1972 in Wales in a fashion similar to *Lay-By*. The mainspring of *England's Ireland* was a passionate conviction of the need to say something about the situation in Ireland. Politically it was dynamite: 'Fifty-odd theatres refused to take it. Many lied quite directly; we knew they lied. We came up against great forces that wouldn't let it happen.'

The play was episodic in structure, including twenty scenes with songs, 'attempting to bring home to British audiences the stench of the Irish troubles'. It encompassed a brief history of British political involvement in Northern Ireland since 1920, with a presentation of the Loyalist viewpoint, the civil rights march of 1969 led by Bernadette Devlin, a television interview with an elderly British Colonel in 1992 looking back on the army's involvement, and an illustration of British military regulations on firing on civilians. There was a scene in which an innocent Irishman is picked up as an IRA suspect, tortured by British soldiers, finally emerging from the experience as a Provisional. There was an Irish comic telling 'racist' anti-Irish jokes, while giving his audience instructions on home-made gelignite bombs. There was a scene in which a priest gave the last rites to two dying women, one in childbirth with her umpteenth pregnancy, the other a civilian shot in the belly by British soldiers. There was the confession of an IRA bomber, and a Protestant Masonic ceremony followed by a UDA military exercise.

The play ended with 'stories to tell our children' in the form of grisly anecdotes about the Irish situation.

The impossibility of finding a place to produce *Lay-By* and *England's Ireland* – particularly the effective censorship of not being able to produce the latter – made Portable writers acutely aware of the need for a theatre of their own – a recurrent preoccupation for Brenton in subsequent years. Indeed, Brenton was instrumental in several attempts to found just such a new theatre. There was an application to the Arts Council in 1969 to set up a writers' theatre within the Combination at Brighton. Then, in 1975, one of Brenton's plays called *Government Property* was done in Denmark. It was a re-working of parts of *The Churchill Play*, and it prompted another attempt to find a theatre:

> We came back to England and we were very pleased with it, and wanted it done in English in England. We went to the Arts Council and said this is an environmental show which needs its own space. We need to take over a place. We had the idea of it changing, like a living newspaper about Ireland. The Arts Council said that it involved bricks and mortar and the bricks and mortar of the London theatre was set. No more spaces. They said there was no reason why we couldn't go to the Cottesloe or Riverside Studios. They offered us instead individual grants as artists – enormous grants of £10,000 each. That meant £40,000, just £20,000 short of the £60,000 with which we could have created a new theatre.

Brenton said they got 'very bloody-minded' about the Arts Council's attitude 'of this is how it is; we are content with the landscape as it is – we have our touring theatres, our studios, our big subsidised stages. They are content with that till the end of the century now.'

With the Joint Stock production of Brenton's *Epsom Downs* (a study of class society in Britain set during a day at the race course) there was another attempt to set up a new theatre, this time at the Roundhouse:

> There was an enormous debate inside Joint Stock. Some of us had the notion that we could rip off the grant for Joint Stock, stop touring, work out the economics so that we could open a big new space in London – transform the Roundhouse into a big new public showplace for popular political entertainment of a kind that's not been seen. But the Arts Council immediately put Joint Stock on an almost monthly stop or go with their money because they were worried that we were going to run up bills of thousands. But you could run a big theatre on a shoestring, you could turn that to advantage. We concluded that there was enormous conservative resistance in the Arts Council and

the theatre itself to forging a brand new public theatre out of what had been learnt in the small theatres.

Brenton's quest for a new theatre came from the belief that 'the theatre belongs to the centre of public life – and should be as loud as parliament. That is what a big theatre should be ... big in order for large numbers of people to see it and for it to begin to reverberate, for it to be discussed, for it to be a national event, for it to be news.' Brenton felt that *Weapons of Happiness* began to function in that fashion: 'You felt the play was actually entering into an argument in a way a play of mine hadn't done before. I dreamed *Magnificence* would do it, but it didn't.' Though Brenton felt that David Edgar's *Destiny* did. Brenton regarded a significant part of his own career (as well as that of others of his generation) as an 'endless dialectic towards a real people's theatre. That is what we are all engaged in, and building that is very, very difficult – building a theatre that is exclusively a popular socialist theatre.'

His vision was not unlike Joan Littlewood's ambitions or those of Wesker's Centre 42 which were, Brenton felt, before their time:

> They didn't have the ... experience of rough theatre behind them. Their only models were West End theatres – they could only think of the local Odeon or the Shaftesbury Avenue theatre transformed. The notion of how to do it on a shoestring was not available to them. But it is to us, our experience in the past ten years has given us the practical knowledge of how to stage, how to keep economies down, how to run a company that is self-governing. The ideas of a Fun Palace or a Roundhouse Transformed seem less grandiose and less ludicrous after our experience.

Brenton also thought that the state of the nation in 1978 was very like the time when Littlewood and Wesker tried to start – especially the consensus politics:

> The deterioration of working-class politics in the country is very similar to the fifties. It's like an endless plain of mud. Nothing on the horizon at all, just decline. Late capitalist decline. No parties on the left of any size which are working-class parties. The Labour Party in ruins. So outside, the consciousness in the theatre is high, and is increasing about political matters – the desire to make a political theatre as politics itself has decayed in this country.

One of the achievements of the political theatre movement had been the accumulation of experience and commitment required to build such a theatre as Littlewood and Wesker had dreamed of – but in a suitable political climate.

The anger that informed the very existence of Portable and the anti-establishment ideology that motivated the search for a new theatre was the same anger that characterised the work of Brenton and his fellow writers. The actual subject matter of Brenton's plays is often crime and corruption in politics – resulting in acts of violence. This was apparent as early as 1969 in *Christie in Love*, where two policemen resurrect the murderer Christie who recounts the history of one of his crimes. Peter Ansorge in *Disrupting the Spectacle* isolated a recurrent device in Brenton's work:

> As Christie rises from the dead different kinds of horror effects take place. The stage is plunged into darkness and we are prepared for the rising of a Dracula figure which might occur in a Hammer Horror picture. But the eventual appearance of Christie is a deliberate anti-climax. The murderer seems to be a sad, apparently respectable middle-aged man. The policemen are, in a real sense, disappointed.[9]

Ansorge concluded that 'Brenton is concerned with showing the surface of social life in England as something of a sham'. Brenton made the point in the play that Christie killed whenever he loved. He used similar shock tactics and similar means of upending expectations in his other plays. *Revenge* (1969) also dealt with the police. Brenton: 'Politically I had no ideas, I was very immature. But I had an instinct that there was a conflict I wanted to get at, between public figures, between figures who meant something in public, like a criminal, an old lag from the East End of London, and a religious, almost ancestral policeman from Scotland.'[10] The play inventively opened with the 'Voice of Brixton Prison' and charted 'the career of a criminal Hepple, pursuing a fanatical desire for revenge against the Assistant Police Commissioner Macleish, who first brought him to justice and Brixton Prison'. At the end 'they are both declared redundant in the new world of moral lawlessness. For the first time Macleish confronts Hepple and, of course, comes to understand that his enemy has really just been the reverse, repressed side of himself'.[11] For Brenton, the criminal subculture in his early plays and its confrontation with the forces of law and order provided the means of displaying a society devoid of any unifying moral code or political ethic. From *Revenge* onwards, Brenton's plays became more overtly political.

Fruit, written for Portable in 1970, was a direct response to the 1970 General Election victory of the Conservatives. Brenton:

> *Fruit* was written in an area which said that the Prime Minister was a homosexual. It's a development of that idea and the fact that, if he

is a homosexual good luck to him. The attack on the Prime Minister should be something else. A blackmail attempt is made by the central character who is twisted and bitter and has it in for the world. For reasons which are quite clear in the play – he's a thalidomide child – he goes for the Prime Minister. He becomes a quack doctor, he gets into a position where he can get at the Prime Minister and secures a tape. The attack is completely misfounded; when confronted with his homosexuality, the Prime Minister says, 'So what?' And then the play ends by pointing out that there could have been another attack, mounted from a different angle, a much more political, realistic one. [12]

The play ended with the trades unionist throwing a petrol bomb into the auditorium. Later, in *A Saliva Milkshake* (1975), Brenton's protagonist found a 'more political, realistic attack': the Home Secretary was actually assassinated. The play then explored the dilemma of a liberal intellectual who becomes literally caught up in the crossfire and is forced to choose which side he is on. He opts for the forces of law and order and conspires with the Special Branch to catch the friend who committed the assassination. But at the end – with his ear drums pierced in an act of retaliation – he is far from sure that he made the right choice.

Hitler Dances came about in 1972 as a result of talking to members of the Resistance in Holland:

> I saw children in Eindhoven, which was flattened twice during the war, first by the Germans and then by the Allies, and is now the home of the world headquarters of the Philips Electrical Company. And at night in Eindhoven the huge Philips sign, like a weird emblem, flashes everywhere in the sky. I saw a bomb-site there with children playing on it ... and there the idea was lodged in my mind, because it was like children playing on this heap of rubble – history. And the idea of a German soldier coming out of the ground became meaningful. [13]

In 1972 there was the film *Skin Flicker* – 'a 40-minute exposition of urban guerilla warfare in which a group of disillusioned young people kidnapped, tortured and murdered a prominent politician', [14] which began the exploration of political terrorism which Brenton continued in *Magnificence*, *A Saliva Milkshake*, and indirectly in *The Churchill Play* and *Weapons of Happiness*.

The Paris Events of May 1968 had an important impact on Brenton and were directly relevant to the writing of *Magnificence* for the Royal Court in 1973.

> May '68 was crucial. It was a great watershed and directly affected me. A lot of the ideas in *Magnificence* came straight out of the writing

of that time in Paris, and the idea of official life being like a screen. There's a long speech in *Magnificence* about that. May '68 disinherited my generation in two ways. First, it destroyed any remaining affection for official culture. The situationists showed how all of them, the dead greats, are corpses on our backs – Goethe, Beethoven – how gigantic the fraud is. But it also, secondly destroyed the notions of personal freedom, freak-out and drug culture, anarchist notions of spontaneous freedom, anarchist political action. And it failed. It was defeated. A generation dreaming of a beautiful utopia was kicked – kicked awake and not dead. I've got to believe not kicked dead. May '68 gave me a desperation I still have. It destroyed Jed in *Magnificence*.[15]

Jed was blown up by the gelignite he was going to use to destroy a former Tory Government minister: they were both blown up. *Magnificence* was important in being directly about the generation of the sixties: the naturalistic first act for example, involved a squat, put down as effectively – and as violently – as the Paris events by the police. The play was also significant in marking a philosophical turning point for Brenton, whereby previously anarchic anger became directed – towards identified enemies. Despair and disillusionment put the necessity of terrorist violence as a means to change society on to Brenton's political map.

In *The Churchill Play*, Brenton's anger was more constrained, but the attack in political terms more concerted. The play was produced at Nottingham in 1974, but had to wait until 1979 for a London showing. And whether that five-year delay in reaching a wider audience related to the vehemence of the play's political stance was worth a passing thought. The idea came from a coincidence of images – Churchill lying in state in Westminster Hall, and the truth about Long Kesh Prison in Northern Ireland. Brenton wrote a radio play about an internment camp in England in a few years' time – 'but they wouldn't do it on radio'. That became *The Churchill Play*, set in a concentration camp in England in 1984. Brenton:

> . . . it's about 'What is Freedom?' The idea that Churchill is universally admired by people who went through the war is not true, but what they always say . . . 'He gave us freedom'. And the question of freedom becomes paramount – you say 'What freedom? What do we do with the freedom? What have we done with it?' And the answer at the moment is, we are in danger of throwing it away – and also that it's not freedom. That was the gut feeling behind the play.[16]

And he wanted to make the point that 'the pleasant roads in southern suburbs are as much of the wire in Long Kesh as the wire itself'. And so Brenton transferred the not so far-away world of Northern

Ireland to England in the not so distant future to show the forces of facism operating in the name of freedom.

The development through Brenton's plays – from his earliest short 'plays for public places' (*The Education of Skinny Spew*, *Scott of the Antarctic*, *Heads*, *Gum and Goo*) – was from a politically unconscious anger (with its arbitrary undirected violence) to an option in favour of socialist politics and the response of the left (including the response of terrorism with its ambiguous victories). Then on – in *Weapons of Happiness* – to an analysis of the dilemma of the left and its Stalinist inheritance. This he presented in the character of an elderly exiled Czech, caught up in the occupation of a South London factory by the angry anarchist-oriented young workers and their confrontation with a complacent boss-class. By connecting the old communist tradition with the activities of the left in contemporary Britain, Brenton attempted to find some realistic, pragmatic approach to socialist change. He did not get very far – a counter-culture cop-out in the Welsh hills – but he confronted the problem of 'politicos without a party', and he did so on the biggest public stage in Britain. Brenton: 'At the centre of *Weapons*, I think, is an intolerable pain, over sixty years of communist struggle. And the character of Josef Frank to me represents such pain.'

Brenton felt that *Weapons of Happiness* and other such socialist plays in the establishment theatre fulfilled an important function of political theatre, that of speaking to the left about the left.

> Writers on the left have to be a vanguard. They have to provide survival kits for people who are active politically. That is how I've seen the work so far. Also their work has to be at the service of the working class. But in ways that are difficult to describe because you are not performing to the working class. Therefore you are addressing them to people who are a potentially political vanguard. And that is why the plays often have painful issues. Like Stalinism; what the party is; what violent action is; the actual reality of working-class life; working-class consciousness, which a lot of people on the left have to be told – that people are up to their knees in concrete out there – which is the subject of *Weapons of Happiness*.

In writing about Stalinism, communism, socialism, said Brenton, 'you have no alternative but to tell the truth' – even though there is the risk of what you say being abused by the right-wing press, or even by the production system of subsidised theatres. 'Like if you write a play with a communist in it, which is about people discovering that the communist tradition can help them in their work and the state they are in, you just cannot not mention Stalin. You begin to tell lies.'

It was one signal achievement of socialist writers, said Brenton, to have maintained effectively (and arrogantly), that 'the most important plays in the theatre are new plays with a left perspective. They are more important than classics. Therefore they should be on the same stages. They must dominate the theatre. That is really what we are saying.' He defended a policy of 'strategic penetration':

> Because the plays themselves and the people who are writing them assume and presume that socialism and a socialist society are a norm – even though daily experience contradicts this all the time – it begins to become part of a norm. So you make the drift of the arts socialist.

Brenton also felt that the state of the nation, the political climate of concensus politics in the seventies, contributed to making political theatre important: 'People can become radicalised in the theatre.' For Brenton political theatre and political activity could not be separated:

> Theatre doesn't actually argue politically, that is done in meetings and parties and unions. But the theatre can illuminate what matters in those political meetings. So they go hand in hand. But theatre itself is not a political act the political act is voting.

In 1978 Brenton had just completed *The Romans in Britain* for the National Theatre. And this had, in fact, increased his imperative to find a new theatre – but in the mainstream and not the alternative:

> I'm under no illusions about the National. By its nature the National can't succour writers. You can't sustain a body of work there, which gets heavier and heavier in its political content and intent. But a socialist theatre could sustain a body of work like that.

Brenton thought a socialist theatre without subsidy was necessary and feasible – 'a 600-seat theatre, once you got the bricks and mortar sorted out, could sustain an *Epsom Downs* style operation financially. It could do it. But getting there ... getting the building ... I'm a writer, do I give up five years of writing in order to do this?'

Finally Brenton remained convinced that 'there is only one society, therefore there is only one theatre':

> And the question is: what dominates that theatre? Just as who dominates the government is the crucial thing. We don't have a socialist government. You can't grow a socialist government in community work, because we are in an advanced society and you can't go back to some ill-defined village society. A socialist government has to run the country,

before a socialist theatre can dominate the theatre. And if socialist work doesn't dominate the arts, something else will.

That in a nutshell was the essential contradiction of socialist theatre in a capitalist society.

'*A revolutionary theatre without its most vital element, a revolutionary audience, is a nonsense on which we should not embark.*' Erwin Piscator, quoted by Gavin Richards.[1]

Belt and Braces Roadshow

The Belt and Braces Roadshow was formed in 1973 by Gavin Richards who had previously worked at the Everyman Theatre in Liverpool in the early seventies when John McGrath was writing for it, then with the Ken Campbell Road Show, and finally with 7:84 Theatre Company, directing and acting in the ill-fated production of Margaretta D'Arcy's and John Arden's *The Bally-gombeen Bequest*. An important inspiration for Belt and Braces came, however, from the work of Ken Campbell. Richards:

> Everyone was going around talking about playing to the people, but no one except Ken Campbell – and Ken Dodd – was actually doing it. Ken Campbell was totally apolitical and totally popular. It was like being an entertainer in cowboy land. You just went into pubs and made them laugh. I learned an enormous amount about the duplicity of being a performer, the intellectual game you play with the audience. The real point for me was to perform in a different way to working-class people in their own environments, to find a way to interest them, attract them, get them to enjoy it and learn something.

Richards wanted to use traditional acting techniques combined with elements of variety and pantomime, to use music as a vital ingredient in performance rather than as decoration. So the Belt and Braces Band came to be an autonomous, but integral part of Belt and Braces Roadshow,[2] which aimed at 'a synthesis of form in order to develop a way in which the political life of our society could be experienced and communicated'.

7:84 Theatre Company had also provided some useful lessons in political theatre, particularly in the production of *The Ballygombeen Bequest*. Richards: 'It was a politicising experience for everyone involved, and it also taught many of us the real problems of political theatre.' Certainly, like the work of Albert Hunt at Bradford, it crystallised in one production important strands of experience and developments – the work of Margaretta D'Arcy and John Arden, John McGrath, the actor Stephen Rea and Gavin Richards. With its songs, satire, music hall and agitprop techniques, the play was, according to Albert Hunt, 'a new dimension of political theatre' and an early example of a kind of theatre that was developed by many companies in the seventies, not least by Belt and Braces. Richards:

> A lot of people came onto the stage, appearing as half a dozen different characters, so the audience by the end had got to know you, what the group was feeling about the subject. So the audience came away thinking the group and their opinions were very interesting and wanted to know what sort of people they were and what were their aims.

Belt and Braces' policy was to 'strive to present entertainment which is articulate and socialist – that is to say, created from the viewpoint of working and progressive people who look for a socialist culture of all kinds':

> We do this through our theatre productions, club and community centre performances, music and song ... We have made it our job to present socialist entertainment in as wide a variety of venues as possible, including the Half Moon Theatre in London and the Crucible Studio Theatre in Sheffield ... The Socialist Workers' Party Conference, The American Farmworkers, Gateshead Boilermakers Club, etc.

By the time Belt and Braces came to be formed, it was on a solid foundation of theory and practice. For its first production, the company applied for and got a small Arts Council grant and produced, in 1973, a political pub show called *Ramsay McDonald: The Last Ten Days*:

> It was a revue about Ramsay MacDonald and how he sold out the working class. We played it in pubs in Edinburgh and Glasgow and drew such a response from the audience that we felt we were one of them. We'd open them up and they'd end up talking about their political views and discussing the Labour movement. Suddenly you weren't just an actor, you were a performer like you would have been 200 years ago. We could see the strength of being able to go into those places and perform. It was really a prejudiced little show, extremely funny, but with no analysis.

It was, however, according to Richards, a fairly successful attempt to combine politics with a popular art form. It was followed in 1973 by *The Reign of Terror and the Great Money Trick*, an adaptation of Robert Tressell's *Ragged Trousered Philanthropists* produced jointly with 7:84 Theatre Company. In 1974 there was *The Recruiting (Liaison) Officer*, a study of modern recruiting. In 1975, there was

Weight, based on the 1942 strike at Betteshanger Colliery in Kent, and *Front Line*, commissioned by a Shop Stewards Committee in Newcastle:

> Here we responded to something from a group of working-class people who wanted a show about the Shop Stewards movement on Tyneside, to play in Working Men's Clubs in Newcastle.

In the summer of 1975, Belt and Braces went to Portugal:

> We wanted to rekindle the fire of being out on the street. So we took a couple of vans and spent seven weeks performing in Portugal – in village squares, sometimes in liaison with the armed forces, sometimes with reconnaissance parties. That was the making of Belt and Braces as a company.

And it was in Portugal that Belt and Braces finally came to grips with the problems of performance style:

> Our performance was politicised, as it were. You can't play popularly, make yourself really there with the audience if you haven't got anything to give them. If your only aim in life is to be funny, which is the case for most comics, you find there is a horrific hole which is filled with megalomania. They're feeding the beast in the people, what the bourgeoisie has created in the working class. The only way to fill that hole is with revolutionary content. You've got to think and feel and fight it through for the rest of your days. Because you've got to create a new human and a new language and that can only go hand in hand with the class struggle.

Fuelled with revolutionary energy from Portugal, Belt and Braces embarked on *England Expects* in 1976:

> The play talked about complex things and made them accessible to a working-class audience. We were talking about the Labour government and the economy, about workers' democracy, worker directors, about the Labour plan which the Labour leadership had sold out with the Social Contract. We knew the spirit was excellent, the music (played by the performers) was excellent, and the script had depth and aggression.

Set in a modern factory and centring on conflicts between management and workers, the play was an ambitious attempt not only to explicate capitalist economic theories, but to present the opposing socialist views on how to combat 'the crisis of capitalism'. Thus the action involves first a strike of workers in protest against redundancies, then their return to work and subsequent, unsuccessful attempt to persuade management to replace 'redundant' machines with new ones. This is followed by another strike which – when the management tries to close down one section of the factory – becomes an occupation. Then while 'working-in' – with access to the firm's files – the workers discover the real management machinations: how the managing director has claimed £900 of expenses for a private party, for example, and how the redundancies and threatened closures are the consequence of multi-national wheeling and dealing of machines and work to more profitable foreign subsidiaries. The crunch comes when the workers are presented with a government-backed proposal for worker participation which splits their ranks. The majority are seduced by what sounds like real workers' control, and eventually vote in favour – only to find management returning to implement the redundancies and closures regardless. A militant minority meanwhile attempts to explain the complexities of multi-national economics and to demonstrate the hyprocrisy of worker participation as opposed to full worker control:

> MAUREEN: ... The only way we can keep our jobs when they are threatened at our place of work is to take over the place of work. And that doesn't mean taking over 50 per cent of the board and leaving the other 50 per cent free to scuttle us. Worker participation? It's like the captain of a sinking ship turning to his first mate who has faithfully served him for the last twenty years and saying, ... 'Here – you may take over the wheel, Mr Mate, and assume command and guide her carefully to the bottom of the sea. Just keep her afloat long enough for me to get to the life boats, there's a good chap.'[3]

The speaker in this instance is the play's heroine (a nice piece of non-sexist casting), who in the first scene has just arrived off the boat from Belfast, 19, ignorant and innocent, who by the end has become politicised by circumstance and personal experience and self-educated in political theory. In this respect *England Expects* was very much modelled on Brecht's *The Mother*[4] (which Belt and Braces were to do the following year): an ordinary working woman coming to understand how the ruling class operates and then taking the lead in revolutionary activity. At the end of the play Maureen has sided with the militants and from her new knowledge is lecturing the workforce on government policy and hypocrisy, footnoted with references to the books she has read.

England Expects was both blatantly didactic and arrogantly entertaining. In its content, it tackled complex issues (the theory of surplus value, capitalist economic theories, socialist alternatives and tactics, the problems of worker participation) and aimed these without reservation at working-class audiences. In its style and theatrical techniques, it attempted to make the issues accessible and acceptable to poorly informed and possibly resistant audiences. Thus music and song were an integral part of the action:

> The stage is set as for a rock show ... The music must be non-acoustic and of a high professional standard. By experience young working-class audiences are far more discriminating in their musical appreciation than in their knowledge of dramatic techniques. For this reason, the show was constructed to form a bridge for these audiences between styles of music with which they were familiar and the less familiar territory of drama and political debate.[5]

The show opened with the refrain – 'money, make money, make money, make money, make more' – to a song which then went:

> for all the teaching that we get
> there's only one thing we can expect
> to live and work just where they put you
> we're all just meat for the butcher.[6]

The last verse questioned how strong 'they' (the working class) had to be to 'smash the power of capital', thus setting the tone of the play. Then throughout the play, the 'message' was summarised in the songs which punctuated the scenes. Thus there was a song about window-shopping in Bond Street, on nine carat gold bicycle clips and mink coats for poodles; a song about the advantages of British investment abroad, with the refrain from the workers 'we cannot make your profits if we don't have new machines'. There was a parody of Nancy Sinatra's 'These Boots Were Made for Walking – All Over *YOU*', sung by a soldier in giant jack boots, with a gold swastika round his neck and a beret badge reading 'Pinochet Is Innocent OK?'. There was 'Smash the Unions' sung by grotesquely caricatured, masked Tories; and a ballad about working-class Joe who received a £6 wage increase from one government hand to find it taken away in taxes and reduced benefits by another. 'The Principle of the Air Balloon' was illustrated with the lines – 'if profits are rising, increase dividends, if profits sink, chuck out some men'. And there was a final statement that 'we can't work in the factories, the factories are shut', with a rousing chorus of 'Fight for the Right to Work'.

Popular entertainment techniques were used to present the more didactic elements. Thus the theory of surplus value was presented in the style of Spike Jones and his City Slickers to flag-waving old men in the dole queue by a German professor of economics:

In order to maintain hiss rate off profid ze capitaleest can eizer put ub hiss prizes or lay off his verkers. Inflation izz ven he iss pudding ub hiss prizes, but ass more unt more verkers are unable to buy ze goods unt realize for ze capitaleest ze surbluss value, he is forced to rezort to ze ozzer messod. Unemployment.[7]

Worker democracy was satirised in a spoof piece of 'Advice to Management' from on high, exposing the duplicity of the participation proposals. The play ended with the arrest and interrogation by the Special Branch of the heroine Maureen and of Desmond, the unsung 'Messiah of the Left', on a demo against unemployment.

In 1977 there was a sequel to *England Expects*, the equally ambitious *A Day in the Life of the World* – 'an everyday story of capitalism in all its global complexity: how HMG, EEC, IMF, TUC, CBI, IBM, ENI, ITT, ICI, GATT, OECD, and CIA are looking after us'. It was an international political conspiracy, multi-national whodunnit with a plot more convoluted than an Agatha Christie thriller. Its various strands included President Carter receiving news of a CIA-backed coup in a South-East Asian country somewhere near Vietnam, and a scene in that fictitious country in which the economics of warfare were spelled out to the peasants. The complicated action involved an attempt by EEC interests to take over a British firm, not unlike the Lucas Aerospace Industry, and one of its subsidiaries, not unlike Fords or Chrysler, foiled by a giant American multi-national called The Foundation who bribe NATO and the Arab countries to support its takeover. In all of this the interests of South African uranium are linked with South-East Asian copper, and the 'war' is cast in a cold economic imperialist light. In the end, it all boiled down to multi-nationals taking over nationals by fair deals or foul. The ultimate point was that the so-called and apparently political problems in the world were at root economic problems: governments were mere pawns in the multi-nationals' global game of Monopoly. The play ended in a nightmare/dream sequence with Carter cornered, defeated by the pressures of the many vested economic interests. The final song had the refrain 'there's a meeting taking place ... and revolution is on the agenda'. Like *England Expects* the play used music and song integrally as well as popular forms such as mock Gilbert and Sullivan and cod Shakespearean dialogue.

Gavin Richards explained the context for Belt and Braces of *A Day in the Life of the World*:

1970 to 1977 was a period of learning. Understanding structures in a capitalist society; losing our naïveté about co-operatives; ... and realising that our unique English problems – social democracy and the recurrent betrayals by the trades union leaderships – had to be seen in an international context. We just couldn't keep on crying about how *our* working class were paying for *their* capitalist crisis. We had to describe the nature of their crisis – which of course meant understanding the history of imperialism and the various theories of late capitalism. A massive task. The show marked the consolidation of a world view; that capitalism as an international historical force would not be finally defeated in the national arena. So we at last blew away the cobwebs of Stalinism, i.e. 'socialism in one country'. What nonsense![8]

Richards described *A Day in the Life* as a 'frontal assault on bourgeois ideas about style':

Without fooling audiences into believing you can create a revolutionary style without a revolutionary audience, we used bourgeois styles – all of them, one after another and sent them up. We exploited the audience's expectations, only to suddenly change course and surprise them. There were about thirty-two different scenes. Each had a different style, always derived from a conventional bourgeois style. So unity of style was destroyed.[9]

Richards said it was middle-class audiences who had trouble with the style of the play, not working-class audiences, 'who took it in their stride, having no problem in seeing the capitalist ethic presented as anything other than antagonistic to their own'. And the show was a great success touring to working-class venues.

In 1977 Belt and Braces also produced *Not So Green As Its Cabbage*, a rock musical entertainment on the subject of Northern Ireland, depicting the struggle of working-class people in a violent world, questioning the nature and source of that violence:

A show about Ireland where it is not so green, where the saints are not much help and the scholars are feeling the education cuts, the whiskey is produced by Americans, the Waterford glass by Belgians and the zinc mines have fallen to the Canadians. Government posters say: 'Seven Years Is Enough'; graffiti on brick walls says: '700 Is Too Much'. Brian Faulkner has become a lord, and Rose McCusker *still* hasn't got a house with a bathroom, an inside toilet and hot water . . .[10]

In 1978 Belt and Braces produced *The Accidental Death of an Anarchist* by the Italian socialist satirist Dario Fo, adapted to relate to the British political situation, one of the most striking of political theatre events of that year.

By 1979 Belt and Braces had established itself as one of the most distinctive of the socialist theatre companies in its style and treatment of political and economic issues, and its commitment to socialist causes. In the summer of 1979 the company took over the organisation of a Benefit held at the Royal Court to raise money for the Blair Peach Memorial Fund and the Southall Defence Fund. Blair Peach, an East London teacher and member of the Anti-Nazi League, had been killed by the police during a demonstration in the largely Asian Southall area of London against a meeting of the National Front there.[11] As well as eye-witness accounts from local people, the Benefit included contributions from Edward Bond, Trevor Griffiths, John McGrath, Alex Glasgow, Alan Plater, Tariq Ali, Paul Foot and the Belt and Braces Band. The Benefit was indicative of the solidarity amongst political theatre workers, and their commitment to real politics as well as to political theatre.

1975

One of the most publicised single-issue political campaigns of 1975 was that to free from prison George Davis, an East Londoner, who in 1974 had been sentenced to twenty years for armed robbery and attempted murder. The Half Moon Theatre joined the campaign to get Davis's case reviewed with its show *George Davis Is Innocent OK?* written by Shane Connaughton and directed by Pam Brighton. The show dealt with the facts of the case from the robbery to the conviction. (Davis had been convicted on identification evidence only – five police identifications and one civilian who identified Davis from the dock, and police 'verbals' i.e. what the defendant was supposed to have said.) It also dealt with attempts by Davis's friends and family to get him out of prison: in desperation Davis's friends had turned over the turf on the Headingley cricket pitch – a heinous crime in its own right which landed *them* in gaol, having been refused bail ten times. But it got them the publicity they wanted.

A similar case came to the stage at the Theatre at New End for the second time in 1975 (it had originally been produced at the Little Theatre in 1972 and was later produced at the Theatre Upstairs in 1977). This was George Thatcher's *The Only Way Out*.[1] The author was serving a life sentence and the play presented the facts of his case. In 1962 Thatcher had been arrested and charged with armed robbery and murder. He was tried, convicted and sentenced to death, the last person in Britain to receive the death sentence before the abolition of capital punishment. He spent three weeks in the condemned cell waiting for his appeal to be heard. The death sentence was commuted to life imprisonment and Thatcher had been in prison ever since, protesting his innocence. His play was set in the death cell during those three weeks and tried to explain how and why an innocent man come to be convicted, what it felt like to be a victim of justice. The play had been smuggled out of prison to David Halliwell who used it to campaign for Thatcher's release.

At the time of the Half Moon's *George Davis Is Innocent OK?* it was unclear whether it would have any positive effect. But along with all the other publicity – the slogan which gave the play its title had appeared as graffiti on hundreds of walls and hoardings – the production did eventually assist in achieving the release of Davis. (Though the George Davis story had a less triumphant postscript when a year later he was again arrested, caught red-handed this time, and sent down for armed robbery.) Thatcher was less lucky. Despite strong recommendations for his parole, he was refused annually and was still being refused in 1979. After the production of *The Only Way Out* at the Theatre Upstairs, the Royal Court attempted to commission another play from him, but he was refused permission by the Home Office, despite a petition from the Theatre Writers Union.

1975 was a year of crisis in the area of arts subsidy. In 1974 the Independent Theatre Council had come into being as an off-shoot of TACT; by 1975 TACT joined forces with ITC for a combined defence against the freezing of funds by the Arts Council and the campaign for an Equity contract for the fringe. Again in 1976, when the arts as a whole were threatened with cuts at government level, TACT joined with ITC and other bodies to create the FACT (Fight Against Cuts in the Theatre) Campaign and to support MP Renee Short's AID (Arts In Danger) Campaign. In 1978 TACT formally affiliated to ITC as a constitutent part of it, and TACT's child became its parent. The history of ITC and of the changes within Equity in the seventies are chronicled in the following essays.

By 1975 a number of new and important political theatre groups had emerged. William Gaskill had left his position as artistic director of the Royal Court to set up – with Max Stafford-Clark, David Hare and David Aukin – Joint Stock Theatre Group, and in 1975 they produced David Hare's critically-acclaimed *Fanshen*. Gay Sweatshop – emerging from and aimed at the homosexual constituency – grew out of a season of lunchtime plays at the Almost Free Theatre. As did the Womens Theatre Group – a feminist company aimed at educating young audiences. Red Ladder underwent internal analysis, dissension and transition, and a break-away group started the Broadside Mobile Workers Theatre.

A number of new writers began to come to prominence in 1975. There was Howard Barker – of working-class origins, whose plays were concerned with class, class conflict and the history of the Labour movement in Britain – who had started writing in the early seventies. There was Barrie Keeffe, who, like David Edgar, began work as a journalist, in his case on an East London newspaper, and left journalism to write for the theatre, often basing his plays on the lives of East End youngsters. His first trilogy of short plays was produced at the Soho Poly in 1975 and 1976, later on television, at the Royal Court and on a national tour. These plays marked Keeffe as a playwright of specific political concerns – a miniaturist rather than a writer of epic breadth, but passionately concerned with contemporary social problems, class conflict and its dangers.

And there was Stephen Poliakoff, who came to the public eye in 1975 with the Bush production of *City Sugar* (and its subsequent transfer to the West End) – about a radio disc jockey and his exploitative relationship with his young listeners. *Heroes*, produced at the Royal Court Theatre Upstairs in 1975, was set in an unspecified country (which might have been Germany or England) at an unspecified time, though presumably in the future and combining elements of 1934, 1974 and 1984. It was concerned very obviously with political issues, not least the kind of soil in which fascism flourished, but its tone was ambiguous. Though critical of fascism, the play also implied that communists were uncouth, the government a failure in creating unemployment, that workers were grubby, grubbing and morally degenerate. This was the case again with *Strawberry Fields* at the National Theatre (Cottesloe) in 1977 which showed two young people (and an unwilling third) caught up in a right-wing terrorist organisation. And again in *Shout Across the River* at the RSC Warehouse in 1978.

There was, in all of Poliakoff's plays, a fascination with fascism, but also an ambiguity of attitude to its sources and its solutions. Poliakoff described his own political position:

> I'm not in any way a Marxist – I hardly would be considering that my father's family fled from the Soviet Union – and I don't think there will be a violent revolution. I think quite a lot of political drama is very remote from anything the audience can identify with. I'm concerned with individuals reacting to the pressures on them – authority, environment, that sort of thing – rather than with political theories or themes. I'm writing about what's happening now, about people searching for beliefs in what is no longer a religious country,

and about how individuals of charisma and power can polarise things
... There's an anarchic streak, a high energy level, a frenetic feel. I'm
not an anarchist, but I'm reflecting the uncertainty of our time. Until
about 1968 or 1970 everyone assumed that things were going to get
better, that there would be inevitable progress towards more freedom,
love not war, all that sort of thing. The belief in the future disappeared
very very quickly – it was killed mainly by violence in Northern Ireland
and by the economic crisis at home. Now people are casting around
to discover where we are going; a lot of students and young people
are very right-wing, even joining the National Front. Look at some
pop stars saying they're quite happy to be thought fascists! I suppose
it's quite possible we may get a right-wing government, and in that
case I'll probably find myself moving further to the left. *Strawberry
Fields* illustrates the dangers of wishy-washy liberal attitudes – it shows
how easily well-meaning people can be defeated by determined, strong-
minded fanatics. I'm very conscious of that danger. My characters
always refuse to be trampled on – even the girls in *City Sugar* are
not totally destroyed or made into zombies.[2]

In his political views and in his plays, Poliakoff was very much a
child of the seventies and a writer of some significance, but outside
the immediate scope of this book.

'You can't be expected to live on social security forever.'
ITC Manifesto, 1974.

The Independent Theatre Council (ITC)

The Independent Theatre Council (ITC) came into being embry-onically in the spring of 1974 at the time that TACT – The Association of Community Theatres – organised its first national conference. The areas of concern were:

1) How to get more money for our kind of work.
2) How to guarantee a minimum wage for people in our kind of work.
3) How to set up a satisfactory negotiating body to standardise grants, terms of employment, rates of pay, conditions, etc.
4) How best to exchange information.
5) How to free the energy, money and time presently absorbed by administration which we need for creative work.[1]

The first circular was a statement of ITC's raison d'être:

Over the last ten years a generation of theatre workers has grown up on 'the fringe' whose work has acted as a creative powerhouse for much established theatre, but which has no particular desire to work in established theatre ... Considerable recognition of its work has been achieved in spite of minimal conditions and a general 'poor relation' attitude towards it. The point has now been reached when this whole gamut of new developments in theatre could be jeopardised, held back by lack of funds from achieving the continuity and development it needs ... In the light of this the time seems ripe to try and form some sort of association to represent the common interest of all non-repertory, non-Establishment theatre – i.e. those self-originated groups whose financial support is dug from the nooks and crannies of the Arts Council's, Regional Arts Associations' and other grant-givers' purses.[2]

The ITC originators recognised the initiative of TACT and in no way wanted to be a substitute, or a competitive force.

Rather they felt it was time for an apolitical umbrella organisation for all the areas of alternative theatre – lunchtime and community theatre then having been joined by a significant amount of small-scale touring. They envisaged an Independent Theatre Council with the scope to embrace 'writers, directors and designers, for whom at present no satisfactory representation exists'. Ultimately they felt 'we could even finish up with an Independent Theatre Workers Union, which might do better than Equity does for our kind of theatre'. It was a grandiose, unrealised vision: but, like TACT, by the end of the seventies, ITC had succeeded in changing the theatre in ways which it could not really have thought possible.

By 1975 ITC had burst onto the theatre scene with fervour and force. At a historic meeting ('the largest and most vociferous ever of "fringe" theatre') organised jointly with TACT in October 1975 at the Oval House, 125 people representing fifty theatre companies plus thirty fringe writers met in response to information 'leaked' from the Arts Council indicating arbitrary, uninformed decisions on subsidy to alternative theatre. As *Time Out* put it:

> ACGB allocations are 'confidential' and its bureaucracy so mystified that its clients live in continual nail-biting ignorance.[3]

The Arts Council had also announced cuts for the last six months of 1975: no funds for new touring, for any community arts projects, for writers' bursaries, for production grants for new plays or for guaranteeing authors' royalties on new plays. This news came just at the time that the RSC had received an emergency grant of £200,000 and the as yet unopened National Theatre's costs had escalated to £16 million. It was a crisis for alternative theatre: its workers were up in arms.

The Oval House Conference made a number of unanimous unilateral demands. As *Tribune* reported:

> Conference unanimously demanded that all frozen money in all schemes be immediately released and that freezing of funds cease to be an instrument of Arts Council policy. It also passed a number of other important resolutions – including a demand for a living wage for fringe theatre workers (£45 a week for the first six months of 1976–77 and £60 in the following six months). Conference additionally asked that the Arts Council *commit* itself to the development of work not ordinarily reached by existing cultural institutions, particularly in the rapidly growing sectors of young people's theatre, experimental drama, small-scale touring, new drama, performance arts and community arts – as the Arts Council's Charter requires it to do. Conference demanded

that the confidentiality of Arts Council panels be lifted, that minutes be published and that representative organisations be allowed to send observers with speaking rights ... Delegates felt that it was time the Arts Council ... stopped regarding fringe theatre as ephemeral and treating it as second class and recognised it as a fast developing and viable alternative force in the theatre, with an important role to play in society.[4]

The meeting was in a militant mood. There was solidarity in numbers and purpose. A demonstration and lobby of the Arts Council was held in November 1975 at the last meeting of the Drama Panel before the new year:

> This was a great success from several points of view: 1) In less than a week and with very incomplete information re: addresses and phone numbers, we were able to achieve a turnout of well over 100, representing more than 40 companies, bearing banners and placards. There were also puppets and street theatre to dramatise the occasion. 2) We leafleted all Drama Panel members and spoke personally to many of them, asking them to bring up the question of a meeting with us if the matter did not appear on the Agenda. 3) The Theatre Writers Group [see below], who had demanded a meeting and had been refused by Linklater [the then Drama Director], circulated letters to the members of the Panel and were asked in to make a statement. 4) There was coverage of the demonstration in *The Guardian*, *Evening Standard*, *Workers Press*, *The Entertainer*, *Case-Con*, and on BBC *PM* and on LBC.[5]

The impact was largely the result of the energetic efforts of the ITC/TACT Joint Action Committee. Then, following a flurry of correspondence, resistance from the Arts Council and persistence from ITC/TACT, an unprecedented meeting of the Arts Council's Experimental Drama Committee (EDC) was held with ITC/TACT *outside* the Arts Council at the Oval House in December 1975. The discussions were sympathetic and seemed productive, and the Arts Council representative promised a report. This did not materialise, nor immediately did the demanded meeting with the Drama Panel.

Part of the problem was re-structuring within the Arts Council, itself the result of TACT and ITC pressure – i.e. the elimination of a special committee dealing with the fringe and a new system whereby the Drama Panel dealt with all companies and applications in the same category of 'drama'. This should have been a major achievement for fringe theatre: the end of second-class citizenship in a second-class category. But in the event, the Council of the Arts Council instituted an alternative plan whereby fringe and repertory theatres were considered by the Drama Panel and *artistic* decisions taken, but with *financial* decisions devolved to a special and very separate Finance Committee. Thus power – i.e. the purse strings – remained firmly within bureaucratic control. The re-structuring also provided the Council with an opportunity to 'purge' the radical elements from the committee and the panel.

With negotiations at stalemate, ITC/TACT were forced to more direct action. From an ITC Newsletter:

> On Thursday, Feb 5th members of your committee 'crashed' the first meeting of the new Drama Panel to question the Supplementary 'exceptions', to voice our worries about the McClellan/Equity proposals [see section on Equity], to express our opposition to the Officers' and Council's plans for reorganisation and to express our disappointment and anger at the new appointments to the Drama Panel. This became a real test of stamina: we were forced to wait over four hours before the Panel would see us. Eventually they admitted us, and we found that the Panel itself was not prepared to accept these 'alternative' plans. All companies who were on-going clients of the EDC are now on 'Standards and Reassessment Committee' along with all the reps. However, they refused to discuss any individual companies with an 'outside organisation', claimed that Panel appointments were nothing to do with them, and offered to look at the McLellan proposals when (if) they came to their notice via the Union! The meeting was then closed.[6]

The same Newsletter summarised the state of the crisis:

> Oh, and in case you're wondering what happened to 'The Freeze', it was quietly forgotten. Only special cases could be considered, so all applications were considered 'special cases'. Apart from the Community Arts Panel, none of the money was ever officially released, but it has gradually been spent. Just letting them know that WE know what they're up to is sometimes enough. The New Drama Panel are now in the position of having a lot of money saved from the first six months to get rid of – they're actually asking people to apply for money. So do, and get it while you can ... We must keep up the pressure, since it seems very clear that it has been our persistent attacks on Arts Council policies that have been largely instrumental in forcing a change of attitude on the part of the Drama Panel as a whole.[7]

Certainly ITC, with TACT, had tested its collective strength with considerable success. On the occasion of the next major crisis almost precisely a year later, they were to be equally successful – this time in taking on the government itself pressing for more government arts funding.

The Independent Theatre Council was still active and strong at the end of the seventies. By 1979 it was itself in receipt of an Arts

Council grant towards administrative costs, in acknowledgement, as ITC put it back-handedly, of 'the fact that the ITC Executive Committee has been doing work that should in many instances have been done by the Arts Council'. And the ITC had also ratified a contract with the Theatre Writers Union that it had spawned, as it had been spawned by TACT.

When ITC started in 1974, it was with a vision of a new Independent Theatre Workers Union – an entirely new organisation to replace existing organisations. Many members of the new Theatre Writers Union held a similar vision of a single Writers Union to replace the four or five overlapping organisations then in existence. With the almost miraculous success of these new organisations, and with Equity, the major theatre union, embattled and still in a state of seige and conflict at the end of the seventies, there was speculation that the eighties would prove to be the decade in which a new Theatre Workers Union might finally be created.

Equity

British Actors Equity was founded in 1930, and in 1967 amalgamated with the Variety Artistes' Federation. Thus it came to be the major union representing the interests of theatre performers (and later directors). But owing to its origins and development (it was a large union with a bureaucratic structure), it tended to be conservative in its outlook and policies. In the seventies, however, Equity was forced by new developments in the theatre to reconsider its constitution and *modus operandi*. And there were attempts to shift union policy in three areas: fringe theatre; the internal structure of the organisation; and referendum voting.

Registration of Equity under the Industrial Relations Act of 1972 was a major issue in the seventies, and it marked the renewal of overt political struggle within the union. In 1972 the Equity AGM voted by an overwhelming majority to de-register: this was in line with TUC instructions, and what 95 per cent of the other union members of the TUC voted to do. But the Equity Council put the issue to a vote through a referendum of all members, suggesting a special case loop-hole. The referendum (as David Edgar had pointed out, often a method of balloting that produces the most reactionary response) favoured registration, thus overturning the AGM vote. As a consequence of this decision, Equity was suspended from the TUC in 1972 and expelled in 1973. With the election of a more progressive Equity Council, the union reversed its referendum decision and de-registered in 1974 just two weeks before the Labour government of 1974 repealed the widely despised Industrial Relations Act.

Another major campaign of the seventies was to democratise Equity itself, and there were periods when the issues were fought in pitched battle between the conservative elements in the union and the left progressives. The campaign took a number of forms. There was an attempt to set up a branch and delegate structure in the union which was thought to be a more democratic method of representation. This started with an undertaking in 1973 to re-write the Equity Rule Book, and a committee was set up to do this. By 1978, however, the branch and delegate campaign had been defeated, though in London six unofficial branches had been set up in conjunction with the committee working on the New Rule Book. These branches had a membership of 13,000 – about a quarter of the whole Equity membership in the region. They met monthly and produced regular news bulletins (in response to the lack of any regular or reliable information service from the central offices of Equity) – and effectively operated as if the branch and delegate structure campaign had not been defeated.

The process – both in the case of the branch and delegate structure and the issue of registration – whereby Equity AGM decisions were overturned by the Equity Council using a referendum ballot became a controversial issue in its own right, and there was a campaign to end the use of referendum voting. The pattern had been that AGM decisions tended to be progressive and referendum decisions conservative. Additionally, the progressive elements in the Union felt that the system of election of the Equity Council was undemocratic, producing generally right-wing Councils which aggravated the vicious circle of decision-making between AGMs and referenda. By the 1979 AGM this struggle within Equity produced the first-ever overwhelming vote of no-confidence in the Equity Council. Thus by the end of the seventies, this battle was at its peak, both sides dead-locked, the issues unresolved but the right winning victories in the courts.

The Independent Theatre Council's battle with Equity – achieving its major victory in 1978 – concerned a fringe contract. The critical period in this campaign was 1975/76 and there was considerable conflict and opposition within Equity. The ITC/TACT Joint Action Committee reported in January 1976:

> The Equity Fringe Committee, created only after a long battle, investigated the way the fringe works, with particular reference to conditions of entry and contracts. The problems are, of course, complex, but not insoluble, and the findings of the Fringe Committee were perfectly acceptable in our view, both practically and theoretically.[1]

The Fringe Committee had reported in 1975 with concrete proposals 'that Equity should ... seek to unionise the subsidised Fringe Companies'.[2] And it outlined in detail the kinds of contracts and conditions appropriate to co-operatives and management companies. But the Equity Fringe Committee did not accept the proposals:

... the chairman of that Committee, one Kenneth McClellan, found himself unable to accept these conclusions ... In such an untenable position he withdrew – after sitting on that Committee for a year. Very right and proper – if somewhat delayed – but he then presented his own set of conclusions as motions which not only demonstrated quite extraordinary ignorance of the very area which he was supposed to be investigating ('... a hotbed of exploitation and undercutting') but which also clearly aimed to destroy the fringe altogether ... This reaction seems to spring from a fear that the people who work in the fringe are just trying to find a back way into the true 'Professional Theatre' – the 'talentless grubby thrusters' of that other well-known fringe expert J. W. Lambert. Anyone with any experience of the fringe knows that exactly the opposite is true – Equity members are increasingly turning to the fringe for work. Indeed, most of the pressure to get ITC to deal with this situation comes from Equity members who are worried about working without the solidarity of the rest of the profession, rather than from those who are not members of the Union and who for the most part see no advantages in joining. After all, most of us are here through choice – and we want to stay here thanks all the same. And *that* is why we want to improve our conditions.[3]

As it happened, the McClellan proposals were defeated, and an experimental fringe contract came into operation in 1978, beginning with block unionisation of the fringe which enabled the backlog of people prevented from getting an Equity card in the seventies to enter the union, and allowing a generous 10 per cent per annum quota for new members of fringe companies.

By 1979 Equity was confronted head-on with the 'political' problems of political theatre and an AGM emergency motion was passed unanimously:

This AGM calls upon Equity Council to take action as a result of the recent decision of Northern Arts Association (NAA) to terminate subsidy to Bruvvers, Major Diversion, Skin & Bones and Wearabout. We call for the following policies to be adopted to fight the attack on members' jobs in the field of community theatre:
1) withdrawal of labour from all entertainment media in the NAA area;
2) a national enquiry into the process of devolution of funding from the Arts Council of Great Britain to Regional Arts Associations;
3) opposition to ACGB's 'centres of excellence' policy being used to attack certain companies, causing artistic stagnation and contraction of employment;
4) fighting for the global subsidy to small-scale theatre to be commensurate with the real needs of the field, especially new developments;
5) demanding that community theatre is assessed by criteria that give

a genuine understanding of the social function of the work and that this is done by practitioners in the field;

6) reinstatement of subsidy in full to the above four companies in the Tyne and Wear region – and draw lessons from attacks on companies such as: Theatremobile, Sidewalk, North West Spanner, Recreation Ground, Mutable Theatre and others.[4]

This was a remarkable event – a direct result of the large-scale development of community and political theatre work among the Equity membership, and a result of the politicisation of a large number of performers and union members. It marked a radical departure from the union's previous pretence of political neutrality. The union was confronting the more subtle problems of censorship in subsidy. For the first time the union was departing from its policy of not questioning the Arts Council. In 1968 the idea that such a motion might be passed by Equity would have seemed impossible. The fact that it was, at the end of the seventies, was evidence of the impact of politics on the theatre.

'*We are not a group that has set out to indoctrinate.*'
William Gaskill, 1979[1]

Joint Stock Theatre Group

'Joint Stock became politicised by doing *Fanshen*,' said William Gaskill, who with David Hare and Max Stafford-Clark was one of the directors of the Joint Stock Theatre Group. The play was written in 1975 by David Hare, based on the book of the same title by William Hinton, about the political education of the peasants of the Chinese village of Long Bow. 'Fanshen' means literally 'to turn over', and in revolutionary China it meant the process of change from feudalism to communism: a peasant person who was effectively 'politicised' was said to have 'fanshened'.

The 'drama' of the play was in the dialectics. For generations the peasants lined the pockets of the landlords, whose power went unquestioned. They are finally forced to ask why. And to answer: because the landlords own the land, and the peasants need the landlords' land in order to live. Did they ever think that the landlords equally depended on them and their work? Suddenly they are made to question who needs whom, who depends on whom, for what and why. The peasants are taught to accept nothing at face value, to question everything until it makes sense or until they can change it so that it does make sense. The play charted the process of change.

The first change is a redistribution of the wealth: but how to do it? What is fair? What is equal? Scales of value are devised, based on just needs and just deserts. The poorest families with children need more; those who put themselves at risk in denouncing the landlords deserve more, as do the ones who do the work; the leaders deserve less. The new values seem to make sense and the wealth is redistributed accordingly. But the village of Long Bow does not settle down to live happily ever after. One problem is that old habits die hard – habits of having more and wanting more and getting more. More means status and power and once again inequality and unfairness. There is the case of the peasant who was at the forefront of the feudal revolution, who, as a leader, accepts less in the first dividend, but who is nevertheless dazzled by his increased wealth and the power of his position and who effectively becomes a new landlord figure. What to do?

Another problem is the seeming necessity of creating a new class system – of poor peasants, middle peasants and rich peasants. Incentive is the rationalisation and the seeds were sown in the original decision to reward just deserts. The peasants are aware of the problems and are asked by the work team from headquarters to find solutions. They try different variations of wealth distribution until they run out of wealth to distribute, which means new wealth must be created, an end for which the incentives of inequality seem particularly necessary. From one point of view, inequality is evil, from another it appears to be a necessary instrument for good. Lapsed communists are dealt with in peasant courts. The accused confess their errors; the peasants pass judgement. It makes sense. Everyone must take responsibility for everyone else as well as themselves. There must be a process for maintaining a fully fanshened system. The obvious answer is to weed out the bad growths (the feudal landlords had been liquidated), but one of the play's points is: why punish if you can re-educate? In theory, if a proper method of constructive self-criticism is inhered and adhered to, a fanshened person should not relapse. In practice people are weak and mistakes are made. What is important is to learn from the mistakes and move forward.

It was precisely by applying these dialectical methods to their actual production of the play that the Joint Stock company became politicised. Gaskill:

> We made a decision before we started rehearsal that because of the nature of the material we would work by methods we hadn't used before. Like making group decisions on everything. Everything went through discussion, analysis, everyone spoke. The image of the meetings in *Fanshen* were mirrored all the time by the meetings of the group.

The company worked on every scene of the play from a political point of view:

> When you say, what is the political point of the scene to an actor, he tries to find out and then tries to demonstrate it. And you start to get epic acting. Something changes. I suppose I've always understood it in a way, but never so simply or profoundly ... When we were working on *Fanshen* we were part of a political process ... you couldn't really do it in any other way, because that is the way the political meaning is made clear ... The aesthetic clarity came as a consequence of getting the political line.

It was the way of working which Gaskill regarded as political. The play evolved out of workshops during which the actors, the two directors (Gaskill and Stafford-Clark) and the writer (Hare) worked closely together. After this exploratory period of research on William Hinton's book and associated material, David Hare wrote the play. Gaskill:

> I think the fact that everyone knew what the play was about at all stages was an absolutely crucial factor in the quality of the acting itself when it appeared. We had an exercise we used to do once a week: we just sat around and in turn said what we thought the play meant, what the point of the book was. Week by week we changed our minds, but each time we heard each other's speech we had to measure our own opinion against the opinions of the rest of the group, so the work was constantly sifted, re-examined and criticised. I've never felt so satisfied with a working method. We also had periods of self-criticism as we believed they had in China. And we did presentations of ourselves as class animals to the rest of the group and were categorised by them. So we were constantly examining ourselves as political, social and economic beings. I think the process was strong and fertile and had a tremendous effect on the finished product.[2]

Gaskill's personal 'politicisation' had come earlier:

> I was really educated politically by theatre and what I've learned about politics I've learned through theatre ... I came to understand that my work had always been political even though I hadn't realised it before ... I was politicised by the Berliner Ensemble when I first saw them in 1956 ... I'd never seen such good theatre before and ... it wasn't just because it was wonderfully directed and wonderfully designed and wonderfully acted, but there was something about the whole process of work which was serious and thoughtful in a way that we had never seen before ... it was a different kind of work ... That was a great revelation ... We thought, 'That's what theatre should be like', not because it was political, but because it had excited us, really deeply, and moved us or involved us ... Serious theatre, a large scale company, subsidised theatre and a group of people working as a permanent ensemble – that image of what theatre could and should be dominated many of our lives for a long time.[3]

From 1956 onwards Gaskill tried to incorporate this revelation into his work at the Royal Court (where he was artistic director from 1965 to 1975) and at the National Theatre. But he thought achieving Brecht's political and aesthetic aims was difficult if not impossible in the major subsidised theatres in Britain. Gaskill: 'I don't think we achieved a kind of political statement because there was no coherent thinking in the actors as a group, or in the management in relation to the work of the group. I think the techniques we learned became just production techniques. I think the political commitment of the writer is the fuelling of the work and that you cannot impose political commitment on a writer just by the way you do his plays.'[4] The whole structure and *modus operandi* of the large subsidised theatres militated against committed political work. Gaskill: 'You can have democracy with a group of eight people, but it's very difficult with a group of sixteen. What I'm really still struggling with at the moment is how to apply some of those things that we first discovered in *Fanshen* to working in a larger theatre on plays not necessarily geared to it.' He compared the National Theatre production of *The World Turned Upside Down* with Joint Stock's *Light Shining in Buckinghamshire* (both were about the seventeenth-century British 'revolution that failed') and felt the former 'was nowhere as good' as the latter: 'That's because the work process was not long or searching enough.' Gaskill had come to believe that one could produce good work only if the conditions were created in which to produce quality, and this was not possible at the National Theatre.

> The National Theatre is as much driven by commercial needs as any other theatre. Perhaps more so. Because of the amount of subsidy, it has to satisfy audiences, has to fill the house, has to turn out a certain amount of work. It's very difficult in the context of running a building to do creative work.

Which is why Gaskill chose to leave the Royal Court and work with Joint Stock: 'I have better working conditions in Joint Stock than I've ever had in any other theatre.'

The production of *Fanshen* not only affected Gaskill personally and politically, it also affected the work of Joint Stock: 'You make political changes within a group and it continues to reverberate.' Though he had often directed Brecht, Gaskill felt he'd never directed Brecht well 'until I did *Fanshen* because that was the first time we found a working method which produced the kind of result that we'd seen all those years ago in the Berliner Ensemble'. It was the work process which was crucial:

> The process, I think, brought us nearer to making a political statement – in the way that the play was acted and directed and designed, not just in what it was saying, but in the way our techniques were being used. I discovered that there is a politics in the way you place people on the stage, there is a politics in the way you light people on the stage, in the way the actors act, in the way you design your plays.[5]

The work process of *Fanshen* and the politicisation fed into all of Joint Stock's subsequent work. In 1976 they produced *Yesterday's News*. Gaskill:

> I wanted to do something about community, and the loss of community identity . . . We started by telling our own life stories, where we'd come from, where our parents had come from, whether we related to any community . . . The material you get is just extraordinary. Everyone will talk about themselves. But we decided that a play about ourselves would be too inward-looking so we decided on a subject outside ourselves – the Angola affair.

The end-product was about the recruitment of British mercenaries for Angola and the effect it had on people at home. Paul Kember, an actor with the company, described that work process:

> Shortly after the workshop began, news began to break of the massacre of the group of British mercenaries in Angola. First reports were confused and confusing, but one thing was clear. A group of British men had formed a community with the object of fighting another community. The action had led to their deaths.[6]

One approach to the subject was for the company to look at themselves as a community, as there seemed at first little connection between the actors and the men who had fought and died in Angola. Yet they felt they must all be 'products of the same forces'. Kember:

> One of the most striking aspects of the story was the case of Keith Jones (as with all the people mentioned in the show we changed the names for obvious reasons). A seventeen-year-old East Ender with no military training, he had gone to Angola thinking he was going to train black troops. He had been presumed dead in the massacre and returned to become a short-lived celebrity. We examined the cuttings. He had felt his own community inadequate, but what needs had that community created in him? What needs had it failed to satisfy? What was the character of the force which had brought him almost to his death? Whatever else it was, it was powerful and brutalising. The newspapers seemed inadequate for our purposes.[7]

So the Joint Stock actors decided to try and contact the people involved and interview them. They found a man named Roche:

> Next day two actors went to meet him with a tape recorder. The following morning the recording was played back to the rest of the group. The 'material' was candid, shocking.[8]

They finally found Jones and some of the others involved. From hundreds of pages of recorded conversation the company – through a process of self-criticism – built up characters 'letting the words speak for themselves'.

With Caryl Churchill's *Light Shining in Buckinghamshire*, also in 1976, the workshop approach was similar.[9] In the first rehearsal period the material was explored. By the second rehearsal period Caryl Churchill had written the script, but the company continued to improvise to solve problems. Ann McFerran described one such session in *Time Out*:

> One scene involving a preacher and an objector at a prayer meeting caused particular trouble – eventually being abandoned till the next day to allow some work to be done on other scenes. The following morning Max Stafford-Clark returned to the scene, asking that Caryl and I should join in too. Producing a pack of Tarot cards, he gave one card to each participant saying that the number on the card would govern whether we were to support the preacher or oppose him. Eight, nine or ten demanded vociferous support. An entirely different subject was given to the preacher for his harangue – Welsh nationalism instead of the theology of God's elected saints. No one knew who had the joker, the objector's card. The meeting began with Colin McCormack speaking eloquently on the rights of Cymru. The objector Jan Chappell found so many hostile to her cries of outrage that she was forcibly thrown out of the room. We then discovered Stafford-Clark had stacked the deck and dealt out three tens. The scene was conducted again, rewritten, and no longer presented problems of motivation.[10]

Such a workshop method requires that the actor thinks. Actor Robert Hamilton: 'It's quite simply that Joint Stock directors assume you have a mind and demand that you use it.'[11]

In 1977 Joint Stock continued with their workshop approach of 1976 and produced four new plays – Tony Bicât's *Devil's Island*, Wallace Shawn's *A Thought in Three Parts*, Barrie Keeffe's *A Mad World My Masters* and Howard Brenton's *Epsom Downs*, which included the company making 'research' expeditions to the race-course. In 1978 Joint Stock produced Stephen Lowe's adaptation of Robert Tressell's novel *The Ragged Trousered Philanthropists*. Gaskill:

> I'd always wanted to do a play about working. At one time I thought of trying to adapt the book by Studs Terkel – that great American interviewer, that old thirties' radical – of interviews with men working, but couldn't get the rights. So we settled on Tressell – a wonderful book. We used workshops and went to Plymouth for a month and actually painted and decorated as preparation for the finished play.

Because of Gaskill's interest in the work element, other strands of the book were abandoned: 'The basic image of the play is one of work. The play wouldn't make sense except in the context of work, and I wanted the whole of the play to exist with the memory of the first scene already there in the minds of the audience.' The first scene was at least five minutes long and showed the painters and decorators arriving for work in the morning, stripping, preparing the walls, painting, each in a separate room. For five minutes there was no script but the 'acting' of work. Sandy Craig previewing the play in *Time Out* described the second half: '... a sudden stylistic shift and a much sharper political focus. Expressionistic and agitprop devices, beautifully rendered lachrymose ballads and jingoistic tub-thumping fuse the entertainment and politics together. And the last third of the play departs entirely (but convincingly) from Tressell to debate the nature of opposition to capitalism and the problem of whether trades unionist and Labour Party social democracy is really the way to defeat capitalism. Joint Stock leave this question open.'[12]

While Joint Stock's work was clearly political in important respects – in the working methods and the subject matter of its plays – Gaskill did not feel it was political in the normally accepted sense. Gaskill: 'Joint Stock does not set out to indoctrinate. I think of alternative theatre as at its most striking when people alter their life styles. Or as some groups who have found roots and become part of a community. They are doing something which is outside the traditions of theatre. I don't think Joint Stock has existed in that way.' For Gaskill and Max Stafford-Clark, Joint Stock provided 'an opportunity to work in a way that other theatre can't offer' – to control their own working conditions. Gaskill's attitude towards alternative theatre was ambivalent:

> I do think 1968/69 was a very historic time politically – and marked a change from the kind of theatre I'd been working in. The Royal Court was always a mainstream theatre, not a fringe theatre, but a theatre in which the best new plays could be done as well as possible. We always thought we were in the main tradition. I think when the whole movement of alternative theatre started, it was by a different generation and one to which I was not wholly sympathetic. Because it seemed to say that there had got to be an alternative and the alternative cannot be in the mainstream. I felt that was disturbing, but I had to go along with it. It was a movement of the time that one couldn't avoid. The founding of the Theatre Upstairs in 1969 was an acknowledgement of something that had already happened that we had to take cognisance of. But it wasn't something that I'd really

activated and I think alternative theatre has produced a split in the theatre.

Though not for Gaskill himself, who continued to work in both 'camps'.

Womens Theatre Group

In December 1978, the following letter from 'A London Teacher, name and address supplied' appeared in the pages of the *Evening Standard*:

> ... many thousands of children of 13 upwards in ILEA schools have been shown a propaganda film encouraging them to go to the Brook Centres for contraceptives. This film called *My Mother Says*, actually encourages under-age children to have sexual intercourse. It is about two 15-year-old girls called Wendy and Terry, who plan to go to a party at the home of Wendy's cousin. Terry tries to persuade her mother to let her go, and her grandmother says: 'Better go see about them tablets they 'ave, no point in taking risks.'
>
> Terry: Do you mean the pill, Gran?
> Gran: That's right, for stopping babies, so as you can *enjoy* yourself.
> Mum: Gran!
> Gran: Just 'cause *you* don't enjoy it ... Well, I liked it when I was fifteen.
> Terry: Gran, you never ...
> Gran: It's only natural i'n' it?
>
> So Terry and Wendy go to the party and Wendy has sexual intercourse with a casual boyfriend. She describes her experience to Terry, including the fact that someone opened the bedroom door and saw them at it, and says she hopes it wasn't her cousin.
>
> 'My dad thinks she's such a nice girl. She's always saying 'ow she's saving 'erself for Bill when they get married.' To which Terry replies: 'Oh, it don't make no difference unless you get pregnant.'
>
> Alas Wendy misses a period and fears that she is indeed pregnant. In the course of a conversation with an older friend called Diane she says: 'I don't think I'm going to do it again. I feel right put off.' Diane says: 'Oh, go on, you can't expect it to be up to much the first time. You wait and see – the more you do it, the better it gets.'
>
> On Diane's advice Wendy goes to the Brook Centre for a pregnancy test. The doctor tells her she is not in fact pregnant, but though Wendy has not suggested that she intends to have sex any more the doctor

puts her on the pill and even offers to do the same for Terry who is a virgin and has only gone along to keep Wendy company.

My Mother Says is a televised recording of a play performed in schools in 1975 and has been transmitted many times since 1976 with the full knowledge and approval of the Education Officer and the Chief Inspector of ILEA. Though transmissions have now ceased, schools which have made videotapes will no doubt continue to show it for many years to come. I wonder if your readers approved of educational television being used to incite children to break the law?[1]

The film referred to was that of the Womens Theatre Group's first play, *My Mother Says I Never Should*, which toured to London schools and youth clubs in 1974 and 1975. It was innovative at the time, but not particularly controversial. It was ironic that the controversy was to arise four years after the original critically-acclaimed production, long after the Inner London Education Authority had judged the play sufficiently good and useful to have it recorded and widely disseminated as one of their official sex education aids.

My Mother Says was specifically designed for and aimed at teenage audiences. The Womens Theatre Group (WTG) felt that theatre-in-education work at that time ignored this 'terribly important' age group and that what was produced 'had no feminist content at all – that this was long overdue'.[2] They decided to do a show 'about being a teenager, about first sexual experiences'. They knew it was a difficult subject to deal with – that sex education classes in schools did not do the job properly. They were very clear about what they wanted to say – basically the opposite of all the sex education which says 'don't'. As Anne Engel, a founding member of the Womens Theatre Group, said: 'We wanted to show what would happen if you do. Because the fact is that teenagers do, and it's silly to pretend they don't. It tapped such a need: everybody wanted it.' The anonymous London teacher's letter to the *Standard* did not reflect the enormous demand and positive response at the time. In a post-play discussion at the Oval House in 1975 there was a 14-year-old girl who thought it would help her friends; a teacher who thought it would have more impact than a dozen lessons (in one scene a 'teacher' had delivered a sex education lesson describing human reproduction in entirely impersonal technical terms); and a Brook Centre doctor who thought it would achieve more than all the leaflets they printed. The play was also important in making it clear that the teenagers had choices – whether or not to have intercourse, whether or not to have a baby and that the inevitable role of women did not have to be unrelieved childbearing, child rearing and housework. The play opened up the educational network for the Womens Theatre Group and for other later groups – the audiences to which they were still performing in 1979, though most of the members of the original group had by then changed.

The WTG was not only innovative in the 'new' content of *My Mother Says*, and in the 'new' audiences to which they were playing. They were also innovative in their origins, in their methods of working and their ideology – which was strongly feminist (at a time when women were still primarily in the traditional housewife role of actress) and slightly socialist (though there was a wide spectrum of political inclination amongst individual members of the group).

While the Womens Theatre Group did not formalise itself until 1974, there had been a loose, *ad hoc* group since 1971 operating as a women's street theatre called Punch and Judies, performing for demonstrations and similar events. They did a touring show in 1972 called *The Amazing Equal Pay Play* (later filmed by the Womens Film Group) – a 'rough agitprop play about Barbara Castle and the Equal Pay Act'. The performers dressed as men – for the first and last time – and performed what was largely a dramatisation of *Hansard* in the form of a debate between a Labour and Tory MP. A case, as often, of real life being more dramatic than drama. That loose group disbanded in 1972.

But in 1973 members of that early group were approached by Ed Berman of Inter-Action's Almost Free Theatre who wanted to hold a 'Women's Festival'. The ensuing lunchtime season was a 'success' – measured by the featuring of women playwrights produced by women directors with women stage-management in a context in which workshops and crèches were provided as well as productions, and by the fact that two companies of women were catalysed by the season – the short-lived Womens Company and the Womens Theatre Group.

For many of those involved, though, the Almost Free venture was not totally successful in achieving its ambitious aims. A decision was taken early on consciously to avoid working in the hierarchical, competitive structures which characterised the male-dominated establishment theatre and media. So the season was organised over a period of six months of 'open' Sunday meetings to which any interested women could come, where scripts were read and discussed. As word spread, the meetings attracted more and more women, some professionals with considerable experience of establishment theatre, some professionals from fringe theatre, and some altogether or relatively new to the theatre. The response was indicative of the neglect of women in theatre and it created 'absolute bedlam' as far as the organisation was concerned. Finally, the pressures of deadlines militated against that 'experimental' process, relatively 'safe' scripts were chosen, and the season was cast and set up in a conventional way. It included plays by Jennifer Phillips, Pam Gems, Michelene Wandor, Sally Ordway, Dinah Brooke and Jane Wibberley: only the latter was a previously unproduced writer. Engel: 'Despite the problems, the event was exciting in focusing attention on the work of women.'

The differences of opinion which arose as to the organisation of the event occasioned the split of the group into two separate companies, the Womens Company, including the previously established, establishment theatre professionals and the Womens Theatre Group, the alternative theatre workers, who as history had it, went on to produce the innovative work.

After the Almost Free season, the WTG decided immediately to get a show together. They were involved in the production of *The Three Marias* – readings from the letters and writings of three Portugese women who had been persecuted and imprisoned for their progressive stance on oppressive social issues affecting women. Then early in 1974 they were offered the opportunity (by John Ashford) to take part in a festival at the Oval House. In a very short time they applied to the Arts Council for a project grant, got it and put together the ambitious multi-media *Fantasia* ('the kind of thing we wouldn't dream of undertaking now') – about women's fantasies, contrasting those of a lonely single girl in London with those of a harassed housewife. Engel: 'It actually worked, not wonderful, but not bad. It was newish and at least the commitment shone through.'

The group got a lot of energy and enthusiasm from *Fantasia*, went to see the Arts Council and started to plan for the next year. Both the Womens Company and the Womens Theatre Group applied for grants, and it was the so-called 'amateur' WTG which got one. The group then – Anne Engel, Lynne Ashley, Sue Eatwell, Clair Chapman, Julia Meadowes, Mica Nava – started work on what was to become *My Mother Says*. The blind folk-singer Frankie Armstrong later joined them to write and sing the songs in the show, opening with Peggy Seeger's 'I'm Gonna Be an Engineer'. In conscious opposition to working hierarchically, the group decided to write and produce the show collectively. So they experimented with the method they eventually went on to use on further shows: 'We improvised, went away and scripted, came back, read it out, discussed it and went away and re-wrote.' It worked, in part because they wrote out of their own experience.

Following the success of *My Mother Says* 'everybody wanted them', and they decided to do a follow-up about teenagers going out to work: what happened to the girls next, but not using the same characters. This was *Work To Role* – simply about the kind of jobs female school-leavers could expect to find, if they were lucky. Engel: 'It was a much more complicated play, with really too much in it. Too many characters with complex stories that weren't fully developed. But we deliberately intended to relate individual experience to economic conditions in this play. To show that women were forced into the worst working conditions. One member of the company researched her role by working in a hamburger joint wearing shorts and fish-net tights.'

By then, the group felt they'd had enough of touring youth clubs and decided to embark on a touring adult show. Several topics were considered – including a show on advertising. But deliberations were superseded by a strike at the Trico windscreen-wiper factory in Brentford over the issue of equal pay. The women were payed significantly less than the men for the same work ('Triconometry – £46 equals £52') and had gone out on strike – in the end for 22 weeks. Engel: 'We went down to the picket line, saw what was happening, talked to some of the women and decided then and there to do a play about the strike. It was a historical first – and inherently dramatic. We started writing the show without even knowing the outcome of the strike.' *Out! On the Costa del Trico* was then written in consultation with the strikers.

The *Trico* show intended to celebrate the strike of that famous heatwave summer of '76 when 'the picketers stood their ground, fighting the police, scab lorries and hostile press' not to mention the black-leg office staff who crossed the picket line daily. Seven women characters were shown mostly on the picket line (sun-tanning, brewing cuppas, sweeping up, chatting) and occasionally off – at home (once), at a South Wales car factory meeting seeking solidarity. The performers impersonated the American owners of Trico, the cat-calling men in Cardiff, and the Kangaroo tribunal which arbitrated, and at which the boss's representatives gave evidence for both sides, the Trico women having refused to acknowledge the tribunal.

When the show opened at the Bush in 1976, the strikers and shop stewards came to see it. There were discussions, arguments: the women loved it, but the union officials (men) objected, 'said the feminist consciousness had been imposed where there was none, that the WTG didn't know anything about working-class women'. The WTG did, in fact, do some re-writing as a result of those discussions. They had left the end ambiguous – showing a moral, if not a literal victory (the Trico strikers got equal pay, but with all the usual loopholes about night work and shift work). They had deliberately avoided emphasising a feminist consciousness that wasn't really there (there was in fact only one feminist on the picket line), but they did want to show the solidarity that had developed. But the play had feminist perspective if not a feminist bias, if only because the WTG was constituted entirely of women and never used men.

After the *Trico* show there was a big turnover in the membership of the group when four people left. And they decided to go back to the teenage audience, but with all the changes there was no longer the shared context, the common premises, the assumed way of working. So with *Pretty Ugly* in 1977, the group stopped working in their former collective fashion and used a freelance director and designer, though they still co-wrote it. The intention was to talk about the images on which women base their lives: the importance of physical appearance, obsession with looking 'pretty', what that meant to mothers and their daughters. Engel: 'I think we failed. We skimmed the surface and produced a glossy show. The teenagers loved it, but for the wrong reasons. They liked the costumes, the gear: they wanted to know where they could get some like it! Exactly the opposite of what we wanted. We had failed as a group to deal with our own attitudes, though we succeeded in creating a so-called successful polished piece of work.'

There was another big turnover in the group, followed by *In Our Way* in 1978, an attempt to show the shop-floor discrepancies in the anti-discrimination legislation. It was structured on the awkward device of a lady journalist interviewing the lady manager (successful in a man's world with hair on her chest to prove it) of a progressive company and discovering the gap between preaching and practice. It too was not entirely successful. In 1979, the WTG had again reformed and were working for the first time with a writer – Donna Franceschild on *Soap Opera*, thus developing in a different direction. But the group had had an impact – in producing an exciting new kind of play for a new kind of audience, using a relatively new kind of working method. Engel: 'Though the WTG and other former collectives have gone on to a more labour-divided method of working, many principles and practices of the collective method have continued. This is important.'

'We have met fear, outrage, prejudice and blind, petty ignorance.' Drew Griffiths, Gay Sweatshop, 1979[1]

Gay Sweatshop

Gay Sweatshop, like the Womens Theatre Group, started in 1975 out of one of the 'constituency' lunchtime seasons organised by Ed Berman at the Almost Free Theatre. Berman's Inter-Action advertised in *Gay News* for gay theatre workers to take part in a gay theatre season, and the response from homosexuals was enthusiastic. The season included *Limitations* by John Roman Baker, *Ships* by Alan Wakeman, *Thinking Straight* by Laurence Collinson and *Passing By* by Martin Sherman (whose *Bent* later broke box office records in 1979 at the Royal Court). The season was a great success – sufficient to warrant an extended run (with three additional plays by Robert Patrick, author of *Kennedy's Children*), and to catalyse members of the original group to continue working as the independent theatre company Gay Sweatshop (which had been the umbrella title of the season, chosen in favour of 'Revolting Homosexual Spectacles').

After the Almost Free Season, Gay Sweatshop were invited to perform at the Campaign for Homosexual Equality (CHE) Conference at Sheffield. They applied for an Arts Council grant and got together the group-written *Mister X*. This was based on a combination of the personal experiences of the group and a book entitled *With Downcast Gays: Aspects of Homosexual Repression*. Drew Griffiths, a founder member of Gay Sweatshop, said: 'And that's what it was about. It was a simple agitprop show about a boy who becomes aware of his sexuality, and aware that it's different. It was about all the ways gay people put themselves down, put obstacles in the path of their own liberation, believing all the lies that society tells about homosexuals. It was about getting rid of self oppression so you can start fighting society's oppression.' *Mister X* toured with considerable success and then became part of a Gay Sweatshop season at the ICA in 1976. That season also included

Jill Posener's *Any Woman Can*, about a lesbian coming to terms with her sexuality, *Randy Robinson's Unsuitable Relationship* by Andrew Davies, *The Fork* by Ian Brown, *Indiscreet*, a follow-up to *Mister X* written by Roger Baker and Drew Griffiths, and Edward Bond's *Stone*.

The ICA season was a turning point for Gay Sweatshop. Their Arts Council grant had multiplied in one year from £1500 to £15,000. *Mister X* broke box office records for lunchtime theatre. Women homosexuals were participating for the first time, and the question of whether all those participating in Gay Sweatshop should be homosexual had to be confronted. Edward Bond's *Stone* brought the company wide critical attention – and nearly wrecked it, according to Drew Griffiths.

The company had written to Edward Bond asking if he would write a play for them, had heard nothing and then received the script of *Stone*. The play was contentious within the group as it was not directly about homosexuality, but rather about capitalism. Bond was asked to write a prologue making reference to homosexuality as one of the many forms of repression in capitalist society, which he did, but there was a feeling in the group that it 'was a sell-out to do a play by Edward Bond, a means of courting popularity'.

The women joined the group by invitation. None had come forward at the time of the Almost Free season and the men members of Gay Sweatshop felt that there was an imbalanced view of human homosexuality in the company, that gay women had to be included 'to give a fair view'. The women mounted *Any Women Can*, and the men and women then went on later that year to produce a gay panto *Jingle Ball* together. But they found their methods of working were incompatible, and by 1977 the men and women had become two artistically autonomous companies sharing the same administration. Griffiths: 'We had a policy of non–interference. We offered criticism and mutual help, but left each other alone artistically.'

The major issue to arise from the ICA season was whether Gay Sweatshop should be constituted entirely of homosexuals. Since the Almost Free season, they had used some straight writers and performers working with gay directors. After the ICA season it became company policy only to involve homosexuals. They had concluded that 'only a gay man or woman who had lived the life they had led could truthfully portray it'. And Gay Sweatshop's aims became clearly defined – 'to change the media misrepresentation of homosexuals, to present themes to liberate rather than oppress'. The ICA season was both a critical and popular success, however, and established the company firmly. Griffiths: 'These plays were the first of their kind. They were flawed but were breaking fresh ground. We were creating a culture that hadn't existed before.'

After the ICA season the company took *Any Woman Can, Mister X* and *Indiscreet* on tour. Griffiths: 'Wherever we went, we made people talk. We used the plays as the basis for discussion. The theatrical dialogue started a "real" dialogue.' At the invitation of the Irish Gay Rights Association, they performed in Dublin in 1976 – to great public hue and cry. There were bomb threats at the theatre and 'disgusted' front page headlines, and they were threatened with lawsuits for obscenity. But Gay Sweatshop were not unhappy as homosexuality was being aired in public in a country reluctant to discuss even heterosexuality. While the response to the new company was generally open, if tentative, there were instances of 'fear, outrage, prejudice and blind, petty ignorance'. Griffiths quoted the example of the drama officer from a regional arts association who left the ICA season saying, 'I'm blasted if I want to hear how men fuck,' and promised that under no circumstances would the company ever be seen in his region.

In 1977 both the men's and women's companies produced shows which were critically acclaimed. The women did *Care and Control*, scripted by Michelene Wandor from documentary information and interviews with lesbians who had been deprived of custody of their children. And the men, joined by Noel Greig (formerly with The Combination and The General Will in Bradford), did *As Time Goes By*, with a first part set in 1896 after the Oscar Wilde trial, a second part set in Berlin in the thirties, culminating with the 'Night of the Long Knives', and a third part set in 1969 when Gay Liberation was born. The latter was performed as part of a 'Gay Times Festival' at Action Space's Drill Hall with lectures and discussion, which in turn spawned a number of new groups including 'Gays in Media'.

By the time Gay Sweatshop made a return visit to Dublin in 1978 with *As Time Goes By* they were regarded as respectable, an indication of the impact of the group in that two year period. Griffiths: 'We didn't create a demand. We answered a need. And we didn't single-handedly break down prejudice, but we contributed to that. The first time we went on tour with *Mister X* we were terrified. We thought the experience would relate to no one except male homosexuals. We were greatly surprised that it was universal. Straight audiences would come up to us afterwards, shake our hands and say we were the first homosexuals they'd ever met. We would tell them we weren't, that they just hadn't realised before. So we opened a lot of eyes, and we opened a new area of discussion. We started people thinking and asking questions. Gay Sweatshop went some way towards ending that automatic response of "pooftah".'

In 1978 Gay Sweatshop revived *Jingle Ball*, the men produced *Iceberg*, about gays and fascism, and the women *What the Hell Is She Doing Here?* By the end of 1978 most of the original members of the company had left and the group was changing direction. But Gay Sweatshop had shown there was an audience for plays about public about a formerly taboo subject.

> '*They told us afterwards that what we described as taking place under fascism in Portugal was now taking place in Liverpool.*' Kathleen McCreery, April 1978

Broadside Mobile Workers Theatre

Broadside Mobile Workers Theatre was the group formed by Kathleen McCreery and Richard Stourac who left Red Ladder in 1974. Their first independent play, in 1975, was *The Lump* about the building trade.

> Here we tried something we'd been aiming for – we decided we actually wanted to make the play with workers. After some effort we got together with half a dozen building workers. They didn't take us seriously at first – they asked if we were 'Trots'. But the battle won – we were not Trots – they were giving up their Sunday mornings and more. They knew the Lump, they knew the building industry, they had been experiencing the struggle for a long time, they taught us a lot. For example, we wanted to put a work-to-rule in the play. We didn't know what a work-to-rule in the building industry was, so we asked them and they said, 'Well, first we dust down the bricks'. So we had a bloke with a feather duster and an apron round his waist, dusting the bricks while the boss is stewing.[1]

Broadside wanted to play to building workers. They didn't get on to the non-unionised Lump building sites – that would have been impossible. But they played to other building sites and reached the apprentices, card-carrying union men who had been or might have been attracted to the Lump.

Their next play, in 1976, was *The Participation Waltz* (following an earlier version in 1975 dealing with nationalisation and phoney participation) about the Lucas Aero-Space Industry. The Lucas workers had produced a corporate plan for their industry, showing how they could make socially useful products as opposed to military equipment; this was counter-posed with worker participation. The play was made with the help of members of the Combine Committee of Lucas who supplied the basic research material and helped to shape the play. For example, there was a character, George, who started out as a militant, but got drawn into the worker participation process, so that by the end he was playing the Boss's game – trying to get the work force to accept redundancies without any struggle. Broadside wanted to show George seeing through the fraud of worker participation. But the Combine Committee disagreed: they wanted to show that there was no going back for George once he'd decided to co-operate with management. A Committee member had said: 'The blokes who get sucked up into participation deals don't deserve to be resurrected. Let them stew in their own juices. Show them for what they have become.' So instead of showing that militancy could triumph, Broadside were more 'realistic' in their portrayal than they might have been. Later they changed the emphasis, to show the positive side of the corporate plan. This time the employer started out as an old-fashioned authoritarian and then came to take off his jacket, to roll up his sleeves, to sit with the workers in the bar and talk about their wives. This was intended to show the workers co-operating in their own exploitation, in voluntary redundancies.

Also in 1976 Broadside did *Now You See It, Now You Don't*, their 'Magic Circus', first performed when the Labour government broke their side of the Social Contract with the first round of cuts, at a time of temporary passivity in the working class in the face of wage restraint and heavy unemployment. The play was intended to counter the 'tighten your belts' and 'get the country back on its feet' line, and the economic viewpoint being put over by the media – that high wages cause inflation, that investment can be stimulated by the transference of funds from the public to the private sector. It was an attempt to put over an alternative economic analysis in simple and entertaining terms, to demystify such bogeys as the International Monetary Fund, inflation and the National Debt and to reallocate the blame for the crisis to those responsible for control of the country's wealth. It was done in a traditional agitprop style with the ladder and its hierarchies, money bags, etc, but also incorporated puppets, circus, clowning and conjuring. Kathleen McCreery:

> We used clowns because we were interested in explaining apparently complex concepts such as alienation (in the Marxist sense) in a simple and entertaining way, utilising the 'naivety' of clowns. A woman worker employed by Desmond Dough sits down to eat the bread she has produced, his long arm (a hand on a stick) stops her, she protests that she has made the bread, so why can't she eat it? Dough replies that she has made it but the flour and ovens and her hands belong to him, he's bought the *time* she made them in. Andre van Gyseghem, a

veteran of the Workers Theatre Movement, saw the play and talked of how much better a political play it was than the crude 'agitprop' of the thirties.[2]

It was performed at trades union branch meetings (NUPE, AUEW/ TASS, NALGO, ASTMS), Labour Party, Co-op and Cuts Campaign meetings, the NUPE anti-cuts demonstration and lobby, for Hounslow hospital workers, for the Chloride and Greenwich Reinforced Steel Services occupations, at weekend schools, Workers Education Associations and at colleges.

There followed a Working Women's Charter Show, a Race Play and then a play about Portugal – *We Have the Power of the Winds*, written in co-operation with the Portuguese Workers Co-ordinating Committee, 'to show the learning process of a revolutionary movement of several classes – workers, peasants – and at the same time to make that process relevant to Britain'. One of its scenes dealt with the multi-national Plesseys, to show the need for workers in Britain and abroad to combine against multi-national companies. Plesseys had plants in Britain and Portugal, with a strategy of maximising profits by closing factories and shifting production around the world when workers in any particular country became too militant or too expensive.

Broadside performed the play for the Plesseys occupation in Kirkby. A woman character in the play in Portugal gets the sack when her eyes go bad. Broadside were shown the equipment the English Plessey workers used – and which involved connecting hundreds of little bits of coloured wire. Broadside were anxious to draw a parallel with the poor working conditions in Portugal. During the performance a woman in the audience shouted to the sacked woman in the play, 'Never mind, dear, Lily Allen's here', Lily Allen being their convenor. The identification was strong:

> They told us afterwards that what we described as taking place under the fascist government in Portugal was now taking place in Liverpool and Kirkby. They have to ask permission to go to the toilet, they have to write their names on a blackboard, their productivity is listed up at the end of the week. They were encouraged to compete with each other for no extra pay.

Other scenes showed the way Portuguese workers and peasants organised after the overthrow of fascism, their direct action to take control of housing, the land, their factories, the setting up of the popular assemblies. There was the 'Trial of Social Democracy' – Mario Soares put on trial somewhere between heaven and hell, with the audience as the jury of workers, to decide whether he'd devoted his life to the exploited or the exploiters. Broadside's work with the Portuguese Workers Co-ordinating Committee and a performance of the play to migrant workers in West London prompted the Portuguese to translate the play and perform it themselves, and to start work on their own play on the exploitation of migrant labour in Britain.

Broadside ran a number of shows in repertoire, which in 1978 included a short 20-minute agitational piece, *Divide and Rule Britannia*, in which Sir Jack Boot (with a giant-size boot pumping the workers from the ladder top in a production-line rhythm), with the help of his ally in Parliament, Kid Glove, and of television and the press, set the workers at each other's throats, using racial hatred to divide them and smash their strike. The message was to fight for class unity against racism and fascism.

Broadside's policy was always to hold discussions after their shows; at one time they would tape record these and play them back as part of their learning process, often incorporating comment and criticism into rewrites. Or they would take turns taking notes. They believed 'that the workers theatre movements of the past proved that art can become an effective tool in the class struggle, that theatre can become a dynamic part of a revolutionary cultural arm of the workers movement and its organisations, that workers *can* create proletarian culture (which is something that Trotsky disputed), a culture that serves the workers'. By returning to the old agitprop forms from Russia after the Revolution (the Blue Blouses, for example) and to German agitprop in the twenties and thirties, they saw themselves as developing new forms. 'You can't put new content into old forms, or store new wine in old bottles' was their philosophy. Kathleen McCreery:

We have researched and studied the workers theatre movements of the past and have learned from their *mistakes*, as well as from the best examples of their work. But far more important and fundamental to our aesthetic approach are the methods developed by Brecht and Eisler. We have also been influenced by contemporary playwrights such as Peter Weiss, by writers and art critics such as John Berger; we learn from today's filmmakers, from groups such as Bread and Puppet, from dancers, musicians, journalists and from other theatre groups. We are continually experimenting with new forms. The objective difficulties we face as a small, underfunded group, determined to continue to play for working-class audiences, and attempting to develop a genuine company or ensemble approach, are the main stumbling blocks.[3]

The key question for Broadside was where and for whom do you perform? They made a conscious decision to perform to the working class, preferably in situations of struggle when they were open to new ideas, were looking critically at the world in which they lived and were attempting to change that in some way. A not untypical day for Broadside would involve performing for Grunwick pickets in the morning and to Garner Steak House strikers in the evening.

'I'm much more interested in the effects of political decisions on people, than in people making political decisions.' Barrie Keeffe, 1979[1]

Barrie Keeffe

Barrie Keeffe grew up in East London and after a variety of jobs, started work in 1964 as a news reporter on an East End newspaper. (Keeffe, in fact, drew directly on this experience in *Scribes*, about a newspaper strike and its effects on the journalists involved, produced at Greenwich Theatre in 1976). He drew a sharp distinction between East London and the East End, the former more prosperous, the latter

> still tenements, slums in the sixties at the time of Rachmanism ... I'm talking about seven people living in one room, like shanty towns we see in other countries and don't realise it is just behind the Tower of London. That was my political awakening, in those years in the East End ... the sheer incredible poverty ...

Keeffe went into journalism just as the Labour government came into office in 1964. Keeffe:

> I remember being excited at the prospect of a long period of what I thought would be a socialist government. I thought there was going to be enormous social change. And I remember, not disillusionment, but absolute despair, at the end of it, that so little ... nothing ... had changed. I became extremely cynical about Labour Party politics.

He had not got caught up in the events of 1968:

> The Vietnam experience had an effect, of course, the feeling of horror and the rude awakening to the adult world. But I thought Paris in 1968 was totally unrelated to England. I could see no similarity at all. The different thing about England to most other countries in the world is the class structure. I could never see the students and the working class uniting in England – ever.

He thought the 'small battles' in the East End were more important for those involved than the 'big battles' in Vietnam: 'The rent strikes, for example, were actually achieving things, not in great romantic ways, but pushing centimetre by centimetre in a united effort.'

Keeffe wrote very much from his own personal experience – about the people of the East End, and particularly the young people: 'I wanted to give a voice to people whose voices aren't heard. I think the people I've been writing about deserve to have as much voice in the theatre as middle-class dilettantes with problems of adultery.' He regarded himself, therefore, as outside the political mainstream. Brenton and Hare were epic writers: he, Keeffe, was a miniaturist. 'I'm much more interested in the effects of political decisions on people, than in people making political decisions.'

When he turned to playwriting in 1969, he started writing for the National Youth Theatre: *Only a Game* in 1973, about a star footballer at the end of his career, in a physical and moral decline, and *A Sight of Glory*, about East End kids finding comradeship and purpose in a boxing club as the East End crumbles around them. But it was not until 1975–1976 with his short plays first produced at the Soho Poly and later expanded into two trilogies at the Royal Court and Greenwich Theatre, that Keeffe began to make an impact. In those plays – *Gimme Shelter* consisting of *Gem*, *Gotcha* and *Getaway*; and *Barbarians* consisting of *Killing Time*, *Abide With Me* and *In the City* – Keeffe adopted the role of spokesperson for dispossessed youth, the victims of an inegalitarian social and educational system, the future unemployed, the unemployable.

It was *Gotcha* which first captured the imagination of the public most vividly. It is structured on what David Edgar described as one of the most striking theatrical images of seventies theatre, an expression of 'sustained fury in which a working-class teenager holds three teachers hostage in a school boxroom by threatening to drop a lighted cigarette into a motorcycle petrol tank'.[2] The situation alone sums up the anger of a generation who had been deprived not just of any meaningful kind of education, but even of a 'ticket' into the adult world of work. When the 'kid' finally confronts the headmaster, it is to point out that he's been sold a pack of lies about life, that though the headmaster has signed the end-of-school report he does not even know the boy's name. The kid's basic human dignity is affronted: he is a cipher, anonymous, at most a number on an over-crowded school role, soon to become a government statistic on unemployment. He's been through a so-called comprehensive school, but the class structure has operated as inexorably there as in the outside world. The boy's action is a call for help, an attempt to claim some kind of meaningful identity in society. As he says in despair, he's only got one life and can't wait for the fruits of progress, nor presumably for a revolution around the corner. In the end, the kid is overpowered: his attempt to blow it all up has failed.

Gem, the first play of the *Gimme Shelter* trilogy, is set on a cricket pitch on the occasion of a firm's annual, ritual cricket match with another branch of the company. Cricket itself is a symbol of class society – it is the bosses' game. Keeffe focuses on a group of young people, the working-class kids at the bottom of the work hierarchy. They – led by Kev, the bolshiest of the lot – have set themselves apart from the bosses by sitting on the opposite side of the pitch, by not participating, though theirs is made to look a feeble form of rebellion, especially when one of them is persuaded to join in the game (a form of 'selling out'). The student, who is only there for a vacation job, highlights the lack of opportunity for the others: he'll be going on to bigger and better things because of his education. The girl is a sex object.

In *Getaway*, the last play of the trilogy, the characters from *Gem* meet the kid from *Gotcha*. By now even Kev has sold out, though he keeps up a running patter about 'tactics', 'infiltration', 'fifth column' and not 'letting apparent appearances deceive'. The girl is wed and pregnant. And the kid has been to Borstal and back and he's 'changed':

> Well, now all the fuss has died down ... served me time ... 'repaid society my debt to it' ... well, got a nice job ... learned about gardening in Feltham ... nice job ... found ... something ... a ... peace ... now forget it ever happened.[3]

Kev remembers him from the newspaper publicity and tries to make a revolutionary hero out of him, but the kid won't wear it. He's seen a boy suicide himself on a bed of razors, he's had nightmares – of burning flesh – about actually dropping the fag into the petrol tank, and he's wet the bed in Borstal while the others were outside leading a normal life.

Keeffe wrote *Gotcha* at the time of the big comprehensive education debate. He'd heard 'politicians and experts talking, but never a kid, a pupil'. He'd remembered

> ... when I left school, people talking about what they were going to do for a career, how they were going to spend their life, and there seemed to be enormous choice. But now there is no choice, the reality is youth unemployment.

He'd liked kids and hated seeing them get so cynical:

It's hateful that the kids I've written about become so old so young, so cynical, so mistrusting, so wholly unromantic and shockingly pessimistic. But they are protecting themselves from the brutalities and they're not going to be crushed and disillusioned by the lies. I think the plays are asking questions of the people who are running the world, who have forgotten what it's like, or who never knew.

The *Barbarians* trilogy showed what life is like on the streets for unemployed school leavers: nothing to do except fantasise about another bloke's 'bints', and spot cars for heisters to supplement social security; nowhere to go except the odd nip up West to steal bubbly from the Lord Mayor's banquet. The plays were an impassioned plea for attention to be paid to an increasing and ignored sector of society. Like *Gotcha*, the second play, *Abide With Me*, ended with Paul on his knees making an anguished cry just to be noticed. He's not, and by the third play, *In the City*, his anguish has turned to anger, worse than undirected, mis-directed against his own (black) mate. He's had the boot once too often: up against the wall (the slogan-sprayed corrugated iron of inner city decay) he kicks back. The irony is that he puts the boot in the face of his friend, not his foe. He is hard done by, but he is hard pushed to identify by whom.

What these kids lack as much as work and money, suggested Keeffe, is a sense of belonging. They are always outsiders, locked out, looking in – in pursuit of an unattainable 'community'. In the first play – aptly titled *Killing Time* – the only available work is that traditionally done by women in the local factory. Beneath their dignity it might be, but they take it and they soon come to enjoy the female company, even to take pride in being employees of the Company. By *Abide With Me*, they've given themselves heart, soul, pocket and gear to Manchester United, following their heroes religiously (hence the title) from one end of the country to the other. But they can no more get into the Cup Final (despite their devotion) then they could get into the Lord Mayor's do. That is the betrayal that finally breaks their unfounded but persistent optimism.

By the third play, Louis has left Lewisham and found his black roots in the hip community of Notting Hill. Jan has joined the army, one of the few areas of work so unpleasant that it is wide-open to the working class. The uniform is his badge of belonging, but he's not comfortable in it, and he's uneasy about the motives of an organisation that is sending him off to Belfast to be sniper fodder. Less easily pigeon-holed, Paul is still drifting, now after the black 'bints' advertising in *Time Out*. And it is that quest which ironically precipitates the violent confrontation between the old friends.

Keeffe was concerned that young people

are rarely truthfully portrayed. Documentaries don't get them right because they are playing to the camera or the journalist, and when they are in court they don't say anything.

And he wanted to introduce to middle-class theatre audiences 'people they wouldn't normally come into contact with or get to find out about, to try to create a better understanding'. *Barbarians* had been accused of being pessimistic, but Keeffe disagreed:

I thought it was very optimistic. The wall was there, but there was a way to get through it. Next time they would find a more devious way of getting through to the other side. That is the lesson they learned from that brutality. They didn't accept anything, they challenged those who rejected them, and that is optimistic I think.

Certainly in *Frozen Assets* (produced at the Warehouse in 1978) he'd got the kids he'd been writing about 'to cross the wall and get into the other world and start finding out'. In that play, the boy in Borstal, who accidentally kills a 'screw', escapes. While on the run he gets involved with his small-time-criminal brother-in-law and the middle-class people he burgles. The boy actually ends up in the drawing room of a government minister, as a guest. Keeffe:

In *Frozen Assets*, the victim met the people who had created the life he endured and would have to go on enduring. The hero finally met the enemy face to face.

Keeffe said many middle-class people had hated *Frozen Assets* because they felt the middle-class characters were portrayed less sympathetically, treated unfairly. But he said the play had been written as though through the boy's eyes, that the portrayal was therefore truthful, that middle-class characters got more than their fair share of fair treatment in the theatre by other writers. But there was a dilemma in Keeffe, a conflict between the naturalism necessary to portray the people he'd been writing about and the society they lived in, and the non-naturalism (the grotesque) that started to emerge in *A Mad World, My Masters* written by Joint Stock in 1976, and, to a certain extent, in *Frozen Assets*. But, said Keeffe, the subject matter and his intentions for a play dictated its style: to create an emotional response, naturalism seemed a most effective approach.

This was borne out by *Sus*, produced at the Soho Poly in 1979, set on the eve of the General Election of that year in the interrogation room of a local police station where two detectives interview a

Jamaican on 'suspicion'. The Jamaican, who's been harassed before on 'sus' (the nineteenth-century law which was increasingly used in the seventies to detain people – often blacks – for no particular reason), thinks he's getting the same old racist run-around. The audience, however, knows that his wife has died a most bloody death in circumstances which look like murder, and he's going to be charged with it. The cops are keen to get home and watch the election results come in – heralding the new 'dawn', as the sergeant puts it, when 'The Thatch' wins, and they can cut all the good race relations crap and get down to serious business. When they finally release him (after a beating) on the news that his wife died a natural death, they warn him off making any complaints. It happens all the time, they say, and they'll testify he was only there for the usual 'sus'. Keeffe made it clear that such dramas were happening daily, that the new Conservative government would make matters worse for the working class and the blacks.

Keeffe regarded himself as a political writer and he talked about 'doing my bit for the revolution in trying to change people's attitudes, in trying to contaminate audiences with the anger of the people I write about. There are a lot of people who are good at working out political solutions, but I hope I can create a flickering of energy: if an audience *feels*, if it is angry or compassionate, then, I think that is a legitimate contribution.' The major problem was that 'the people I'm writing about, writing for, wouldn't be seen dead in a theatre'. Keeffe, like many writers of the seventies, showed the system at work, the damage that the capitalist system does to the young, and thereby demonstrated the need for change.

'There are more juvenile delinquents than there are Young Socialists.' Howard Barker, 1978[1]

Howard Barker

John Ford, reviewing Howard Barker's *Claw* in *Plays and Players* in 1975, wrote:

> The third act opens with an even more extreme stylistic jolt than the second. Two waiters serve Claw breakfast. They do not speak to him. They speak to the audience about themselves. They are both men of violence. One tells the story of the first time he planted a bomb in Northern Ireland. The second tells of his experience as an apprentice hangman before the abolition of the death penalty. Both speeches are written with an extraordinary clarity and sympathy. The men also gossip about the grubby sexual origins of pop stars, and it gradually becomes clear that they are not waiters but warders. This is a mental institution of a very special nature, and they have been selected to work there because of their particular experience. Claw appeals to his warders, but gets no response. He appeals to a vision of his father. Old Biledew, now dying, condemns Claw's individualism, regrets that he did not have the vocabulary necessary to pass on his experience, and advises Claw not to despise his class but to win them. Claw again appeals to his warders. They swiftly and efficiently drown him in a bath.[2]

David Edgar felt that it was 'not easy to think of a series of images that say so much in so little time as those of the last half hour of Howard Barker's *Claw*, the tale of a working-class boy who rejects the politics of his class, becomes a pimp to the aristocracy and, after a scandal involving the Secretary of State for Home Affairs, is arrested by the Special Branch'.[3] Edgar used *Claw* as an example of formal developments in political theatre in the seventies, 'the upending of received forms and the techniques of shock and disruption ... to confront the gap between the objective crisis of the system and the subjective responses of the human beings within it.'

And Howard Barker was certainly at the forefront in the innovation of techniques and styles. Barker: 'I don't like naturalistic situations. I like events which are metaphorical not commonplace. The language is no longer naturalistic, the situations are deliberately unfamiliar.' Ironically, because Barker was so successful as a stylist (and he addressed himself particularly and deliberately to this aspect of his work), because the emphasis on style – aesthetics – created an inevitable degree of ambiguity in the content, the bedrock socialist politics of his plays was not fully appreciated.

Barker regarded himself as 'unquestionably a socialist writer':

> I've always been a socialist, and have actually been on the Stalinist wing of socialism. A lot of my work is quite clearly pessimistic and I think the reason for that is that it is very difficult to be an optimistic socialist in England.

Barker was not particularly politicised by events in the sixties. He had come from a very political working-class background and had received his political 'education' at home. My father was an active trades unionist, an old hard-line Stalinist. I was brought up to be interested in politics.' Barker was educated out of the working class, but his background remained integral to his work:

> I was aware at all times of the conflict between labour and the employers. My father works in a very paternalistic family company where the men call the bosses Mr. Jack or Mr. Leslie, and they call the workers by their surnames, so I was very much aware of the basic relationship between the working class and the employer class. Although I didn't join the CP, I was much more aware that change had to come through industrial conflict rather than through consciousness-changing.

Class and class conflict were basic to Barker's plays, 'because I believe conflict is the most powerful element in the theatre, as class conflict is the essential truth of English society'.

> I was consciously concerned to write about class. And my four or five earliest plays were about class warfare. Any person who goes through grammar school and university and then moves into the theatre obviously experiences a lot of the English class system at first hand.

As he developed as a writer, Barker became increasingly interested in the aesthetic elements of playwriting: 'My first instinct is not to write a political play in the sense that its didactic purpose is paramount, but to write a play in which politics happen to be the arena for the action. Classical aesthetic values – style, language, character – are primary over the political ends of the play.' At the same time, all of his plays were set in the political arena and

Barker couldn't 'think how a serious writer could not place his characters in a political context; it's irresponsible if he's not continually brushing against politics, the quality of society and how individuals respond to it'.

Barker's plays were also very much 'state of the nation' plays – reflecting England in decline:

> I heartily believe that some societies do actually tragically go into decline. I think England is going into decline. The thing that makes me pessimistic is that I see no way out of it. Jack London describes in *The Iron Heel* a society where the working classes aren't able to take control and the country falls into the hands of a savage bureaucracy and remains so for several hundred years. Now because we're Marxist, we talk about progress as inevitable, but of course Marx never put a time scale on these things. It's quite conceivable that England could – because of the myths that sustain a capitalist system, because working-class consciousness hasn't developed sufficiently – spend a hundred years in decline. We are lumbered with dead and immovable institutions. That's why I'm pessimistic.

Even Barker's early plays, though 'they weren't exactly political plays in the conventional sense', were about 'social disintegration'. Some of his early plays were for radio. There was one about the alienation of youth, and another about Eleanor Rigby, who she really was, with a John Lennon character exploiting her problems for the benefit of his own songwriting. Barker: 'The first radio play I wrote was about a strike organised by the slaves on the pyramids, called *One Afternoon on the 63rd Level*. The second one was *Henry V in Two Parts*, a pastiche on Shakespeare referring to Henry's speech just before the battle of Agincourt where he says that "every man who fights with me today shall be my brother". In my play a common soldier at the front rank hears that speech and decides to put it into practice. After the war's over he goes to the king for fraternal help and Henry rejects him, sends him away with a flea in his ear. And there was one about a bloke who tries to avoid committing himself to work.'

Working-class attitudes towards work were recurrent themes in Barker's plays:

> It's very important to the working class to avoid work. It's a very middle-class, puritanical concept to see evils in working-class habits like gambling. For them it's a means of not working and the avoidance of the work experience is very basic to the working class. It annoys me when socialists glorify work, when all the work available is of a soul-destroying nature, and always likely to be.

The working-class alternative to work – often crime – was also a recurrent theme for Barker. He regarded crime as a natural response to capitalism:

> If you're working class and you have a real resentment, crime is one of the ways in which you operate it. Political knowledge is another, but because political knowledge is not widespread in the working class, crime is a very natural and legitimate outlet. That's why my characters more often drift into crime than politics. After all, there are more juvenile delinquents than there are Young Socialists.

Cheek, produced at the Theatre Upstairs in 1970 and Barker's first stage play, was very precisely about working-class avoidance of work:

> A young bloke who's just left school with no work, with friends in a similar situation and a father who's dying, is persuaded to make a living, not exactly by crime, but by developing a way of life in which they don't have to work – what he calls work by cheek. If you're cheeky enough you can get by doing very little in life, succeeding by exploiting other people. Capitalism is, basically, a great swindle. An immense cheek.

Barker had been influenced by Bond's *Saved* which he thought was powerful, but which he felt underestimated the working class. Barker: 'The monosyllabic responses didn't do much justice to working-class dialogue which I rather fancied I could write. The leading character in *Cheek* is articulate and witty.' Barker thought that the working class was witty, with a tremendous verbal imagery, that the idea of an inarticulate working class was a false one.

In *Alpha Alpha* at the Open Space in 1972, the subject was again the working class and crime:

> I don't think crime is a revolutionary activity, though there are some left-wing individuals who would argue that it is. I see it as being quite the opposite. *Alpha Alpha* was about the Kray twins: I was trying to show that by carrying out acts of violence, running a criminal syndicate, they were performing a mirror image of the ruling class. There is no question but that criminals such as the Krays and the Great Train Robbers aspire towards living the style of life of the ruling classes. For many of those criminals going fox-hunting, Jaguars, the vulgarity of the squirearchy, are the evidence of success.

Stripwell, produced at the Royal Court in 1975 was the first of Barker's plays to reach a main stage; and again the play was concerned with crime and culture. Stripwell is a judge, married to the daughter of a very elderly, very eminent 'old socialist' politician resonantly named Jarrow. Ironically, Stripwell has fathered a silver-spooned, free-enterprising, absolutely amoral son and keeps (or tries to keep up with) a mistress who's a go-go dancer with literary aspirations – sexy, independent-minded and young enough to be his daughter. At the beginning of the play, Stripwell passes judgement and sentence on a minor offender named Cargill who vows from the dock to take revenge. He says he's going to kill Stripwell. The threat prompts Stripwell to question his role and function in society – and he decides to quit judging. The play was very much about dropping out and stripping away. Barker chose his characters carefully so that politics, education, work, money, marriage, sex, class were all exposed (the 'stripping' metaphor was very effectively woven right through the play), particularly capitalist society and all its consequential structures, not to mention people.

What was funny – and the play was very funny, with the verbal wit of a Tom Stoppard – was that every respectable character and convention was rendered (sometimes outrageously) incongruous and shown to conceal a mass of contradictions: the judge slumming with a stripper, a county wife claiming to be a socialist yet whose fondest memory is having copulated twenty years earlier with a Tory MP on the floor of the House, a son whose socialist background brings him up to be a capitalist, a socialist grand-dad who's become lord of the manor, and so on. Barker didn't resolve the contradictions, except perhaps implicitly in the violent death of Stripwell at the end.

In response to a review of the play in *Tribune*, Barker wrote:

... the contradictions form the vital backbone both of the play and the society it's trying to describe ... Stripwell is a warm-hearted and rather winning character (i.e. he invites your sympathy). That is the very nature of middle-class society – it is literate and amusing – after all, it has had so many years of uninterrupted power in which to cultivate those assets. The fact that he is pleasant as an individual does not weaken the fact that he exists in a world of contradiction and inherent decadence – he is unable to make a moral decision because of his class character ... I don't resolve the contradictions; Cargill's decision at the end to reject the compromise attitude of a ruling class which effectively castrates the working-class movement (in and out of Parliament) necessarily involves violence. I am deeply depressed about the only alternatives we seem to have before us – either to accept a perpetually treacherous social democratic Labour Party (which simply cannot deliver the goods), and to live with that hypocrisy – or to destroy it. I am not certain which gives the greater pain.[4]

Fair Slaughter, produced at the Royal Court in 1977, was a startlingly original play. It told the story of a failed revolutionary Gocher, who struggled unsuccessfully through two world wars to the collapse of the welfare state. The play cleverly interspersed the end of the life of the old man (finally a convicted murderer on his death bed in Wandsworth Prison hospital) with scenes from his past life chronicling his development from youth onwards. The play traced Gocher's quest for a socialist society beginning with his communist conversion while a private in His Majesty's army stationed in Siberia where he meets Trotsky's train driver and takes the man's dismembered hand home to England as a souvenir and a symbol of his socialist aspirations. Indeed he carries the gruesome totem to his deathbed. Gocher never quite succeeds as Lenin's self-appointed British vanguard, and in the end he decides to bury his dreams by returning the hand to its native soil. He doesn't get all the way to Siberia, just the South Downs; but it was the thought that counted.

Barker felt the criminal aspects of *Fair Slaughter* were different compared to his other plays: 'He hasn't done a criminal act; the murder he commits at the old people's home is justifiable as a form of localised *Realpolitik*.' Barker described the play as about 'the tragedy of being English: the old man has spent a lifetime fighting for socialism, and he keeps saying in the play (and I agree with him) "I'd have been better off living in Eastern Europe, at least I'd have been shot". He has this aspiration to be "historical". It's very hard to be "historical" in England.' So often accused of being pessimistic, Barker argued that the end of *Fair Slaughter* was optimistic:

> At the end of the play Gocher has converted the prison warder; he hands the prison warder the talisman of socialism (Trotsky's train driver's hand) and he runs off with it – like the Olympic torch. I believe in that. I believe the working class learns its politics at the knee of its parents and in the factory. Each generation tells the next what working in the capitalist system is like. So the handing on of the bottle in that play is symbolic and positive.

That Good Between Us, produced by the RSC at the Warehouse in 1977, was about life in England under a repressive Labour government at the time of a putative left-wing coup in the armed forces. On one level the play was a timely attack on moderate Labour government – and the compromises that go with it – working hand in glove with a civil service establishment, using a mixed economy which supports and perpetuates a status quo whoever is in power. The play was about the tweedledee, tweedledum system of British parliamentary democracy, a system in which political principle succumbs to expediency and simple survival.

On the advice of her MI5, the 'liberal' lady Labour Home Secretary imposes repressive legislation of a sort that gets her labelled fascist by Liberal and left interests. She is disgusted by the measures she takes but can come up with no alternative within the system she governs by. The MI5 man is only doing his job. In 'real' life he is the nice suburban daddy of a spina bifida daughter whom he adores and tries to protect from precisely the public life filth he is responsible for – blackmail, murder and worse. The Home Secretary's daughter uses anarchist rhetoric to abuse her mother and the Labour movement. However much she thumbs her nose, though, she is still secure in the privileged class into which she was born. In the end a combination of her anarchy – at least her sexual anarchy – her political fence-sitting and fortuitous accident gets her a bullet in the brain.

All of the characters were interesting, but Barker's tandem heroes most so. McPhee is a Scottish sort of Brendan Behan, a dosser blackmailed into the spy game. Before he gets politicised by the People's Democratic Movement, he's oblivious of whose pawn he is and why, or who he's pawning and why. Godber, the MI5 hitman, on the other hand, goes into the spy game precisely because he knows what the social system game is all about and he intends to win at whatever the cost. Godber believes that life is about surviving and that the end justifies any means.

Accused of being nihilistic in *That Good Between Us*, Barker responded:

> I don't think I am nihilistic ... What I wanted to show in *That Good Between Us* was a world in which morality has evaporated, has gone into abeyance. In which human goodness as we understand it, has been eroded by the prevailing corruption of a truly decadent society ... The characters in my play are, with only one exception, people unable to fulfil their sense of moral responsibility, or like Godber, the other spy, a creature of a world without moral values. The only person who is actually fully connected to his ideals is McPhee and McPhee is betrayed through his simplicity and honesty. Taken at face value, that is pessimistic. On the other hand McPhee is the sole survivor, and his last words are an affirmation of the spirit of survival, of coming through. Godber and Rhoda [the Home Secretary], unmotivated products of a motiveless world, are swept aside. The army conspiracy is still on. The play is a picture of a declining world and its disordered human products ... What both *That Good Between Us* and my other recent

play *Fair Slaughter* show, I think, is that without political change, human nature deteriorates. And England is not changing ...[5]

Barker explained the working-class boy who became a professional government spy with strong fascist tendencies not as a criminal but as 'someone who's come through that particular mill, grammar school, which makes working-class boys lose contact with working-class ideology – the grammar school was a very cynical attempt to recruit the best brains of the working class to service the lower echelons of the ruling machine'. Barker felt that *That Good* might have seemed ambiguous because his portrayal of all the characters was sympathetic:

> If you're going to say that all fascists are hobbling about in boots, it tells you nothing about fascism ... Can one go on showing Labour Party people as bombastic twits? I don't think you can. There's more to the Labour Party than that. So many people say, yes but you're being sympathetic with the enemy, you blur the focus. This is a terrible crisis for anyone who quits agitprop for serious writing.

In 1978 Barker wrote *The Hang of the Gaol* for the Royal Shakespeare Company using a prison as a metaphor for English society. It was about an arson, the fire that destroyed one of Her Majesty's prisons and the official investigation which 'came, saw and whitewashed'. Again the concern was the decline of imperial England and the failures of a Labour government and movement. Barker pitted the prison governor (of the old 'honourable school') against a deeply cynical Labour Home Secretary and a tragically weary 'socialist' Royal Commission. Barker:

> Prisons are very catholic descriptions of English society, they are very colonial, as England is colonial. There is the governor, the staff of NCOs, the class of oppressed prisoners, and the way the prison operates is not unlike the way we used to run our colonies – a pyramid with a cultured, Christian apex. The governor wants to 'civilise' the inmates. I don't think that's possible. I don't believe in people making themselves better by willpower. It's a very Victorian notion of goodness. The play shows the contradictions of the liberal stance, the impossibility of personal morality in an immoral political system.

Barker, personally as well as through his plays, thought the 'state of the nation' was bleak:

> The real tragedy of England is the fact that the population subscribes to a myth of freedom, a notion that freedom is about universal suffrage and the parliamentary system, and they are aided and abetted in this

by the capitalist press. Freedom is something different. In communist and East European countries freedom means freedom from unemployment, racial prejudice, exploitation, bad health and housing – all the things we have here. But this is accompanied by a stultifying bureaucratic repression. Here freedom means ballot-boxing. We are still lumbered with nineteenth-century concepts. And they are stiff with materialism. Neither is right. Neither is adequate.

He felt that the political prognosis was equally bleak:

> I'm not sure that things are polarising. If they were I think one would have grounds for being optimistic. I know the National Front has appeared and the Tory party is careering to the right. On the other hand the working class has not strongly moved to the left in its own defence. The most significant event of the last five years has been the Social Contract, the fact that the union movement succeeded in convincing the working class that it should cut its living standards in the interests of international capitalism.

Barker was anxious to be a popular dramatist, to reach as wide a middle-class audience as possible. He did not worry about being absorbed by the system:

> That's the argument that's put against all kinds of political activity in the west – that you're being tolerated, that you're being turned into the conscience of the bourgeoisie, that your freedom is a product of their repression. I don't accept that argument because I don't want to. The alternative is simply to shut up.

He didn't think the working class would ever, given the state of the nation, see his plays.

Barker, unlike other writers of his generation, did not think there had been much change in the theatre or outside it:

> I think it's a very disappointing generation on the whole. I'm very disappointed myself. I think the end products of the apparent upheaval of the sixties and seventies have been negligible. I don't think the prevailing values of our generation are fundamentally any different from the prevailing values of the previous generation – the intellectuals are broadly left, the masses are broadly right. You could say about them, at least, they fought the war and defeated fascism, though even that is to glamorise their motivations. But there's very little we could claim at the moment. It's yet to come, this major struggle, or it isn't coming at all.

Subsidy had made a material change, but he questioned how long the Arts Council would continue to subsidise propaganda against themselves. The most significant changes he thought had been in the area of content rather than form – in breaking with the naturalistic conventions located in domestic environments:

> One of the ways of evading this was to annexe a wider territory for theatre, to describe political pressure not in terms of closely-observed personal dilemmas, but to open up wide-ranging vistas of English society. To chuck overboard any concern with unities and pillage the entire stock of forms and conventions.[6]

Thus in *Claw* Barker had written three very disconnected acts, each of which was a buckled and beaten version of some existing form, put to the service of a very urgent didactic idea. Barker:

> I think on the whole the smash-and-grab we as a body of writers have carried out on areas previously hogged by Rattigan or Coward or Pinter and the collision we have forced between this and the already existing world of working-class realism, has sent blood racing through the veins of a sclerotic theatre. Where we have not won, however, is in bringing a crowd to witness the results of the accident.[7]

1976

At a meeting at the ICA in 1976 a full-scale broad-based campaign was launched to 'Fight Against Cuts in the Theatre'. An alarming number of theatres and theatre companies had been threatened with closure: Bolton TIE, Humberside Theatre Hull, Sheffield Crucible, Phoenix Leicester, the ICA, the Royal Court. The Theatre at New End in Hampstead had already (temporarily) closed. The outcome of the ICA meeting was FACT. As *The Stage* put it: 'Doing, not talking, therefore appears to be the order of the day from now on.'[1] One of FACT's first efforts was to join with AID (MP Renee Short's Arts in Danger campaign) at an all-party meeting at the House of Commons on 25 January 1977 where the issue of cuts in arts subsidy was discussed in the context of the government's Social Contract and other cuts in public services. The crisis was precipitated by the likelihood that the government allocation to the arts for 1977/78 would not be enough to match even the level of inflation, running then at 21 per cent. FACT representatives were feeling militant, suggesting the possibility of strikes and theatre occupations. In response to pressure, the government allocation for the arts turned out to be at least inflation-linked and the AID campaign died away. Not, however, FACT, which documented further cuts over the next six months. As the situation worsened, FACT attempted to organise a one-day strike in the entertainment industry. In favour of the strike FACT received over 700 signatures on a petition, plus letters and telegrams. An Equity AGM voted overwhelmingly in favour of strike action. But as a result of the internecine struggles within Equity, the Council refused to implement the AGM resolution and the strike never took place. But an occupation did – at the University Theatre Newcastle in the summer of 1977, and this did, unprecedentedly, receive official Equity support. The Newcastle occupation was a historic occasion and the theatre was re-opened as a consequence. As a front-line fighting force, FACT faded away after 1977, as the subsidy crisis became less acute. But the campaign was yet another manifestation of the collective strength of the politicised elements of the theatre.

There were two particular events in 1976 which illustrated attitudes towards political theatre at this point in the seventies. One was the visit to the Roundhouse of Peter Brook's International Centre for Theatre Research with their production of *The Ik*. The play was based in part on a book about the Ik, *The Mountain People*, by Colin Turnbull, an English anthropologist, and in part on a trip to Africa by the members of Brook's international centre. The Ik, the subject of the play, were a nomadic African tribe who were forced by the Ugandan government in 1946 to settle down into an agricultural life – a process normally taking centuries but which the Ik were expected to achieve in twenty years. They were herded onto an arid, infertile hillside, deprived of access to the green valleys, and had nearly been starved into extinction. Brook documented the effects on the Ik of their new life-style. On the level of information provided, the play was of some interest. But Brook did not document the causes, so the important political aspects of the plight of the Ik were ignored completely. As Kenneth Tynan pointed out in a revaluation of Brook in *Theatre Quarterly*,[2] a documentary film would have done the job better. As it was the Ik had been twice exploited, once by the Ugandan government for financial gain, and then by Brook for artistic gain. Brook was not taken seriously by the political theatre movement, nor, indeed, by many people outside it.

Across London at the ICA the real-life drama which came to surround the production of Roger Howard's *History of the Tenth Struggle* – an account of post-revolutionary China, spanning the years 1938 to 1971 and focusing on the developing and then disintegrating relationship between Mao and his minister Lin Piao – soon overshadowed the drama of the play itself. Purely by chance, the production coincided with the death of Chairman Mao and the cast of the play and the staff of the ICA started to receive death threats during the dress rehearsals. The company were faced with the decision whether to go ahead, and in a secret ballot, the majority voted to continue (though none was under contract to be killed), but one voted against. With emergency recasting and the offer of blanket security from the police (who took the threats seriously), the show eventually went on. Whilst no one involved (the play was directed by Malcolm Griffiths who was active in political theatre from the days of Portable Theatre) really knew why there had been such a 'drama', it seemed that someone, for the first time in decades, might have taken political theatre as seriously as it is taken in South Africa or Chile where it is censored, silenced and sometimes liquidated.

1976 was a big year for the theatre. It marked the opening of the new National Theatre on the South Bank – 128 years after the idea of a National Theatre was first conceived, 27 years after £1 million was first granted for it by Parliament, seven years after building began, two years after it was due to open. The Lyttleton Theatre (890 seats with an adjustable proscenium stage) opened on 16 March 1976; the larger, grander Olivier (open stage with revolve, a fan-shaped auditorium seating 1160) on 4 October 1976. The 'experimental' 400 seat 'arrangeable space' Cottesloe was, symptomatically, delayed until March 1977.

The opening of the National Theatre occurred in a blaze of publicity – more critical than congratulatory, but publicity nevertheless. The Queen came to open it, with the Duke of Edinburgh and Princess Margaret, greeted by the Mayor of Lambeth (the deprived inner London borough in which the ostentatious NT was located) and by Lord Cottesloe, Lord Rayne, Lord Olivier and Peter Hall (soon to be knighted). It was quite a cast, quite a performance.

With little comment, in the same year, almost coincidental with the opening of the Olivier, was the closing (temporarily) of the ICA theatre – an open space seating 150 at one end of the Institute of Contemporary Arts. The issues behind the opening of the National Theatre and the closing of the ICA Theatre – two ends of the theatre spectrum – illustrated in nutshells the 'politics of the theatre' in the seventies, in relation to aesthetics, audiences and subsidy.

Foco Novo, the theatre company started in 1972 by Roland Rees, Bernard Pomerance and David Aukin, also became the subject of some considerable controversy in 1976 with its production of *The Nine Days and Saltley Gates*, about the 1972 miners' strike celebrating the bi-centenary of the 1926 General Strike. As The *Daily Telegraph* reported:

The Government is handing out £18,000 to a theatre group about to tour the coal fields with a play that shows the virtues of militant trades unions. It is co-written by a Marxist and opens at Abertillery, South Wales, tomorrow. It shows how in the 1972 strike the miners got their revenge for their defeat in the 1926 strike.[3]

In the play's defence, John Hoyland, who co-wrote the play with Jon Chadwick, said to the *Telegraph*: 'Some of the characters are extremists and some are moderates. Neither side is presented as more worthwhile or better than the other. We are telling people what happened, not spreading propaganda.' And Don Hayward, Chief Executive of the South Wales Miners' Executive, which had collaborated on mounting the play, said: 'We hope the play will encourage people to be trades union conscious. It shows what can be done by a strong, militant union.'

The *Daily Telegraph* 'news' was picked up by other papers and a Conservative MP in Scotland, who kicked up a lot of fuss without ever having seen the play. The big question was why the Arts Council was subsidising a so-called left-wing play written by Marxists. The implied criticisms in the press led the Arts Council to 'investigate', with a letter to the Drama Panel advising all of its members to see the play. According to Roland Rees, artistic director of Foco Novo, 'the whole of the Arts Council came to see the play – right from the top'.[4] Rees thought in retrospect that the only ramifications had been the publicity and discussion it initiated, though many alternative theatre workers felt the incident was a worrying omen of potential repression.

The Nine Days and Saltley Gates actually came into being at the request of miners, as had the previous Foco Novo show *Arthur Horner* by Phil Woods. The President of the South Wales National Union of Miners, Dai Francis, had seen a pantomime directed by Rees at the Sherman Theatre in Cardiff. As a consequence, he wanted Foco Novo to do a play which the NUM could present themselves. The miners then suggested Arthur Horner as a suitable subject, as he spanned a period of time from the mid-twenties to after the war and saw the formation of the national union. It was the success of this venture that prompted Rees to think of doing a play about the 1926 General Strike, to coincide with the fiftieth anniversary. It was put to the executive committee of the Welsh miners and they voted twelve to one in favour.

Throughout the writing, the authors referred back to the miners with scenarios for discussion, and they met members of the National Executive of the NUM in London. As well as writing, John Hoyland was responsible for the bookings. Armed with letters of recommendation from Dai Francis and the National Executive, he went to Yorkshire to try to persuade them to put on the play:

> I just drove around the coalfields from pit to pit. I'd go to a pit, ask for the NUM office, walk in and say, 'I've got some people who want to put on a play.' A total stranger. I had tip-offs about the blokes who were good and how to approach them. Of course, they always talked. I'd tell them about the project and they'd talk about 1926 and 1972, and all that became material for the play.[5]

Again the result was a success:

> What evenings we had with that play around those clubs, in Yorkshire and Scotland particularly! The miners were out of their minds over it. They'd all be sitting in their clubs, tables piled with booze. They laughed, they cried ... the biggest cry was at the end when the General Strike got smashed.[6]

The Saltley Gates 'scandal' proved to be a storm in a teacup, but Foco Novo only did one more show directed at the Labour movement: *Tighten Your Belts*, again co-written by John Hoyland and Jon Chadwick.

There was another new company which was founded in 1976 – the socialist/feminist Monstrous Regiment. They were to work closely with Caryl Churchill. The work of both Monstrous Regiment and Caryl Churchill is dealt with in the following essays.

'... *the empty radicalism of metropolitan counter-cultural chic ... edging over into the dismissal of quality itself, as an authoritarian idea.*' Michael Kustow on the ICA, Guardian, 1976

The ICA Theatre

The Institute of Contemporary Arts, founded in 1947, moved to the Nash Terrace in The Mall behind Trafalgar Square, in 1968 when it opened as an arts centre with facilities for exhibitions, lectures, cinema and catering. In the late sixties – at the time of the hey-day of the Drury Lane Arts Lab – under the direction of Michael Kustow, it became identified with the emergence of the counter-culture and its associated arts activities. When the ICA Theatre opened in 1973, it was in the context of a policy appealing to the highbrow, intellectual sector of the middle class. In 1975, however, there was a radical change in the ICA's image, policy and programming when Mike Laye was appointed director of the theatre and began to present an ambitious repertoire of the best of alternative theatre and to attract new audiences. In twelve months, Laye turned the ICA into one of the liveliest alternative theatre venues in London, presenting over 60 companies to over 22,000 people, including children's theatre, an international experimental season and a socialist theatre season. His initiative created more work (and larger audiences) for more Arts Council subsidised companies than any other London venue. But Laye's tenure was short-lived. His adventurous programme was brought to an abrupt halt in circumstances which forced many people to conclude that an important platform for alternative theatre had been censored for political reasons.

The governing Council of the ICA decided in November 1976 to close the theatre and to dismiss the staff from the end of December. The reasons given were an overall deficit (of which the theatre was only one part of the many arts activities) of £25,000; a demand from the Arts Council (the subsidiser of the ICA as a whole) that the deficit should be cut back; and indications from the Arts Council that the grant for 1977/78 could not cover continuing loss on that scale. This was in fact the period prior to the cut-backs, and threatened closures on a national level that stimulated the FACT and AID campaigns.

On close scrutiny, however, the sums that seemed to necessitate the closure didn't add up very well: closing the theatre looked like saving at most £2500 of the total £25,000.

So, to save the theatre, the staff set up a fund-raising campaign which, within a month, matched the theatre's deficit and collected 2500 signatures on a petition to save the theatre. They felt that if the closure really was for economic reasons, then cancelling the deficit would logically mean the theatre could stay open. On the other hand, if the economic arguments were a subterfuge (as they suspected), then the theatre would be closed regardless. The answer came from the ICA's Chairman, Robert Loder, in a letter on 21 December 1976:

> The Council has every sympathy with the ... efforts you have made to mobilise support for saving the theatre programme in its existing form ... Nevertheless the Council ... are not able to change their decision.[1]

He added that he appreciated 'that the closing of the theatre programme adversely affects the presentation of small-scale theatre in central London'.[2]

There was obviously more to the closure of the ICA theatre than met the eye – certainly more than money. The key lay in Loder's own words when he referred to the 'theatre programme in its existing form'. The intention was clearly to end the specific theatre activities which had been taking place there over the past year.

The ICA theatre story (punctuated by some dramatic moments) dated from the appointment of Mike Laye. The first public indication of hostility towards the ICA's new image and function came in an article by Michael Kustow in *The Guardian* in the spring of 1976.[3] It was an innuendo-ridden piece alluding to 'anarchy', 'turbulence' and 'disorder in the house', which carefully avoided saying what, if anything, was wrong – though it was well-known that Mike Laye had tried to improve communications between the ICA Council and staff as well as the public. Kustow's piece referred nostalgically to the 'good old days' of the sixties, when, under his direction, the ICA had been a showcase for the very middle-class, intellectual tradition of the avant-garde. It regretted the changes that had turned the ICA into a gathering place much more in the experimental arts lab tradition of the sixties.

Certainly, there had developed a much more hospitable ambience, an air of informality, with the inventive use of partitions and colour, with a 'café' atmosphere in the restaurant area, with folk-singing entertainment, with a regular clientele who seemed less well-heeled, more casual than West End night-outers. And the ICA had acquired its distinct identity as a theatre, housing outside companies consistently and so regularly – both lunchtime and evening – that it was difficult to keep pace with the repertoire. In the 'Socialist Theatre Season' there had been a Gay Sweatshop lunchtime play and Brian Phelan's *Article Five* showing torture as an integral part of 'civilised' society, a play which had been commissioned and filmed for BBC TV and then cancelled. There had been Foco Novo's *The Nine Days and Saltley Gates*, the play about the 1972 miners' strike. There had been the Womens Theatre Group's *Work to Role* and Monstrous Regiment's *SCUM – Death, Destruction and Dirty Washing*, the play about the women of the 1871 Paris Commune which had introduced Monstrous Regiment as one of the exciting new companies of the seventies. CAST had performed *Samuel Keir Hardie Muggins*, followed by a discussion on the Labour Party and socialism, Broadside Mobile Workers Theatre had presented *Now You See It, Now You Don't*, their agitprop explanation of inflation, and the exiled Chilean actors group, Teatro Popular Chileno, did *Chile 11973*, about the defeat of the Allende government and conditions in the concentration camps after the coup. And there had been the *Realpolitik* surrounding the production of Roger Howard's play about Chairman Mao.

This was the ICA's new theatre programme, which Kustow described as 'the empty radicalism of metropolitan counter-cultural chic; automatic underdogism, mindless espousal of oppressed minorities (the elevation of homosexuality or Third World art into heroic undertakings *per se*), Pavlovian anti-elitism edging over into the dismissal of quality itself as an authoritarian idea'.[4] From the other side, however, it was regarded as an alternative, political (with a small 'p') policy in the best sense. But it was obviously a policy which the ICA Council wished to end with the 'closure' of the theatre.

That this was, indeed, the case – a purge, as it were, with the Arts Council 'passively' participating, inverting the liberal arguments it later used in support of North West Spanner, by saying it could not interfere with the policies of its clients – was made clear by the manner in which the decision to close the theatre was implemented. As *Tribune* reported at the time, Mike Laye arrived after the 'closure' to deal with his outstanding business to find that the management had made a 'clean sweep' in his absence, and indicated that his presence was not required. And there was the fact that the theatre immediately re-opened in January 1977 – significantly with a different programme and policy. Finally, there was the fact that large amounts of money were spent over the next two years in improving the ICA theatre facilities, hardly an indication of financial crisis. And the ICA returned (eventually under the artistic direction of John Ashford) to being the bland, arguably elitist arts centre of its early years.

'I'd rather have a bad night at Bootle ... I would run about twenty-five miles from the National Theatre.' John McGrath, Theatre Quarterly, 1975

The National Theatre

Coinciding with the controversial closure of the ICA theatre was – at the other end of the spectrum – the equally controversial opening of the new National Theatre. To mark the occasion the dozens of alternative theatre companies who were deprived of the ICA venue – the member companies of ITC and TACT – organised a campaign ending with a demonstration under the banner 'A National Theatre ... For whom? At what cost? At whose expense?' They pointed out that there were *two* national theatres:

> One stands on the South Bank of the Thames, cost £16 million to build, is subsidised to the tune of £2 million per year and will eventually employ 500 staff and just over 100 actors. The other exists in workshops, community centres and short-life premises all over the country. It performs everywhere and anywhere from parks and art galleries to schools, trades union halls and arts centres, taking theatre to people where they want to see it, helping them to celebrate, to organise campaigns, to enjoy themselves, bringing old and new ideas to their notice. This national theatre, using existing buildings often many years old, is subsidised to the tune of £700,000, employs over 1000 people and is still expanding.[1]

At this stage, the alternative theatre movement was not advocating the 'demolition' of the new National Theatre (it was too late anyway), but 'demanding that the second national theatre, the Fringe Theatre, should be considered for subsidy on the same basis, that of its needs and vast potential'.[2]

When the National Theatre was due to open in 1974 (before the endless building delays and escalation of costs), Michael Kustow, who left the ICA to become one of the NT directors, had written to 'fringe' companies expressing a desire that the NT should 'reflect the nation' and inviting them to perform on the South Bank. It seemed a generous gesture, but the reply from most alternative theatre companies was 'no'. Their view was best summed up by John McGrath when he said 'better a bad night at Bootle than a good one at the National'.

There were in fact very real ideological reasons for the indifference of fringe theatre and their polite refusals. Performance on the South Bank was a fundamental contradiction for many community and political companies. How could companies – with work created for a particular audience – meaningfully uproot from that audience? They felt too, that to direct funds to the National Theatre, who would then *indirectly* fund the companies with fees, would be to undermine their campaign for direct revenue-funding from the Arts Council. They concluded, and communicated to Michael Kustow, the following:

> The contradiction in the National Theatre's desire to involve us 'at the outset' is that we were not involved 'at the outset' in the decision to spend the enormous sums of money required to build the South Bank complex – a sum of money that could, in our view, have been much more productively spent on increasing the grant-aid made available to our companies to an adequate level for the work to function properly, without making undue demands on our staff, regarding poor wages and conditions, such as they now have to put up with.[3]

And they wondered whether the National Theatre's interest in their work was a recognition of their vitality and relevance, whether the NT needed them more than they needed the NT.

The story of the National Theatre was much longer than the ICA's – more an epic novel than a short story. Historically, the physical concept altered radically over the 150-year period of gestation, in response to events and particularly to technological developments. But by the time it was built, the concept of its role in the world of theatre, not to mention society at large, had hardly changed from that proposed by Henry Irving and Matthew Arnold in the nineteenth century – as an independent public corporation and as a means of cultural evangelism respectively. Society, however, had changed between 1848 when Effringham Wilson first put forward a *Proposition for a 'House for Shakespeare'* and 1976 when the NT opened, particularly between 1948, when the first National Theatre Bill passed through the post-war Parliament, and 1976 – indeed, between 1969 when building began and 1976. When John Elsom wrote in his *History of the National Theatre* that 'while the theatre drifted, society moved somewhat away from it',[4] he was referring to the 1870's. How much more true of the 1970s. As a cultural concept the National Theatre did not reflect the changes, except in a token fashion with the Cottesloe and with Kustow's approaches to fringe theatre, for example.

When Harley Granville Barker and William Archer campaigned for a National Theatre at the turn of the century, nationalism had a significance it no longer held in the seventies. Then was a time when things national were enshrined in monuments. In the early sixties (a period of economic growth and national self-satisfaction) when the National Theatre Company was formed under the direction of Laurence Olivier, one company representing the 'best' of the nation's theatre was still a credible concept. In the late sixties, when building began, 'theatre' still meant theatre *buildings* – conspicuous consumption (and nationalism) in concrete. By the mid-seventies things had changed so much that the new National Theatre building – and the company and its structure – was seen by some as anachronistic, regarded by others as extinct even before it opened.

It was certainly a technological miracle – though with technical teething troubles still by the end of the seventies. But in many ways it was still rooted in the nineteenth century. Laurence Olivier was a classic actor-manager; Peter Hall a classic director-manager. The rigid hierarchies of the NT's internal structure were precisely what the new theatre movement had reacted against and created alternatives to. The bricks-and-mortar boom of the sixties had become, in recession's retrospect, a much-questioned policy, creating the kind of situation described by Peter Hall in *The Observer*: 'The NT building alone, before anything is put on the stage, gobbles up more than 33 per cent of our present total subsidy.'[5] By this time, the distinction between subsidising *theatre* as against theatre *buildings* had become crucial.

Criticism of the National Theatre did not come only from the alternative theatre. The building itself came under attack from *The Architectural Review* and *The Architect's Journal*:

> Earnest, gloomy and depressing ... Like a hotel foyer at floor level and a car park at ceiling level ... The logic is impeccable but the results disappointing ... Where in a city has concrete ever weathered beautifully? ... reminiscent of an airport ... nowhere to put an empty glass ... one is overwhelmed by architecture ... the leit-motif of grey, wirebrushed concrete has become an unimaginative cliché.[6]

There was specific criticism of the lighting in the foyers from Peter Hay, a theatre consultant: 'It is in many areas quite inadequate from a purely functional point of view ... one cannot read a programme or tell whether the British Rail sandwiches are of yesterday's vintage or the day before! One can hardly find one's way to the men's lavatories without the aid of a pocket torch ...'⁷ And criticism of one auditorium: 'From the balcony one strains and does not hear ... The actor seems very distant and, in fact he is. From the proscenium to the back wall measures 20 metres. In the immense Drury Lane, seating 2283 as against the Lyttleton's 890, it is 25 metres. To achieve the situation of an audience sitting full square to the stage, the proscenium has had to be made immensely wide ...'⁸

The NT was also criticised for its administrative structure and for waste of money by Vivian Nixon, formerly manager at the Victoria Theatre, Stoke on Trent:

> The National Theatre's management outlook and its response to financial accountability are alien to much of the profession it purports to lead. Designers spend on one production more than the full year's grant received by two thirds of the other theatre companies in England ... Every time an annual budget is exceeded, supplementary grants are given. The underlying assumption being that, as a prestige symbol, the Government wouldn't dare to close them down. Until the Treasury presents the National with that possibility, nothing will ever change ... Most of the actors, stage managers, wardrobe mistresses, box office staff, have worked in other less wealthy theatres. They have been involved in the struggle to make ends meet, which engenders a concern about the National's indiscriminate use of both men and materials. But the hierarchical structure concentrates all real decision-making at the very top.⁹

Nixon was 'cost executive' at the new National. He resigned.

And the NT was criticised for its policy and its productions from many quarters. Steve Grant in *Time Out* was typical:

> The National Theatre shows no capacity whatever for genuinely transforming the theatregoing practices of the masses, nor does it seem interested in promoting new or experimental talent ... Why has it consistently refused to present the best of foreign and British fringe companies? Isn't the work of the Bread and Puppet Theatre, Tenjosajiki or Pip Simmons as much a reflection of the best of world theatre as Ibsen or Jonson in the Olivier?¹⁰

And Grant concluded that 'its function has been largely superseded by the RSC's brilliance and the Royal Court's imagination'.

Criticism hit the banner headlines with the publication of John Elsom's *The History of the National Theatre*, with *The Evening News* heralding 'A National Disaster'. Elsom's book was, in fact, a model of liberality, with constrained and constructive criticism – documenting the history of the NT and including information about the replacement of Olivier with Peter Hall ('When Olivier left, the National was an excellent and buoyant company. Under Hall I feel it is being led on a disastrous course that could ultimately ruin all of British theatre.'[11]); the administrative and artistic staff who were either dismissed or resigned ['These include Patrick Donnell, Anthony Easterbrook (policy committee members) and directors Jonathan Miller and Michael Blakemore. The last of Olivier's old guard to leave was associate director Blakemore. Hall offered him a contract that would have guaranteed him no more than £20 a week. The people from Olivier's reign who opposed Hall are, for a variety of reasons, no longer at the National'][12]. And there was the matter of Peter Hall's large and secret salary, the size being less important than its secrecy. The implication was that a dictatorial directorship of three major theatres was perhaps not the best, and Elsom suggested an alternative – an 'intendant' on the lines of continental theatres.

A far more radical alternative was also proposed:

> The building is there but ... its function and use could be radically reconceived. It need not be Peter Hall's and the National Theatre Company's sole facility, with the attendant costs of over-subsidising that one company. It could even be used as a multi-purpose building in quite different ways from those Peter Hall proposes (which is to invite companies to perform under his roof and his overheads). It could, for example, be managed and used jointly by a number of different theatre companies whose different needs could be fulfilled by the variety and expanse of facility ... In practice Peter Hall might be the artistic director of a part of the facility presenting the kind of theatre he does so brilliantly in, say, the Olivier. Then let Joint Stock run the Lyttleton; let 7:84 run the Cottesloe; let Welfare State have the foyers – all for limited periods of time, on a rota with an almost endless list of other artistic directors and theatre companies. Let them all rotate in the use of the different spaces, so Peter Hall would have his turn as artistic director of the foyers, and so forth.[13]

This was a deliberately provocative proposal when it was first put forward in *Theatre Quarterly* in 1975, much less so when it was further advanced in *Tribune* in 1976 and 1978. In August 1978 *The Guardian* reported that 'Sir Peter is thinking about a series of arrangements by which responsibilities are shared, with different associate directors taking responsibility for different theatres.'[14] It was suggested that Peter Hall would then concentrate on experimental studio work in the Cottesloe (which was not metaphorical miles from artistically directing the foyers, after all). As it happened, the *radical* changes were rumours, and introducing new blood in the form of director

Michael Rudman from the Hampstead Theatre and up-grading director Bill Bryden, already there, was what actually materialised. But it indicated that a collective management of the National Theatre – a way of letting the nation's theatre define the National – was not simply a fantasy from the left.

The real point of such proposals was a reflection of the fundamental political issues: subsidy (redistribution of the theatre wealth), aesthetics (kinds of theatre) and audiences (where it is performed). Or in the words of the alternative theatre movement: A National Theatre for whom, at what cost, at whose expense? These issues were largely unresolved at the end of the seventies, but still in the central arena of debate. And perhaps symptomatically there was the launching of a 'National Theatre Enquiry' by the Arts Council in July 1978: 'to examine the operation of the National Theatre now and in the future, the financial implications of current policies and practices and the level of funding, with particular reference to the operational and maintenance requirements of the National Theatre building; and to make recommendations.'[15] Only the eighties would tell whether the recommendations would be a sufficiently radical reflection of the realities of seventies theatre, or more of a cosmetic nature.

'We see ourselves not as seeking to reproduce bourgeois ideology, but to undermine it, to challenge it ... the personal is political.' Susan Todd, Monstrous Regiment, 1978[1]

Monstrous Regiment

Monstrous Regiment – the name comes from a sixteenth-century pamphlet by John Knox entitled 'The First Blast of the Trumpet Against the Monstrous Regiment of Women' – was started in 1975 by a group of women who had been working in the fringe and the establishment theatre, and who had come to realise the limited opportunities for women in all areas of the theatre, including socialist and political theatre. The women were first and foremost committed feminists, but they were also committed socialists (three members of the company until 1978 were members of the Communist Party) and both perspectives informed their aims as a theatre company:

> In Monstrous Regiment we are engaged in trying to shift consciousness in the area of women's relation to society.

The means by which Monstrous Regiment tried to achieve their aims involved conscious experimentation with old forms and a search for new ones, 'which integrate with and reflect our perception of the world as women, and the often very dislocated nature of women's experience now.' And the company's concern with form was reflected in their productions and their methods of working.

Their first production was *SCUM – Death, Destruction and Dirty Washing*, a touring show 'set in a laundry in Paris in 1870, about the Paris Commune and the part that women had played in those revolutionary events'.

> Our strongest impetus in SCUM was a desire to convey a kind of passionate sense of the joyousness of women's solidarity. A joyous quality, within the framework of a set of larger political events of quite wide significance within the socialist tradition as a whole.

The company were presented with a script by writers C. G. Bond and Claire Luckham – 'a large, rambling, heavily padded naturalistic kind of script and we decided to use it in some way. But we started off by throwing the whole of the second act out of the window, because there was no way that this nice, but cumbersomely architectural second act could give any expression to the way we felt the women experienced the real emotional and political change at the point when the Commune was established.' They wanted a second act that said it was possible to change in very important dynamic ways. And with endless discussions they constructed a second half 'that showed the rapidity of the impetus of those events and a sense of the possibility of a radical change of consciousness occurring for the women'. They used the existing plot and the characters, though they elaborated a lot of the characters, always emphasising the possibilities of a change of consciousness. This approach set a precedent for future productions.

As none of the women of the Commune was making strategic political decisions (nor were they in the direct line of political fire, though they were caught up in the political crisis), it was necessary to find a means of conveying the political events from a personal point of view:

> There was a device used to bring the area of major power politics into the play, a soliloquy device in which an aristocratic French woman broke into the vigorous and very active group scenes, and talked about what was going on at Versailles. She ate all the time, nibbling as she was talking. It was unlikely that political figures would come into the laundry and have relationships with those women, so an alternative had to be found. And the formal dislocation of the solution pointed up the real gap between the arena in which political decisions were made and the experience and the challenges and the struggles of the people whom those political decisions affected. I think they found a very interesting way of doing it.[2]

Monstrous Regiment's second show was a play by Caryl Churchill, *Vinegar Tom*, about seventeenth-century witchcraft.[3] As a company Monstrous Regiment were pre-occupied with the subject, as was Churchill. They had several meetings, read some books and then Churchill presented them with 'a very nicely tailored terse piece of work, with a very clear through line, quite clear character definition, considerable depth of analysis, a really nicely made piece'. Monstrous Regiment wanted to present the material 'in terms of the economic pressures and the role of women in that society' and Churchill tried to accommodate. With some considerable success. The contemporary parallels were implicit except in the songs which interspersed the scenes. These were deliberately and provocatively modern:

Quite consciously, in a very perverse manner, we decided to break the form completely apart by putting songs between the scenes. And though the rest of the play was set in the 1640's, performers appeared in their own contemporary clothes for the songs which were really very aggressive and extremely difficult to communicate. We didn't want to allow the audience to ever get completely immersed in the stories of the women in the play. We wanted to make them continually aware of our presence, of our relationship to the material, which was combative, anguished. The songs had to contain what we sensed as a connection between the past of the play and our present experience.

From the beginning, Monstrous Regiment intended to use music in an experimental fashion. 'We had been very conscious of music having a life of its own, not just being used decoratively. But we have done it differently in every show. We have tried the song within the action, or the song that comments on the action or draws some parallels. We have tried many different ways of giving music a status within theatrical performance. Our musicians have had a lot of responsibility in our work.'[4]

Their next show *Kiss and Kill* was devised entirely within the company, scripted by Susan Todd and Ann Mitchell, a play about 'violence between the sexes and what the springs of that violence were, and intended to show how new models of social and sexual relationships between men and women, between adults and children, might be sketched, implied, suggested':

Connections between romanticism and violence, connections between relationships of dependence and violence, connections between men's militaristic emotional heritage and violence.

The result was a dislocated, rambling piece, showing such situations as a wife treated by her husband as a piece of furniture until she walks out of housework and into 'real work', an ex-wife receiving obscene telephone calls from a hurt husband, a mistress manicuring herself for a married-man lover. But the play was deliberately contradictory in its form. The company wanted to 'imply quite different sorts of relationships from those we are accustomed to seeing'.

There's one sequence of scenes in the play where a woman is seen in bed with two different men. Originally those scenes were separated by another – she was in bed with one bloke, there was a scene, and then she was in bed with another bloke. Audiences would say things like 'I thought she was a different character', although it was clear she was the same character, she had the same dressing gown on, for example. Even at that level it was impossible for audiences to accept that a woman might have two lovers. We wanted to suggest, without making a production number about it, that different structures of relationships are possible, that a multiplicity of relationship was possible between men and women, men and men, women and women.

The concept of different relationships extended to those of adults with children: 'I was quite anxious that the various children who figure in the play should end up not with their own parents, but in the hands of some other adult with whom they'd had a relationship.' In the end, the company found that audiences were confused. 'Whether it was because it was written badly or whether it was because they were unaccustomed to making new assumptions' the company couldn't be sure.

With their next project *Floorshow*, co-written by Caryl Churchill, Bryony Lavery, Michelene Wandor and David Bradford, they embarked on a completely new area and a new form – cabaret:

> It was an attempt to use a working-class form, a form that's used in clubs, in pubs, in the kind of places where working-class people go to be entertained. It's often very reactionary in content, so the challenge was to use that form in a way that challenged the audience's pre-conceptions about the relation of women to stand-up comedy, and their own sexist assumptions.

Certainly cabaret with its girlie orientation and glitter and its stock-in-trade of wife and mother-in-law jokes is traditionally anti-feminist, but Monstrous Regiment managed to turn the sexist content inside out. There were throwaways like 'Dober-person pinschers' and 'cock-pecked wives' and 'My boss is a woman ... is he really?' And there were sketches on female bus drivers, house-husbands and women wolf-whistlers which exposed the bedrock of sexual dis-crimination. One of the funnier sketches was a father's description of a day of child-minding his three kids, feeding them fish fingers (like ice lollies), slapping them about and slipping out for a quick drink. It was funny: but if a mother had delivered the same patter, she would probably have been regarded with horror.

To crack the form of cabaret and to inject a different sort of content, the company had to be very aggressive and dare 'not to be nice' – which they regarded as a challenge. And they made use of untapped areas of feminine experience:

> ... material drawn from the kind of subterranean female humour that exists, but that is never made public, the kind of humour between women that often occurs in factories. Jokes against men – often quite nasty jokes against men.

Monstrous Regiment followed *Floorshow* with another cabaret in
1978 called *Time Gentlemen Please*, a piece of slick, sophisticated
entertainment performed with exceptional polish, but weak on
content and feminist bite and sabotaging its intentions by reinforcing
its stereotypes. On this occasion they were less successful at
manipulating the form, more controlled by it. By the end of 1978
they were working again with a writer, this time with David Edgar
co-writing with Susan Todd: *Teendreams* opened in 1979. It shared
similarities of approach with *Kiss and Kill*, and also some of the
problems. It was a retrospective view of the seventies in which the
heroine moved from the heady days of 1968 (they meet at the Demo,
he whispers sweet dialectics in her ear and they walk off into the
sit-in) to disillusionment and despair in 1978 (we thought we could
change people, we were wrong). But the treatment of the material
had more in common with *Love Story* and *West Side Story* than
with Edgar's *Destiny* or Monstrous Regiment's *SCUM*. The
audience were asked to question the convictions of left politics over
the past ten years without the substance to warrant that questioning.
It was not obvious how – or why – the heroine/teacher's relationship
with her teenage students tipped them to suicide and vandalism;
the reasons suggested in the play – a need for consumerist props
and romantic fantasy, without which they had no identity – were
presented too glibly to be truly credible. The tone, too, was of
unbalanced bleeding-heart feminism – all 'woe is woman and what
a rotten world with all those beastly men'. But one of the pitfalls
of experimentation is the occasional right to fail. And, despite ups
and downs, by 1978 Monstrous Regiment had established a strong
identity as a socialist/feminist company and a deservedly high
reputation for the quality of their work.

'What politicised me was being ... a wife ... at home with small children.' Caryl Churchill, 1979[1]

Caryl Churchill

Like many women Caryl Churchill's political consciousness came slowly and subjectively, and grew out of her own personal experience rather than as a response to public political events. Churchill: 'I didn't really feel a part of what was happening in the sixties. During that time I felt isolated. I had small children and was having miscarriages. It was an extremely solitary life. What politicised me was being discontent with my own way of life – of being a barrister's wife and just being at home with small children.' And the most politicising event was – with her husband – changing her life-style, when her husband left the bar and started working for a law centre: 'We did not want to shore up a capitalist system we didn't like.' And there was 'that decision of having no more children', when, after another miscarriage, her husband had a vasectomy. And there was the packing up lock, stock and barrel for six months, three in Africa and three on Dartmoor, where she wrote *Objections to Sex and Violence*: 'me living with David and coping with things so that he could work for ten years, so why didn't he take time off to do what I wanted to do?' Like Edward Bond, Churchill came only gradually to be able to intellectualise what was always an intuitive socialist (and feminist) perspective – to analyse and to understand her own personal experience in terms of class society. Churchill: 'My attitude then was entirely to do with self-expression of my own personal pain and anger. It wasn't thought out.'

And she remained in 1979 still reticent about talking about politics with a capital 'P'. 'If pushed to labels, I would be prepared to take on both socialist and feminist, but I always feel very wary.' She said she still had 'a massive sense of my own political uneducatedness – a feeling of having started personally and emotionally and still groping towards finding what that means in political terms.'

But if political commitment is measured by the adage of actions speaking louder than words, then Churchill rated high. Not just with the content of her stage plays, but with the stances she took, for example, against the BBC's censorship in 1978 of her TV play *The Legion Hall Bombing* – an edited transcript of the trial and conviction in 1976 of Willie Gallagher who was sentenced to twelve years imprisonment and who was then in the sixth week of a hunger strike at Long Kesh – a play intended to draw attention to the juryless 'Diplock Courts' in Northern Ireland. The BBC had intervened at the eleventh hour and re-written the voice-over prologue to the play and cut an epilogue. Requests to consult over the cuts had been ignored, as well as suggestions that the play might go out uncut but with a disclaimer that the commentary did not represent the BBC's editorial viewpoint. The BBC claimed they had been advised the play might aggravate tensions in Northern Ireland and had therefore decided to 'tone down' the commentary at beginning and end. According to the BBC:

> The feeling was that what was needed was an explanation that would tell the public the situation of the trial factually. The objection to the opening as written was that it was very opinionated. It was less concerned with fact than with opinions about rightness.[2]

It was a case of censorship so blatant that it hit the newspaper headlines and prompted the Defence of Literature and the Arts Society to condemn it as a 'perversion of art to serve the purpose of political orthodoxy' and to ask writers and directors to withdraw their services from the BBC until its executives provided an impartial system of appealing against their censorship decisions.

As originally written, the prologue read:

> This is a British court in Northern Ireland. It is different from any court in England. In 1972 a committee was set up under Lord Diplock, an English judge, to find ways of dealing with terrorists other than by internment without trial, which was causing widespread disapproval. According to the Diplock Committee, it was difficult to get convictions in the courts, because of the intimidation of potential witnesses and the difficulty of finding impartial jurors for sectarian crimes. They therefore recommended a different kind of trial for political offences, which was adopted under the Northern Ireland Emergency Provisions Act 1973. There is no jury. The judge sits alone. And the rules of evidence have been altered so that a confession is allowed as evidence even if it was obtained by threats or force.

This was the opinionated, non-factual commentary to which the BBC objected. The following was the version they wrote on behalf of the author:

This is a special criminal court in Northern Ireland. It is different from the normal criminal courts in Northern Ireland and elsewhere in the UK. In 1972 a commission was set up under Lord Diplock, an English judge, to find ways of bringing terrorists to justice. The main problem for the courts in Northern Ireland had been the intimidation of witnesses and jurors and the finding of impartial jurors. The Diplock Commission recommended a modified form of trial for terrorist offences which was adopted under an Act of Parliament passed in Westminster in 1973. Under this Act a judge may admit as evidence a confession obtained under intense interrogation. There is no jury. The judge sits alone.

The play's epilogue had been completely removed. It read:

> The Diplock Courts were set up to make it easier to get convictions, and they have been successful. Recent research at Queen's University Belfast shows that the rate of acquittals in these courts has dropped steadily each year. If courts can accept unsigned statements put forward by the police with no corroborative evidence and reject the evidence of a defence witness without explanation it is reasonable to ask whether it is worthwhile for the defence to put a case at all. The courts have a tradition of independence, but at the same time they carry out the will of Parliament. In peaceful times the role of the courts is generally accepted. In times of stress their role may change.

Bernard Gallagher, Willie Gallagher's father, was coming to London for the screening of the play and was detained for 36 hours under the Prevention of Terrorism Act, in order, he said, to prevent his comments on the play. Caryl Churchill and director Roland Joffe tried to prevent the censorship. When they were unsuccessful, they removed their names from the credits.

Churchill was diffident about the function of political theatre and her function as a political playwright. 'I'm not sure what it all means,' she said, 'I just do it.'

Churchill started writing radio plays in the early sixties, having written some plays as a student which she described as 'broadly groping towards anti-capitalist plays'. The radio plays, said Churchill, 'tended to be about a bourgeois middle-class life and the destruction of it.' There was *Identical Twins*, played by the same 'voice'. One of the characters was a landlord – a theme in many of Churchill's plays. *Not Enough Oxygen*, a play about ecology, was set in the future, in which some young people plan to set fire to themselves – 'sort of to do with the Vietnam protests at the time'. *The Judge's Wife* was written for television – 'the last of the self-destructing plays, because I was self-destructing reality by then and it wasn't necessary to do it in the plays'. Churchill described the play as rather like Howard Barker's *Stripwell*, about a judge and his wife. The judge sentences a man to prison and when he comes out he shoots the judge. The wife is very critical of their whole way of life, and after the death of her husband claims that he had been disillusioned with his role and had deliberately given oppressive sentences in order to inflame opposition, that he had deliberately gone to his death with the young man. And there had been a radio play called *Henry's Past*, 'about someone coming to terms with awful events in his past and yet able to live in the present'.

Landlords and tenants, time and the past, madness and sanity were recurrent themes in Churchill's work. *Schreber's Nervous Illness*, written for radio and made into a lunchtime play at the Kings Head, was based on one of Freud's case histories, about a schizophrenic who at the end of his life 'wrote these amazingly intelligent memoirs about his illness – talking about being a woman and that God was using him for an alien purpose'.

Owners, Churchill's first major stage play produced at the Royal Court Theatre Upstairs in 1972, was about housing, but combined personal preoccupations – 'coping with time' – with a perspective of things on a larger scale, 'with a more political view'. Churchill:

> I wrote it in three days. I'd just come out of hospital after a particularly gruesome late miscarriage. Still quite groggy and my arm ached because they'd given me an injection that didn't work. Into it went for the first time a lot of things that had been building up in me over a long time, political attitudes as well as personal ones.

Objections to Sex and Violence produced at the Royal Court in 1975 concerned a middle-class woman coming to political consciousness and trying to break away from her class roots. The heroine has been seduced by anarchists, and is somehow involved with and committed to indiscriminate civilian bombings, though the cause is never specified. Her friends and family attempt to woo her back to non-violence, without success. In the play Churchill equated repressive sexuality with violence. In one scene a middle-aged couple are on their annual seaside holiday. The man slips away from his wife, sets up his deck chair and settles down with his porn magazine to masturbate. His wife catches him in the act, discovers his pathetic little source of pleasure (the magazine), tears it to shreds, tries to burn it and ends up burying it in the sand. Later the man comforts a lonely old woman on the beach, but can't resist the temptation to expose himself. It was poignant. But the development was rather

simplistic: sexually repressed middle-aged man becomes National
Front flasher, middle-class intellectual turns terrorist because sex
is better with working-class lover. Churchill regarded it as her least
successful play. It had been triggered by Wilhelm Reich's ideas about
sexual oppression and fascism – by the Angry Brigade and Patty
Hearst. The attraction of terrorism was connected with her preoccupations with images of destruction, and angry rejection, with
being trapped by class and work.

The play marked a transition for her from writing in isolation
to meeting other writers and theatre workers, which Churchill
regarded as important (she was instrumental in founding the Theatre
Writers Union), and to writing with theatre companies, specifically
Joint Stock and Monstrous Regiment. In 1976, using a workshop
approach, she wrote *Light Shining in Buckinghamshire* with Joint
Stock, set in 1647, about the Levellers and the Ranters and their
struggle with Cromwell. The original idea for *Light Shining* had in
fact been the Crusades, but 'we were getting into rather a mess
thinking about people clanking about in armour'. Churchill and Joint
Stock were taken with the idea of the millennium and ended up with
the Commonwealth rather than the Crusades, but also with an
emphasis on the religious nature of the revolutionary feelings at the
time. Churchill:

> We had debates in the workshops and talks about specific historical
> characters. We read a lot and talked about moments of amazing change
> and extraordinariness in our own lives, things turned upside down.
> We got ourselves fluent with the Bible, so the whole area was opened
> up and everyone knew what it was about.

'More Light Shining in Buckinghamshire' was the title of a Digger
pamphlet from 1649 arguing the lack of logic in hanging a man for
stealing a loaf from the man who stole the land which the hanged
man had worked to produce the loaf which . . . etc. – in other words
the vicious house-that-jack-built circle of capitalism. The play
focused on the seventeenth-century conditions of working-class and
ruling class life which led to England's great revolution-that-never-
was. It traced the lives of six people, all on the boot end of an
economic system of privileged and poor, documenting how they rose
up against the system.

Churchill emphasised the 'millennium' element of the uprising and
portrayed the English Civil War more as a Medieval Crusade than
a Marxist revolution. Jerusalem did not get founded in England's
green and pleasant land. The break-away faction ended up likened

to hash-smoking hippies, dropouts wondering why Christ (Godot?) didn't turn up, thinking that maybe he had, and they'd missed him. The revolutionaries (the leaders who betrayed the cause) became, with the Restoration, the new squires, the new ruling class. Churchill suggested the religious non-dialetic was ultimately influential in defeating the possibilities of real revolution. Churchill:

> A revolutionary belief in the millennium went through the Middle Ages and broke out strongly in England at the time of the civil war. Soldiers fought the king in the belief that Christ would come and establish heaven on earth. What was established instead was an authoritarian parliament, the massacre of the Irish, the development of capitalism . . . [3]

The play was an attempt to show the other side of history, that under-written in the history books. The revolutionary-fervour-that-failed appealed to Churchill, as did the parallels with the present:

> The simple 'Cavaliers and Roundheads' history taught at school hides the complexity of the aims and conflicts of those to the left of Parliament. We are told of a step forward to today's democracy but not of a revolution that didn't happen; we are told of Charles and Cromwell, but not of the thousands of men and women who tried to change their lives. Though nobody now expects Christ to make heaven on earth, their voices are surprisingly close to us. [4]

With Monstrous Regiment, also in 1976, she wrote *Vinegar Tom*, a play about seventeenth-century witchcraft but with contemporary songs. The play was very much about sexual politics: Churchill's witches were shown to have been scapegoats of poverty, pseudo-religious persecution, superstition and fear – hanged because of their sexuality and their place in the economic pecking order. The modern parallels were implicit, but extremely powerful. There was the case of Alice Noakes and her mother, poor enough to starve, not quite poor enough to be stigmatised by being on the parish's social security.

Mother Noakes tries to borrow a bit of yeast from her ambitious neighbour Margery, a woman so sexually frigid and self-righteous that the butter she churns and which won't 'come' (sexual imagery pervaded the play) wouldn't melt in her mouth. Margery refuses. There was the case of Susan, the young married woman with one toddler, one child on the breast and another on the way. She opts reluctantly for a 'back-street abortion' which leaves her physically sick and mentally deranged with guilt.

There was the case of Miss Betty, daughter of the manor, about to be married off to a man of her father's choosing. For refusing, she is locked up, bled with leeches and about to be charged with witchcraft for her independent stance. There was the case of Jack, Margery's husband, so besotted with an unrequited passion for Alice, that he can't make it with Margery. In the hysteria of the witch-hunt he concludes that Alice has bewitched his private parts.

There was the case of the 'cunning woman' whose herbal home pharmacy is as busy as a GP's surgery. All the characters consult her and she is hanged for providing a community health service. There was the case of Mr Packer, the witch-hunter, who in the name of God prods women's private parts with sharp metal in search of the devil's mark. And there was his 'Goody' helper who assists in the obstetrical torture because the wages are good. At one point the cunning woman explains the art of sinking without drowning. The play showed that sinking without drowning was the art of survival as a woman, whether in the seventeenth or the twentieth century.

Vinegar Tom and *Light Shining in Buckinghamshire* marked Churchill's departure from the expression of personal anger and pain to the expression of a public political perspective, which was itself the source of the anger and pain. The group approach on the part of the two companies helped her in this development: 'Discussing with Monstrous Regiment helped me towards a more objective and analytical way of looking at things. Their attitude towards witches was in terms of economic pressure and the role of women in that society. They ensured that I approached the witchcraft in a cool analytical frame of mind. I was more aware than I had been before of what I was doing.'

In 1977, Churchill's *Traps* was produced at the Royal Court Theatre Upstairs. It was a departure in style from the specifically political, group-created work in that it centred on the personal relationships of six people in a room, in the city, in the country, in the present, in the past. Churchill posited that everything was 'real while it happened', but the play effectively questioned realities. Churchill described the play as an 'impossible object' and compared it to a painting by Escher 'where the objects can exist ... on paper, but would be impossible in life'. *Traps* showed Churchill to be a writer of rich, imaginative talent.

Churchill worked again with Joint Stock in 1978/79 on *Cloud Nine* starting again with workshop sessions. The research was fairly limited, and included Churchill looking through some children's books about explorers, 'just to confirm this was the era we wanted to be in' and a talk in rehearsals from a man who had been in India. Otherwise it was a matter of everyone involved 'exploring' themselves with the help of background readings in sexual politics. Churchill:

'People talked about themselves and their own lives. They talked about their sexuality, and we did improvisations about stereotypes. One person would have a stereotype they would lay on another, and the first person would find themselves becoming like that – how people would expect them to be. A wife expects her husband to be dominating and he expects her to be hysterical. We made those things happen.' Caryl Churchill wrote the script, but a lot came out of the workshops (as it had done with *Light Shining*), 'and the company took a lot of responsibility for what it was like and what it was saying'.

What it was saying was strong medicine. The first act was set in colonial Africa in the nineteenth century ('it was deliberately historically imprecise'), where restless natives are shaking the foundations of Her Majesty's dominions. But it is a domestic drama that is acted out, the foundations of 'the family' that are crumbling, as much as the empire. The second act was set in a London park in the present, but with the same characters – 100 years on in history, 25 years older (yet again Churchill was 'playing' with time). The disjointing juxtaposition – shattering all unity of time and place – was what finally married the 'external' and the 'internal'.

Churchill's real coup, though – thematic and theatrical – came from having a man play the mother in the first act, a doll her daughter, a girl her son, and a white the black servant. And in the second act a grown man plays a little girl – thereby conclusively and very comically exposing double sexual standards. Having set her scenes, Churchill then hilariously up-ended expectations. Clive, the colonial governor and rigidly authoritarian husband and father, keeps his wife subjected but has a 24-hour hard-on for a neighbouring lady of independent manner and means. The wife pines romantically and unrequitedly for the heroic explorer Harry Bagley, a closet gay whose idea of conquering the natives is not quite the same as his Queen's, and who is having it off with the servant and Clive's young son (who prefers dolls to daddy). In order to salvage his honour, Bagley conveniently marries the governess (herself a lesbian in love with the wife) at the suggestion of Clive, whose absolute horror at a homosexual advance from his friend is one of the high points of the play. All the latent sexuality comes to the surface in the second act and Churchill shows her characters starting to come to terms with themselves. The final moment when the mother of the first act and the mother of the second (in fact, one and the same person) meet and embrace was an extraordinary image.

Churchill: 'I had the image of a black man aspiring to white values and literally being a white negro. And the idea of a woman who has taken on men's values, a sort of man-made woman who has no sense of herself as a woman.'

Cloud Nine was profoundly political, with a small 'p', characteristic of Churchill's style: not agitprop, but art, with powerful images that couldn't be argued with. It disturbed the most deep-seated assumptions about sexual roles and role conditioning, linked sexual repression with capitalist oppression, related economic imperialism to sexual imperialism. Churchill: 'For the first time I brought together two preoccupations of mine – people's internal states of being and the external political structures which affect them, which make them insane.'

1977

The extent to which the consciousness-raising of political theatre had, by 1977, affected the consciousness of mainstream theatre and its writers was demonstrated by the production of Robert Bolt's *State of Revolution* at the National Theatre. Bolt admired Lenin, but felt he was 'possessed by a terribly wrong idea'.[1] So he presented a version of the Russian Revolution which aimed to show how and why. The play showed events from 1910 (where at Gorky's home on the island of Capri, Lenin, Lunacharsky, Dzershinsky and Kollontai were preparing for a school of Party activists) to Lenin's death in 1924 (after which the remaining revolutionaries discussed Lenin's last will and testament, recommending the removal of Stalin for being 'a trifle' too crude, and warning of the dangers in the personal relations between Stalin and Trotsky). The story unfolded in ironic flashback narrated by Lunacharsky within the framework of a speech to the Young Communists on the anniversary of Lenin's death. Bolt used particular historical events, such as the German invasion of the Ukraine, the Kronstadt uprising, the demands of the peasants for property, the setting up of the Cheka, to show how ideology was undermined by expediency. Bolt implied that the reactionary post-revolutionary measures in Russia suggested that human nature was 'capitalist' rather than 'communist'.

What was wrong with Soviet Marxism, argued Bolt, was that it produced a Stalinist dictatorship despite Lenin's socialist ideology. One reason was Lenin's failure to resolve the contradictions of the 'cult of personality' in a proletarian revolutionary context. Bolt even quoted Lenin claiming categorically no contradiction between 'socialist democracy and the exercise of dictatorial powers by individuals'. Implicit in Bolt's argument was that Marx may not have been absolutely right in believing that individuals do not make history, but rise instead to the occasions provided by society. Stalin would seem to have contradicted Marx's axiom.

Not surprisingly, *State of Revolution* was cast in a Cecil B. De Mille mould similar to Bolt's earlier history play *Vivat! Vivat! Regina*. The play perpetuated the myth that Russia had been the only significant attempt to realise a socialist society and that communism should be judged solely on the success or failure of the Soviet Union. From the left, the play and production were criticised for the glorification of the individual, for the reduction of mass revolution to the idiosyncratic actions of a few individuals, and for the presentation of historical events as indisputable historical fact, of 'creating the fantasy of fact'.[2]

Where Bolt questioned communism in *State of Revolution*, Eric Bentley questioned anti-communism in *Are You Now or Have You Ever Been ...?*, a dramatised documentary derived from the transcripts of the House Un-American Activities Committee (HUAC) hearings during the McCarthy era in the USA. The play was produced at the Bush Theatre in 1977 and transferred to the Mayfair. It appeared shortly after the deportation of the 'dissidents' Agee and Hosenball for their campaign to expose the CIA, and at the time that the two *Time Out* journalists Crispin Aubrey and Duncan Campbell – with ex-soldier John Berry – were facing prosecution under the Official Secrets Act. The play was devastating in its condemnation of the post-war McCarthy witch-hunts of Hollywood 'reds', and a timely warning of the possibilities of a new McCarthy era emerging in Britain.

A number of new writers had become established by 1977. There was Pam Gems, not so much a socialist writer as one concerned with sexual politics. Gems was one of the first – and the very few – women to write a serious play that reached the West End (though later Mary O'Malley's comedy, *Once a Catholic*, transferred from the Royal Court to a long West End run). Like Caryl Churchill, Gems started writing later in life after raising four children, and she was closely involved in organising and participating in the Women's Season at the Almost Free in 1975, which included her play *The Amiable Courtship of Ms. Venus and Wild Bill*. She had previously had two lunchtime plays – *My Warren* and *After Birthday* – commissioned and produced by the Almost Free. The brief had been for some 'sexy pieces', but Gems didn't precisely oblige: 'The first was about a girl who shoves her baby down the lav, the other about an older lady living in a bed-sitter who is sent a vibrator as a mean joke. I remember an argument with someone who thought them depressing, and therefore politically suspect. To me, these two women were tough survivors.'[3]

1977 saw Gems's first big success, *Dusa Fish Stas and Vi* transferring from the Hampstead Theatre to the Mayfair to (mostly male) critical acclaim. Gems: 'I wanted to write about women now, women in their twenties who would almost certainly be mothers but for the pill. I do think that when the pill came in it was fantastic, now we can have equality, now we can have the phallic freedoms to screw where and when we want. But there is also the chemical and existential mutation. I wanted to show some women as they are now, against mechanised, urban backgrounds, isolated in eyries, breeding sometimes, more often divorced from their mothers, reacting against modern commercial brutality by becoming anorexic – a female disease which is a rejection of sexuality. Women who are the pathfinders of the new breed, trying to live the revolution with their fellers, and so often getting knocked back in what is still so inexorably a man's world.'[4] Gems went on to write *Queen Christina*, which was produced at The Other Place in Stratford by the Royal Shakespeare Company in 1977. It was based on the Swedish queen who was groomed for the throne as though she were a man. *Queen Christina* had been rejected by the Royal Court who said it 'was too sprawly, too expensive to do and anyway it would appeal more to women. That got to me. I mean, would they ever have said, "We can't do this play, it will appeal to men"?'[5] As a feminist playwright, it was this kind of attitude in society that Pam Gems was writing against. In 1979 her play *Piaf* – a musical biography of the singer – was produced by the RSC at The Other Place and the Warehouse to great critical acclaim.

The 1977 John Whiting Award was won by David Lan, a young expatriate South African anthropologist and playwright, for his *Winter Dancers*, produced at the Royal Court Theatre Upstairs. Lan first came to attention in 1974 with a lunchtime play at the Almost Free entitled *Painting a Wall*. One of the most politically oriented of the new generation of playwrights, Lan was closely involved in the Theatre Writers Union and with issues of censorship, and he was active in the campaign against apartheid in South Africa and how that affected writers. He had strong feelings about the function of political theatre:

A play is not political simply because it is about politicians, but only when it tries to demonstrate a political process, an actual moment of particular change. There are many ways of dividing up what constitutes progressive art or reactionary art. And perhaps the most useful way of doing that is to think about work which shows the possibility of change and work which doesn't. Political theatre demonstrates that things need not be how they are, that there is nothing natural about the way we live. One doesn't have to provide prescriptions for change, how it is to be done, but to show that the forces that created what we have are also capable of producing quite different things.[6]

Lan saw his plays as relating very much to contemporary England, even when set in South Africa or in some primitive society, because 'you can't understand what is happening in England at the moment without a historical perspective of England as an imperialist power'. To understand how England might change, Lan felt a wider historical perspective was required than was usually found in English theatre. The very language and imagery of the theatre could contribute to that change:

All writing for the theatre is an attempt to arrive at a dialogue with one's audience. It is dialogue that is dialetical in that it alters by what emerges in it, from it. And what lies behind that is the fact that language is a real thing, language is something powerful which changes things. One of the extraordinary insights of Levi-Strauss which is really lifted straight out of Marx is that metaphors do change the world.[7]

Thus the metaphors of the theatre could change the world: 'Language is something which makes experience real and whole, through which you can understand what is happening, and how it can be changed.'[8]

It was also 1977 in which North West Spanner, a socialist theatre company aiming to reach shop floor audiences in the north of England which had started in the early seventies, became the subject of one of the major political theatre controversies of the seventies, when local authorities attempted to cut their grant. That story and the history of North West Spanner is chronicled in the following essay, side-lighting the thorny issue of devolution of arts subsidy.

And 1977 was a historic year for a previously ignored sector of theatre workers – the theatre writers who in 1975 had formed themselves into an embryonic union. By 1977 the Theatre Writers Union was successfully blacking the new National Theatre in an attempt to start negotiations on a standard contract for writers which would provide them with a living wage. The quite extraordinary history of the TWU is described in the following essay.

'I don't believe in Chairman Mao. I mean God bless him, he was a good man and he did a lot of good for China. But he doesn't appeal a lot to the people we play to. And if the sun shines over Red China, God bless it. But it has a hard job rising here . . .' Member of North West Spanner, Manchester, 1978[1]

North West Spanner

Late at night on 7 October 1977, North West Spanner Theatre Company in Manchester (or Mossley to be precise) received a telephone call from the Drama Director of the North West Arts Association (NWAA) telling them that the Management Council of NWAA had decided to freeze their grant and to strike them off the estimates for 1978/79 altogether. The reason given was that the Management Council thought North West Spanner was a 'Marxist revolutionary' company, that public funds should not be used for that purpose. There was to be a committee of enquiry into Spanner's political aims and ideas. This was, said Spanner, one of the few times in the history of the theatre that anyone had been overtly attacked for their politics. People were getting sacked every day, they said, for political reasons – because they were encouraging people to join the union, for example. But that was not the reason given – it was because they put too much salt in the mashed potatoes, or whatever. This was the beginning of a witch-hunt.

The move to cut North West Spanner's grant came from a new Conservative Councillor and supporter of the extreme right-wing National Association for Freedom (NAFF). The decision was taken in direct opposition to the advice of the NWAA advisory drama panel who had recommended the company highly. David Mayer of the University of Manchester Drama Department, assessing their work, commented:

> . . . the plays are pithy, direct, rather un-polished, but humorous, tough and astringent. The subject matter is timely. There is no trace of condescension. The performers have strong political convictions, but they recognise that their audiences are conservative (not Tory) and view work and economics and politics in terms of their pragmatic experience.[2]

The Management Council's action was aggressive and unprecedented. The NWAA Drama Panel (at its next meeting on 17 October) was outraged and passed a unanimous resolution:

> The members of the Theatre Panel of North West Arts have learnt with concern the decision of the Management Council to withdraw funding from North West Spanner Theatre Company, contrary to the recommendation of the Theatre Panel, on the basis of the alleged political views of its members and the political content of their work. The Theatre Panel remain convinced of the value to the region of the work of this company in bringing theatre to a public who would not normally see theatre of any sort. Furthermore, they reiterate their conviction that they should receive support both now and in the future for their work.[3]

David Scase, Artistic Director of the Library Theatre Manchester and Chairman of the Drama Panel, considered resigning over the issue:

> It came as a great surprise to us ... No one just rubber-stamps grants applications. We have spent months assessing the artistic standards of this group. Their material is exactly geared to the audiences they are working for. We do not have a critical role as to what the content should be. This is not the thin end of the wedge, it is the wedge itself.[4]

The Arts Council of Great Britain stepped forward to support North West Spanner and Secretary General Roy Shaw issued a statement:

> It is my impression that most of the people who are condemning North West Spanner have not seen its work. Members of our Drama Panel and Drama Officers have seen its work and speak well of it. The Arts Council gives it a grant because it believes it does useful work in bringing entertaining theatre to non-theatrical venues. The Council makes no political judgements, only artistic ones, and it would deplore the introduction into the world of the arts of any form of political discrimination. I would prefer the judgement of our expert panel and our specialist officers rather than that of local politicians of whatever party. If devolution puts clients at the mercy of political pressures we shall have to reconsider the whole question.[5]

North West Spanner decided to refuse to co-operate with the investigating committee and called a conference on 'Political, Bureaucratic and Economic Censorship' in Manchester on 4 December 1977. More than 250 rallied to attend: and the North West Spanner supporters read as a roll-call of political theatre in the seventies. The conference was sponsored by Northern Equity, the Independent Theatre Council, The Association of Community Theatres, Theatre Writers Union, Writers Guild and North West Trades Union

Council. Theatre companies represented were: 7:48, Belt and Braces, CAST, Red Ladder, Broadside, Recreation Ground, Counteract, Roadgang, Theatremobile, M6 Theatre Company, Lancaster Theatre-in-Education, Itinerant Theatre, Midland Red Theatre, Avon Touring, North West Children's Touring Company, Liverpool Children's Theatre, Key Perspectives, 'The Factory', Shuttle Theatre Company, Merseyside Unity Theatre, Everyman Theatre, Theatre Royal Stratford East, and from Manchester, the Contact Theatre Company, the University Theatre, the Royal Exchange Theatre and the Library Theatre. Also present were dozens of organisations and individuals such as David Edgar, John McGrath, Trevor Griffiths, David Hare, Howard Brenton, Henry Livings, David Scase and Alan Dossor. The solidarity and support for Spanner was truly formidable, and indicative of the seriousness of the issue.

The conference passed a resolution proposed by David Mayer stating 'that an investigation of political content is not a valid test of a theatre company's suitability for financial subsidy', urging the 'rejection of the Management Council's report, and the full restoration of North West Spanner's grant for 78/79'. If this did not happen, the conference urged the *en bloc* resignation of all NWAA advisory panels, alternative direct subsidy from the Arts Council itself and action by Equity in this and similar instances to protect the rights of its members. Another unanimous resolution proposed by John McGrath and seconded by Henry Livings demanded that the 'Arts Council suspend the process of devolving funding powers to Regional Arts Associations, that RAAs constitutionally accept that the political views of their clients should not be a criterion of assessment and that the Arts Council should withhold its financial support from NWAA until the political censorship of North West Spanner was abandoned'.[6]

The result of the protest from all quarters was that North West Spanner's grant was re-instated (though there was a further unsuccessful rearguard action by the troublesome Councillor). The strength of the combined forces of the left in the arts had been demonstrated. And having been thrust so unexpectedly into the national limelight, Spanner returned to its normal graft of providing 'shop-floor' theatre nationally, but particularly to the greater Manchester area.

But some very important issues had been raised. The Arts Council's support (given the overall structure of arts subsidy, whereby money passed from the Arts Council to Regional Arts

Associations for local allocation) was helpful. But as Spanner pointed out:

> They supported us from the purely liberal grounds that political criteria are not appropriate for art, that artistic criteria only apply. That is a liberal argument, and it was very influential in winning the day. But Roy Shaw had to say that, even if he hated us. Even if he really wanted to get rid of us, he had to say that. Anybody concerned with the arts bureaucracy had to support us on that level.

That was one irony in the situation. Another involved the crucial issue of devolution – the official Arts Council policy which the North West Spanner 'witch-hunt' prompted Roy Shaw to question. Ironically, in a report to NWAA in August 1977 (just two months earlier) Spanner had discussed the issue of devolution whereby the Regional Arts Associations would take full responsibility for funding the arts in their geographical area. And while they had been 'confused and uncertain' about the relative merits, they had presented some arguments in favour of devolution as a means of minimising bureaucracy and 'removing a bottleneck in their funding', though aware that 'North West Arts was more vulnerable to potentially hostile Councils'.[7] Not surprisingly the attempt to cut their subsidy set Spanner's mind absolutely against devolution and they outlined the long-term dangers:

> The Arts Council's support for us is deceptive. Because in reality the whole concept of devolution suggests that we are such a piddling little company, they can't really be bothered. One argument for devolution is de-bureaucratisation, and there's no question that the Arts Council is just a huge bureaucratic machine. You can't imagine the amount of paper work we do – weekly box office quota forms to fill in – kilos, tons. Last year we got £12,500 from the Arts Council, but they must have sent us a grand's worth of paper. Multiply that eighty, a hundred times for small-scale companies. But the dangerous thing is that devolution is a way that the arts in this country can be cut back.[8]

Such cuts in subsidy would be subtle and the consequence of conservative elements in local government – eyes on the ballot box rather than the stage. Spanner pointed out that it was all very well for the Redcliffe-Maud Report on devolution to talk about replacing the 'distant hand' of centralised subsidy, with a friendly helping hand locally, but that it was the hand round your throat you had to watch out for – as they learned from experience.

By 1979 North West Spanner was an active shop floor theatre company – performing at building sites, dry docks, works canteens and factory gates and doing evening plays in clubs and pubs based on the insights and experiences gained during visits to the workplace. But in 1970, in its early days, it was part of Inroads, a community arts project aimed at children and based in York.

Inroads moved to Salford in 1971 'because it was less conservative, traditional, more fluid. Basically, the idea was to set itself within a working-class community that was in change. And it did so by settling in a slum clearance area called Lower Broughton – a classic slum.' The early theatre work was entirely for children – 'street theatre, doing plays about Dracula and Frankenstein'. They used 'gang session techniques' attracting large groups of kids on an estate or school, attempting to get them to interact. Penny Morris, founder member of Inroads:

> It's best illustrated by some of the plays. There was a play for very young kids called *Dummies* – four people dressed up in white boiler suits with stockings over their heads. The children would manipulate the kids as robots – they would be dummies. And a story would evolve by asking the children 'what happens next?'

The adult theatre work grew directly out of this – specifically a King Kong Festival which coincided with the Tory Housing Finance Bill of 1972 raising rents.

> The parents said – we've got Dracula and Frankenstein on our door-step – at County Hall, and they've put the rents up. There was quite a thriving tenants' association and they said why don't you do a show for us? It would help to attract people to the meetings. They said it would help convince people not to pay the rent increases if we did a show. So we did our first play – *The Rents Play*.

The group felt they couldn't avoid doing a play on rents. Rent strikes were a national movement which took root in 1972, a backswell against the Tories. The parents were fighting evictions and refusing to pay the 50p increase:

> It was the first time you could really sense on an estate that they were really coming together, after the classic problem of people not knowing each other. For years they'd lived in the old terraces, and they were suddenly in this amazing futuristic slum, or what was to become a slum. It was really a sort of a social activity, not paying the rent.

The Rents Play was first played at the festival with over 3000 people present. At the end they burnt the giant King Kong the kids had made:

> The fire brigade came to hose down the King Kong because it was

getting out of hand. They couldn't hose down the tenants who were
also getting out of hand.

The Rents Play was typical of the early work:

> It was a series of sketches, with lines like 'I'm not prejudiced, but how
> would you like to live next door to one?' And it also had a famous
> papier-mâché head of Edward Heath. The scenes showed how the
> tenants were involved and why they wouldn't pay the rent. There was
> an agitprop didactic element – what proportion of the rent was actually
> paying off interest, who got the contracts to build the flats. It was very
> simplistic, but it was also very effective.

Working with tenants' associations, they used to knock at doors, leaf-
leting estates and inviting the people to a performance followed by
a discussion and 'organising' for resistance against rent rises:

> We were actually attractive. We used to go around in gaily coloured
> uniform – we were those funny people in four different coloured boiler
> suits with loud hailers – and act as a focus of attention. We were like
> commandos, arriving at a place, jumping out of the van, ready to go
> on when the tenants' association gave the cue.

With some success and a broadening of interest, the theatre nucleus
of Inroads formed an independent group in 1973, but still within
Inroads.

The Rents Play led to a *Nurses Play* (all the shows had generic
titles). One of the tenants who'd seen them was a nurse and at the
time of the nurses' strike in 1973, she asked them to do a show for
the strike:

> The request came from the Manchester Nurses Action Group, and
> again we used a simplistic agitprop form. The kids' stuff helped a lot:
> you couldn't keep their attention for long, so you had to be really quick –
> at the most 20 minutes – and precise. And you had to be entertaining.
> If you were rubbish, they wouldn't want you.

In 1973 the nurses were going on strike for a higher basic wage.
Like the rent strike, it was the first national strike within the health
service. And the nurses had to break down big barriers, for example
that their strike was killing people on the wards. The difference for
Spanner was that they were basically persuading tenants *to* strike,
whereas the nurses were already on strike. So their show had to act
as a morale booster and also to 'spread the word'. As it happened the
nurses' strike was historic in the development of Spanner because it
took them on to the shop floor where they were to remain:

> The nurses themselves said it was ridiculous just going around the

hospitals – what about the dockers, the miners, the big battalions. And although there was a lot of support – the nurses were doing a good job, working a hundred hours a day, not getting much money, we're right behind you lasses, sort of thing – it was often patronising. The nurses said they'd been going round with a collection slip, but only ever speaking to the stewards, and they thought they'd get more money and support if we did our play and went into the canteens and had a whip round after. So we went in and said you've got to support the nurses: we used a simple format – the old one of 'sinking the HMS NHS' for which we used an old zinc bath tub. We had an amazing response.

They worked closely with the nurses, and they discovered a lot about their future audiences: 'just ordinary blokes from the shop floor who had got all the prejudices you can imagine, like we had at the time about them'. If the nurses weren't allowed in the factories Spanner would say, 'Well why bloody well not?' They learned to be aggressive. They 'dared to perform in these places'. Later they were to write:

> To dispel one myth: playing to workplace/union/community centre audiences is not a case of 'preaching to the converted'. Our audiences are as broad a cross-section, if not broader, as the audiences for most theatre, and may often be cynical at the beginning of a Spanner play. We have to win them over.'

They had no trouble winning workers over in the cause of the nurses: it was a 'heart throb issue'. But the next show – about the Shrewsbury pickets – was less successful. Spanner were changing in a number of ways at this point. They were 'developing their own political sense', largely as a result of performing in factories. They'd built up contacts with *The Rents Play* and *The Nurses Play* and they found 'they had a foothold in factories'. They were changing their style, as Ernie Dalton, a founder member of Spanner described:

> I can remember I used to stuff this shirt with a dollar sign on it, like a big fat capitalist. But then I thought – I don't need to stick anything up there, I'll just go on as I am. That was a big thing.

The Spanner identity had become stronger than Inroads, which in any case was winding down from 'natural' causes:

> It was geographical really. Because Lower Broughton began to be cleared away. The people we had cemented a relationship with were being moved out and the houses were all being knocked down. So Inroads began to be demolished.

It was a turning point, and the theatre group came to a surprising decision: to stop theatre work in order to do 'real' work:

> We thought if we were really serious about playing to workers, we'd
> better find out about work, not just peddle the old 'Smash the State'
> line. So we said, let's go into hospitals, we'll find out what it's really
> like and then do a really big play about hospitals. We had performing
> experience, but no 'real' experience. So we all got jobs in hospitals: I
> was a theatre porter and Penny a nursing auxiliary at Ashton General,
> someone else at Salford Royal. We really got into it, especially unionisa-
> tion. I led a famous strike at Ashton General over the condition of the
> toilets!

To everyone's surprise, some members of the company got into
hospital work so much, they decided to stay. On the basis of this
experience, Spanner eventually came to recruit 'escapees from the
shop floor' – Newman Smith, for example, an ex-electrician, and
Chris Tupman, ex-labourer and circus boy. Ernie Dalton and Penny
Morris decided they didn't 'want to be inside factories, but playing
to them'. And they now wanted nearer the £38.50 they'd been earn-
ing than the £2 a week pocket money from Inroads. They managed
to get a grant from North West Arts in the spring of 1975:

> Someone from NW Arts came with us for three days, and we managed
> to do eight performances in four factories, and one on a Trades Council
> demo in Liverpool for the release of the Shrewsbury pickets. And we
> took her down to the dry docks where we had built up a really good
> relationship. There were about 100 people in an incredible shed with
> a giant joist gear and great huge metal sheets for lining the sides of ships
> and us at one end. It must really have affected her, because we got
> funded.

From that point Spanner 'began to take seriously what they wanted
to do'. And they produced a show that was to stay in their repertoire
until 1979, *Safety First or Last*, with Bruce Fosdyke and the Alienation Game, the Indestructible Worker and the Human Body Clocks:

> It was a short half-hour show dealing with the problems of health and
> safety at work. And again it was a hybrid of those earlier agitprop plays
> on issues. It was someone in the dry docks suggested the issue of safety.
> There would be blokes limping round the yard – and he said 'because of
> them'. It was an incredible success.

As the *Oldham Evening Chronicle* testified, reviewing a performance
for manual workers at a local factory:

> The play explored problems met by workers on the shop floor ...
> problems such as shift work and irregular hours, and their consequence
> on married life, were presented with comic ingenuity; the name of
> profit-making was deftly handled without sinking to the level of merely

nasty capitalist pigs exploiting the poor workers. Dangers of the over-prescription of drugs to bored housewives and exhausted workers came across through a series of clear images and uncomplicated dialogue ... Raymond McBride, a sheet-metal worker at Dronsfield's, said: 'This play has certainly made me think. We did not really know what to expect when the players first came, but I am sure I represent many who saw the show in agreeing that it was well worth while and it worked.' One of the managers commented that he was glad that the play had been given, because there was something for everyone to learn in what it said.[10]

And Derek Newton, Head of Drama at Padgate College, saw Spanner in Warrington performing their 'safety' play on a picket line as the factory where they had booked to perform was actually out on strike over an issue of industrial safety:

It was electric, entertaining and exciting. Though this was self-confessed 'political theatre' it was well-constructed, satirical and light-hearted; it was critical of management, establishment and worker ... The audience was a study and I regretted that I had no video camera with me.[11]

At this point, the Company were joined by an older person, Elsie, a middle-aged millworker, who proved to be a strong influence on the group. With her they produced a 'well-researched' play – *Winding Up* – about the textile industry, and Courtaulds in particular:

It centred on the Empress Mill in Wigan where there had been an historic attempt by trades unionists to stop it closing. We showed a solution – that the workers should sit in, occupy, however unrealistic. It was in fact totally unrealistic for most mill workers at the time, but we wanted to get across that they should attempt to fight back. And we made the point that it was better to have fought and lost than never to have fought at all.

Winding Up also provided critical information about the textile industry and Courtaulds' development of synthetics, the use of cheap materials from Hong Kong and Portugal, import controls, and the closures: '12,000 jobs in the last four years have gone out the window through Courtaulds'.

Courtaulds opened a weaving plant in Skelmersdale. This was a new town in a development area outside Liverpool, so they got government grants. These were worth at least £4 million. Then when they had stayed there long enough not to have to repay the grants they moved out, opening up a new weaving plant in Londonderry – another development area. They left Skelmersdale a ghost town, and one thousand in the dole queues.

The play combined agitprop with nationalism – the story of a family in the mills. With the show, Spanner got involved in the closure of the Adelphi Mill in Bollington, Cheshire:

> We took it to Bollington two weeks before the mill closed. Because we knew there was incredible bitterness and anger against Courtaulds. They were closing down the only operative mill in that town. It meant job suicide for 400 people. Some had been offered jobs in Wrexham – thank you Courtaulds! The main thing was that we held out the belief that the play could change those audiences' lives, could have an effect, that they could see it was happening everywhere and they weren't alone. It was a really memorable performance.

Again there was a good response locally.

Next came *Dig For Victory*, in the summer of '76, a 25-minute play about unemployment. This was followed by *Just a Cog*, the story of four workers at MEL Engineering Ltd and their fellow workers down the road at Automat's, fighting for trades union recognition.

> There was a dispute for union recognition of the AUEW in a very small plant called Automat – a forerunner to Grunwicks. It was a very interesting strike, about a year long. In 1969 there had been a similar situation with the Arundel Strike which the AUEW won. The firm became bankrupt and moved out and a special agreement – the Manchester day work agreement – was won for Manchester. In 1976 this poxy little firm had been out for nine months – and where was the AUEW? Things had changed. It was a totally different political period – when wage cuts had become the norm and redundancies were accepted on a wide scale. So we wrote a play about the spirit of collaboration and tried to show why the generation of militants who fought the Arundel Strike in '69 now tended to accept the situation. So it was a propaganda play for the strike, but also gave a broader analysis of shop floor attitudes. I think we found our form. It was critically acclaimed. It was quite an achievement.

David Mayer reviewed the play enthusiastically in *Plays & Players*:

> I caught up with *Just a Cog* in the upstairs disco of the Allied Engineering Union Club in Eccles, barely a distinct Lancashire town and rather a continuation of the terrace sprawl north of Salford, where Spanner's performance before an audience of 150 was sponsored by the strike committee of a local electrical components firm. By sheer coincidence, negotiations in the strike, deadlocked for nearly a year, had come to life with hopeful meetings in the preceding two days, adding to the play a dimension of immediacy ... Although somewhere there are em-

ployers and governments who must be presumed to be adversaries or callous bystanders, no bosses, MPs or civil servants, caricatured or otherwise appear, and are instead represented by impersonal – and for that reason heartless – efficiency studies, unrealistic productivity quotas, bugged strikers' meetings, evidence of trans-shipping blacked goods, and out-of-the-blue redundancy notices. The four employees are not drawn as stereotypes, but as individuals who, in attempting to cope with the sequence of demands, come gradually and separately to recognise the problems, not the solutions, and equally to recognise themselves.[12]

Mayer confessed that 'Spanner's politics are not my politics' but nevertheless concluded that they 'must now be taken seriously for their artistry as much as for the vehemence and clarity of their politics'. And he praised them for 'none of the smug self-congratulatory prolier-than-thou condescension towards audiences so endemic in performances by 7:84, Belt and Braces, Red Ladder and similar companies'.

By this time Spanner had begun to tour more nationally; though about half their work was in the North West. They made a brief excursion into cabaret – more general entertainment – and *Sign Here* for a strike at a Batchelors pea factory:

> ... a short throwaway piece, back to street theatre, it was done on two trestles and a plank. Mind, we are more likely to have two workers on a ladder, rather than a boss and a worker. There was a strike, too, at a factory making Jubilee corgis, so we did a spoof on the Jubilee and the Social Contract.

Then there was *Out of Control* in 1977, set in the Jetchem Plant, looking at urban violence and the ultimate hazard – nuclear power:

> We lived on the edge of the greatest time bomb on earth – Windscale: nuclear power, infinite and godlike. How the hell are you going to control a power like that? A perfect analogy for the sort of power structures we live with – powers from above. Again, though, it was rooted firmly in the industrial mould – a strike at a chemical factory over a safety issue. And it was also loosely based on a strike at ICI who were out over a guy who'd got his arm caught in a machine.

After the NW Arts controversy, Spanner returned in 1978 to the direct action themes of *Just a Cog* in *Partisans*, about the occupation by the workers of a Chrysler subsidiary at the time of the Peugeot takeovers.

North West Spanner believed in what they were doing. With their local success and the national limelight of the subsidy controversy, they found themselves in a position to change direction, even encouraged to do so. Maureen Ramsey, who was responsible for co-ordinating the development of Spanner's audiences:

> There is enormous pressure on us to become like 7:84, with the glory and kudos of playing to 500 people in large centres. It would be much easier for us to be doing that. Easier to arrange – all you have to do is ring up the Arts Association. To go into a factory means 95 phone calls to one person, someone inexperienced in putting on theatre. You've got to tell them how to go about it, sometimes print their tickets for them, go and see them, spoon-feed them.

But however successful they became, they said 'we'll still be doing it on the shop floor'.

> When it doesn't work, it's really terrible. Six people turn up and it's a real downer and we think what the fuck are we doing this for anyway? But when it does work, it's magic. You go into a factory, play to 20 people. Maybe two of those will come to an evening performance, next time maybe six, or their wives will see us and say why don't you come down to our hosiery factory. It's the snowball effect – slow, but it builds up.

They carried on slogging quite simply because they wanted to change the world:

> We started playing to working-class audiences whether they wanted us or not: it was a challenge, to make a belief of what we do. We're frightened of the National Front marching in the streets, of the conservatism that exists; we're frightened because we want a different future for our lives and our kids. Now is not what we always want it to be and we want to change the world.

And they felt they created the demand for their work:

> That is important. We hinge on the cornerstones of these people's lives. And that is why they want to book us. We do a play about safety – that concerns them. We do a play about nuclear power – that concerns them. So they book us on that basis. We aren't the Ballet Rambert.

And they believed profoundly in the future and function of political theatre:

> What we show is the dialectic between their – and our – lives and hopes and dreams. And of course, we are political and point to the way forward. But we are not didactic: the kind of audience we play to – all layers of political consciousness from conservatism to whatever, but rarely ultra-leftism – we'd go down like a lead balloon. We actually see the real life or death struggle within the increasing conservatism.

They didn't believe the revolution was further away: 'I can't put a date to it, but there is a polarisation taking place, changes, developments'.

If you believe in the fight for socialism, then, of course, political theatre is relevant. And it is your job to make it so. When you drive through places like Skelmersdale, when you know that kids of 16 will never get a job and are likely to turn to the National Front, then you know what you've got to tap into. And you know you've got to fight. Theatre is a way you can do it.

'Theatre Writers Unite. A Living Wage for Theatre Writers.' TWU slogan during NT Strike, 1977

Theatre Writers Union (TWU)

At the meeting in October of 1975 at the Oval House when the ITC closed ranks to confront the Arts Council on the issue of cuts in subsidy, a group of thirty playwrights joined forces to form the Theatre Writers Group. Within twelve months it had become the Theatre Writers Union representing over 150 playwrights who were successfully blacking the new National Theatre in an attempt to force the major subsidised theatres to negotiate a minimum standard contract for theatre writers. The rapid growth of the Theatre Writers Union and its radical activities epitomised the political principles operating in the theatre in the seventies. It was significant that such well-established playwrights as Steve Gooch, Caryl Churchill, David Edgar, Snoo Wilson and Ken Campbell were instrumental in starting the Theatre Writers Group; that such major writers as Edward Bond, Trevor Griffiths, Howard Brenton, David Hare and John Arden immediately joined and devoted impressive amounts of time and energy to the early months of the TWU and to its industrial action. For the first time, playwrights – notoriously individualist and traditionally isolated – combined and used their considerable collective strength to improve the working conditions of the worst paid of British theatre workers.

What precipitated the formation of the Theatre Writers Group – as with ITC – was the threatened cuts from the Arts Council: much of the end-of-1975 freeze directly affected theatre writers – writers' bursaries, guarantees against authors' royalties on new plays and production grants for new plays. Within a fortnight of the October 19th meeting at the Oval, an inaugural meeting of the Theatre Writers Group was called to organise its campaign against the Arts Council. There immediately followed a delegation of writers direct to the Drama Panel of the Arts Council. Under pressure, the Arts Council agreed to a full meeting with playwrights who were campaigning under the banner of 'Theatre Writers Unite!' and 'A Living Wage for Theatre Writers!'[1]

Within months, the TWG had thrashed out its policy and formulated its demands. These included the immediate release of money for all Arts Council writers schemes, the raising of minimum royalty guarantees, the payment of writers on a parity basis with Equity, the distribution of information about subsidy to writers, and the acceptance of a theatre company's judgement on the artistic merit of work. The demands, put to the Arts Council, were by no means fully met, but the Council agreed to co-operate in re-thinking and revising its schemes for subsidising new writing in consultation with the Theatre Writers Group.

Then over the next six months, TWG thrashed out an even more demanding minimum policy for Arts Council subsidy to writers. TWG wanted contract writing and attachments paid at £60 per week, with supplementary performance fees to bring the total to not less than £1500 per full length play. TWG wanted a bursary scheme for a period up to a year calculated at £60 per week. TWG wanted a guaranteed performance fee, based on acceptance by a theatre company of £1500 for a full-length play and £750 for a short play. TWG wanted a dramaturge's scheme calculated at £60 a week. TWG wanted rehearsal attendance calculated at £60 per week. TWG also asked for regional centres for the duplication of scripts and £6000 set aside for that purpose, plus full access to Arts Council information relating to grants, awards and applications. TWG's demands boiled down to their rallying cry of a living wage for writers – of £60 per week. Almost overnight TWG won some important victories: commission fees for its members of £1200 and £1500 and 12 month bursaries up to £2500. The TWG demands remained a continuing element in discussions with the Arts Council.

In 1978, the Theatre Writers Union was still trying to influence Arts Council policy, but the bureaucracy was proving less accessible. 'Fun and games at 105 Piccadilly', as a TWU newsletter put it, involved concern about size of delegations, cancelled meetings and flat refusals to meet at all.[2] It was the same old story, the same problems faced by TACT and ITC, with the Arts Council putting up barriers to discussion and positively paranoiac about the numbers in delegations. But things had changed for the TWU by 1978. It was still interested in the Arts Council's role in new writing, but its energies in 1977 and 1978 had been diverted to negotiating a minimum standard contract with the Theatres National Council (representing the National Theatre, Royal Shakespeare Company and Royal Court) and with the ITC. The Arts Council was temporarily out of the direct line of fire, though there would be consequences eventually for the Arts Council from the contracts being negotiated with the major subsidised theatre and the alternative theatres.

The Theatre Writers Union was, from the beginning, able to function with flexibility and force in large part because of its constitution and structure. David Edgar explained why in a report arguing the case for the Theatre Writers Union as a new and independent union separate from the Writers Guild of Great Britain:

> From the start, we took the view that writers are difficult people to organise and that the only way to create and keep an organisation together was to make it as democratic as possible. To this end, we evolved a constitution with the following characteristics:
> a) TWU holds general meetings at least every three months.
> b) The Committee is elected from the general meetings and is directly responsible to and dismissable by it. The committee acts at all times on the mandate of the general meeting as delegates rather than representatives.
> c) Further to avoid the creation of an unrepresentative bureaucracy, no committee member may serve more than two delegate sessions – no more than six months. We believe that this system works, and works better than more hierarchical and bureaucratic structures.[3]

TWU, additionally, had none of the 'commercial' restrictions on membership (the Writers Guild required a certain number of hours of broadcast or produced work, implying that a management gave writers their status and identity): TWU membership was open to anyone who wrote plays whether performed or not. That proved to be one of the union's strengths, though it also created one of the stumbling blocks to achieving official (as opposed to *de facto*) trades union status – an effort which the Theatre Writers Group initiated in 1976. David Edgar:

> ... things became clear to us very rapidly. First, that writers were appallingly treated throughout the theatre. Two, that there was a need for a trades union to fight to redress this situation. Three, that no existing organisation could fulfil this role ... We became aware very quickly that a pressure group alone could not redress this situation. Pressure on the subsidising body was vital; but there was a severe limit to what the Arts Council could do. The very fact of the appalling situation of writers proved that the good offices of a government body were not enough. The economic state of the vast majority of writers proved that the status and riches of a few did not aid the many. Clearly, despite all the difficulties of organising individual, disparate and atomised writers, some kind of union was necessary.[4]

So the Theatre Writers Group decided to pursue unionisation. The crucial questions were: 1) Should the Theatre Writers Group become a trades union in its own right affiliated to the Trades Union Congress? 2) Should TWG become a part of another body already affiliated to the TUC? 3) Or should TWG continue to exist as already constituted? The TUC response was categorical rejection, as they encouraged new groups to affiliate to existing unions. The TWG tried Equity who said no. At that stage there were two remaining options – to join the Writers Guild of Great Britain or to become a properly constituted Independent Trades Union. And though the Writers Guild was at that time lobbying for TWG to amalgamate with them, the TWG decided to pursue unionisation as an independent union, under the Government's 1974 Trades Union and Labour Relations Act, by applying to the Certification Office.

The issue of whether or not to join the Writers Guild precipitated a great deal of daggers-drawn debate in TWG. David Edgar:

> We discovered at once that although the Guild did, nominally, organise playwrights, and had done so for some years, that they had not done so effectively. Writers had, indeed ... been allowed to become the whipping boys of the theatre. And in addition to their derisory financial rewards, they also lacked many other basic rights, like control over their work in rehearsal and performance. We discovered that the Guild had secured no agreements at all in any sector of the theatre (though there were rumours that they were now opening talks with the Society of West End Theatre, which employed the richest writers). We concluded from this that a) theatre writing was virgin territory, and that, therefore, we could not be seen as muscling in on someone else's patch were we to remain autonomous, and b) that there must be a reason for the Guild's apparent incapacity to represent their playwright members. It is our view that there is a reason for this, and that it lies in the very structure of the organisation itself. The Guild's structure may be very suitable for its film, television and novel writing members: we believe it is not suitable for the representation of playwrights.[5]

So the Theatre Writers Group decided there were but two possible options:

> One is to disband gracefully, and leave theatre writers back out in the cold. The other is to fight to build our organisation and to secure agreements with managements. We view the first course as grossly irresponsible. We are going to go on fighting.[6]

As it happened, TWG's attempt to register as a trades union came unstuck over the legal definition of a 'worker'. When the Certification Officer asked point blank whether TWG members were workers, the question was greeted with great hilarity at the general meeting which discussed it, not least because of the anomaly whereby the Writers Guild had registered as a trades union in 1976, apparently certified as an 'organisation of writers'. But at that stage it seemed impossible for TWG to *prove* to the satisfaction of the law that its members were workers without altering its constitution in an unacceptable fashion, so registration was abandoned.

Official trades union recognition soon became irrelevant, in any case, when the Theatre Writers Group changed its name to the Theatre Writers Union, agreed to operate as a *de facto* union and, indeed, immediately did so in its effective blacking of the National Theatre – a state of industrial affairs ironically brought about as much by further difficulties with the Writers Guild as with the National Theatre itself.

In pursuit of its aim of a living wage for writers, the Theatre Writers Group decided early in 1976 to focus its energies on contracts. An ad hoc committee was set up including TWG members Steve Gooch, Mike Stott, Edward Bond, David Halliwell, Howard Brenton, various interested agents, the Society of Authors and the Writers Guild and the National Theatre to discuss a standard subsidised theatre contract. The National Theatre seemed open to approaches, if not proper negotiations, but the Writers Guild put a spanner in the works:

> The Writers Guild of Great Britain have mounted a campaign to take over the Theatre Writers Group. They are refusing to meet the National as equal partners with the TWG, but are insisting that they alone have the right to represent theatre writers. They have told us: we will only work with you if you join the Guild. The NT are laughing all the way to the South Bank.[7]

The National Theatre's response came in a letter to the Theatre Writers Union in January 1977. The NT's membership of SWET (the Society of West End Theatre) – a curious membership for a major subsidised theatre – required them to recognise the Guild as the negotiating union for dramatists:

> ... Our present position is, therefore, that while we are anxious to begin constructive negotiation as soon as may be convenient and we are always ready to talk to you about matters of mutual concern, we cannot recognise TWU as the *sole* representative of dramatists for the purposes of negotiations.[8]

The Theatre Writers Union had little choice. In order to force the Writers Guild to recognise it, it had to force the National Theatre to do so first. In short, it had to demonstrate that it *did* represent theatre writers in ways in which the Guild did not. It had to use the industrial muscle the Guild lacked.

At a historic meeting of TWU in January 1977 at the Royal Court Theatre Upstairs, two important things happened. First, the meeting of over eighty writers spent eight hours quite literally dotting the i's, crossing the t's and analysing every comma of the minimum standard contract that TWU intended to negotiate with the National and other major subsidised theatres. It was an impressive event, with playwrights sufficiently concerned about their working conditions to devote the time to working out the final contract for themselves. A draft contract had already been through many meetings with equal care, but the perfection of the final contract was important and imperative because, given the democratic structure of the Union, TWU negotiators would not be in a position to do any horsetrading around the negotiating table. They would negotiate what the full membership had approved and nothing else. This meeting and its work was another indication of the strength of the collective.

And it was at this meeting that the decision was taken to black the National Theatre, and strike instructions were circulated to TWU members:

> In the absence of any house agreement with the National Theatre, we instruct our members not to sign any contract for an individual play. THIS MEANS THAT YOU CANNOT SIGN ANY CONTRACT FOR AN INDIVIDUAL PLAY WITH THE NATIONAL THEATRE UNTIL OTHERWISE INSTRUCTED.[9]

In fact, in voluntary solidarity nine TWU members had already been refusing to sign their individual contracts. TWU was in a solid and militant mood: its writers could not afford not to be. From *The Stage*:

> Since January 16, the TWU has been blacking the NT – which amounts to strike action – over the specific issue of what is seen as ludicrously low commissioning fees and the broader issue of the NT's refusal to recognise the TWU as a negotiating body for theatre writers. The writers immediately concerned are Edward Bond, Howard Brenton, Trevor Griffiths, Robert Holman, Paul Thompson, Howard Barker, Julian Mitchell, Christopher Hampton and Barrie Keeffe. TWU's idea of a standard contract for writers will allow among other clauses, for a playwright's direct involvement in the choice of a director and cast for his play, some measure of control over the emphasis placed on its theme, and payment of about £1500 per play rather than the NT's offer of a basic £150 plus royalties.[10]

By March the blacking was still in force and receiving outside support – from the Royal Court Theatre which opened negotiations with the Theatre Writers Union and the writers' section of the ACTT which posed a resolution, proposed by David Mercer:

> We publicly support the position of TWU in dispute with the National Theatre and as a logical consequence no ACTT writer will contract to work with the National Theatre during the period of the dispute.[11]

Both events were significant: for both another theatre and another union gave TWU the recognition it was being denied. Indeed David Mercer was even a member of the troublesome Writers Guild, and over the months of dispute TWU membership increased significantly with renegade Writers Guild members.

By March, however, there were indications that negotiations might be sanctioned 'with the Writers Guild in association with TWU', and the TWU were 'optimistic for a successful outcome to our dispute'...[12] But negotiations to negotiate were still going on in April when the TWU emphasised to its members that 'the blacking of the National Theatre was not to be lifted' until after negotiations had started.[13] TWU was taking no chances. It had discovered its muscle and it would continue to use it. Then, at the end of May, after four months of dispute, the blacking was lifted. *The Stage* reported:

> On May 25, the Theatre's National Committee ... agreed to negotiate with the TWU and the Writers Guild of Great Britain for standard minimums. Accordingly the TWU has lifted the blacking of the NT they imposed in January, which stirred up such a flurry of publicity for the union ...[14]

Ironically, it was through the blacking of the NT that TWU found itself officially recognised as a union. Then, from the summer of 1977, negotions with the Theatres National Council took place regularly. By the autumn of 1979, the minimum standard contract had been agreed, marking a major victory for theatre writers and the Theatre Writers Union.

Simultaneously negotiations were taking place with ITC and TACT for a fringe theatre writers contract. There was, from the beginning a willingness on behalf of ITC member companies to arrive at a contract (a number of fringe theatres had signed an interim agreement) and negotiations were more in the vein of mutual effort and interest than a battle. ITC and TWU shared common interests and aims – and a common problem, shortage of money. By the autumn of 1979 a contract for all writers writing with ITC companies had also been signed.

The signing of the two agreements – with the major subsidised and the alternative theatre – was a genuinely revolutionary event. For the first time in the history of the country, playwrights would by right receive a living wage for their work. Quite as significantly, the agreements recognised writers as workers. In practical terms, playwrights would be paid on a calculation of six months' work per play, at least £2000 whether the produced play had been commissioned or not. The case of Howard Brenton's £350 commission from the National Theatre for *Weapons of Happiness* in 1976 provided a standard of comparison for the improvements in working conditions that the new contract achieved.

Rates for alternative theatre companies would be calculated on the basis of six months' work, but at the level which respective companies paid their other workers, thus taking into account variations in subsidy in the different sectors of the theatre, and the often collective, or at least non-hierarchical, working and wage structures in alternative theatre. The minimum wage was a major achievement, but so were other improvements in the agreement. Writers would have the right (not just the privilege by management invitation) to attend rehearsals (for which they would be paid just as the director and performers were) and to be fully involved with artistic decisions such as casting, directing and publicity. In addition, writers would begin to approach a ten per cent level of royalties – a contentious, but fundamental principle in the unions' platform – and the contract started to redistribute the profit that managements took from the future success of a writer's work, giving playwrights access to and some control over subsidiary rights (where lies the real money and just reward for successful plays).

1979 also saw the beginning of a Theatre-in-Education and Community Theatre Writers Scheme set up by the Calouste Gulbenkian Foundation in negotiation with TWU since 1976:

> Following a suggestion from the Standing Conference of Young People's Theatre at Aberystwyth in September 1976, the Calouste Gulbenkian Foundation has consulted with writers' organisations to establish an initial fund of £10,000 to assist Theatre-in-Education and Community Theatre Companies to commission new work from writers who have shown evidence of ability, and/or have experience in this form of theatre. If the scheme is successful it is hoped to extend it in due course with further funds.[15]

All three contracts – the major subsidised, the alternative theatre and the TIE – marked a concrete achievement in British theatre history which could hardly have been conceived of in 1968. They were concrete proof of the force of 'alternative theatre' in Britain in the seventies. As far as TWU was concerned, they would set precedents for similar contracts in regional theatre and no doubt eventually in commercial theatre. And they would inevitably further alter patterns of subsidy in the eighties. For the onus in the subsidised area would fall back onto the Arts Council, who would have to come to terms with the fact that subsidy to theatres included a living wage for writers. Above all the contracts were a measure of the political commitment of the Theatre Writers Union and its members, a commitment which was an integral part of the Union's policy and practice.

For, though the Arts Council and theatre managements had been the main targets of TWU activity, the union had also consistently taken stands on political issues specific and general – and particularly on Northern Ireland, South Africa and censorship. In response to requests from Amnesty International, TWU had regularly written to repressive Latin American governments about the imprisonment and torture of individual writers. It took up the case of the Czech dissidents who were on trial in 1977 – including playwright Vaclav Havel – liaising with Equity to organise statements of protest from the stages of the RSC and the National Theatre. When Red Ladder was threatened by the National Front, TWU wrote to Leeds newspapers on their behalf, to the Leeds Chief Constable and the Arts Council. It supported the Newcastle Theatre occupation, with an official TWU representative taking part. It supported North West Spanner when its grant was cut. It supported members of Theatremobile who were sacked because of their controversial play on asbestosis.

In 1978, when the apartheid situation in South Africa had become especially complicated and confusing to writers (many TWU members including Barrie Keeffe, Caryl Churchill and David Lan were seeking advice on what to do when South African managements asked to do their plays), David Lan prepared and presented a fact paper for TWU (and subsequently for wider distribution) on how apartheid operated at the end of the seventies and what writers should do about it. As a result TWU voted to advise its members to implement a total boycott – no productions of plays in South Africa under any circumstances.

By 1978 problems of censorship had become widespread and severe: Caryl Churchill had brought to TWU the case of the cuts made by the BBC to her television play *The Legion Hall Bombing*, based on a Northern Ireland trial transcript. This prompted TWU to join with ITC to hold a one-day conference on 'Political Censorship in Alternative Theatre', which resolved:

> ... the right of artists, writers and all theatre workers like all citizens, to free speech and public discussion of politics except where these freedoms are used to propogate racial hatred or for discrimination on grounds of gender and sexual orientation.[16]

The conference served as a useful preliminary to a larger and broader-based 'Extent of Censorship Conference' organised by TWU in January 1979, attended by more than 400 people from the communications media. This conference heard of censorship in the areas of Industrial Affairs, Sexual Politics, Racism, Northern Ireland and State Security. At the end of the day a swingeing resolution was passed, with profound political implications:

> This conference urges union members to raise issues of censorship and self-censorship and social, sexual and racial discrimination at branch level – with the aim that the TUC should *implement* a policy to prevent censorship attacking the political consciousness and social progress of the working class.[17]

And a new all-media, multi-union action committee was set up to counteract censorship in what the conference felt was a forthcoming period of 'McCarthyism' in political censorship – what Lillian Hellman described as 'the time of the toad'. With this commonly held view of the eighties, one of the Theatre Writers Union's future functions was clearly to be in the area of stopping censorship.

1978

In 1978, Paul Thompson, who had previously worked primarily for the National Youth Theatre and in collaboration with Steve Gooch, made an impact in his own right with *The Lorenzaccio Story* produced by the RSC at the Warehouse to considerable acclaim. The play was adapted from Alfred de Musset's play of 1833, and Thompson's treatment of the original, relatively apolitical material illustrated one of the several ways in which a socialist perspective had begun – towards the end of the seventies – to inform work which would previously have been presented outside any kind of overt political context. The historical situation – and Musset's handling of it – had always been interpreted as 'a view of history which glorified the individual and denigrated the mass'. And Lorenzaccio was always presented as 'the archetypal bourgeois hero, romantic, individualistic and self-obsessed'.[1] Thompson wanted to focus on the economic conditions at the time of that particular tyranny, to show 'how this act of tyrannicide failed to precipitate an uprising and remained the isolated action of one individual, the motivation for which is questionable'. So Thompson emphasised the class structure of Florentine society in the sixteenth century and filtered the story through the eyes of 'the poor man' who assassinates the assassin, and who appears at the beginning and the end and 'in all the servile roles throughout the action simply to remind an audience of his presence'. *The Lorenzaccio Story* was one of the many indications of the impact of political theatre on establishment theatre.

Again in 1978 the theatre joined in a campaign to free a prisoner –

in this case Jimmy Boyle, at one time known as Scotland's most violent prisoner, but who had been rehabilitated by an experimental Special Unit at Barlinnie Prison in Scotland. On this occasion the campaign called into question the whole concept of punitive imprisonment and challenged the ideology and methods of the prison system. As part of the campaign poet Tom McGrath, with Jimmy Boyle, wrote a play called *The Hardman* which showed the brutalisation of prisoners and prison officers in conventional prisons, and argued the case for prison alternatives such as the Barlinnie Special Unit. The play toured the country and played at the ICA, drawing considerable support for the cause. Certainly Boyle's case and the case for prison alternatives was still being pleaded in 1979 in the letter pages of *The Guardian* with such eminent signatories as Lord Gifford, Christopher Hill and Alan Sillitoe.

In the summer of 1978 the Albany Empire, one of the most popular of community theatre venues, was destroyed by arson. It was an incident which highlighted the nature and importance of political theatre work in the seventies. An account of the circumstances surrounding the fire is included in the following essay on the work of The Combination, in 1968 one of the first fringe theatre companies, presenting in Brighton the early work of Portable Theatre and the new generation of playwrights, by 1978 having expanded its work into the deprived area of Deptford in South London.

The Combination – though possibly more overtly political than some – typified the work of other community theatre companies. There was East End Abbreviated Soapbox Theatre (the agitprop arm of an East London Community Action Centre), Free Form Arts Trust, also based in East London, and Covent Garden Community Theatre. Outside London there was the Interplay Community Theatre in Leeds, Word and Action in Dorset, Medium Fair Theatre Company operating in rural areas of Devon, The Emerging Dragon, serving Somerset and the South West, Open Cast in Wales, Key Perspectives in East Anglia. Red Ladder, the seminal socialist company, had acknowledged the value of this kind of theatre in its move to Leeds in 1974, as had Ed Berman in building his community arts empire.

In demonstrating the commitment of The Combination against considerable odds, this book concludes on an optimistic note. At the same time there is a note of pessimism in the essay on the work of another notable Portable writer, David Hare, who by 1978 was acknowledging the significant extent of the political theatre movement, but calling into question its aims and achievements. Whilst

Hare was in a minority with his views, his was undoubtedly a necessary element in any assessment of a decade which had produced so much, and so much of a controversial and contentious nature.

'*GOT YOU*.' Letter from Column 88, the paramilitary or terrorist wing of the fascist movement in Britain, to The Combination at the Albany Empire, Deptford, July 1978

The Combination

On the night of Thursday 13 July, the Albany Empire was gutted by fire. Officially, Fire Service investigators were unable to ascertain the cause, but arson has not been ruled out. The theatre is totally destroyed.[1]

The news of the Albany fire in the summer of 1978 was greeted with dismay in the theatre and out. The Combination – the theatre company based at the Albany – had been Britain's first and foremost community theatre, as that kind of theatre had come to be widely known and practised by the end of the seventies. From its origins in Brighton in 1967, it had provided a platform for the new generation of English playwrights (Howard Brenton and John Grillo, in particular) and a venue for early touring companies like Portable, The People Show and Freehold; it had been a source of inspiration for the work of John McGrath, Ed Berman and others; and it had pioneered a unique new form of entertainment.

The many activities at the Albany Empire in Deptford from 1973 represented the culmination of ten years of politically committed, highly original and very successful community work – of which theatre was just a part. Indeed, the fire itself could be taken as a measure of both the commitment and the success, for despite official claims to the contrary, there was strong evidence that it had been deliberate arson by an extreme right-wing group aiming to stop any future such anti-racist, anti-fascist work in the area. The likely cause of the fire and its cover up in a curious way illustrated the whole raison d'être of this kind of political theatre – its theory, practice and role – the needs to which it was responding, and the varying responses to it. Certainly The Combination were determined to resist defeat, to start again, 'to rise phoenix-like from the ashes': and the Albany *did* re-open in December 1978.

Following the fire, Greenwich police issued a statement which specifically ruled out the possibility of arson. Officials suggested that an electrical fault was to blame, but the electricity had been turned off at the mains. The local fire officer's views – as well as the facts – did not accord with the police verdict. The fire official concluded that arson could not be ruled out: 'We can't say it's arson – only a court can say that.'[2] But the courts never had the opportunity because there was no further official investigation.

Instead it fell to the All Lewisham Campaign Against Racism and Fascism (ALCARAF[3]) to investigate and on 1 August 1978 to issue a report:

> ALCARAF believes the fire was started deliberately. We have said we think there is every probability that this was the work of the National Front or their supporters. We are aware that in saying this we are directly contradicting the official statements of the Greenwich police ... We are in fact gravely concerned at the apparent indifference to this attack. We intend to try to bring pressure to bear on the Home Office and to insist that suspected racist and fascist crimes are treated with the seriousness they deserve. Before doing so, however, we must explain our reasons for reaching the conclusions above. These can be summarised as follows:
>
> 1) The expert opinion of the fire officer in charge of the case is that the fire was almost certainly started deliberately.
> 2) The Albany Empire and the Combination theatre group who are based there are well-known for their work in the field of race relations.
> 3) The Albany Institute is affiliated to ALCARAF and they played the major part in staging with us the 'All Together Now' festival in Deptford in the three weeks prior to the May local council elections. We believe this helped significantly in bringing about the National Front's resounding electoral defeat in Lewisham.
> 4) A note claiming to come from 'Column 88' (believed to be the paramilitary wing of the fascist movement in Britain) and indicating responsibility was delivered to the Albany shortly afterwards.[4]

Certainly, The Albany Empire had been at the front line of local, anti-rascist, anti-fascist activities. One of their most popular shows had been their then current *Restless Natives* by John Burrows, a series of satirical songs and sketches on racism. There was, for example, a *This Is Your Life* on the death of David Oluwale, for which the police had 'no case to answer' in the scandalous real life event of 1969, and a music-hall style monologue by a lady on how hard it is to be a Nazi; there was a dramatisation of the rise and fall of the Third Reich, including the Second World War, performed outdoors during the interval in the 'Smallest Theatre in the World'; audience participation in a 'Discrimination Game'; and the politics of race prejudice among kitchen appliances. All in all it was the kind of knees-up evening packed with political punch that The Albany Empire's faithful followers (and there were many) had come to love.

The last public performance at The Albany Empire before the fire had been a music benefit for the SUS Campaign. (The SUS Law was the out-dated and abused 1824 Vagrancy Act which allowed anyone to be arrested 'on suspicion of being about to commit an arrestable offence' and which was being used alarmingly often against young blacks.) Rock Against Racism (with Red Saunders, who had been with CAST at its beginning) had recently concluded a series of concerts at The Albany, and in April 1978, The Combination had, as ALCARAF explained, been closely involved in the local festival. In these circumstances, the ALCARAF conclusions of right-wing arson were not surprising.

The way in which The Combination came to be the centre of such a political controversy exemplified the development of politically committed community theatre. The Combination was started in 1967 by Jennie Harris (still the director in 1979), Ruth Marks (later an Arts Council officer) and Noel Greig (who went on in 1973 to work with The General Will and later Gay Sweatshop). They had all been at university together (LSE and Kings College respectively) until 1966 and had been strongly influenced by Jim Haynes and his Edinburgh Bookshop and Traverse Theatre (even before Haynes moved to the Drury Lane Arts Lab in London, which coincided with the opening of The Combination in Brighton); by Stephen Joseph's concept of community theatre-in-the-round in Scarborough; by a powerful negative reaction against the hierarchical establishment theatre opportunities in rep and the BBC; by student political ferment in the United States (where Jennie Harris visited in 1967); and by music. Jennie Harris:

> In 1960 if you were interested in theatre you had to climb the ladder, go into rep, be an ASM, then a DSM. Or you went into the BBC and became a floor manager, or if you were one of the five lucky ones, you became an ATV trainee. And if you were interested in politics, you went into the Labour Party. There was no sense that creative work had any link with the real world. The amazing thing about the sixties was that there was this very utopian, possibly misguided belief that there was a generation who might do something. I think that came out of the music.'[5]

They had also been influenced by The People Show performing in Better Books' basement, and they had seen CAST. The original idea of The Combination was to have a 'dance hall, not a theatre, because we had all been anti the institution of theatre. The crucial thing was to find a new audience. We were trying to create a new context. We were trying to create something that wasn't a theatre, but which was a place where you could put on plays. And have a very sympathetic and positive atmosphere. Very casual, without all the protocol, without all the red plush and booking tickets – the middle-aged, middle-class thing.'

In 1967 they were ready to find a place to try the idea out. They rejected London 'because at that point it was "swinging London". Very tough and competitive, brash and big and you needed money. And I just knew we would never survive. And there was Jim Haynes coming down to London, and he was very much more experienced, much tougher, a wheeler-dealer. We wanted to get out of London. Brighton was just a pin on the map.' They named themselves The Combination on the principle that they would be combining different forms of entertainment for different audiences. And they found a tiny café in Brighton – open all the time, with live music – with a little old school hall at the back for shows.

The audience they were aiming for was important:

> Then we really believed that there was a generation that could cross class boundaries. I think we were very naive. Now I think that can only work with a certain age group. Although at times it really did work in Brighton. In fact, it worked ever such a lot. We had a very mixed class range within the age range of 16 to 30. We were getting to the kids who were on the beaches and unemployed. And if the professionals and the students came too, that was great. As long as it mixed.

The way they worked was also important:

> We were trying at that point to be political in a very day to day active way. We were trying to run the company as a co-operative, which I don't think a lot of people who just came in understood. It seemed very chaotic – there wasn't a director. We didn't want the hierarchical, authoritarian structure of a rep. The company ran the whole operation – cooked the meals, did everything.

And from the beginning, the theatre was only a part of the whole scene:

> We did shows six nights a week – ever such a lot of plays. I don't know how we did it. The films and the discos were after the plays. And there was poetry reading and performance art, bookstalls, poster workshop, dance classes, kids' dance classes – and anything anybody wanted to do. We did make mistakes about what we were doing – what plays we were putting on. But at the best of times, there was a total fusion.

By 1968–69, The Combination at Brighton was sufficiently successful to attract playwrights like Howard Brenton: 'They saw it and thought great, an ideal place to put on our plays. And I really think that is all they saw, not the whole thing, not the new audiences. They just saw a little company to put on their plays. But none of them actually stayed because we weren't interested in what they were interested in – which was a literary field. Howard stayed with us a time and we did a number of his plays. But after a while he decided he wanted to write plays for theatre audiences. We were more interested in the *process* and the young people that were coming in.' Nevertheless Brenton and director Chris Parr were sufficiently enamoured with it to want to turn it into a place for new playwrights and actually went so far as to put a scheme to the Arts Council. Brenton:

> We didn't really know what we were doing at The Combination, we were feeling our way. But all the elements that are in the fringe, that have developed since, were there. There was the idea that theatre should be communicative work, socially and politically active. There was the idea of very aggressive theatrical experiment.[6]

But it was the local community that interested The Combination:

> Just kids, dossers actually. Like Colin and Dave who ran the coffee bar. They didn't have a higher education. Colin was literally a young dosser of 23-24, Dave had done a year at art school and left and was dossing on the beach. It sounds romantic, but it's true that people like that really grasped what we were doing. They contributed a lot and criticised a lot, either by implying that we were shits or that we had our heads in the clouds. I actually came into contact with people who came from a completely different class and found that communication with them was very strong. And that really gave us confidence. I never wanted the audience to be the classic working-class audience which is what John McGrath really wanted. We wanted kids in jeans and sweatshirts, not the miners. We were getting to a *real* working-class audience who were out for a knees-up and a good time. And we were going into the places that they knew and not the places *we* knew, which were theatres. That's what The Combination was about really – creating a place that people could feel was their own. We thought drama should be something else than didactic. A very clear statement of life, I suppose. And meaning. Within a very clear context.

When the local Brighton community began to change in 1969, The Combination decided to move out and on. Brighton was getting 'too intellectual, too tight and too rigid, smart and trendy – horrible. There wasn't a strong working class ... it was a seaside town, very mobile population. We didn't want that.' The summer before they left Brighton they turned the disco over to the Skinheads and their music. The students' reaction when they came back in the autumn was that the 'yobbos' had been let in. Jennie Harris: 'That was my final disillusionment.'

They decided they'd go round the country and find somewhere else to settle. They 'wanted a much stronger community to work in'. So they spent the summer of 1971 working in 'one of the toughest areas of Liverpool – an Irish Catholic community'. They had, in Brighton, just got together one of their better plays, *The NAB Show* – about social security, which conveniently coincided with the Claimants Unions that were starting then:

> We were getting fed up with our student audience, and we'd had all those kids in who were on the NAB – the old word for social security, and we wanted to make a statement to them. So we said, let's do a show about being on the dole. So we did and suddenly had people from all over the country asking us to do the show – for community workers and political people and Claimants Unions. And we suddenly realised we were performing to groups of people who had a very direct relationship with the material in the show. It was a constituent audience. They were the ones who really understood it. It was a mixture of agit-prop and music hall – quite shambolic really, but it was aimed at a popular audience.

In Liverpool The Combination did a lot of community work – 'street theatre, going out with the kids to their summer camps'. Then they went on tour all around England (1971 was still early days for small-scale touring) with shows for both children and adults:

> We tried to explore new venues, that was the crucial thing. By that time the fringe circuit had started building up – the arts centres. We were doing all the places that Portable and Freehold were doing. But at the same time we were trying to build up a circuit of community venues – youth clubs, schools, community centres. You'd get your money from the arts centres and use it for the youth clubs. We were constantly trying to find that new audience.

Unlike CAST and Red Ladder, and later The General Will and 7:48, The Combination didn't aim for the trades unions. Politically they were non-aligned:

> We regarded our politics as Marxist or socialist – definitely yes. But definitely non-aligned. We came under pressure from the IS (International Socialists) in Brighton who tried to get a hold on The Combination. But we resisted, because we felt the left had a lot of blind spots about things that are crucial to what socialism is about.

Jennie Harris's position was typical of many political theatre workers:

> I would never have joined one of those organisations and probably never
> will. I would be terribly worried even now if someone came to the
> Albany and they were good and said they were from any of those groups
> – WRP, SWP. I would be worried and would have to talk with them
> for days about it. When I was at LSE I got a great dose of 'the move-
> ment' and got terribly disillusioned. By nature I am very non-
> theoretical. Of course we saw ourselves as part of a movement on the
> left, involved in the Vietnam demos, the LSE sit-in. Our politics weren't
> just about putting ideas into art, but actually being involved in left
> politics. But there was a need for real action, not just sitting around in
> coffee bars and printing pamphlets. I still distrust so much of the
> pamphleteering and theorising of the left. I think they are terribly
> patronising and puritan and don't know the working class and don't
> know where it's at.

The move to the Albany came at the end of 1971. The Albany
Trust, of which The Combination and later The Albany Empire,
were a part, was a long-standing community action centre.

> It was one of the old Victorian charities, going since 1894. In the
> sixties it became a much more active, quite radical and progressive
> social action centre, pioneering a lot of work. Squatting was pioneered
> from the Albany for example. And work with single-parent families,
> short-life housing, community work and radical youth work. And
> it had a really good director who was so radical that he realised that
> art had a place in a deprived urban area like Deptford. So he got
> the Gulbenkian Foundation to fund a three-year arts project, which
> must have been about the first community arts project the
> Gulbenkian funded. He put an ad in *New Society* which said the
> Albany wanted to start a community arts project and wanted two
> people to run it. We saw it and thought, Christ, if we went, they
> would actually pay us to do what we were doing. So we said we'd
> do a deal: you employ us and we'll bring along our own company
> which has got its own funding from the Arts Council. And that is
> basically what happened. They were terribly far-sighted and said, you
> come along and run this project, bring your company and you can
> have the use of the hall on condition you do stuff that is good for
> Deptford. We thought it was amazing, the chance to work closely
> with community workers. The chance to establish a project in a build-
> ing that wasn't an art house, that had its own identity, that was
> known by the people in the area. We had found our base.

The set-up was perfect for The Combination's purposes, because
the Albany Trust was involved with pre-school playgroups, youth
work, alternative education, student training, work with the elderly,

community work (welfare rights counselling, short-life housing for single-parent families, issue-oriented work with tenants' associations and other local groups), arts and crafts workshops, the SE London Claimants Union and the Lewisham Family Squatting Association.

Before opening The Albany Empire, The Combination did two years of work 'on demand out in the streets':

> We were on the end of a phone. And we said to people, if you want something give us a ring. Whether it's an entertainer for a children's party, a play about a rent strike to tour, a piece of street stuff ... whatever. At first local people didn't understand what we were doing because they had had no first hand experience of live performance or accessible art. If we started talking about theatre they just clammed up. They only know about what's on TV. We had an enormous job to do: we needed to reinterpret what art was all about. We needed to make people confident that it was relevant, accessible and part of the mainstream of life. We were trying to stimulate. We started pottery workshops, video and film projects, mural painting ... everything that is now called community arts.

The last thing Jennie Harris wanted to do was start a theatre in the conventional sense. But under pressure from the company, she compromised by 'opening a place that had music and drink and that would appeal to our generation'. The Arts Council refused to help, but in 1973, The Albany Empire opened:

> I think what we have created is the *place*. You can eat and drink and watch the show and you can dance afterwards. It's very casual, you don't have to book tickets. And we've got a new young audience. It's worked. I am now confident to go to anyone – like the National Theatre with their Cottesloe and say they've done completely the wrong thing. What they should be doing is a version of The Albany Empire. You can do serious work there, and I'm absolutely sure that it works. I've no idea why people who run places like the Cottesloe don't do it.

Jennie Harris was convinced of the success of the context and also of the content of the shows, which from the beginning attempted to combine music, music hall, cabaret and political comment in the right mixture for local audiences. 'I think we have definitely worked out how to integrate good music into a show. That isn't just schmaltzy West-End-musical type music. Super music, with good lyrics. That has been very exciting. And working with good contemporary musicians, and having them work with the writer and director. It's getting better and better.' In 1978 The Combination were still trying to perfect their work:

We are still trying to find a new audience – a non-theatre-going, non-intellectual, non-literary, non-middle-class, non-higher education audience. And to find a popular form of drama, that is not just mock-music hall, but contemporary and valid and strong. We are still trying to create a context that isn't a theatre or a literary club or a commercial rip-off, a place the people feel is theirs and that has an identity. And we are still trying to tell the community we are there. Trying to have some political affect.

In their quest, The Combination realised the limitations of political theatre, and because they were working in the much wider context of the Albany Trust, they could accept the limitations:

When we realise it is better to produce a poster than do a bit of theatre, then we produce a poster. If people come and say to us can you do a show on something, nine times out of ten we say, look go and use the video project – it's much better, faster, cheaper and you don't have to spend eight weeks with eight people shut up in a room rehearsing a play. We can say, you don't need a play but a film, slide show, tape, series of posters, pamphlet. And as an arts project we can help them get all that together. I think we have been lucky because we have been liberated from the need to try to make our art do *everything* political.

The Combination also learned that social change is a slow process, that the revolution is not around the corner. Jennie Harris: 'When we first went to Deptford, we said this is a three year project. Then after three years, we said five years, and after five, twenty. I suddenly realised it is a huge arrogance to think that you can change the last 100 years of history – of exploitation and alienation – in two or three or four years. It's an amazingly slow process – through the revolution or to the revolution or to the ten years before the revolution or whatever.'

This was the achievement that the fire of 1978 threatened. But the phoenix did rise from the ashes – in six short months: yet another measure of The Combination's commitment. *Time Out* welcomed the grand re-opening:

The gutted interior has been gloriously reconstructed to recapture that cosy community-centre knees-up atmosphere so many people came to love over the years. The balcony is still there – painted pink now – and the bar, the café tables, the stage – tinselled silver. It's good and gaudy with a touch of art nouveau and the walls are lined with mirrors – to reflect the fun.[7]

The reconstruction work was done with the support and solidarity of the local community and from theatre workers:

... with the help of countless friends, they started straightaway to re-build. Insurance covered the cost of the structure and a Manpower Services Grant provided previously unemployed labour. Equipment hadn't been insured, but money came pouring in – from theatres and fringe theatre companies (though the NT's £10 and the Royal Court's fiver looked a bit mean next to cheques from Welfare State, Croydon Warehouse and Hull Truck to the tune of £100), from Unions (NUPE, SOGAT, the Writers Guild), from local authority and local groups. The Gulbenkian Foundation gave £4000 while the Arts Council was conspicuously absent from the long list of those who donated to the Fire Fund.[8]

The Combination was not to be intimidated by arson or any other attacks. In 1979 it was continuing its committed work with the Deptford community and preparing to open a new, purpose-built theatre.

'We have looked. We have seen. We have known. And we have not changed ... It is hard to believe in the historical inevitability of something which has so frequently not happened.' David Hare, 'A Lecture Given at King's College, Cambridge' 1978

David Hare

David Hare was one of the more radical figures in the British theatre of the seventies, not just in the content of his plays (*Fanshen*, written with Joint Stock was one of the classic achievements of political theatre) but in the conduct of his work – in starting Portable Theatre; initiating and organising the groups of writers who co-wrote *Lay By* and *England's Ireland*; in starting Joint Stock with William Gaskill and Max Stafford-Clark. Yet with the exception of *Fanshen*[1] Hare's plays were primarily concerned with middle-class life, often brilliantly dramatised, but with a degree of cynicism, showing *that* life enduring despite attempts to alter it. And in 1978 he delivered a lecture at a conference on political theatre in Cambridge (later published as an appendix to the text of his TV play *Licking Hitler*) which called into question the fundamental aims and achievements of political theatre. He did so with such an air of contempt that it left many members of the political theatre movement reeling as if from an unexpected, undeserved blow. Hare had not quietly sold out (he had arguably not sold out at all), but aggressively put himself on a platform to point an accusing finger. Was he a renegade, or a harshly realistic re-evaluator during a period of self-criticism and consolidation?

In his retrospective, Hare acknowledged the inclinations of the theatre towards politics over the previous ten years:

> One of the reasons for the theatre's possible authority, and for its recent general drift towards politics, is its unique suitability to displaying an age in which men's ideals and men's practice bear no relation to each other; in which the public profession of, for example, socialism has often been reduced by the passage of history to wearying personal fetish, or even chronic personality disorder.[2]

'Exposing the difference between what a man says and what he does' was, said Hare, what the theatre had always done best. Which was why there was nothing on stage so exciting as a great lie – and why *Brassneck* (written jointly with Howard Brenton) weakened as a play when its greatest liar was killed off at the end of the first act.

One of the functions of the theatre was similar to that of the satirist, based on the principle of 'If only you knew', and providing information:

> If only you knew that Eden was on Benzedrine throughout the Suez crisis, stoned out of his head and fancy-free; if only you knew that the crippled, stroke-raddled Churchill dribbled and farted in Cabinet for two years after a debilitating stroke, and nobody dared remove him; if only you knew that Cabinet Ministers sleep with tarts, that Tory MPs liaise with crooked architects and bent offshore bankers: if only you knew.[3]

The problem with the information-providing approach of theatre, and particularly of political theatre, was the audience replying 'Well we do know now; and we don't believe it will ever change. And knowing may well not affect what we think.' The level of sophistication with regard to information received – in the theatre, if not generally – had risen over ten years and had proved of relatively little relevance.

Consciousness-raising had been the claim of many (if not all) political theatre workers and companies since 1968. 'Yet,' said Hare, 'consciousness has been raised in this country for a good many years now and we seem further from radical political change than at any time in my life. The traditional function of the radical artist – "Look at those Borgias; look at this bureaucracy" – has been undermined. We have looked. We have seen. We have known. And we have not changed.'[4] In short, political theatre had had very little effect as far as consciousness-raising was concerned:

> The urban proletariat in this country knows better than we ever can that they are selling their labour to capital; many of them know far better than we of the degradations of capitalism. Of the wretched and the inadequate housing into which many of them are born; of the grotesque, ever worsening imbalance in the educational system whereby the chances of progress to examinability even at 'O' level, even at CSE level, is still ludicrously low; of the functional and enslaving work they are going to have to do; of the lack of control they are going to suffer at their own workplace. Of all these things they know far more than we, and, most importantly, they are familiar with socialist ideas which see their sufferings as part of a soluble political pattern.[5]

Given all that, asked Hare, why had the level of revolutionary activity been so miserably low? Worse still, he said, 'we have lived through a time of economic depression which classically in Marxist theory is supposed to throw up those critical moments at which the proletariat may seize power ... It is hard to believe in the historical inevitability of something which has so frequently not happened.'

Hare made a specific attack on the techniques of political theatre as employed by 'the slaves of Marxist fashion'.

> Why do we so often have to endure the demeaning repetition of slogans which are seen not as transitional aids to understanding, but as ultimate solutions to men's problems? Why the insulting insistence in so much political theatre that a few gimcrack mottoes of the left will sort out the deep problems of reaction in modern England? Why the urge to caricature? Why the deadly stiffness of limb? Brecht uncoils the great sleeping length of his mind to give us in everything but the greatest of his writing exactly that impression, the godlike feeling that the questions have been answered before the play has begun.[6]

And there was the matter of Marxist writers wearing their political credentials on their sleeves:

> The Marxist playwright ... thinks that because the play itself is part of the class struggle, an object, a weapon in that struggle, that he must first say which side he is on and make that clear, before he proceeds to lay out the ideas of the play as fairly as he may. To me this approach is rubbish, it insults the audience's intelligence; more important, it is also a fundamental misunderstanding of what a play is.[7]

If a play was going to be a weapon in the class struggle, then it would be so in 'the interaction of what you are saying and what the audience is thinking'. Hare concluded that 'dramatists have lately taken to brandishing their credentials' precisely because their theatre was failing as theatre.

Hare outlined what he'd been trying to do as a playwright:

> For five years I have been writing history plays. I try to show the English their history. I write tribal pieces, trying to show how people behaved on this island, off this continental shelf, in this century. How this Empire vanished, how these ideals died ... When I first wrote, I wrote in the present day, I believed in a purely contemporary drama; so as I headed backwards, I worried I was copping out, avoiding the real difficulties of the day. It took me time to realise that the reason was, if you write about now, just today and nothing else, then you seem to be confronting only stasis; but if you begin to describe the movement of history, if you write plays that cover passages of time, then you begin to find a sense of movement, of social change, if you like: and the

facile hopelessness that comes from confronting the day and only the day, the room and only the room, begins to disappear and in its place the writer can offer a record of movement and change.[8]

Hare distinguished his outlook from 'the Marxist writers': he recognised the real changes that had taken place in the past thirty years, while 'the Marxist writer spends a great deal of time rebuking societies for not behaving in the way that he expected them to'. Hare:

> We are living through a great, groaning, yawling festival of change – but because this is England it is not always seen on the streets. In my view it is seen in the extraordinary intensity of people's personal despair, and it is to that despair that as a historical writer I choose to address myself time and time again: in *Teeth 'n' Smiles*, in *Knuckle*, in *Plenty*.[9]

Instead of seeing a socialist silver lining in the clouds of change, Hare had, in his plays, assumed that some of the changes in society may have been for the worse, that changes for the apparent good may have been illusory or of less importance than they might have seemed in the heady moments of their happenings. Within the perspective of a historical panorama, Hare had chronicled the life and times of that almost mythological generation of the sixties in plays which repeatedly symbolized the state of the nation, microcosms of a country in decline, its citizens in despair.

Teeth 'n' Smiles was a good 'early' (1975) example of this approach. The play was set in 1969 when a pop group is performing at a Cambridge ball. 'Let's smash the place up', says one of the musicians, and that is what they do, smashing themselves in the process. Maggie, the heroine and lead vocalist, burns down the tent in a deliberate attempt to go to prison. The group is busted for drugs. The group's manager is more interested in the group as a capital asset than for their art; the group is beset by internal strife. Arthur, the composer, is torn between the dreams of the group and his establishment background. The play functioned as a swan-song to the sixties and its various kinds of rebellion – through politics, sex, music, drugs. When the play ends, the group has come to an end and implicitly everything they have stood for. The play ends with a musical coda: 'The ship is sinking/And time is running out/But the music remains the same.' Clearly Hare was sceptical about the impact of the sixties and chose to use the liberated and liberating forces to symbolise the futility of the protests. England – the ship – was sinking before the sixties, and was still sinking after the counter-culture had come and gone. As Peter Ansorge pointed out, the 'hierarchical dated values of

Cambridge will survive long after the classless anarchy of the band has drowned in a sea of self-contempt and bitterness'.[10] Hare, referring to *Teeth 'n' Smiles*, said:

> ... all I was doing was observing the passing scene, its stridency, its hysteria, its obscenity, and trying to put it in a historical context which the literary community seems pathologically incapable of contemplating. In *Teeth 'n' Smiles* a girl chooses to go to prison because it will give her an experience of suffering which is bound in her eyes to be more worthwhile than the life she could lead outside: not one English critic could bring himself to mention this central event in the play, its plausibility, its implications. It was beyond their scope to engage with such an idea. And yet, how many people here have close friends who have taken control of their own lives, only to destroy them?[11]

Plenty, which opened at the National Theatre in 1978 directed by Hare himself, was a similar exposition of this world view, if anything more persuasive for the post-war history it spanned. The play opened and closed in war-time France where the heroine Susan 'fought' as an undercover agent and had 'the major positive experience of her life – it is her peace, the substance of the play in fact, which ruins her.'[12] As she remembers it: 'People I met only for an hour or two. Astonishing kindness. Bravery. The fact you could meet someone for an hour or two and see the very best of them and then move on.' For her, those two hours contained more of value than the whole of the following twenty years, during which she drifted in and out of jobs, married (and divorced) a diplomat whose career (like the empire) declines before her eyes. In a futile attempt to recapture the past, she 'returns' to France at the end of the play to 'relive' the momentary illusion that great changes were afoot. But it *was* an illusion, as the play has demonstrated. The post-war period may have been one of material 'plenty', but it was also one of moral bankruptcy. But the play was a parable of the economic and political decline of the English middle-class: Susan comes to realise how little was won in the war. Susan's response was the intense personal despair that Hare remarked upon as the subject to which he addressed himself, the play a summary of the disinheritance which so many of the writers of the sixties became aware of.

Licking Hitler, which Hare wrote for television in 1978, similarly used the Second World War to question the quality of post-war change. And Hare again exploited the intensity of war-time experience (as in *Plenty*) to indicate the potential (political and personal) which is never subsequently realised. Here the setting is an English country house in 1941 where the British are broadcasting anti-Nazi propaganda to Germany – 'encouraged to lie – to spread a network of deceit, rumour and havoc across Europe'.[13] Hare showed the seedier side of the war effort, the lack of scruples necessary to 'win the war'. But what was won? The end of the play reveals what happened later to the major characters. One became a cabinet minister in the 1966 Labour government – the government that sold out the socialist values of the Labour movement. Another became a famous writer of spy fiction. The main character made sentimental movies about his working-class childhood in Glasgow. The heroine dropped out of advertising and into the 'fringes of radical protest, an outcast from her class and upbringing. For her the war has been a painful journey towards truth – away from the "30-year-old deeply corrosive national habit of lying".'[14] Her final words are: 'While we all knew what we were fighting against – none of us had the whisper of an idea of what we were fighting for.' Like *Plenty*, the play questioned the values of post-war English society. If the war had been fought against fascism and for socialism (as it was for many of Hare's characters), it had failed in the latter and possibly the former.

Brassneck, which Hare co-authored with Howard Brenton in 1973, also tackled the state of the nation after the war, exploring bribery and corruption in the industrial Midlands during 'the last days of capitalism' – the kind of corrupt business which provided the peace-time 'plenty'. And in *Knuckle* in 1974, Hare took an equally cynical look at the corruption of 'big business' and the moral bankruptcy of the middle-class – this time using a 1940's Mickey Spillane framework for a stock-broker Surrey setting. As one of the characters in *Knuckle* says:

> Those who wish to reform the world should first know a little about it. I told her some stories of life in the city – the casual cruelty of each day. I talked across the breakwater. The drizzle had stopped. We talked – takeover bids, redundancies, men ruined overnight, jobs lost, trusts betrayed, reputations smashed, life in that great trough called the City of London, sploshing about in cash. And I asked what I have always asked. How will that ever change?[15]

In all his plays – with the significant exception of *Fanshen* – Hare wrote eloquently of the middle classes, of the people trapped in that class and of its durability – the durability of capitalism. People might wish it to change, but were foolish to think that it had. In the meantime Hare would try to do what a playwright could: 'put people's sufferings in a historical context, and by doing that . . . help to explain their pain'. *He* was careful to point out that what he meant by history was not 'the mechanised absolving force theorists would like it to be'.[16]

On one occasion only did Hare write with enthusiasm about the possibilities of radical revolutionary social change: that was in *Fanshen*. But then the history was of the East – in China during the Revolution – and not of the West. And a realistic assessment of the historical processes in China showed that revolutionary change was not illusory but actual. England, however, was not China, and Hare had never been prepared to presume that it was. In the West, revolution had never been around the corner. This view explained Hare's contempt for what he regarded as the facile sloganising of political theatre and its adherents who appeared to peddle easy and often irrelevant answers.

For Hare, the problem with political theatre was its assumption that all the questions had been asked and answered, when in fact, the crucial questions had not been asked at all.

> I write about politics because the challenge of communism, in however debased and ugly a form, is to ask whether the criteria by which we have been brought up are right; whether what each of us experiences uniquely really is what makes us valuable; whether every man should really be his own cocktail; or whether our criteria could and should be collective, and if they were, whether we would be any happier. However absolute the sufferings of men in the totalitarian Soviet countries, however decadent the current life of the West, the fact is that this question has only just been asked, and we have not even the first hundredth of an answer. To give up now would be death.[17]

Hare had not given up on his kind of political theatre. If anything he felt the need for it was more imperative than ever before because he now found 'a generation who are cowed, who seem to have given up on the possibility of change, who seem to think that most of the experiments you could make with the human spirit are likely to be doomed or at any rate highly embarrassing'. He felt that 'it would be sad if this historical period had no chroniclers'. And so he would continue to chronicle, with the degree of harsh realism and cold cynicism that the history of the Western world and the demands of late, but still lasting, capitalism required.

Postscript

1979 and the Future

At the end of the decade, there remained some pressing questions about the political theatre movement and its many diverse workers. What had been achieved? What would the future hold? What was changed? Certainly not the world. So, assessed on its own terms – on its desire to achieve a socialist society – the political theatre movement could only have been judged a failure. At the end of the sixties, there had been revolutionary fervour at all levels of society, the feeling that things were changing and could be changed. At the end of the seventies, the forces were reactionary and showed signs of becoming positively repressive. The political climate was becoming increasingly unsympathetic to socialism and to socialist theatre.

The Conservatives won a landslide victory in the General Election of 1979, an event which was clearly to mark the beginning of the end of the post-war era of British social and economic history. It was not just a Conservative government, but a right-wing Conservative government, and the Tory intentions were clear: to alter the tax system to favour the wealthy rather than the workers, to denationalise industries, to dismantle the National Health Service and the Welfare State, to cut public spending, particularly in the areas of health, education, welfare and the arts. Within months of coming to office, the Conservative axe had begun to hack the heart out of such socialist structures as had been built within Britain's mixed economy after the war. Barrie Keeffe, in his short play *Sus*, set on the election night (and written within weeks of the election), demonstrated the kind of attitudes that would prevail in the future. As the police sergeant interrogates (with physical as well as emotional violence) the victimised black, wrongly accused of killing his wife, he eulogises the new Conservative dawn which the victory of 'The Thatch' would herald. The pretence of good race relations could go, and the cops, at least, could put the racialist boot in with the full blessings of the powers to be. It was in the spring of 1979 during a demonstration at Southall (an area of London with a large Asian population) against the racism of the fascist party The National Front, that a teacher and member of the Anti-Nazi League was killed by the police, or so it seemed to many people.[1]

Thus in 1979 while the right went from strength to repressive strength, the left became weaker and increasingly defensive. From its perspective (crusading for a wholly and truly socialist society), the left had been consistently critical of the rightist elements in the Labour governments of the seventies, and had thereby in no way contributed to the continuance of the Labour Party in power. In 1979, not only was the left divided, but also the Labour Party and its allies, the unions. The foundations from which the forces of repression could be fought were unstable, if not crumbling. In retrospect some of the best work of the seventies had been prophetic of this state of affairs. Howard Brenton in *The Churchill Play*, set in 1984, had predicted the use of internment camps for 'political dissidents' in England, much like Long Kesh in Northern Ireland in the seventies. Brenton had also posited a Con/Lab Coalition Government, comprised of the right-wing of the Labour Party with the Conservatives, with the left of the Labour Party in minority impotence. Trevor Griffiths in *Bill Brand* had looked to a similar future for the Labour Party and the Labour movement.

With the Conservatives in power and the left in disarray, the future of left theatre was uncertain. Theatre workers talked of biding time, analysing theory and practice, consolidating achievements. There were forecasts of repression and censorship, the closing down of channels of communication (in theatre and television), even of a new era of McCarthyism. As Trevor Griffiths put it: 'The future is clearly one of struggle, and absolutely unremitting commitment to that struggle.' Most people shared Griffiths' views, and opinion was virtually unanimous that there would not be the 'selling out' of previous generations. What form, however, the action to the reaction would take was not clear.

The political theatre movement had failed to reach and convert or mobilise the mass of the population, even if it had managed to raise the consciousness of many individuals in pubs, clubs and work-places. It had, however, succeeded in 'penetrating the bourgeois theatre' with content and personnel. But, as it had not succeeded in changing the structure and power base of the bourgeois theatre, in a period of repression, the power of the penetrators would be tested, and likely to be found limited.

The dream of a popular socialist theatre had been around since the war – with Arnold Wesker's Centre 42 and Joan Littlewood's 'fun palaces for the people'. And in a very real sense the political theatre movement of the seventies made those dreams come true – by taking theatre to the people on a scale that had never happened before. But the dream of a popular socialist theatre building (space or place) of their own had not materialised, though the National Theatre – apotheosis of establishment theatre aspirations – had. It was Howard Brenton who pointed out the sad irony – that his generation had got the experience to realise the dream, experience lacking in the previous generation, but true to historical form: no money.

As subsidy had been crucial to the growth of political theatre, so it would be instrumental in its decline. And there were signs in 1979 that subsidy to alternative theatre would be reduced. In their first budget, the Conservatives cut the government allocation to the Arts Council, increased Value Added Tax (VAT) to 15% and enforced reduction in local authority expenditure. The theatre industry responded with anger (there was a 4000-strong Equity demonstration in July 1979) and action (The Theatres Advisory Council – TAC – launched a National Arts Campaign to protect the theatre). At this stage even the establishment theatre was concerned about the fate of alternative theatre, given the cuts and its relatively low priority in the subsidy hierarchy. It was not inconceivable that subsidy to this area of theatre would dry up altogether by the mid-eighties. Whether the theatre itself would disappear depended on the quantity and quality of commitment to the cause and to the struggle of which Trevor Griffiths spoke.

It was perhaps the image of Edward Bond's Lear that was most appropriate to political theatre at the end of the decade: still scaling the wall (symbolic of capitalist society and still most definitely in existence) and still likely to be shot down. Only time would tell whether foundations had been laid for future growth (politically and artistically), or whether political theatre in the seventies would simply become a chapter in a book. If only the latter, it would still have proved to have been an impressive achievement.

A balanced perspective, however, was hopefully that of David Edgar when he concluded that 'the realisation that socialist playwrights cannot themselves change the world might yet help them to discover ways of contributing, and in no small measure, to the work of those who can'.

Notes

Preface

1. 'At Ease in a Bright Red Tie', by John Whiting, *Encore*, September 1959. In *The Encore Reader, A Chronicle of the New Drama*, Methuen & Co. Ltd, London, 1965, pp. 105–6.
2. From an unpublished lecture given by John McGrath at King's College, Cambridge, Conference on Political Theatre, April 1978. See John McGrath, 'The Theory and Practice of Political Theatre', *Theatre Quarterly*, Vol. ix, No. 35, 1979.
3. Richard Seyd, 'The Theatre of Red Ladder', *The New Edinburgh Review*, August 1975.
4. *The Knotty*, A Musical Documentary, introduction and notes by Peter Cheeseman, Methuen and Co, London, 1970; *Fight for Shelton Bar*, A Documentary from the Victoria Theatre, Stoke-on-Trent with introduction and notes by Peter Cheeseman, Eyre Methuen, London, 1977.
5. Peter Cheeseman, 'A Community Theatre-in-the-Round,' and Production Casebook on 'The Staffordshire Rebels', *Theatre Quarterly*, Vol. I, No. I, 1971.
6. Gulbenkian also assisted financially in the publication of three collections of TIE scripts: *Theatre-in-Education: Five Infant Programmes, Theatre-in-Education: Four Junior Programmes*, and *Theatre-in-Education: Four Secondary Programmes*, all edited by Pam Schweitzer, Eyre Methuen, London 1980.
7. See Tony Coult, 'Class Struggles, an appraisal of theatre in education', *Platform* 1, 1979, p. 18.
8. For further information on alternative theatre see the *British Alternative Theatre Directory 1979* (and updated annually), ed. Catherine Itzin, John Offord Publications Ltd, Eastbourne, 1979.
9. David Edgar, 'Political Theatre, Parts One and Two', *Socialist Review*, April and May 1978.
10. Martin Esslin, *The Theatre of the Absurd*, third edition, Eyre Methuen, London 1974, p. xv.

Introduction

1. David Triesman, 'Culture Conflict and Political Advance in Britain', *Marxism Today*, May 1978, p. 164.
2. Eric Hobsbawm, '1968 – A Retrospect', *Marxism Today*, May 1978, p. 131.
3. From a letter to Catherine Itzin, from David Mercer, 22 October 1977.
4. For further useful information see David Bradby and John McCormick, *People's Theatre*, Croom Helm, London, 1978.
5. From an interview with Catherine Itzin for the purpose of this book, May 1978.

1968

1. From a leaflet entitled 'Quipu, A Brief Summary of its History, Policy and Plans', 1971. p. 2.
2. *Ibid*, p. 1.

CAST (Cartoon Archetypical Slogan Theatre)

1. From an unpublished interview with Roland Muldoon by Catherine Itzin, 1978. Unless otherwise indicated all quotations from Muldoon are from that interview.
2. *Plays & Players*, January 1977, 'CAST Revival', a report by Roland Muldoon, pp. 40–1.
3. *Ibid*.
4. *Ibid*.
5. *Ibid*.
6. *Confessions of a Socialist*, a play by CAST, Pluto Press, 1979.
7. *Plays & Players*, op. cit.
8. Anon., 'Grant Aid and Political Theatre', *Wedge*, Summer 1977.
9. *Plays & Players*, op. cit.
10. Albert Hunt, *Arden, a Study of His Plays*, Eyre Methuen, London, 1974, p. 127.
11. *Arden, a Study of His Plays*, op. cit.
12. John Arden, *To Present the Pretence: Essays on the Theatre and its Public*, Eyre Methuen, London, 1977, pp. 83–4.
13. Margaretta D'Arcy's and John Arden's comments on reading the MS. of *Stages in the Revolution*:

    Roland Muldoon's interview is great stuff to read and we're sure he does really remember it like that: a swift zippy retrospective hard-sell ad for the laid-back lads sailing Clint Eastwood-like through the activist aggro and agitprop of the late sixties. Hostile gun-slingers fall left and right beside their track – so apparently do women. Margaretta D'Arcy vanishes almost completely from sight except for a forlorn caption-bubble reading 'Ridiculous' and is replaced in the fantasy by the eccentric 'great playwright' John Arden, riddled with guilt from the privileged echelons of the Royal Court, willing to be instructed by the young lions, and offering his precious gift to the service of 'resistance'; while Tamara Hinchco, the professional actress who took over the notorious nude-scene when all the others were afraid of prosecution, loses her name in favour of an inaccurate joke about a political party. As a result, the basic reason for our breakdown of communications with CAST in the later stages of rehearsal (over the nude-scene, significantly) is (a) misunderstood, and (b) paradoxically highlighted.

Facts. Margaretta D'Arcy saw *John D Muggins Is Dead* and was enthusiastic: impressed, particularly, by the continuity of fast-moving images. CAST put an ad in *Peace News* for premises in which to rehearse. Margaretta D'Arcy was away at the time, but asked John Arden (who had not seen CAST perform) to contact them and let them use the house in Muswell Hill. A couple of months later, when both D'Arcy and Arden were in London, we gave a party for La Mama from New York, to which CAST, and Michael Kustow, were invited. Roland was seeking premises for a permanent cultural socialist centre: we said we were interested (because of our recent anti-Vietnam War agitprop experiences in the USA), and so did Kustow. Kustow cried off shortly afterwards to take over the ICA: but contact was made with George Clarke in Notting Hill, as being a likely community for such a project. He found a hall there, where we began some improvisations on the take-over of a café by gangsters, à la Kray–Richardson, using Muggins as the central character. This was to have been an environmental play set in a practicable café, and directed towards the local community. But the Notting Hill hall proved not to be available, so we dropped the project.

In spring 1968 Roland told us that Unity Theatre was available. D'Arcy said she still wanted much of the original café community-environment idea kept, and got in touch with John Fox and others to help make this. We had to write a *draft* script very quickly. Roland was given overall control of the production, which was to have slide-shows, music etc. CAST for this production was Roland and two others – the rest of the company was from Unity, plus various others, odd Americans etc. Two people from the San Francisco Mime Troop were working with us on children's plays etc. and later pioneered street-theatre in London. We had told Roland that the draft script was only a basis for improvisation – we had worked in this way before, in Yorkshire, and America. As it turned out, there was no time for any improvisatory development (we only rehearsed three nights a week). Roland spent most of that time replacing music and slides with elaborate lighting-plot and tableaux, which prolonged the brief script to two and a half hours and contradicted the speech-rhythms.

The breakdown over the nude-scene. Roland objected to this episode:

he did not understand its purpose, to analyse sexual exploitation of women. We later found that Unity had put the clamps down on this scene. We successfully resisted: said 'no nude, no play'. All communication between us and Roland ended there. We took it that neither Roland nor Unity was serious about D'Arcy/Arden's actual *work* but only wanted John Arden's name for prestige purposes. D'Arcy concentrated on her original concepts of external community/environment activities and children's theatre: in an atmosphere of indifference from CAST, and Unity (who did not want to be identified with the local working class lest it impede their vision of representing the whole of the Labour movement). This work was not hindered so long as we took full responsibility for safety – Unity not being insured for outside events. Throughout this period there were no political discussions: Roland appeared terrified of Margaretta D'Arcy and never opened his mouth . . .

In hindsight the main differences between us were ones of previous experience: (1) D'Arcy coming from Ireland, was very sensitive to authoritarian steam-rolling, censorship, denigration and suppression of women: and D'Arcy/Arden had both been in the Committee of 100 with its commitment to civil disobedience. (2) Arden coming from Yorkshire was imbued with Messianic rage about the thinness and feebleness of language in the media, regarding this as theft of the working class's natural heritage. Ironically had Roland paid attention to the vigorous and poetic improvised plays of the pre-pubertal children from the Somers Town estate, he would have understood what Arden was getting at. (3) Roland's attitude to Arden was misleadingly based on the bourgeois media's treatment of the so-called Angry Young playwrights, and we did not appreciate how effective this had been: and what blocks it made for younger theatre-workers trying to collaborate with us. Unfortunately this still goes on.

We got a lot out of the Unity project: because we had done such a variety of things in it, culminating in an improvised version of the play for local kids on a Sunday afternoon as part of a big party. Roland dropped his lighting-plot and tableaux, we dropped the written script, and the result was a fast-moving, funny panto, with the actors influenced but not enslaved by the rhythms of the original language.

Note: the poem JA read at the Vietnam Rally (1967) was by Ginsberg and was about *America*: Civil Rights blew up in Ireland in *1968*.

John Arden and Margaretta D'Arcy

1. John Arden, *To Present the Pretence, Essays on the Theatre and its Public*, Eyre Methuen, London, 1977, p. 48.
2. Albert Hunt, *Arden, A Study of His Plays*, Eyre Methuen, London, 1974, p. 18.
3. John Arden, *Serjeant Musgrave's Dance*, Introduction by John Arden, Methuen & Co. Ltd, London, 1960, p. 7.

4. *To Present the Pretence*, pp. 157–8.
5. Albert Hunt, p. 22.
6. *To Present the Pretence*, pp. 49–50.
7. *Ibid*, p. 48.
8. John Arden's response to reading the MS. of *Stages in the Revolution*.
9. *Ibid*.
10. *To Present the Pretence*, p. 47.
11. *Ibid*, p. 46.
12. *Ibid*, pp. 59–60.
13. John Arden, *Left Handed Liberty*, Author's Note, Methuen & Co. Ltd, London, p. xii.
14. Albert Hunt, p. 107.
15. John Russell Taylor, Introduction to *John Arden Three Plays*, Penguin, 1967, p. 10.
16. 'Building the Play', Interview with John Arden, *Encore*, July–August 1961, p. 31.
17. John Russell Taylor, *Anger and After*, Methuen & Co. Ltd, 1962, p. 84.
18. John Arden, *Encore*, Sept. Oct. 1964.
19. *To Present the Pretence*, pp. 155–6.
20. *Ibid*, p. 83.
21. *Ibid*, p. 149.
22. *Ibid*, p. 150.
23. Albert Hunt, p. 143.
24. *Ibid*.
25. From an unpublished interview with Catherine Itzin, January 1978.
26. *To Present the Pretence*, p. 157.
27. *Ibid*, p. 84.
28. *Ibid*, p. 166.
29. John Arden, *The Workhouse Donkey*, Author's Preface, Methuen & Co. Ltd, London, 1964, p. 8.
30. 'On Comedy: John Arden Talks to Albert Hunt about *The Workhouse Donkey*', *Encore*, Sept.–Oct. 1965, p. 18.
31. John Arden's response to the MS. of *Stages in the Revolution*: 'More precisely, D'Arcy has ceased to be invited: and Arden, *if* he insists on continuing to work with her. His own work, he has been informed through the usual subterranean British channels, would always be welcome provided it is divorced from hers.'
32. Margaretta D'Arcy and John Arden, *The Non-Stop Connolly Show*, Pluto Press, London, 1978.
33. See *To Present the Pretence*, p. 108.
34. Eamonn Smullen, 'Another View of *The Non-Stop Connolly Show* in Dublin', *Theatre Quarterly*, Vol. II, No. 25, 1977, p. 94.
35. Albert Hunt, 'Passions and Issues', *New Society*, 18 January 1979.
36. From a speech at the Conference on Censorship organised by the Theatre Writers Union, Riverside Studios, January 1979.
37. Margaretta D'Arcy and John Arden, Introduction to *The Little Gray*

Home in the West, Pluto Press, London, 1980.
38. From notes taken by Catherine Itzin at *The Ballygombeen Bequest* trial November 1977.
39. *Ibid.*
40. Albert Hunt, p. 153.
41. Interview with Catherine Itzin, January 1978.
42. John Arden's response to reading the MS. of *Stages in the Revolution*: 'Margaretta D'Arcy's protest at the Ulster Museum was primarily sparked off by the fact that the 7:84 Theatre Company, presenting *Vandaleur's Folly* in Belfast, had ceased to put up the posters about H-Block and other modern Irish agitation which had been determined from the beginning as part of the presentation of the play. The full political impact of our production had thus been blunted, in Northern Ireland, by a British political company, and this of course bore out Margaretta D'Arcy's views on the Belfast Festival.'
43. Interview with Catherine Itzin, *Tribune*, 29 December 1978, p. 13.
44. *Ibid.*

AgitProp Street Players/Red Ladder

1. From an unpublished interview with John Hoyland by Catherine Itzin, 1978.
2. *Ibid.*
3. *Ibid.*
4. *Ibid.*
5. AgitProp Information Service Brochure, 1968. Available from Red Ladder, New Blackpool Centre, Cobden Avenue, Lower Wortley, Leeds LS12 5PB.
6. From an unpublished interview with Chris Rawlence by Catherine Itzin, 1979.
7. John Hoyland, *op. cit.*
8. Chris Rawlence, *op. cit.*
9. From an unpublished lecture given by Kathleen McCreery at King's College Cambridge, Conference on Political Theatre, April 1978.
10. *Ibid.*
11. From an AgitProp Newsletter. Available from Red Ladder at the above address.
12. John Hoyland, *op. cit.*
13. Kathleen McCreery, *op. cit.*
14. Chris Rawlence, *op. cit.*
15. Kathleen McCreery, *op. cit.*
16. From an unpublished interview with Kathleen McCreery and Richard Stourac of Broadside Mobile Workers Theatre by Catherine Itzin, 1978.
17. Chris Rawlence, *op. cit.*
18. *Ibid.*
19. John Hoyland, *op. cit.*

20. Kathleen McCreery, *op. cit.*
21. From an unpublished article by Chris Rawlence and Steve Trafford on Red Ladder.
22. From Broadside's response to reading the MS. of *Stages in the Revolution*.
23. Chris Rawlence, Steve Trafford, *op. cit.*
24. *Ibid.*
25. *Ibid.*

Ed Berman and Inter-Action

1. Unless otherwise indicated all quotations are from an unpublished interview with Ed Berman by Catherine Itzin, 1978.
2. See Appendix 'Chronological List of Productions 1968–1978' for further information on plays produced by Inter-Action.
3. From an unpublished interview with Roland Rees by Catherine Itzin, 1979.

1969

1. Ann Jellicoe, 'Royal Court Theatre Writers Group,' *Ambit 68*, a quarterly of poems, short stories, drawings & criticisms, 1976, p. 61.

Albert Hunt and the Bradford College of Art Theatre Group

1. Albert Hunt, *Hopes for Great Happenings, Alternatives in Education and Theatre*, Eyre Methuen, London, 1976, pp. 66–7.
2. *Ibid*, p. 46.
3. *Ibid.*
4. *Ibid*, p. 99.
5. *Ibid*, p. 106.

Welfare State

1. 'The Tenth Anniversary of Welfare State', booklet published 1977 by Welfare State.
2. 'Theatre to Liberate Fantasies, The Welfare State and The Cosmic Circus', by John Fox, *Theatre Quarterly*, Vol. II, No. 8, 1972, p. 4.
3. *Ibid*, p. 5.
4. *Ibid*, p. 10.
5. *Ibid*, p. 10.
6. Theodore Shank, 'The Welfare State', *Arts in Society*, Vol. 12, No. 1, May 1973.
7. *Ibid.*
8. *Theatre Quarterly*, No. 8, pp. 11–12.
9. Interview with John Fox by Brancko Matan, *Prolog 27*, Poland, August 1976.

10. *Ibid.*
11. *Ibid.*
12. 'Artistic Commitment is Social Commitment', interview with John Fox by Theodore Shank, *TDR*, March 1977.

Pip Simmons Theatre Group

1. Peter Ansorge, *Disrupting the Spectacle, Five Years of Experimental and Fringe Theatre in Britain*, Pitman Publishing, 1975, p. 30.
2. *Ibid*, p. 33.
3. *Ibid*, p. 34.
4. *Ibid*, p. 35.
5. See Clive Barker, 'Pip Simmons in Residence', *Theatre Quarterly*, Vol. ix, No. 35, 1979, for documentation on WE.

Edward Bond

1. B. A. Young, *Financial Times*, 4 November 1965.
2. Edward Bond, *The Bundle*, Introduction, Eyre Methuen, London 1978 p. xvii.
3. From Edward Bond's notes to Catherine Itzin in response to reading the MS. of *Stages in the Revolution*.
4. *Ibid.*
5. From an unpublished interview with Catherine Itzin, 1978.
6. *Ibid.*
7. Edward Bond, *Saved*, Methuen & Co. Ltd, 1966, Preface by Edward Bond, p. 5.
8. From Edward Bond's notes to Catherine Itzin in response to reading MS. of *Stages in the Revolution*.
9. Interview with Catherine Itzin, *op. cit.*
10. *Ibid.*
11. Edward Bond, *Lear*, Eyre Methuen, London, 1973, Preface by Edward Bond, p. v.
12. *Ibid*, pp. vi–vii.
13. *Ibid*, p. xiii.
14. Edward Bond, *Bingo*, Eyre Methuen, London, 1974, Preface by Edward Bond, pp. ix–x.
15. *Ibid*, p. xii.
16. Edward Bond, *The Fool*, Eyre Methuen, London, 1976, Preface by Edward Bond, p. vi.
17. *Ibid*, pp. vi–vii.
18. *Ibid*, p. xii.
19. *Edward Bond, Plays: One*, Eyre Methuen, London, 1977, Author's Note 'On Violence', p. 11.
20. *Ibid*, p. 12.
21. *Ibid*, p. 14.

22. *Ibid*, p. 17.
23. From Edward Bond's notes to Catherine Itzin in response to reading the MS. of *Stages in the Revolution*.
24. Edward Bond, *The Bundle*, Eyre Methuen, London, 1978, Preface by Edward Bond, p. viii.
25. *Ibid*, p. xiii.
26. This and all the remaining quotations in this chapter are from the interview with Catherine Itzin already cited.

David Mercer

1. D. A. N. Jones, 'Mercer Unmarxed', *The Listener*, 14 May 1970, p. 652.
2. 'Birth of a Playwriting Man', David Mercer interviewed by the Editors and Francis Jarman, *Theatre Quarterly*, Vol. III, No. 9, 1973. All subsequent quotations are from this source unless indicated otherwise.
3. *Flourish*, (RSC Newspaper), Interview with David Mercer, Autumn 1966.
4. *Ibid*.
5. David Mercer, 'Outline of a Memorandum to Myself', 24 August 1978 – an unpublished response to an interview with Catherine Itzin, August 1978.
6. David Mercer, *The Generations, A Trilogy of Plays*, John Calder, London, 1964.
7. David Mercer, *On the Eve of Publication and Other Plays*, Methuen & Co. Ltd, London, 1970.
8. 'Political Theatre in Britain: An Interview with David Mercer and Geoffrey Reeves', *Gambit 20*, Calder & Boyars Ltd, 1971, p. 80.
9. D. A. N. Jones, *op. cit.*
10. *Ibid*.
11. David Mercer, *The Listener*, 28 May 1970.
12. 'Mercer's *Cousin Vladimir*, A Review and Interview' by Ronald Hayman, *Plays and Players*, November 1978, p. 11.
13. From an 'Outline of a Memorandum to Myself', *op. cit.* Unless otherwise indicated all remaining quotations are from this source.
14. *Gambit 20*, *op. cit.*

Arnold Wesker

1. 'John Arden Talks to Albert Hunt', *Peace News*, 1963, reprinted in *Encore* September–October 1965. The reference to Wesker's description of Arden as a 'wishy-washy liberal' is in Albert Hunt, *Arden: A Study of His Plays*, Eyre Methuen, London, 1974, p. 148.
2. In response to reading the MS. of *Stages in the Revolution*, Arnold Wesker made the following point: 'This suggests there was a time they ever did succeed commercially. They *never* did. No play apart from *Chips* (which ran a year in the West End mainly because the audiences saw it as a comedy about the forces) ever ran longer than a few weeks

in a subsidised theatre. *The Kitchen* ran for four weeks twenty years ago. *The Trilogy* ran for three months at the Court, heavily subsidised. The transfer of *Roots* to the West End flopped! The plays never succeeded commercially and so I've always viewed myself as a kind of fringe writer! The paradox was that they were done so much abroad that one was really very well off, and continued to be despite the English climate.' Wesker's point reinforces the fact that some of the major British writers of the post-war period were virtually unproduced in Britain and yet regarded as classics and studied on school syllabuses.

3. *Tribune*, interview with Catherine Itzin, 13 October 1978.
4. *The Merchant* was produced in New York in a cut version. Zero Mostel, who played Shylock, died during rehearsals. The play was thus faced with enormous problems, and it was a financial and critical failure.
5. *Tribune*, interview, 13 October 1978.
6. *New Manchester Review*, interview with Arnold Wesker, Autumn 1978.
7. 'A Sense of What Should Follow', interview with Catherine Itzin, Glenda Leeming and Simon Trussler, *Theatre Quarterly*, Vol. VI, No. 28, p. 20.
8. *Ibid.*
9. John McGrath, 'A Review of *The Friends*', *Black Dwarf*, 12 June 1970.
10. 'Roots in Norfolk', *Encore*, May/June 1960, p. 30. Albert Hunt's brief summary of the BBC broadcast of *Roots* and the letters it prompted to the *Eastern Daily Press* in Norfolk would reinforce McGrath's criticism of Wesker's treatment of the working class.
11. From unpublished correspondence between Arnold Wesker and John McGrath, June 1970, printed by permission.
12. /*Ibid.*
13. *Ibid.*
14. *Ibid.*
15. See Arnold Wesker, 'Casual Condemnations', *Theatre Quarterly*, Vol. 1, No. 2, 1971.
16. From unpublished correspondence, see note 11. Unless otherwise indicated all subsequent quotations are from this source.
17. Arnold Wesker, *Chicken Soup with Barley* in *New English Dramatists 1*, Penguin, 1959, p. 236.
18. Arnold Wesker, 'Let Battle Commence', *Encore*, November 1958.
19. Programme for Centre 42 Festival in Nottingham.
20. Geoffrey Reeves, 'The Biggest Aunt Sally of All', *Encore*, Jan.–Feb. 1963, p. 14.
21. From *Black Dwarf*, *op. cit.*
22. Geoffrey Reeves, *Encore*, *op. cit.*
23. *The Encore Reader: A Chronicle of the New Drama*, Ed. Charles Marowitz, Tom Milne and Owen Hale, Methuen & Co. Ltd, London, 1965, p. 230.
24. *Theatre Quarterly*, *op. cit.*, p. 22.

25. *Ibid*, p. 20.
26. *Ibid*.
27. *Tribune*, 13 October 1978.
28. *Ibid*.

1971

1. Catherine Itzin, 'The Case for a British Theatre Institute', *Theatre Quarterly*, Vol. I, No. 3, 1971, p. 2.

John McGrath and 7:84 Theatre Company

1. From unpublished correspondence between John McGrath and Arnold Wesker, June 1970, printed by permission.
2. *Ibid*.
3. John McGrath, 'Better a Bad Night in Bootle', interview with Catherine Itzin, *Theatre Quarterly*, Vol. V, No. 19, 1975, p. 43.
4. *Ibid*.
5. *Ibid*, p. 44.
6. *Ibid*, p. 48.
7. *Ibid*.
8. John McGrath's response to reading the MS. of *Stages in the Revolution*.
9. John McGrath, *Theatre Quarterly*, *op. cit.* p. 49.
10. From an unpublished lecture given by John McGrath at the King's College, Cambridge Conference on Political Theatre, April 1978.
11. *Fish in the Sea*, Introduction by John McGrath, Pluto Press, London, 1977.
12. See 'Breaking Free of the Troubled English Giant', interview with John McGrath by Catherine Itzin, *Tribune*, 30 December 1977.
13. *Theatre Quarterly*, *op. cit.*, p. 54.
14. *Ibid*.
15. From the Cambridge Lecture, *op. cit.* All subsequent quotations are from this source.

Hull Truck

1. Catherine Itzin, 'Articulate Lorry' (interview with Mike Bradwell), *Time Out*, 5 November 1976, p. 9.
2. From an unpublished interview with Mike Bradwell by Karin Gartzke for an MA thesis on 'Alternative Theatre in Britain' for Manchester University Department of Drama, printed by permission. All subsequent quotations are from this source.
3. Hull Truck, *Bridget's House*, TQ Publications Ltd, 1977.

1972

1. *Time Out*, 18–24 August 1972.
2. From the Constitution of the Association of Lunchtime Theatres. Available from Kenneth Chubb, Wakefield Tricycle Theatre Company, Tricycle Theatre, Foresters Hall, 269 Kilburn High Road, London NW6.
3. From an unpublished interview with Roland Rees by Catherine Itzin, 1978.
4. See pp. 261–63.

David Edgar and The General Will

1. From an unpublished interview with Catherine Itzin, 1978. Unless otherwise indicated, all other quotations are from this source.
2. 'Theatre, Politics and the Working Class', interview with David Edgar by Catherine Itzin, *Tribune*, 22 April 1977.
3. 'Exit Fascism, Stage Right', interview with David Edgar, *The Leveller*, June 1977, p. 22.
4. *Ibid.*
5. *Tribune, op. cit.*
6. *Ibid.*
7. *The Leveller, op. cit.*, p. 23.
8. David Edgar, 'Political Theatre, Part One and Part Two', *Socialist Review*, 1 April and 2 May 1978. Also in *Theatre Quarterly*, Vol. VIII, No. 32, 1979, pp. 25–34.

Subsidy

1. The Charter of Incorporation Granted by Her Majesty the Queen to the Arts Council of Great Britain, 7 February 1967.
2. Malcolm Griffiths, 'The Drama Panel Game,' *Theatre Quarterly*, Vol. II, No. 25, 1977, pp. 3–30.
3. *Ibid*, p. 25.
4. Hugh Jenkins, *The Culture Gap, An Experience of Government and the Arts*, Marion Boyars Publishers, Inc., 1979, p. 189.
5. *Ibid*, p. 198.
6. *Ibid*, p. 192.
7. 'Minister for the Arts: an Interview with Hugh Jenkins, MP', *Gambit 24*, John Calder Publishers, 1974, p. 7.
8. Memorandum from Hugh Jenkins, Minister for the Arts, to the Current Arts Policy Advisory Group, 1974–75, p. 1. See also *The Culture Gap*, p. 178.
9. *Ibid.*
10. *Ibid.*, p. 4.
11. John Elsom, *The Arts, Change and Choice*, published by the Liberal Party, 1978, p. 15.

12. *The Arts, a Discussion Document for the Labour Movement*, published by the Labour Party, Transport House, Smith Square, London SW1, September 1975, p. 13.
13. *The Arts and the People: Labour's Policy Towards the Arts*, published by the Labour Party, September 1977, p. 47.
14. *The TUC Working Party Report on The Arts*, a TUC Consultative Document, published by the Trades Union Congress, Congress House, Great Russell Street, London WC1B 3LS, July 1976, p. 1.
15. *The Redcliffe-Maud Report*, published by the Calouste Gulbenkian Foundation, 98 Portland Place, London W1, 1976.
16. *The Guardian*, 13 October 1977.
17. Colin McArthur, 'The arts in society; not leisure escapism but a major means of change and growth', *Tribune*, 23 July 1976.
18. *The Guardian*, 12 July 1978.
19. *Ibid*.
20. *Time Out*, 31 March 1979, p. 29.
21. Arts Council of Great Britain, *Annual Report*, 1975/76.
22. *Ibid*, p. 18.
23. Arts Council of Great Britain, *Annual Report*, 1976/77.
24. Douglas Hill, *Tribune 40: The First Forty Years of a Socialist Newspaper*, Quartet Books, London, 1977, p. 38.
25. *Gambit 24*, John Calder Publishers, 1974, p. 33.
26. *The Guardian*, 30 September 1978.

1973

1. From a pamphlet published by the Half Moon Theatre, with introductions by Maurice Colbourne and Steve Gooch, 1979.
2. Steve Gooch's *Will Wat? If Not, What Will*; *Female Transport*; *The Motor Show*; and *The Women Pirates: Ann Bonney and Mary Read*, all published by Pluto Press, London.
3. 'Christopher Hampton's *Savages* at the Royal Court Theatre', interview with the editors, *Theatre Quarterly*, Vol. III, No. 12, 1973, pp. 67–74.

Trevor Griffiths

1. From an unpublished interview with Catherine Itzin, 1979.
2. Interview with Raymond Williams, *The Leveller*, March 1979, p. 26.
3. Interview with Trevor Griffiths, *The Leveller*, November 1976, pp. 12–13.
4. 'Transforming the Husk of Capitalism', interview with Trevor Griffiths by the editors, *Theatre Quarterly* Vol. VI, No. 22, 1976, p. 40. For a more detailed analysis of *The Party*, see Leonard Goldstein, 'Trevor Griffiths' *The Party* and the Left Radical Critique of Bourgeois Society', in *Political Developments on the British Stage in the Sixties and Seventies*, Wilhelm Pieck-Universität, Rostock, 1976.

5. *Ibid*, p. 45.
6. From an unpublished interview with Trevor Griffiths by Karin Gartzke, for an MA thesis on 'Alternative Theatre in Britain' for Manchester University Department of Drama, printed by permission.
7. From an unpublished lecture by John McGrath given at King's College, Cambridge, Conference on Political Theatre, April 1978.
8. *Ibid*.
9. *Theatre Quarterly 22, op. cit.* p. 45.
10. *Ibid*, p. 46.
11. *The Leveller* interview with Trevor Griffiths, *op. cit.*
12. *Ibid*.
13. From an interview with Karin Gartzke, *op. cit*.
14. *The Leveller, op. cit.*
15. David Edgar, 'Political Theatre', *Socialist Review*, April and May 1978.
16. From an interview with Karin Gartzke, *op. cit.*
17. From an unpublished interview with Catherine Itzin, 1979.
18. *Theatre Quarterly 22, op. cit.*, p. 46.
19. From an interview with Karin Gartzke, *op. cit.*
20. *Theatre Quarterly 22, op. cit.*, p. 37.
21. *Gambit 29*, interview with Trevor Griffiths, John Calder Publishers, 1976, p. 33.
22. *Ibid.*, p. 34.
23. From an interview with Catherine Itzin, *op. cit.*
24. From an interview with Karin Gartzke, *op. cit.*
25. From an interview with Catherine Itzin, *op. cit.*

The Association of Community Theatres (*TACT*)

1. Manifesto of The Association of Community Theatres (TACT). Available from Bruce Birchall, 60 Edgedale Road, Sheffield 7.
2. Amended Constitution, The Association of Community Theatres, published 4 August 1978.
3. A Report of the 4th National Conference of TACT. Available from Bruce Birchall at the above address.
4. Catherine Itzin, 'Arts Council Eyes Still Fixed on Higher Things', *Tribune*, 20 January 1978.
5. TACT Press Release, December 1978.
6. Copy of a letter from Richard Hoggart, Chairman of the Drama Panel, Arts Council of Great Britain, 22 December 1977.
7. Letter from TACT to Richard Hoggart, 15 January 1978.
8. Letter from Richard Hoggart to TACT, 8 February 1978.
9. TACT Report, compiled by the Executive Committee, April 1978.
10. Official Conference Report TACT by Terry Ilott, December 1978.

1974

1. *The Guardian*, letter from Helen Mirren, November 1974.
2. Catherine Itzin, *British Alternative Theatre Directory*, John Offord Publications Ltd, 1979, p. 125.
3. David Rudkin, *Ashes*, Introduction by the author, Pluto Press, London, 1978.
4. 'Ambushes for the Audience: Towards a High Comedy of Ideas', interview with Tom Stoppard, *Theatre Quarterly*, Vol. IV, No. 14, 1974, p. 12.
5. Garry O'Connor, *Travesties*, *Plays and Players*, July 1974, p. 35.
6. From an unpublished interview with Catherine Itzin, 1978.
7. See Peter Ansorge, *Disrupting the Spectacle, Five Years of Experimental and Fringe Theatre in Britain*, Pitman Publishing, London, 1975 for further information on Snoo Wilson, an important playwright, but one who lies outside the specific terms of reference of this book.

Howard Brenton and Portable Theatre

1. 'Petrol Bombs Through the Proscenium Arch', interview with Howard Brenton by the editors, *Theatre Quarterly*, Vol. V, No. 17, 1975.
2. From an interview for *Theatre Quarterly*, (unpublished), 1974.
3. *Theatre Quarterly* 17, *op. cit.*
4. *Ibid.*, pp. 10–11.
5. *Gambit 23*, John Calder Publishers, 1973, p. 31.
6. From an unpublished interview with Catherine Itzin, 1978. All subsequent quotations are from this source unless indicated otherwise.
7. *Theatre Quarterly* 17, *op. cit.*, p. 16. And Howard Brenton Checklist compiled by Tony Mitchell, *Theatrefacts*, Vol. II, No. 1, 1975.
8. *Ibid.*, p. 18.
9. Peter Ansorge, *Disrupting the Spectacle, Five Years of Experimental and Fringe Theatre in Britain*, Pitman Publishing, 1975, p. 4.
10. *Theatre Quarterly 17*, *op cit.*, p. 8.
11. *Disrupting the Spectacle*, *op. cit.*, pp. 5–6.
12. *Gambit 23*, *op. cit.*, p. 26.
13. *Theatre Quarterly 17*, *op. cit.*, p. 14.
14. Peter Ansorge, *op. cit.*
15. *Theatre Quarterly 17*, *op. cit.*, p. 20.
16. *Ibid*, p. 15.

Belt and Braces Roadshow

1. From an unpublished interview with Gavin Richards by Catherine Itzin, 1978. All subsequent quotations are from this source unless indicated otherwise.
2. The songs from Belt and Braces shows have been recorded and are available from Belt and Braces, 22 Vicars Road, London NW5.
3. Gavin Richards, *England Expects*, Journeyman Press, 1977, p. 54.

4. See introduction to 1973, p. 162.
5. Gavin Richards, *England Expects*, p. 64.
6. *Ibid.*, p. 7.
7. *Ibid.*, p. 18.
8. Gavin Richards' response to reading the MS. of *Stages in the Revolution*.
9. *Ibid.*
10. From the programme of *Not So Green As Its Cabbage*, including a perspective on Ireland, some relevant economic, political and military considerations.
11. See Postscript note 1.

1975

1. George Thatcher, *The Only Way Out*, TQ Publications Ltd, 1977.
2. Quoted from an interview in: Oleg Kerenski, *The New British Drama*, Hamish Hamilton, London, 1977, pp. 261–62.

The Independent Theatre Council

1. ITC letter, May 1974.
2. ITC Manifesto, May 1974.
3. *Time Out*, 22 October 1976, p. 9.
4. *Tribune*, 31 October 1975, p. 7.
5. ITC/TACT Joint Action Committee Report, January 1976.
6. ITC/TACT Newsletter, March 1976.
7. *Ibid.*

Equity

1. ITC/TACT Report, 2 January 1976.
2. *Ibid.*
3. *Ibid.*
4. ITC Journal, January 1979.

Joint Stock Theatre Group

1. From an unpublished interview with William Gaskill by Catherine Itzin, 1979. All subsequent quotations are from this source unless indicated otherwise.
2. From an unpublished lecture given by William Gaskill at King's College, Cambridge, Conference on Political Theatre, April 1978.
3. *Ibid.*
4. *Ibid.*
5. *Ibid.*
6. *Ambit 68*, a quarterly of poems, short stories, drawings and criticisms, 1976, *Yesterday's News*, introduction by Paul Kember, p. 11.
7. *Ibid.*

8. *Ibid.*
9. See section on Caryl Churchill for further details about *Light Shining in Buckinghamshire*, pp. 283–4.
10. *Time Out* No. 340, 24–30 September 1976, *Fringe Beneficiaries* by Ann McFerran, p. 11.
11. *Ibid.*
12. Sandy Craig, 'The Mugsborough Game', *Time Out*, 13 October 1978.

Womens Theatre Group

1. *Evening Standard*, December 1978.
2. This and all subsequent quotations from an unpublished interview with Anne Engel of the Womens Theatre Group, by Catherine Itzin, 1979.

Gay Sweatshop

1. This and all subsequent quotations from an unpublished interview with Drew Griffiths, founder of Gay Sweatshop, 1979.

Broadside Mobile Workers Theatre

1. From an unpublished interview with Kathleen McCreery and Richard Stourac of Broadside Mobile Workers Theatre, 1978. All subsequent quotations are from this source unless otherwise indicated.
2. Broadside's response to reading the MS. of *Stages in the Revolution*.
3. *Ibid.*

Barrie Keeffe

1. This and all subsequent quotations, unless otherwise indicated, from an interview with Barrie Keeffe by Catherine Itzin, 1979.
2. David Edgar, 'Political Theatre, Part One', *Socialist Review*, No. 1, April 1978; 'Political Theatre, Part Two', *Socialist Review*, No. 2, May 1978.
3. Barrie Keeffe, *Gimme Shelter and Abide with Me*, Eyre Methuen, London, 1977, p. 53.

Howard Barker

1. From an unpublished interview with Howard Barker by Catherine Itzin, 1978. All subsequent quotations are from this source unless otherwise indicated.
2. John Ford, *Claw*, *Plays & Players*, March 1975, p. 35.
3. David Edgar, 'Political Theatre Part One', *Socialist Review*, No. 1, April 1978, and Part Two, *Socialist Review*, No. 2, May 1978. Also in *Theatre Quarterly*, Vol. VIII, No. 32, 1979, pp. 25–34.
4. Letter from Howard Barker, *Tribune*, 1 September 1975.

5. Letter from Howard Barker, *Tribune*, 23 September 1977.
6. From a letter to Catherine Itzin from Howard Barker, 17 June 1978.
7. *Ibid.*

1976

1. *The Stage*, 13 January 1977.
2. Kenneth Tynan, 'Director as Misanthropist: on the Moral Neutrality of Peter Brook', *Theatre Quarterly*, Vol. VII, No. 25, 1977.
3. *Daily Telegraph*, 1 February 1976.
4. From an unpublished interview with Roland Rees by Catherine Itzin, 1978.
5. From an unpublished interview with John Hoyland by Catherine Itzin, 1978.
6. *Ibid.*

The ICA Theatre

1. Letter from R. B. Loder to Mike Laye, 21 December 1976.
2. *Ibid.*
3. *The Guardian*, April 1976.
4. *Ibid.*

The National Theatre

1. Press Release from ITC/TACT Joint Action Committee, 1976.
2. *Ibid.*
3. Letter from ITC/TACT to the National Theatre, 13 February 1974.
4. John Elsom & Nicholas Tomalin, *The History of the National Theatre*, Jonathan Cape, London, 1978.
5. 'Failure or Triumph? Sir Peter Hall Answers the National Theatre's Critics', *The Observer*, 2 April 1978.
6. *The Guardian*, 12 January 1977.
7. *Ibid.*
8. Victor Glastone, architect and author on Victorian and Edwardian theatres, *ibid.*
9. Vivian Nixon, 'National Blackmail', *The Guardian*, February 1978.
10. *Time Out*, review of John Elsom's book by Steve Grant, 28 April 1978, p. 27.
11. *Evening News*, 30 March 1978.
12. *Ibid.*
13. *Tribune*, 2 January 1976 and 5 May 1978.
14. 'Fly Away Peter?', *The Guardian*, 10 August 1978.
15. Arts Council of Great Britain Press Release, July 1978.

Monstrous Regiment

1. From an unpublished lecture given by Susan Todd at King's College, Cambridge, Conference on Political Theatre, April 1978. All subsequent

quotations are from this source unless otherwise indicated.
2. From an unpublished lecture given by Michelene Wandor at King's College, Cambridge, Conference on Political Theatre, April 1978.
3. For further discussion of *Vinegar Tom* in the context of Caryl Churchill's own work, see pp. 284–5.
4. From an unpublished interview with Sue Beardon, administrator of Monstrous Regiment by Karin Gartzke, 1978, printed by permission.

Caryl Churchill

1. Unless otherwise indicated all quotes are from an unpublished interview with Caryl Churchill by Catherine Itzin, 1979.
2. 'Writers urged to blacklist BBC in censorship row', *The Guardian*, 22 August 1978.
3. Caryl Churchill, *Light Shining in Buckinghamshire*, introduction by Caryl Churchill, Pluto Press, London, 1978.
4. *Ibid.*

1977

1. Robert Bolt, *State of Revolution*, Preface by Robert Bolt, Heinemann Educational, London, 1976.
2. See Catherine Itzin, 'Bias Masquerading as Fact', *Tribune*, August 1977. Also 'State of Revolution' – Robert Bolt Replies', *Tribune*, 9 September 1977, p. 14. And Catherine Itzin, 'Political Theatre and the Facts in Context', *Tribune*, September 1977.
3. 'Women Are Uncharted Territory', interview with Pam Gems by Michelene Wandor, *Spare Rib*, September 1977, p. 12.
4. *Ibid.*
5. *Ibid.*
6. From an unpublished interview with David Lan by Catherine Itzin, 1979.
7. *Ibid.*
8. *Ibid.*

North West Spanner

1. From an unpublished interview with North West Spanner by Catherine Itzin, 1978. All subsequent quotations are from this source unless otherwise indicated.
2. Rosemary Heesan, North West Arts Association promotion leaflet, 1977.
3. Minute 4, Theatre Panel Meeting, North West Arts Association, 17 October 1977.
4. Robin Thornber, 'Spanner in the Works of North West Arts', *The Guardian*, 13 October 1977.
5. *Ibid.*

6. 'Political, Bureaucratic and Economic Censorship' Conference Report, December 1977.
7. North West Spanner, 'Statement of Policy' for the Officers and Panel Members of North West Arts, August 1977.
8. Interview with Catherine Itzin, *op. cit.*
9. From 'Shop Floor Theatre' a press release by North West Spanner.
10. *Evening Chronicle Oldham*, 6 November 1975.
11. A Report to North West Arts Association by Derek Newton, Padgate College.
12. David Mayer, 'Light of Lancashire', *Plays & Players*, January 1977, pp. 28–9.

Theatre Writers Union (*TWU*)

1. Theatre Writers Group Newsletter, November 1975.
2. Theatre Writers Union Newsletter, July 1978.
3. David Edgar, Report on the Theatre Writers Union, 1977.
4. *Ibid.*
5. *Ibid.*
6. *Ibid.*
7. Theatre Writers Union Leaflet, September 1976.
8. Letter from Peter Stevens, General Administrator of the National Theatre to the Theatre Writers Union Delegate Committee, 27 January 1977.
9. Notice to Theatre Writers Union members, January 1977.
10. *The Stage*, 24 February 1977.
11. *The Stage*, 10 March 1977.
12. Theatre Writers Union Letter, 14 March 1977.
13. Theatre Writers Union Minutes of the Meeting of 24 April 1977.
14. *The Stage*, 16 June 1977.
15. Pamphlet on the Gulbenkian Scheme, 1979.
16. Theatre Writers Union Newsletter, Autumn 1978.
17. *Tribune*, 2 February 1979.

1978

1. Paul Thompson, *The Lorenzaccio Story*, Introduction by Paul Thompson, Pluto Press, 1978, p. vii.

The Combination

1. The Combination Press Release, July 1978.
2. 'Why ALCARAF Believes the Albany Fire Was Deliberate', statement published by All Lewisham Campaign Against Racism and Fascism, 1 August 1978.

3. ALCARAF was a broad-based organisation in the London Borough of Lewisham, formed by local people to tackle racialism in the borough. 80 local organisations were members including political parties, trades unions, church groups and voluntary organisations. It should be remembered that the Lewisham March in 1977 was one of the bloodiest confrontations between the National Front, the police and left-wing organisations.

4. ALCARAF Statement, *op. cit.*

5. From an unpublished interview with Jennie Harris and Noel Greig by Catherine Itzin 1978. Unless otherwise indicated all quotations are from this interview.

6. Howard Brenton, 'Petrol Bombs Through the Proscenium Arch', interview with the editors, *Theatre Quarterly*, Vol. V, No. 17, 1975.

7. Catherine Itzin, 'The Albany Rises from the Ashes', *Time Out*, 12 January 1979, p. 28.

8. *Ibid.*

David Hare

1. See essay on Joint Stock Theatre Company for further information about *Fanshen*, pp. 220–1.

2. David Hare, 'A Lecture Given at King's College, Cambridge', in *Licking Hitler*, Faber, 1978, p. 60.

3. *Ibid.*

4. *Ibid.*, p. 61.

5. *Ibid.*, pp. 61–2.

6. *Ibid.*, p. 63.

7. *Ibid.*

8. *Ibid.*, p. 66.

9. *Ibid.*

10. Peter Ansorge, 'David Hare: A War on Two Fronts', *Plays & Players*, April, 1978, p. 13.

11. David Hare, *Licking Hitler*, *op. cit.*, p. 68.

12. Peter Ansorge, *Plays & Players*, *op. cit.*, p. 15

13. *Ibid.*, p. 14.

14. *Ibid.*, p. 15.

15. David Hare, *Knuckle*, Faber & Faber, London, 1974.

16. David Hare, *Licking Hitler*, *op. cit.*, p. 69.

17. *Ibid.*, pp. 69–70.

Postscript

1. The death of Blair Peach was a controversial issue. Many people believed that the Metropolitan Police's Special Patrol Group (SPG) was responsible. An unofficial committee of enquiry was set up by the National Council for Civil Liberties and published a report in April

1980 entitled *Southall 23 April 1979*, which concluded: 'it is a matter for astonishment that a man has died in suspicious circumstances; that the police investigation into the allegation that he had been killed by a police officer resulted in no criminal proceedings against any officer ...' The verdict of the official inquest in May 1980 was, however, that Blair Peach had died by 'misadventure', but among the riders the jury added to their verdict were 'that there should be more liaison between SPG and the ordinary police and that the SPG are wherever possible more controlled by their officers' and 'that no unauthorised instruments should be available in police stations ...'

Chronology of Productions

'Alternative' theatre in Britain in the sixties and seventies was so fertile and productive, and with the growth of small scale touring so geographically far-flung (performing so often to non-theatre audiences in non-theatre spaces), that the need for a precise record of work done, wherever it occurred became increasingly apparent as research for this book progressed. This was also a period when London fringe venues were a vital part of the theatre scene – in atmosphere and ambience and also in mounting dozens and hundreds of new plays. The most suitable 'history' of those venues seemed to be a record of their productions. All this, together with the fact that playwrights worked in so many different areas of theatre during this period, suggested the need for an extensive chronology of productions.

So the chronology which follows includes the major productions of playwrights, theatre companies and theatres discussed in this book, listing author's name, title of the play, when and where it was first performed. The bulk of the chronology therefore falls between the years 1968 and 1978, and for these years the entries are as comprehensive as it was possible to make them within the terms of reference of the book – with the full (and greatly appreciated) co-operation of all those writers, theatres and companies involved. The work of some writers and theatres included in the book started before 1968, and information has been provided about them, though the entries from 1957 to 1968 are extremely selective. Entries are arranged within each year by alphabetical order of author.

The chronology ends in 1978, the end of the period covered in the book. It was tempting, in retrospect, to try to up-date the chronology to as near as possible the eventual publication date in 1980, but this was not practicable. In future editions of the book, the chronology will be up-dated and corrected: any emendations or additional information would be gratefully received, addressed to me, c/o the publishers, Eyre Methuen.

Catherine Itzin

1957

| John Arden | *The Waters of Babylon* | 20 October 1957 | Royal Court Theatre |

1958

John Arden	*When Is a Door Not a Door?*	2 June 1958	Embassy Theatre, Swiss Cottage
John Arden	*Live Like Pigs*	30 September 1958	Royal Court Theatre
John McGrath	*A Man Has Two Fathers*	1958	Oxford
John McGrath	*The Invasion* (adaptation of Arthur Adamov play)	1958	Edinburgh
John McGrath	*The Tent*	1958	
Arnold Wesker	*Chicken Soup with Barley*	7 July 1958	Belgrade Theatre, Coventry

1959

John Arden	*Serjeant Musgrave's Dance*	22 October 1959	Royal Court Theatre
John McGrath	*Why the Chicken*	1959	Edinburgh
Arnold Wesker	*The Kitchen*	13 September 1959	Royal Court Theatre
Arnold Wesker	*Roots*	25 May 1959	Belgrade Theatre, Coventry

1960

John Arden	*Soldier, Soldier*	16 February 1960	BBC TV
John Arden/ Margaretta D'Arcy	*The Happy Haven*	14 September 1960	Royal Court Theatre
John Arden/ Margaretta D'Arcy	*The Business of Good Government: A Christmas Play*	December 1960	Church of St. Michael, Brent Knoll, Somerset
Arnold Wesker	*I'm Talking about Jerusalem*	4 April 1960	Belgrade Theatre, Coventry

1961

| John Arden | *Wet Fish* | 3 September 1961 | BBC TV |
| David Mercer | *Where the Difference Begins* | 15 December 1961 | BBC TV |

1962

Edward Bond	*The Pope's Wedding*	9 December 1962	Royal Court Theatre
David Mercer	*A Climate of Fear*	22 June 1962	BBC TV
David Mercer	*A Suitable Case for Treatment*	21 October 1962	BBC TV
David Rudkin	*Afore Night Come*	June 1962	RSC, Arts Theatre, London
Arnold Wesker	*Chips with Everything*	27 April 1962	Royal Court Theatre
Arnold Wesker	*The Nottingham Captain*	11 September 1962	Wellingborough, Centre 42 Festival

1963

John Arden	*Ironhand*	12 November 1963	Bristol Old Vic
John Arden	*The Workhouse Donkey*	8 July 1963	Chichester Festival Theatre
John McGrath	*Basement in Bangkok*	1963	Bristol
David Mercer	*The Birth of a Private Man*	1 February 1963	BBC TV
David Mercer	*For Tea on Sunday*	17 March 1963	BBC TV

1964

| John Arden | *Armstrong's Last Goodnight* | 5 May 1964 | Glasgow Citizens' Theatre |
| John Arden/ Margaretta D'Arcy | *Ars Longa, Vita Brevis* | 1964 | London |

1965

John Arden	*Left-Handed Liberty*	14 June 1965	Mermaid Theatre, London
John Arden	*Play Without Words*	1965	Glasgow
Edward Bond	*Saved*	3 November 1965	Royal Court Theatre
Howard Brenton	*Ladder of Fools*	1965	Cambridge University
David Halliwell	*Little Malcolm and His Struggle Against the Eunuchs*	30 March 1965	Unity Theatre, London
David Mercer	*And Did Those Feet*	2 June 1965	BBC TV
David Mercer	*Ride a Cock Horse*	24 June 1965	Piccadilly Theatre, London
Arnold Wesker	*The Four Seasons*	August 1965	Belgrade Theatre, Coventry

1966

John Arden/ Margaretta D'Arcy	The Royal Pardon or The Soldier Who Became an Actor	1 September 1966	Beaford Arts Centre, Devon
CAST (with Roland Muldoon)	John D Muggins Is Dead	Tour 1966/67	London
Margaretta D'Arcy/ John Arden	Friday's Hiding	29 March 1966	Royal Lyceum Theatre, Edinburgh
John McGrath	Events While Guarding the Bofors Gun	12 April 1966	Hampstead Theatre Club
David Mercer	Belcher's Luck	17 November 1966	RSC, Aldwych Theatre
Arnold Wesker	Their Very Own and Golden City	19 May 1966	Royal Court Theatre

1967

CAST (with Roland Muldoon)	Mr. Oligarchy's Circus	Tour 1967/70	London

1968

Paul Ableman	Blue Comedy	October 1968	Open Space Theatre
Agitprop Street Players	Rents Play I	25 November 1968	Open House Tenants Association, Poplar, London E8
John Antrobus	Trixie and Baba	21 August 1968	Royal Court Theatre
John Antrobus	Why Bournemouth	1 October 1968	Ambiance Lunch Hour Theatre
John Arden	The True History of Squire Jonathan and His Unfortunate Treasure	17 June 1968	Ambiance Lunch Hour Theatre
John Arden/ Margaretta D'Arcy	The Hero Rises Up	6 November 1968	Roundhouse, Chalk Farm
Ed. B.	Super Santa	8 April 1968	Ambiance Lunch Hour Theatre
Ed. B.	The Nudist Campers Grow and Grow	15 July 1968	Ambiance Lunch Hour Theatre
Edward Bond	Early Morning	31 March 1968	Royal Court Theatre
Edward Bond	Narrow Road to the Deep North	24 June 1968	Belgrade Theatre, Coventry
John Bowen	Little Boxes	26 February 1968	Hampstead Theatre Club
Bertolt Brecht	The Life Edward II of England	1968	National Theatre at the Old Vic
Bertolt Brecht	The Tutor	1968	Royal Court Theatre
Ed Bullins	The Electronic Nigger	July 1968	Ambiance Lunch Hour Theatre
Ed Bullins	A Minor Scene & It Has No Choice	5 November 1968	Ambiance Lunch Hour Theatre
CAST (with Margaretta D'Arcy & John Arden)	Harold Muggins Is a Martyr	Spring 1968	Unity Theatre, London
CAST (with Roland Muldoon)	Muggins' Awakening	Tour 1968/69	London
Paddy Chayevsky	The Latent Heterosexual	16 September 1968	RSC, Aldwych Theatre
David Cregan	The Houses by the Green	2 October 1968	Royal Court Theatre
Stanley Eveling	The Lunatic, The Secret Sportsman and the Woman Next Door	November 1968	Open Space Theatre (previously at Traverse, Edinburgh)
Stanley Eveling	Come and Be Killed	November 1968	Open Space Theatre (previously at Traverse, Edinburgh)
Stanley Eveling	The Strange Case of Martin Richter	31 October 1968	Hampstead Theatre Club, (previously at Close Theatre, Glasgow)
Jules Feiffer	God Bless	23 October 1968	RSC, Aldwych Theatre

Christopher Hampton	*Total Eclipse*	11 September 1968	Royal Court Theatre
John Herbert	*Fortune and Men's Eyes*	10 June 1968	Open Space Theatre
John Hopkins	*This Story of Yours*	11 December 1968	Royal Court Theatre
Neil Hornick	*Can't Help Loving You*	22 October 1968	Ambiance Lunch Hour Theatre
Arthur Kopit	*Indians*	4 July 1968	RSC, Aldwych Theatre
D. H. Lawrence	*A Collier's Friday Night*	29 February 1968	
(directed by	*The Widowing of Mrs Holroyd*	14 March 1968	} Royal Court Theatre
Peter Gill)	*The Daughter-in-Law*	7 March 1968	
John McGrath	*Bakke's Night of Fame*	25 January 1968	Hampstead Theatre Club
David Mercer	*The Parachute*	21 January 1968	BBC TV
David Mercer	*On the Eve of Publication*	27 November 1968	BBC TV
John Osborne	*Time Present*	23 May 1968	Royal Court Theatre
John Osborne	*The Hotel in Amsterdam*	3 July 1968	Royal Court Theatre
John Osborne	*Look Back in Anger* (revival)	29 October 1968	Royal Court Theatre
Colin Spencer	*Spitting Image*	4 September 1968	Hampstead Theatre Club
Megan Terry	*Keep Tightly Closed in a Cool Dry Place*	1968	Open Space Theatre
Peter Terson	*Mooney and His Caravans*	6 May 1968	Hampstead Theatre Club

1969

An American Package (plays by Van Itallie, Megan Terry, John Guare, Terence McNally)		1969	Open Space Theatre
Agitprop Street Players	*Rents Play II*	8 January 1969	Frampton Park Estate, London, E9
Agitprop Street Players	*Stuff Your Penal Up Your Bonus*	March 1969	Ford's, Dagenham, Essex
Agitprop Street Players	*Rents Play III: Rose Tinted Spectacles*	April 1969	Tower Hamlets, London
Agitprop Street Players	*Squatters Play I*	July 1969	Ilford, Essex
Agitprop Street Players	*Rents Play IV: The Apple*	Autumn 1969	Tower Hamlets, London
Agitprop Street Players	*Squatters Play II*	Winter 1969/70	Tower Hamlets, London
Edward Albee	*A Delicate Balance*	14 January 1969	RSC, Aldwych Theatre
Peter Barnes	*Noonday Demons*	1969	Open Space Theatre
Barry Bermange	*No Quarter & The Interview*	1 June 1969	Hampstead Theatre Club
Edward Bond	*Narrow Road to the Deep North* (revival)	19 February 1969	Royal Court Theatre
Edward Bond	*Saved* (revival)	7 February 1969	Royal Court Theatre
Edward Bond	*Early Morning* (revival)	13 March 1969	Royal Court Theatre
Howard Brenton	*Gum and Goo*	January 1969	The Combination at Brighton
Howard Brenton	*Heads*	June 1969	University of Bradford Drama Drama Group
Howard Brenton	*The Education of Skinny Spew*	June 1969	University of Bradford Drama Group
Howard Brenton	*Revenge*	2 September 1969	Royal Court Theatre
Howard Brenton	*Christie in Love*	23 November 1969	Portable Theatre at Oval House
Ed Bullins	*The Gentleman Caller & How Do You Do*	18 March 1969	Ambiance Lunch Hour Theatre
David Cregan	*A Comedy of the Changing Years*	24 February 1969	Royal Court Theatre Upstairs
Stanley Eveling	*Dear Janet Rosenberg, Dear Mr Kooning*	17 September 1969	Royal Court Theatre Upstairs
Clive Exton	*Have You Any Dirty Washing Mother Dear?*	6 March 1969	Hampstead Theatre Club
Paul Foster	*Tom Paine*	1969	Open Space Theatre (previously at Edinburgh Festival, 1967)
Peter Gill	*Over Gardens Out*	4 August 1969	Royal Court Theatre Upstairs

Trevor Griffiths	*The Wages of Thin*	13 November 1969	Stables Theatre Club, Manchester
John Grillo	*The Fall of Sampson Morocco*	18 February 1969	Ambiance Lunch Hour Theatre
John Guare	*Muzeeka*	1969	Open Space Theatre
David Halliwell	*A Who's Who of Flapland*	11 November 1969	Ambiance Lunch Hour Theatre
James Leo Herlihy	*Bad-Bad Jo Jo*	29 December 1969	Soho Poly
Israel Horovitz	*Rats & The Indian Wants the Bronx*	1969	Open Space Theatre
Jean-Claude Van Itallie	*War*	1969	Open Space Theatre
Henry Livings	*Variable Lengths & Longer*	4 March 1969	Ambiance Lunch Hour Theatre
John McGrath	*Comrade Jacob* (adapted from the novel by David Caute)	1969	Falmer, Sussex University
David Zane Mairowitz	*The Law Circus*	1969	Open Space Theatre
Frank Marcus	*The Window*	4 February 1969	Ambiance Lunch Hour Theatre
Charles Marowitz	*Hamlet* (revival)	1969	Open Space Theatre
Leonard Melfi	*Birdbath & Halloween*	1969	Open Space Theatre
Leonard Melfi	*Stimulation*	9 December 1969	Ambiance Lunch Hour Theatre
David Mercer	*Let's Murder Vivaldi*	27 August 1969	BBC TV
Slawomir Mrozek	*Strip Tease*	25 November 1969	Ambiance Lunch Hour Theatre
Frank Norman	*Inside Out*	24 November 1969	Royal Court Theatre
Michael O'Neill & Jeremy Seabrook	*Life Price*	9 January 1969	Royal Court Theatre
Harold Pinter	*Landscape & Silence*	2 July 1969	RSC, Aldwych Theatre
Barry Reckord	*Don't Gas the Blacks*	1969	Open Space Theatre
James Saunders	*Dog Accident*	6 November 1969	Ambiance Lunch Hour Theatre
Sam Shepard	*La Turista*	18 March 1969	Royal Court Theatre Upstairs
David Storey	*In Celebration*	22 April 1969	Royal Court Theatre
David Storey	*The Contractor*	20 October 1969	Royal Court Theatre
Mike Stott	*Erogenous Zones*	2 April 1969	Royal Court Theatre Upstairs
Mike Weller	*And Now There's Just the Three of Us*	1969	Open Space Theatre

1970

Agitprop Street Players	*Race Play*	July 1970	Greenwich People's Festival
Agitprop Theatre	*The Big Con*	24 September 1970	The Institute for Workers' Control Conference, Birmingham
Agitprop Theatre	*The Cake Play*	8 December 1970	Industrial Relations Bill Demonstration, Tower Hill
Edward Albee	*Tiny Alice*	15 January 1970	RSC, Aldwych Theatre
Fernando Arrabal	*Orison & The Solemn Commission*	28 April 1970	Soho Poly
John Arden	*The Bagman or the Impromptu of Muswell Hill*	27 March 1970	BBC Radio 3
Howard Barker	*Cheek*	10 September 1970	Royal Court Theatre Upstairs
Howard Barker	*No One Was Saved*	19 November 1970	Royal Court Theatre Upstairs
Edward Bond	*Black Mass*	22 March 1970	Part of the Sharpeville Massacre 10th Anniversary Commemoration Evening held by Anti-Apartheid Movement, Lyceum Theatre London
John Bowen	*The Waiting Room*	7 July 1970	Soho Poly
John Bowen	*The Disorderly Women*	5 November 1970	Hampstead Theatre Club
Howard Brenton	*Wesley*	27 February 1970	Eastbrook Hall Methodist Church, Bradford
Howard Brenton	*Fruit*	28 September 1970	Royal Court Theatre Upstairs
Howard Brenton	*Heads & The Education of Skinny Spew* (revival)	2 March 1970	Ambiance Lunch Hour Theatre
Howard Brenton	*Christie in Love*	12 March 1970	Royal Court Theatre Upstairs
Ed Bullins	*It Bees Dat Way*	21 September 1970	Ambiance Lunch Hour Theatre
John Burgess/ Charles Marowitz	*The Chicago Conspiracy*	24 August 1970	Open Space Theatre
Alan Burns/ Charles Marowitz	*Palach*	11 November 1970	Open Space Theatre

CAST (with Roland Muldoon)	*Hilda Muggins*	Tour 1970	London
Vic Corti	*Arrest*	21 September 1970	Ambiance Lunch Hour Theatre
Rosalyn Drexler	*Hot Buttered Roll & The Investigation*	1970	Open Space Theatre
David Edgar	*Two Kinds of Angel*	July 1970	Bradford University
David Edgar	*A Truer Shade of Blue*	August 1970	Bradford University
Günter Grass	*The Plebeians Rehearse the Uprising*	21 July 1970	RSC, Aldwych Theatre
John Grillo	*History of a Poor Old Man*	April 1970	Soho Poly
John Grillo	*Number Three*	14 June 1970	Soho Poly
David Halliwell	*Muck from Three Angles*	14 May 1970	Traverse Theatre, Edinburgh
Christopher Hampton	*The Philanthropist*	3 August 1970	Royal Court Theatre
Christopher Hampton	*When Did You Last See My Mother?* (revival)	11 August 1970	Royal Court Theatre Upstairs
David Hare	*Slag*	2 April 1970	Hampstead Theatre Club
David Hare	*What Happened to Blake*	28 September 1970	Royal Court Theatre Upstairs
James Leo Herlihy	*Midnight Cowboy*	12 January 1970	Soho Poly
Barry Hines	*Billy's Last Stand*	30 June 1970	Royal Court Theatre Upstairs
John Hopkins	*Find Your Way Home*	12 May 1970	Open Space Theatre
Donald Howarth	*Three Months Gone*	28 February 1970	Royal Court Theatre
Ann Jellicoe	*The Sport of My Mad Mother* (revival)	4 May 1970	Royal Court Theatre Upstairs
LeRoi Jones	*The Baptism*	31 July 1970	Ambiance Lunch Hour Theatre
Mike Leigh	*Bleak Moments*	1970	Open Space Theatre
Henry Livings	*You're Free*	4 May 1970	Ambiance Lunch Hour Theatre
John McGrath	*Random Happenings in the Hebrides or The Social Democrat and the Stormy Sea*	1970	Lyceum Theatre, Edinburgh
Charles Marowitz	*A Macbeth*	1970	Open Space Theatre
Mustapha Matura	*Black Pieces*	17 August 1970	Ambiance Lunch Hour Theatre
David Mercer	*The Cellar and the Almond Tree*	4 March 1970	BBC TV
David Mercer	*Emma's Time*	13 May 1970	BBC TV
David Mercer	*After Haggerty*	26 February 1970	RSC, Aldwych Theatre
David Mercer	*Flint*	5 May 1970	Criterion Theatre, London
David Mercer	*White Poem*	17 August 1970	Ambiance Lunch Hour Theatre
David Mowat	*The Normal Woman*	27 April 1970	Ambiance Lunch Hour Theatre
Pip Simmons Theatre Group	*Superman*	1970	Open Space Theatre
Pip Simmons Theatre Group	*The Pardoner's Tale*	12 March 1970	Soho Poly
David Selbourne	*Samson*	1 June 1970	Soho Poly
Sam Shepard	*Red Cross*	30 April 1970	Soho Poly
N. F. Simpson	*How Are Your Handles?*	16 February 1970	Ambiance Lunch Hour Theatre
Tom Stoppard	*After Magritte*	6 April 1970	Ambiance Lunch Hour Theatre
David Storey	*Home*	17 June 1970	Royal Court Theatre
Peter Weiss	*The Tower*	11 February 1970	Soho Poly
Mike Weller	*Cancer*	14 September 1970	Royal Court Theatre
Arnold Wesker	*The Friends*	19 May 1970	Round House, London
Heathcote Williams	*The Local Stigmatic*	19 January 1970	Soho Poly
Heathcote Williams	*AC/DC*	11 November 1970	Royal Court Theatre

1971

Paul Ableman	*Hank's Night*	1971	Kings Head Lunchtime
Michael Almaz	*The Anarchist*	27 April 1971	Royal Court Theatre Upstairs
Michael Almaz	*Inquisition*	11 May 1971	Soho Poly at Kings Head Lunchtime
Ed. B.	*Two Wheeler*	27 December 1971	Ambiance Lunch Hour Theatre
Edward Bond	*Passion*	11 April 1971	Alexandra Park Race Course
Edward Bond	*Lear*	29 September 1971	Royal Court Theatre
Bertolt Brecht	*The Informer*	2 March 1971	Kings Head Lunchtime
Bertolt Brecht	*Man is Man* (translated: Steve Gooch)	1 March 1971	Royal Court Theatre

Bertolt Brecht	*The Elephant Calf*	1971	Royal Court Theatre Upstairs
Howard Brenton	*Gum and Goo* (revival)	22 March 1971	Open Space Theatre (lunchtime)
Howard Brenton	*A Sky Blue Life*	18 November 1971	Open Space Theatre
Howard Brenton	*Scott of the Antarctic*	1971	Bradford Festival, Mecca Ice Rink, Bradford
David Cregan	*If You Don't Laugh, You Cry*	1 November 1971	Ambiance Lunch Hour Theatre
David Cregan	*The Problem*	1 November 1971	Ambiance Lunch Hour Theatre
David Cregan	*The Daffodil*	1 November 1971	Ambiance Lunch Hour Theatre
David Cregan	*Sentimental Value*	1 November 1971	Ambiance Lunch Hour Theatre
Margaretta D'Arcy/ John Arden (with the Socialist Labour League)	*Two Hundred Years of Labour History*	April 1971	Alexandra Palace
Margaretta D'Arcy/ John Arden (with Muswell Hill Street Theatre)	*Granny Welfare and the Wolf*	March 1971	Ducketts Common, Turnpike Lane, London
Margaretta D'Arcy/ John Arden (with Muswell Hill Street Theatre)	*My Old Man's a Tory*	March 1971	Wood Green, London
Margaretta D'Arcy/ John Arden (with Writers Against Repression)	*Rudi Dutschke Must Stay*	Spring 1971	British Museum, London
Keith Dewhurst	*Corunna*	17 May 1971	Royal Court Theatre Upstairs
David Edgar	*Bloody Rosa*	August 1971	Manchester University at Edinburgh Festival
David Edgar	*Acid*	July 1971	Bradford University
David Edgar	*Still Life: Man in Bed*	May 1971	Pool Theatre, Edinburgh
David Edgar	*The National Interest*	August 1971	General Will on Tour
David Edgar	*Conversation in Paradise*	October 1971	Edinburgh University
David Edgar	*Tedderella*	December 1971	Pool Theatre, Edinburgh
Stanley Eveling	*Our Sunday Times*	2 June 1971	Royal Court Theatre Upstairs
Athol Fugard	*People Are Living There*	3 February 1972	Kings Head Evening
Athol Fugard	*Boesman and Lena*	19 July 1971	Royal Court Theatre Upstairs
Jean Genet	*The Balcony* (revival)	25 November 1971	RSC, Aldwych Theatre
Ronald Graham and Ed B.	*Scrambled*	15 July 1971	Ambiance Lunch Hour Theatre
Herb Greer	*Vernon Hoffman*	1 November 1971	Ambiance Lunch Hour Theatre
Herb Greer	*The Secret*	1 November 1971	Ambiance Lunch Hour Theatre
Trevor Griffiths	*Apricots*	28 June 1971	Quipu Basement Theatre
Trevor Griffiths	*Thermidor*	September 1971	7:84 Theatre Company at Cranston Street Hall, Edinburgh
Trevor Griffiths	*Occupations*	13 October 1971	RSC at The Place
John Grillo	*Blubber*	12 April 1971	Soho Poly
John Grillo	*Gearse and Moira Entertain a Member of the Opposite Sex to Dinner*	27 October 1971	Open Space Theatre
David Halliwell	*A Last Belch for the Great Auk*	27 January 1971	Mercury Theatre, London
Peter Handke	*My Foot, My Tutor*	29 September 1971	Open Space Theatre
David Hare	*Slag* (revival)	24 May 1971	Royal Court Theatre
Donald Haworth	*Enlightenment of the Strawberry Gardener*	22 April 1971	Kings Head Lunchtime
Donald Haworth	*A Hearts and Minds Job*	12 July 1971	Hampstead Theatre Club
Roger Howard	*The Meaning of the Statue*	27 December 1971	Ambiance Lunch Hour Theatre
Roger Howard	*Writing on Stone*	27 December 1971	Ambiance Lunch Hour Theatre
Albert Hunt *et al.*	*John Ford's Cuban Missile Crisis*	15 March 1971	Open Space Theatre
Michael McClure	*Spider Rabbit*	15 February 1971	Soho Poly at Kings Head Lunchtime
John McGrath	*Trees in the Wind*	August 1971	7:84 at Edinburgh Festival and Tour

John McGrath	*Unruly Elements (includes Angel of the Morning, Plugged into History. They're Knocking Down the Pie Shop, Hover Through the Fog, Out of sight)*	1971	Everyman Theatre, Liverpool
John McGrath	*Soft or a Girl?*	1971	Everyman Theatre Liverpool
David Zane Mairowitz	*Flash Gordon and the Angels*	16 March 1971	Open Space Theatre
Tom Mallin	*Curtains*	19 January 1971	Open Space Theatre
Tom Mallin	*The Novelist*	1 October 1971	Hampstead Theatre Club
Tom Mallin	*As Is Proper*	20 October 1971	Soho Poly at Kings Head Lunchtime
Frank Marcus	*Formation Dancers*	21 January 1971	Hampstead Theatre Club
Charles Marowitz	*The Critic as Artist* (adapted from Oscar Wilde)	26 May 1971	Open Space Theatre
Mustapha Matura	*As Time Goes By*	14 September 1971	Royal Court Theatre Upstairs
Roy Minton	*Death in Leicester*	20 October 1971	Kings Head Evening
David Mowat	*Anna-Luce and the Diabolist*	2 September 1971	Kings Head Evening
Slawomir Mrozek	*Enchanted Night*	15 April 1971	Soho Poly at Kings Head Lunchtime
Clifford Odets	*Awake and Sing* (revival)	27 September 1971	Hampstead Theatre Club
John Osborne	*West of Suez*	17 August 1971	Royal Court Theatre
David Parker	*The Collector* (adapted from John Fowles)	8 February 1971	Kings Head Evening
The People Show	*People Show/No. 39*	19 August 1971	Open Space Theatre
Neville Phillips	*Upper Street, Supper Treat*	29 December 1971	Kings Head Evening
Harold Pinter	*Old Times*	1 June 1971	RSC, Aldwych Theatre
Harold Pinter	*Night School* (revival)	25 May 1971	Soho Poly at Kings Head
Bernard Pomerance	*High in Vietnam, Hot Damn*	1 November 1971	Ambiance Lunch Hour Theatre
Bernard Pomerance	*Hospital*	1 November 1971	Ambiance Lunch Hour Theatre
Bernard Pomerance	*Thanksgiving Before Detroit*	1 November 1971	Ambiance Lunch Hour Theatre
Portable Theatre Company	*Lay-By*	20 October 1971	Open Space Theatre
Peter Ransley	*Ellen*	25 February 1971	Hampstead Theatre Club
Peter Ransley	*Disabled*	6 May 1971	Hampstead Theatre Club
Barry Reckord	*Skyvers* (revival)	23 June 1971	Royal Court Theatre Upstairs
James Saunders	*Savoury Meringue*	14 April 1971	Ambiance Lunch Hour Theatre
Sam Shepard	*Icarus's Mother*	20 March 1971	Open Space Lunchtime
Pip Simmons	*Do It* (adapted from Jerry Rubin)	February 1971	Traverse Theatre, Edinburgh, then Royal Court Theatre Upstairs, 17 August
Tom Stoppard	*Dogg's Our Pet*	8 December 1971	Ambiance Lunch Hour Theatre
David Storey	*The Changing Room*	9 November 1971	Royal Court Theatre
Paul Thompson	*Captain Swing at the Penny Gaff*	19 February 1971	Unity Theatre, London
Paul Thompson	*The Farmworker*	16 October 1971	National Union of Agricultural Workers Demonstration, Trafalgar Square, London
Boris Vian	*The Empire Builders* (revival)	18 December 1971	Kings Head Evening
Martin Walser	*Home Front*	29 September 1971	Open Space Theatre
Mike Weller	*Grant's Movie*	29 March 1971	Open Space Theatre
E. A. Whitehead	*The Foursome*	17 March 1971	Royal Court Theatre Upstairs
Chris Wilkinson	*I Was Hitler's Maid*	3 August 1971	Kings Head Evening
Chris Wilkinson	*Dynamo*	1 July 1971	Soho Poly at Kings Head Lunchtime
Snoo Wilson	*Blow Job*	10 November 1971	Kings Head Evening
Snoo Wilson	*Pignight*	27 February 1971	Kings Head Evening
Olwen Wymark	*Neither Here Nor There*	29 March 1971	Soho Poly at Kings Head Lunchtime
Olwen Wymark	*The Technicians*	18 November 1971	Soho Poly at Kings Head Lunchtime

1972

| Edward Albee | *All Over* | 31 January 1972 | RSC, Aldwych Theatre |
| Michael Almaz | *The Cut* | 16 February 1972 | Kings Head Lunchtime |

Michael Almaz	*Monsieur Artaud*	August 1972	Bush Theatre
John Antrobus	*Crete and Sergeant Pepper*	24 May 1972	Royal Court Theatre
John Arden	*Live Like Pigs* (revival)	1 February 1972	Royal Court Theatre Upstairs
John Arden/ Margaretta D'Arcy	*The Ballygombeen Bequest*	May 1972	St Mary's & St Joseph's College Drama Society, Belfast and then by 7:84 at the Bush
John Arden/ Margaretta D'Arcy	*The Island of the Mighty*	5 December 1972	RSC, Aldwych Theatre
John Arden/ Margaretta D'Arcy	*Keep Those People Moving*	Christmas 1972	BBC Radio
Chris Bailey	*From the First Day Out*	24 January 1972	Ambiance Lunch Hour Theatre
Howard Barker	*Faceache*	15 February 1972	Recreation Ground
Howard Barker	*Edward the Final Days*	15 February 1972	Open Space Theatre (Lunchtime)
Howard Barker	*Alpha Alpha*	17 September 1972	Open Space Theatre
Wolfgang Bauer	*Shakespeare the Sadist*	25 October 1972	Ambiance Lunch Hour Theatre
Brendan Behan	*Richard's Cork Leg*	19 September 1972	Royal Court Theatre
Bertolt Brecht	*In the Jungle of the Cities*	1972	Half Moon Theatre
Bertolt Brecht	*The Threepenny Opera*	10 February 1972	Prince of Wales Theatre
Howard Brenton	*Hitler Dances*	20 January 1972	Traverse Theatre, Edinburgh and then at Royal Court Theatre Upstairs
Howard Brenton	*How Beautiful with Badges*	2 May 1972	Open Space Theatre (Lunchtime)
Howard Brenton	*Measure for Measure*	25 September 1972	Northcott Theatre, Exeter
John Burrows and John Harding	*For Sylvia*	1972	Bush Theatre
CAST (with Roland Muldoon)	*Sam the Man*	Tour 1972	National tour
Caryl Churchill	*Schreber's Nervous Illness*	6 December 1972	Kings Head Lunchtime
Caryl Churchill	*Owners*	6 December 1972	Royal Court Theatre Upstairs
David Edgar	*The Rupert Show*	January 1972	General Will on tour
David Edgar	*The End*	March 1972	Bradford University
David Edgar	*Excuses, Excuses*	May 1972	Belgrade Studio Theatre, Coventry
David Edgar	*Rent, or Caught in the Act*	May 1972	General Will on tour, Unity Theatre, June 1972
David Edgar	*Not with a Bang But a Whimper*	November 1972	Leeds Polytechnic
David Edgar	*Road to Hanoi*	October 1972	Paradise Foundry
David Edgar	*State of Emergency*	August 1972	General Will on tour and at Edinburgh Festival
David Edgar	*Death Story*	November 1972	Birmingham Repertory Theatre Studio
Jules Feiffer	*The Unexpurgated Memoirs of Bernard Mergendeiler*	16 February 1972	Kings Head Lunchtime
Tom Gallagher	*Mr Joyce Is Leaving Paris*	18 May 1972	Kings Head Evening
Steve Gooch	*Will Wat? If Not, What Will?*	26 May 1972	Half Moon Theatre
Trevor Griffiths	*Sam Sam*	9 February 1972	Open Space Theatre
Trevor Griffiths	*Occupations* (revival)	Tour 1972	7:84 Theatre Company
John Grillo	*Mr Bickerstaff's Establishment*	9 March 1972	Kings Head Evening
Wilson John Haire	*Within Two Shadows*	12 April 1972	Royal Court Theatre Upstairs
David Halliwell	*Janitress Thrilled by Prehensile Penis*	5 November 1972	Little Theatre, Garrick Yard
David Halliwell	*Bleats from a Brighouse Pleasure Ground*	5 November 1972	Little Theatre, Garrick Yard
David Hare	*The Great Exhibition*	28 February 1972	Hampstead Theatre Club
James Leo Herlihy	*Terrible Jim Fitch/Laughs*	November 1972	Bush Theatre
Neil Hornick	*Kingdom Come*	November 1972	Phantom Captain at the Bush Theatre
Hull Truck (with Mike Bradwell)	*Children of the Lost Planet*	10 March 1972	Gulbenkian Theatre, Newcastle

Hull Truck (with Mike Bradwell)	*Last of the Great Love Goddesses*	August 1972	Humberside Theatre, Hull
Ken Campbell Roadshow	*Sylveste Again: Yet Another Evening with Sylveste McCoy the Human Bomb*	3 March 1972	Open Space Theatre
Arthur Kopit	*The Hero*	13 April 1972	Soho Poly Lunchtime
Michael McClure	*The Pansey*	11 April 1972	Soho Poly Lunchtime
John McGrath	*Plugged In To History* (revival)	1972	7:84 Theatre Company Tour, then at the Bush
John McGrath	*Out of Sight* (revival)	1972	7:84 Theatre Company Tour
John McGrath	*Underneath*	1972	Everyman Theatre, Liverpool
John McGrath/ John Arden	*Serjeant Musgrave Dances On*	1972	7:84 Theatre Company Tour
Terence McNally	*Witness*	1 August 1972	Kings Head Lunchtime
Frank Marcus	*Blank Pages*	21 November 1972	Soho Poly Evening
Frank Marcus	*Christmas Carol*	December 1972	Bush Theatre
Charles Marowtiz	*An Othello*	7 June 1972	Open Space Theatre
Mustapha Matura	*Bakerloo Line*	10 April 1972	Ambiance Lunch Hour Theatre
David Mercer	*Ride a Cock Horse* (revival)	24 January 1972	Hampstead Theatre Club
David Mercer	*Let's Murder Vivaldi*	24 October 1972	Kings Head Evening
David Mercer	*The Bankrupt*	27 November 1972	BBC TV
David Mowat	*Morituri*	1972	Kings Head Lunchtime
David Mowat	*The Phoenix and the Turtle*	3 August 1972	Open Space Theatre
Harald Mueller	*Big Wolf* (translated: Steve Gooch)	14 April 1972	Royal Court Theatre
Peter Nichols	*Neither Up Nor Down*	24 January 1972	Ambiance Lunch Hour Theatre
North West Spanner	*The Rents Play*	August 1972	Ellor Street Estate, Salford
Edna O'Brien	*A Pagan Place*	2 October 1972	Royal Court Theatre
Mary O'Malley	*Superscum*	15 May 1972	Solo Poly Lunchtime
John Osborne	*A Sense of Detachment*	4 December 1972	Royal Court Theatre
Phantom Captain	*Kingdom Come: The Art and Craft of Pornography*	1972	Bush Theatre
Bernard Pomerance	*Foco Novo*	1972	Street & Garage, Chalk Farm
Perry Pontac	*The Old Man's Comforts*	21 December 1972	Open Space Theatre
Portable Theatre	*England's Ireland*	2 October 1972	Round House
Red Ladder Theatre Company	*The Sack Play*	13 January 1972	AUEW/TASS Social, Ayr, Scotland
David Rudkin	*The Filth Hunt*	27 November 1972	Ambiance Lunch Hour Theatre
David Rudkin	*Burglars*	1972	Oval House, Kennington
Sam Shepard	*Cowboy Mouth*	11 July 1972	Kings Head
Sam Shepard	*The Tooth of Crime*	17 July 1972	Open Space Theatre
Sam Shepard	*Red Cross & Chicago*	16 August 1972	Kings Head Lunchtime
N. F. Simpson	*Was He Anyone?*	4 July 1972	Royal Court Theatre Upstairs
Andy Smith	*Sawdust Caesar*	1972	Half Moon Theatre
Colin Spencer	*Why Mrs Newstadter*	21 November 1972	Soho Poly Evening
Colin Spencer	*The Trial of St George*	8 March 1972	Soho Poly
George Thatcher	*The Hundred Watt Bulb*	28 February 1972	Little Theatre, Garrick Yard
Paul Thompson	*Joseph Arch*	15 May 1972	Soho Poly Lunchtime
William Trevor	*Going Home*	14 March 1972	Kings Head Lunchtime & Evening
William Trevor	*A Night with Mrs da Tanka*	12 June 1972	Kings Head Lunchtime
Arnold Wesker	*The Old Ones*	8 August 1972	Royal Court Theatre
E. A. Whitehead	*Alpha Beta*	26 January 1972	Royal Court Theatre then August at The Bush Theatre
Chris Wilkinson	*Plays for Ruber Go-Go Girls*	15 June 1972	Kings Head Evening
Charles Wood	*Veterans*	2 March 1972	Royal Court Theatre
Phil Woods	*Show Me the Way to Go Home*	16 May 1972	Royal Court Theatre Upstairs
Paul Zindel	*The Effects of Gamma Rays on Man-in-the-Moon Marigolds*	13 October 1972	Hampstead Theatre Club

1973

Michael Abbensetts	*Sweet Talk*	31 July 1973	Royal Court Theatre Upstairs
John Antrobus	*Captain Oates' Left Sock*	11 April 1973	Royal Court Theatre Upstairs
John Antrobus	*Why Bournemouth*	} 18 July 1973 {	Kings Head Lunchtime
John Antrobus	*Why Bournemouth & Links*		Kings Head Evening
Fernando Arrabal	*And They Put Handcuffs on the Flowers*	12 September 1973	Open Space Theatre
John Arden/ Margaretta D'Arcy	*Portrait of a Rebel*	1973	Radio-Telefís Eireann
Howard Barker	*Rule Britannia*	9 January 1973	Open Space
Howard Barker	*Skipper/My Sister and I*	12 March 1973	Bush Theatre
Howard Barker	*Bang*	23 May 1973	Open Space Theatre
Belt & Braces/Gavin Richards	*Ramsay MacDonald – The Last Ten Days*	27 August 1973	Belt & Braces at the Bush Theatre and on tour
Belt & Braces/ 7:84 Theatre Company	*The Reign of Terror and the Great Money Trick* (adapted from Robert Tressel's *Ragged Trousered Philanthropists*)	September 1973	Oxford Playhouse & on tour
Colin Bennett	*Love Story*	11 September 1973	Kings Head Lunchtime
Edward Bond	*The Sea*	22 May 1973	Royal Court Theatre
Edward Bond	*Bingo*	14 November 1973	Northcott Theatre, Exeter
Edward Bond	*The Pope's Wedding* (revival)	3 July 1973	Bush Theatre
Bertolt Brecht	*Drums in the Night*	September 1973	Foco Novo at Edinburgh Festival, then at Hampstead Theatre Club
Bertolt Brecht	*The Mother* (translated: Steve Gooch)	8 May 1973	Half Moon Theatre
Howard Brenton	*Mug*	9 June 1973	Inter-Cities Conference, 'More Power to the People', Manchester
Howard Brenton	*Magnificence*	28 June 1973	Royal Court Theatre
Howard Brenton/ David Edgar	*A Fart for Europe*	18 January 1973	Royal Court Theatre
Howard Brenton/ David Hare	*Brassneck*	19 September 1973	Nottingham Playhouse
Tina Brown	*Under the Bamboo Tree*	20 November 1973	Bush Theatre
George Büchner	*Woyzeck*	19 February 1973	Open Space Theatre
Alexander Buzo	*Rooted*	5 March 1973	Hampstead Theatre Club
Ken Campbell	*Bollix*	March 1973	Belt & Braces at Sheffield Crucible and on tour
Caryl Churchill	*Objections to Sex and Violence*	2 January 1975	Royal Court Theatre Upstairs
Rick Cluchey	*The Cage*	3 May 1973	Open Space Theatre
Richard Drain	*Hudson's Amazing Money Making Steam Driven Railway Pantomime*	16 July 1973	York Shoestring Company at the Bush Theatre
Richard Drain	*Limbo*	8 August 1973	Bush Theatre
Charles Dyer	*Mother Adam*	16 April 1973	Hampstead Theatre Club
David Edgar	*Gangsters*	13 February 1973	Soho Poly Lunchtime
David Edgar	*The Case of the Workers' Plane*	June 1973	Bristol New Vic
David Edgar	*Baby Love*	28 May 1973	Soho Poly Lunchtime
David Edgar	*Liberated Zone*	June 1973	Bingley College of Education
David Edgar	*Excuses, Excuses* (revival)	16 July 1973	Open Space Theatre
David Edgar	*Operation Iskra*	4 September 1973	Paradise Foundry on tour and at Kings Head
David Edgar	*Tedderella* (revival)	January 1973	Bush Theatre
Stanley Eveling/ David Mowat	*Dracula*	1973	Bush Theatre
Paul Foster	*Elizabeth the First*	31 October 1973	Royal Court Theatre Upstairs
Brian Friel	*The Freedom of the City*	27 February 1973	Royal Court Theatre

Athol Fugard	*Hello and Goodbye*	22 March 1973	Kings Head Evening
Athol Fugard	*Sizwe Bansi Is Dead*	20 September 1973	Royal Court Theatre Upstairs
	Fun Art Bus (with short plays by Chris Bailey, Michael Bullock, David Halliwell, Jim Hiley, Michael Stevens, James Saunders)	4 June 1973	Ambiance Lunch Hour Theatre
Tom Gallagher	*The Only Street*	8 October 1973	Kings Head Evening
Tom Gallagher	*Revival*	16 January 1973	Kings Head Evening
Tom Gallagher	*Schellenbrack*	17 April 1973	Kings Head Evening
Tom Gallagher	*Recital*	1 August 1973	Kings Head Lunchtime
Pam Gems	*My Warren & After Birthday*	5 March 1973	Ambiance Lunch Hour Theatre
Pam Gems	*Miz Venus and Wild Bill*	27 October 1973	Ambiance Lunch Hour Theatre
Steve Gooch	*Female Transport*	November 1973	Half Moon Theatre
Steve Gooch	*Dick*	18 December 1973	Half Moon Theatre
Terry Greer	*Ripper*	20 November 1973	Half Moon Theatre
Trevor Griffiths	*Gun*	Spring 1973	Pool Theatre, Edinburgh
Trevor Griffiths	*The Party*	20 December 1973	National Theatre at the Old Vic
Trevor Griffiths	*The Silver Mask*	15 June 1973	London Weekend TV
John Grillo	*Snaps*	16 April 1973	Soho Poly Lunchtime
Christopher Hampton	*Savages*	12 April 1973	Royal Court Theatre
David Hare/ Howard Brenton	*Brassneck*	10 September 1973	Nottingham Playhouse
Jim Hiley	*Lord Mountlady and the Mortal Odours or The Dalai Lama Lies Dead in the Road*	8 January 1973	Ambiance Lunch Hour Theatre
Don Haworth	*The Illumination of Mr Shannon*	12 March 1973	Soho Poly Lunchtime
Robert Holman	*Coal*	22 October 1973	Soho Poly Lunchtime
Hull Truck (with Mike Bradwell)	*The Weekend After Next*	January 1973	Gulbenkian Theatre, Newcastle
Terry James	*Urban Guerilla Boutique*	1 May 1973	Soho Poly Lunchtime
Chris Johnson	*Sex, Cold Cans and a Coffin*	1 October 1973	Wakefield Tricycle at Kings Head Lunchtime
Barrie Keeffe	*Only a Game*	March 1973	Dolphin Theatre Company, Shaw Theatre
Lindsay Kemp/ Jean Genet	*The Maids*	November 1973	Bush Theatre
Lindsay Kemp	*The Turquoise Pantomime*	November 1973	Bush Theatre
Mike Leigh	*Wholesome Glory*	13 February 1973	Royal Court Theatre Upstairs
John McGrath	*Fish in the Sea*	1973	Everyman, Liverpool
John McGrath	*The Cheviot, The Stag, and the Black Black Oil*	1973	7:84 Theatre Company, tour of Scotland
Philip Magdalany	*Section Nine*	9 October 1973	RSC at the Place (then at Aldwych, 23 January 1974)
Tom Mallin	*Mrs Argent*	22 October 1973	Soho Poly Lunchtime
Charles Marowitz	*The Shrew*	1 November 1973	Open Space Theatre
Jonathan Marshall	*How to Survive in the Nick*	May 1973	Bush Theatre
Jonathan Marshall	*A Wet Winter's Night Dream*	December 1973	Bush Theatre
Dave Marson/ Bill Colvill	*Fall In and Follow Me*	1973	Half Moon Theatre
Mustapha Matura	*Nice*	12 February 1973	Ambiance Lunch Hour Theatre
David Mercer	*In Two Minds*	May 1973	Bush Theatre
Roy Minton	*Good Times*	June 1973	Bush Theatre
Roy Minton	*Ag and Fish*	26 February 1973	Soho Poly Lunchtime
Adrian Mitchell	*Man Friday*	April/June 1973	7:84 Theatre Company on tour
North West Spanner	*The Nurses Play*	3 June 1973	Salford Royal Hospital
Richard O'Brien	*The Rocky Horror Show*	19 June 1973	Royal Court Theatre Upstairs
Jennifer Phillips	*Instruments for Love*	8 October 1973	Ambiance Lunch Hour Theatre
David Pinner	*Cartoon*	27 March 1973	Soho Poly Lunchtime
Harold Pinter	*Landscape, A Slight Ache*	17 October 1973	RSC, Aldwych Theatre
John Quarrell/ Brian Phelan	*Get Off My Back*	October 1973	Half Moon Theatre

Red Ladder	*Happy Robots*	February 1973	Swindon
Red Ladder	*Housing Play*	February 1973	Swindon
David Rudkin	*Cries from Casement as His Bones Are Brought to Dublin*	2 October 1973	RSC at The Place
Sal's Meat Market	*Trouble on the Night Shift*	19 December 1973	Bush Theatre
James Saunders	*Triangle*	1973	Kings Head Evening
Sam Shepard	*The Unseen Hand*	12 March 1973	Royal Court Theatre Upstairs
N. F. Simpson	*The Form*	21 August 1973	Kings Head Evening
Andy Smith	*Heroes of the Iceberg Hotel*	1973	Half Moon Theatre
Andy Smith	*Punch and Judy*	1973	Half Moon Tour
Derek Smith	*How Sparks Learned to Fly*	6 November 1973	Wakefield Tricycle at Kings Head Lunchtime
David Storey	*Cromwell*	15 August 1973	Royal Court Theatre
David Storey	*The Farm*	26 September 1973	Royal Court Theatre
George Thatcher	*The Only Way Out*	12 March 1973	Little Theatre, Garrick Yard
Paul Thompson	*Robin Hood*	2 March 1973	NATTKE Demonstration outside Palladium Theatre
Paul Thompson	*The Children's Crusade*	10 September 1973	National Youth Theatre at Cockpit
William Trevor	*The Forty-Seventh Saturday*	3 May 1973	Open Space Theatre
William Trevor	*Marriages & A Perfect Relationship*	24 July 1973	Kings Head Evening
William Trevor	*George Moore's Celibate Lives*	11 September 1973	Kings Head Evening
John Turner	*Grand Opening*	December 1973	The Combination at The Albany Empire
Michelene Wandor, Sally Ordway, Dinah Brook	*Mal de Mer, Lovefood, Crabs*	19 November 1973	Ambiance Lunch Hour Theatre
Irving Wardle	*The Houseboy*	13 June 1973	Open Space Theatre
Jane Wibberley	*Parade of Cats*	3 December 1973	Ambiance Lunch Hour Theatre
Heathcote Williams	*The Local Stigmatic* (revival)	15 August 1973	Open Space Theatre
David Williamson	*The Removalists*	19 July 1973	Royal Court Theatre
Snoo Wilson	*The Pleasure Principle*	22 November 1973	Royal Court Theatre Upstairs
Snoo Wilson	*Vampire*	1973	Paradise Foundry
Stanslislaw Witkiewicz	*The Shoemakers*	September 1973	Half Moon Theatre
Henry Woolf	*Doctor Croak Sends Help and Johesus*	6 February 1973	Kings Head Lunchtime
Olwen Wymark	*Stay Where You Are*	9 October 1973	Wakefield Tricycle at Kings Head Lunchtime
York Shoestring Company	*Life in a Chocolate Factory*	16 July 1973	Bush Theatre

1974

John Antrobus	*Illegal Immigrants*	26 March 1974	Soho Poly Evening
John Antrobus	*Certain Humiliations & The Dinosaurs*	21 January 1974	Soho Poly Evening
John Antrobus	*The Loonies*	10 October 1974	Hampstead Theatre Club
Belt & Braces	*The Recruiting Officer*	April 1974	Oval House & on tour
Belt & Braces	*The Front Line*	September 1974	Tour commissioned by Vickers Shop Steward Committee
Ed B. (with Dogg's Troupe)	*The Last Straw*	26 December 1974	Ambiance Lunch Hour Theatre
Peter Barnes	*The Bewitched*	7 May 1974	RSC, Aldwych Theatre
Colin Bennett	*Fourth Day Like Four Long Months of Absence*	15 October 1974	Joint Stock at Edinburgh
Edward Bond	*Bingo* (revival)	14 August 1974	Royal Court Theatre
Bertolt Brecht	*St Joan of the Stockyards*	1974	Half Moon Theatre
Howard Brenton	*The Churchill Play*	8 May 1974	Nottingham Playhouse
Alexander Buzo	*Norm and Ahmed*	13 May 1974	Ambiance Lunch Hour Theatre
George Byatt	*Kong Lives*	23 September 1974	Soho Poly Evening
Ken Campbell	*The Great Caper*	9 October 1974	Royal Court Theatre
CAST (with Roland Muldoon)	*C.U.T.S.*	Tour 1974–76	National tour

John Chapman/ Tim Fywell/ Nigel Williams	*Marbles*	21 October 1974	Bush Theatre
Caryl Churchill	*Moving Clocks Go Slow*	June 1974	Royal Court Theatre Upstairs
Johnny Clark	*Cindyella*	1974	Half Moon Theatre
Bill Colvill	*Spare Us a Copper*	1974	Half Moon Tour
Bill Colvill	*The Three P Off Opera*	1974	Half Moon Theatre
Richard Crane	*Secrets*	24 June 1974	Bush Theatre, then ICA
Margaretta D'Arcy/ John Arden (with Corrandulla Arts Entertainment Club)	*The Devil and the Parish Pump*	April 1974	Gort Roe, Corrandulla, Co Galway
John Downie	*I Was Shakespeare's Double*	14 June 1974	RSC, The Other Place, Stratford
Alan Drury	*Asides*	9 September 1974	Bush Theatre
David Edgar	*Operation Iskra* (revival)	January 1974	Bush Theatre
David Edgar	*Dick Deterred*	25 February 1974	Bush Theatre, then ICA
David Edgar	*Man Only Dines*	June 1974	Leeds Polytechnic
David Edgar	*The Dunkirk Spirit*	January 1974	General Will on tour
David Edgar	*The All-Singing, All-Talking Golden Oldie Rock Revival Ho Chi Minh Peace Love and Revolution Show (The ... Show)*	March 1974	Bingley College of Education
Stanley Eveling	*Shivvers*	28 April 1974	Joint Stock, Edinburgh, then at Royal Court Theatre Upstairs
R. W. Fassbinder	*Bremen Coffee*	18 February 1974	Hampstead Theatre Club
R. W. Fassbinder	*Cock Artist*	12 November 1974	Foco Novo at Ambiance Lunch Hour Theatre
Athol Fugard	*The Island*	2 January 1974	Royal Court Theatre
Athol Fugard	*Sizwe Bansi Is Dead* (revival)	8 January 1974	Royal Court Theatre
Athol Fugard	*Statements After an Arrest Under the Immorality Act*	22 January 1974	Royal Court Theatre
Athol Fugard	*Blood Knot*	17 September 1974	Kings Head Evening
Jack Gelber	*The Connection* (revival)	5 September 1974	Hampstead Theatre Club
Steve Gooch/ Paul Thompson	*The Motor Show*	19 March 1974	Community Theatre at Leys Hall, Dagenham, then April at Half Moon Theatre
Trevor Griffiths	*All Good Men*	31 January 1974	BBC TV
Trevor Griffiths	*Absolute Beginners*	19 April 1974	BBC TV
David Hare	*Knuckle*	29 January 1974	Oxford Playhouse, then Comedy Theatre in March 1974
Hull Truck (with Mike Bradwell)	*The Knowledge*	January 1974	Hull Art College, then on tour and at the Bush Theatre (11 November)
Ann Jellicoe	*Two Jelly Plays*	29 January 1974	Royal Court Theatre Upstairs
Lindsay Kemp	*Flowers*	2 January 1974	Bush Theatre
Roy Kift	*Hello Sailor*	April 1974	The Combination at The Albany Empire
Franz Xaver Kroetz	*Stallerhof*	6 August 1974	Bush Theatre, then on tour and at Hampstead 4 February 1975
David Lan	*Painting a Wall*	25 March 1974	Ambiance Lunch Hour Theatre
David Lan	*Bird Child*	22 April 1974	Royal Court Theatre Upstairs
Chris Langham	*Retrogrim's Progress*	1 May 1974	Bush Theatre
Chris Langham	*Greasy Spoon*	19 August 1974	Bush Theatre
Mike Leigh	*Babies Grow Old*	27 August 1974	RSC, The Other Place, Stratford
Mike Leigh	*The Silent Majority*	21 October 1974	Bush Theatre
Lumiere & Son	*Jack ... the Flames*	1 April 1974	Bush Theatre
John McGrath	*The Game's a Bogey*	1974	7:84 (Scotland) tour
John McGrath	*Boom*	1974	7:84 Theatre Company tour
Mustapha Matura	*Play Mas*	16 July 1974	Royal Court Theatre
David Mercer	*Duck Song*	5 February 1974	RSC, Aldwych Theatre

David Mercer	*The Arcata Promise*	22 September 1974	Yorkshire TV
David Mowat	*Come*	12 November 1974	Soho Poly Lunchtime
David Mowat	*Collected Works*	13 February 1974	Open Space Theatre
North West Spanner	*The Shrewsbury Play*	1 May 1974	Albert Square, Manchester
Robert Patrick	*Kennedy's Children*	22 October 1974	Kings Head Evening
People Show	*People Show No. 55*	16 April 1974	Hampstead Theatre Club
People Show	*People Show No. 56*	29 August 1974	Kings Head Evening
Jennifer Phillips	*Bodywork*	17 May 1974	Hampstead Theatre Club
Alan Plater/ Willy Russell/ Bill Colvill	*The Hammers*	October 1974	Half Moon Theatre
Stephen Poliakoff	*Clever Soldiers*	21 November 1974	Hampstead Theatre Club
Stephen Poliakoff	*The Carnation Gang*	23 September 1974	Bush Theatre
Bernard Pomerance	*Someone Else Is Still Someone*	16 July 1974	Bush Theatre
John Quarrel/ F. X. Kroetz	*Stakeout/Homeworker*	1974	Half Moon Theatre
Peter Ransley	*Runaway*	11 March 1974	Royal Court Theatre
Barry Reckord	*X*	19 August 1974	Joint Stock at Royal Court Theatre Upstairs
Red Ladder Theatre Company	*A Woman's Work Is Never Done or Strike While the Iron Is Hot*	11 March 1974	AUEW/TASS School, Weston-super-Mare
David Rudkin	*Ashes*	19 January 1974	Open Space Theatre
David Rudkin	*Afore Night Come* (revival)	3 December 1974	RSC, The Other Place, Stratford
Sal's Meat Market	*Phil Teddy's Fun Palace*	15 July 1974	Bush Theatre
Jeremy Seabrook/ Michael O'Neill	*Our Sort of People*	25 July 1974	Soho Poly Lunchtime
Sam Shepard	*Cowboy Mouth* (revival)	19 March 1974	Soho Poly Lunchtime
Sam Shepard	*Little Ocean*	25 March 1974	Hampstead Theatre Club
Sam Shepard	*The Tooth of Crime* (revival)	5 June 1974	Royal Court Theatre
Sam Shepard	*Geography of a Horsedreamer*	18 February 1974	Royal Court Theatre Upstairs
Sam Shepard	*Action*	17 September 1974	Royal Court Theatre Upstairs
Andy Smith	*Big City Confidential*	December 1974	The Combination at the Albany Empire
Andy Smith	*Sawdust Caesar*	20 December 1974	Bush Theatre
Andy Smith/D. M. Samourai	*Insomniac*	28 May 1974	Bush Theatre
Johnny Speight	*The Salesman*	12 June 1974	Kings Head Lunchtime
Carl Sternheim	*Schippel/The Snob*	17 October 1974	Open Space Theatre
Tom Stoppard	*Travesties*	10 June 1974	RSC, Aldwych Theatre
David Storey	*Life Class*	9 April 1974	Royal Court Theatre
Mike Stott	*Other People*	26 June 1974	Hampstead Theatre Club
Mike Stott	*Midnight*	11 February 1974	Ambiance Lunch Hour Theatre
Mike Stott	*Lenz*	6 June 1974	Ambiance Lunch Hour Theatre
Cecil P. Taylor	*Black and White Minstrels* (revival)	17 January 1974	Hampstead Theatre Club
Paul Thompson	*By Common Consent*	9 September 1974	National Youth Theatre at Cockpit
John Turner	*Strangers in Paradise*	February 1974	The Combination at The Albany Empire
John Turner	*Watch It All Come Down*	October 1974	The Combination at The Albany Empire
E. A. Whitehead	*The Sea Anchor*	9 July 1974	Royal Court Theatre Upstairs
Heathcote Williams	*Remember the Truth Dentist*	13 December 1974	Royal Court Theatre Upstairs
Heathcote Williams	*The Speakers*	28 January 1974	Joint Stock at Birmingham
Snoo Wilson	*The Beast*	18 November 1974	RSC, The Place
Womens Theatre Group	*Fantazia*	17 May 1974	Oval House
Henry Woolf	*A Naval Occasion*	15 April 1974	Bush Theatre
Angela Wye	*The Rialto Prom*	21 October 1974	Ambiance Lunch Hour Theatre

1975

Michael Abbensetts	*Sweet Talk* (revival)	24 June 1975	Kings Head Evening
John Antrobus	*Mrs Grybowski's Academy*	11 February 1975	Royal Court Theatre Upstairs
John Roman Baker	*Limitations*	17 February 1975	Gay Sweatshop at Ambiance Lunch Hour Theatre
Roger Baker & Drew Griffiths	*Mister X*	1975	Gay Sweatshop on tour and at ICA Theatre
Howard Barker	*Claw*	30 January 1975	Open Space Theatre
Howard Barker	*Stripwell*	14 October 1975	Royal Court Theatre
Wolfgang Bauer	*Ghosts* (translated: Mike Stott)	10 July 1975	Hampstead Theatre Club
Steven Berkoff	*East*	12 September 1975	Kings Head Evening
Steven Berkoff/ Terry James	*The Fall of the House of Usher*	4 February 1975	Hampstead Theatre Club
Edward Bond	*The Fool*	18 November 1975	Royal Court Theatre
Bertolt Brecht	*The Good Woman of Sctzuan*	14 October 1975	Hampstead Theatre Club
Bertolt Brecht	*A Man's a Man*	September 1975	Foco Novo on tour and at Hampstead Theatre Club
Bertolt Brecht	*Happy End*	October 1975	Lyric Theatre, previously at Oxford Playhouse
Howard Brenton	*The Saliva Milkshake*	23 June 1975	Soho Poly
Broadside Mobile Workers Theatre (with building workers)	*The Big Lump*	14 January 1975	Tower Hill Demonstration to free the Shrewsbury Pickets
Broadside Mobile Workers Theatre (with Lucas Aerospace Combine Committee)	*The Participation Waltz*	13 April 1975	National Conference of AEUW/ TASS, Edinburgh
Broadside Mobile Workers Theatre	*The Working Women's Charter Show*	31 May 1975	ASTMS Division 15 Action Committee on Sex Discrimination, London
John Burrows & John Harding	*Loud Reports*	10 March 1975	Royal Court Theatre Upstairs
Alexander Buzo	*Norm and Ahmed* (revival)	4 December 1975	Kings Head Lunchtime
Caryl Churchill	*Perfect Happiness*	10 March 1975	Soho Poly Lunchtime
Brian Clark	*Post Mortem*	25 March 1975	Soho Poly Lunchtime
Laurence Collinson	*Thinking Straight*	10 March 1975	Gay Sweatshop at Ambiance Lunch Hour Theatre
The Combination	*Future Histories*	February 1975	The Albany Empire
Shane Connaughton	*George Davis Is Innocent OK?*	10 October 1975	Half Moon Theatre
Richard Crane	*Decent Things*	August 1975	Bush Theatre
Margaretta D'Arcy/ John Arden	*The Non-Stop Connolly Show*	Easter 1975	Liberty Hall, Dublin
Margaretta D'Arcy/ John Arden (with Galway Theatre Workshop)	*The Crown Strike Play*	December 1975	Eyre Square, Galway
David Edgar	*O Fair Jerusalem*	May 1975	Birmingham Repertory Studio
David Edgar	*Summer Sports* (later: *Blood Sports*)	July 1975	Birmingham Arts Lab
David Edgar	*The National Theatre*	14 October 1975	Open Space Theatre
Stanley Eveling	*Dear Janet Rosenberg, Dear Mr Kooning* (revival)	1 May 1975	Hampstead Theatre Club
Alfred Fagon	*Death of a Black Man*	29 May 1975	Foco Novo at Hampstead Theatre Club
Trevor Griffiths	*Through the Night*	2 December 1975	BBC TV
Wilson John Haire	*Echoes From a Concrete Canyon*	28 May 1975	Royal Court Theatre Upstairs
David Hare	*Fanshen*	10 March 1975	Joint Stock at Sheffield, Royal Court, Hampstead Theatre
David Hare	*Teeth 'n' Smiles*	2 September 1975	Royal Court Theatre

Hull Truck (with Mike Bradwell)	*Oh What!*	March 1975	Birmingham Arts Lab and at Bush Theatre (4 November)
Hull Truck (with Mike Bradwell)	*Writing on the Wall*	November 1975	BBC TV
Leonard Jenkin	*Kitty Hawk*	17 June 1975	Wakefield Tricycle Company at the Bush Theatre
B. S. Johnson	*Down Red Lane*	29 July 1975	Open Space Theatre
Neil Johnston *et al*	*The Doomducker's Ball*	6 March 1975	Oval House
Barrie Keeffe	*Gem*	7 July 1975	Soho Poly
Barrie Keeffe	*A Sight of Glory*	August 1975	National Youth Theatre at Cockpit Theatre
Barrie Keeffe	*Scribes*	October 1975	Tyneside Theatre Company, Newcastle
Barrie Keeffe	*My Girl*	15 September 1975	Soho Poly
Roy Kendall	*Cornet Lesson*	27 October 1975	Soho Poly
Franz Xaver Kroetz	*Morecambe*	10 December 1975	Hampstead Theatre Club
David Lan	*Paradise*	23 April 1975	Royal Court Theatre Upstairs
David Lan	*Homage to Been Soup*	4 June 1975	Royal Court Theatre Upstairs
Lumiere & Son/ David Gale	*White Men Dancing By*	27 May 1975	Bush Theatre
John McGrath	*Fish in the Sea*	1975	7:84 Theatre Company tour and at Half Moon
John McGrath	*Lay Off*	Tour 1975	7:84 Theatre Company tour
John McGrath	*Yobbo Nowt*	Tour 1975	7:84 Theatre Company tour
John McGrath (adapted by Bill Colvill)	*Soft or a Girl?* (revival)	Tour 1975	Half Moon Theatre
John McGrath	*Little Red Hen*	Tour 1975	7:84 Theatre Company Scotland Tour
Hector MacMillan	*The Sash*	4 January 1975	Hampstead Theatre Club
Charles Marowitz	*Measure for Measure*	28 May 1975	Open Space Theatre
Charles Marowitz	*Artaud at Rodez*	17 December 1975	Open Space Theatre
North West Spanner	*Safety First or Last*	6 July 1975	AUEW House, Salford
North West Spanner (with Ernie Dalton)	*Winding Up*	2 October 1975	Ridington and Blackrod
Mary O'Malley	*Oh If Ever a Man Suffered*	7 May 1975	Hampstead Theatre Club
Mary O'Malley	*A 'Nevolent Society*	13 July 1975	Royal Court Theatre Upstairs
Michael O'Neill and Jeremy Seabrook	*Sex and Kinship in a Savage Society*	28 July 1975	Royal Court Theatre Upstairs
Joe Orton	*Entertaining Mr Sloane* (revival)	17 April 1975	Royal Court Theatre
Joe Orton	*Loot* (revival)	3 June 1975	Royal Court Theatre
Joe Orton	*What the Butler Saw* (revival)	16 July 1975	Royal Court Theatre
Robert Patrick	*Fred & Harold/One Person*	12 May 1975	Gay Sweatshop at Ambiance Lunch Hour Theatre
Robert Patrick	*Haunted Host*	19 May 1975	Ambiance Lunch Hour Theatre
Robert Patrick	*Play by Play*	16 October 1975	Kings Head Evening
Brian Phelan	*Paddy*	1975	Half Moon Theatre
Harold Pinter	*No Man's Land*	23 April 1975	National Theatre at the Old Vic
Stephen Poliakoff	*Hitting Town*	27 March 1975	Bush Theatre
Stephen Poliakoff	*City Sugar*	8 October 1975	Bush Theatre
Stephen Poliakoff	*Heroes*	1 July 1975	Royal Court Theatre Upstairs
Red Ladder Theatre Company	*It Makes Yer Sick*	November 1975	St Pancras Town Hall
Gavin Richards/ David Bradford	*Weight*	February 1975	Belt & Braces at Jeanetta Cochrane Theatre & on tour
George Ryga	*The Ecstasy of Rita Joe*	18 September 1975	Hampstead Theatre Club
Sal's Meat Market	*I'm Not Walking*	9 December 1975	Bush Theatre
Martin Sherman	*Passing By*	11 June 1975	Gay Sweatshop at Ambiance Lunch Hour Theatre
Andy Smith	*Peyton Space*	December 1975	The Combination at The Albany Empire
Andy Smith	*Fist of Frozen Lightning*	15 September 1975	Bush Theatre

Derek Smith	*The Wedding*	29 September 1975	Soho Poly
Derek Smith	*The Athlete*	March 1975	Wakefield Tricycle Company at Soho Poly
Eric Sutton	*Hello Sailor*	21 July 1975	Soho Poly
Ian Taylor	*Cocks and Hens*	24 November 1975	Soho Poly
John Turner	*Hood*	March 1975	The Combination at The Albany Empire
John Turner	*Beggars Can't Be Choosers* (adapted from John Gay)	June 1975	The Combination at The Albany Empire
John Turner	*The Great Smiffo*	October 1975	The Combination at The Albany Empire
Wakefield Tricycle Company	*The End of the World Show*	2 February 1975	Bush Theatre
Alan Wakeman	*Ships*	31 March 1975	Gay Sweatshop at Ambiance Lunch Hour Theatre
Robert Walker	*B Movie*	18 August 1975	Soho Poly
Keith Waterhouse/ Willis Hall	*Celebration*	19 March 1975	Open Space Theatre
Heathcote Williams	*A Christmas Pantomime Party*	1975	Half Moon Theatre
David Williamson	*Don's Party*	27 February 1975	Royal Court Theatre
Christopher Wilkins	*The Late Wife*	4 August 1975	Soho Poly
Snoo Wilson	*The Everest Hotel*	30 December 1975	Bush Theatre
Womens Theatre Group	*My Mother Says I Never Should*	9 January 1975	Touring London schools and youth clubs, also at Bush Theatre (20 February)
Charles Wood	*Jingo*	19 August 1975	RSC, Aldwych Theatre
Charles Wood	*Prisoner and Escort* (revival)	24 June 1975	Open Space Theatre
Phil Woods	*Arthur Horner*	21 January 1975	Foco Novo at Sherman Theatre, Cardiff
Henry Woolf	*Steer Clear of Kafka*	28 October 1975	Ambiance Lunch Hour Theatre

1976

Yemi Ajibade	*Parcel Post*	16 March 1976	Royal Court
Edward Albee	*Zoo Story* (revival)	5 July 1976	Kings Head Lunchtime
Jamal Ali	*The Treatment/Dark Days, Light Nights*	31 March 1976	Soho Poly
Roger Baker/Drew Griffiths	*Indiscreet*	1976	Gay Sweatshop on tour
Nigel Baldwin	*Just a Little Bit Less Than Normal*	25 August 1976	Royal Court Theatre Upstairs
Howard Barker	*Wax*	18 September 1976	Traverse Theatre, Edinburgh
Colin Bennett	*Soon*	5 October 1976	Bush Theatre
C. G. Bond/Claire Luckham/with Monstrous Regiment	*SCUM – Death Destruction and Dirty Washing*	May 1976	Chapter Arts Centre, Cardiff
Edward Bond	*Stone*	8 June 1976	Gay Sweatshop at ICA
Edward Bond	*We Come to the River*	12 July 1976	Royal Opera House, Covent Garden
Edward Bond	*A-A-America! (Grandma Faust/ The Swing)*	25 October 1976 (Grandma Faust) 22 November 1976 (The Swing)	Ambiance Lunch Hour Theatre
Edward Bond	*Bingo* (revival)	3 November 1976	RSC, The Other Place, Stratford, then at Warehouse 9 August 1977
Bertolt Brecht	*Schweyk in the Second World War*	31 March 1976	RSC, The Other Place, Stratford, then Warehouse, 18 July 1977
Bertolt Brecht	*The Breadshop*	2 July 1976	Avon Touring at the Half Moon
Howard Brenton	*Weapons of Happiness*	14 July 1976	Lyttleton Theatre, National Theatre

Broadside Mobile Workers Theatre	*Now You See It, Now You Don't*	23 April 1976	UCATT Branch, Birmingham
Broadside Mobile Workers Theatre	*Divide and Rule Britannia*	3 July 1976	Brent Campaign Against Racism Demonstration
Peter Brook	*The Ik*	15 January 1976	Roundhouse, Chalk Farm
Ian Brown	*The Fork*	1976	Gay Sweatshop on tour
George Byatt	*Soldier Green*	28 September 1976	Soho Poly
Andy Carr	*Hanratty in Hell*	1 July 1976	Open Space Theatre
CAST (with Roland Muldoon)	*Goodbye Union Jack*	1976/77 Tour	CAST on tour
Jon Chadwick/John Hoyland	*The Nine Days and Saltley Gates*	19 January 1976	Foco Novo at Oval House, Kennington
Caryl Churchill	*Light Shining in Buckinghamshire*	7 September 1976	Joint Stock at Traverse Theatre, Edinburgh, then at Royal Court Theatre Upstairs
Caryl Churchill	*Vinegar Tom*	September 1976	Monstrous Regiment at Hull Arts Centre
Brian Clark	*Campion's Interview*	17 May 1976	Soho Poly
Jim Clark	*Long Ball to Nowhere*	October 1976	The Combination at The Albany Empire
Barry Collins	*Judgement*	19 January 1976	Royal Court Theatre
The Combination	*Wit Week Walkabout*	June 1976	The Albany Empire
Shane Connaughton	*The Good Woman of Wapping* (adapted from Bertolt Brecht)	19 March 1976	Half Moon Theatre
Shane Connaughton	*Canning Town Cowboy*	24 July 1976	Half Moon Theatre
Shane Connaughton	*Relegated*	1976	7:84 Theatre Company tour
Margaretta D'Arcy/ John Arden (with Galway Theatre Workshop)	*Sean O'Scrudu*	February 1976	Coachman Hotel, Galway
Margaretta D'Arcy/ John Arden (with Galway Theatre Workshop)	*The Mongrel Fox*	October 1976	Regional Technical College, Galway
Margaretta D'Arcy/ John Arden (with Galway Theatre Workshop)	*No Room at the Inn*	December 1976	Coachman Hotel, Galway
Margaretta D'Arcy/ John Arden	*The Non-Stop Connolly Show* (revival)	17 May 1976	Ambiance Lunch Hour Theatre
Andrew Davies	*Randy Robinson's Unsuitable Relationship*	1976	Gay Sweatshop on tour
Alan Drury	*Sense of Loss*	February 1976	Open Space Theatre
Alan Drury	*Communion*	12 April 1976	Soho Poly
Alan Drury	*Sparrowfall*	2 July 1976	Hampstead Theatre Club
David Edgar	*Destiny*	22 September 1976	RSC at The Other Place, Stratford then at Aldwych, 12 May 1977
David Edgar	*Events Following the Closure of a Motorcycle Factory*	February 1976	Birmingham Repertory Studio
David Edgar	*Saigon Rose*	July 1976	Traverse Theatre, Edinburgh
David Edgar	*The Perils of Bardfrod*	November 1976	Theatre in the Mill, Bradford University
David Edgar	*Blood Sports* (revival)	30 June 1976	Bush Theatre
Stanley Eveling	*Better Days, Better Knights*	9 August 1976	Kings Head Lunchtime
Paul Foster	*Elizabeth I*	3 August 1976	Kings Head Evening
Gilly Fraser	*Do a Dance for Daddy*	28 June 1976	Soho Poly
Gay Sweatshop (with Drew Griffiths)	*Jingle Ball (Parts 1 and 2)*	1976	Gay Sweatshop on tour

Pam Gems	*The Project*	12 July 1976	Soho Poly
Pam Gems	*Dusa, Fish, Stas and Vi*	6 December 1976	Hampstead Theatre Club
Pam Gems	*Guinevere*	11 October 1976	Soho Poly
Peter Gill	*Small Change*	8 July 1976	Royal Court Theatre
Steve Gooch	*Our Land, Our Lives*	1976	7:84 Theatre Company tour
Trevor Griffiths	*Bill Brand* (eleven part television series)	31 March 1976	Thames TV
Christopher Hampton	*Treats*	5 February 1976	Royal Court Theatre
Nigel Hawthorne	*Sitting Ducks*	29 March 1976	Soho Poly
Hull Truck (with Mike Bradwell)	*Bridget's House*	March 1976	Lanchester Poly, then at The Bush (2 November)
Leigh Jackson	*Parking*	4 October 1976	Kings Head Lunchtime
Joint Stock (with Jeremy Seabrook)	*Yesterday's News*	6 April 1976	Aldershot, later at Royal Court Theatre Upstairs
Barrie Keeffe	*Gotcha*	17 May 1976	Soho Poly
Barrie Keeffe	*Here Comes the Sun*	August 1976	National Youth Theatre at Jeanette Cochrane
Barrie Keeffe	*Abide With Me*	28 September 1976	Soho Poly
Roy Kift	*Cakewalk*	31 January 1976	Hampstead Theatre Club
Rick Lloyd	*Kentucky Moon*	March 1976	The Combination at The Albany Empire
John McGrath	*The Rat Trap*	1976	7:84 Theatre Company tour
John McGrath	*Out of Our Heads*	1976	Edinburgh
Frank Marcus	*Carol's Christmas*	6 January 1976	Kings Head Evening
Rosemary Mason	*Sunbeams*	26 April 1976	Soho Poly
Mustapha Matura	*Rum and Coca Cola*	3 November 1976	Royal Court Theatre
David Mercer	*Huggy Bear*	11 April 1976	Yorkshire TV
Adrian Mitchell	*A Seventh Man*	29 September 1976	Foco Novo at Derby Playhouse, later at Hampstead Theatre Club (3 November 1976)
North West Spanner (with Ernie Dalton)	*Dig For Victory*	5 May 1976	St Anne's Church Hall, Ashton-Under-Lyne Lancs
North West Spanner (with Ernie Dalton)	*Just a Cog*	3 November 1976	Nelson & Colne College
Alan Passes	*Mystic of the Western World*	25 October 1976	Soho Poly
Phantom Captain	*Open to Question*	25 August 1976	Bush Theatre
David Pinner	*Shakebag*	10 May 1976	Soho Poly
Pip Simmons	*Dracula*	7 December 1976	Royal Court Theatre
Jill Posener	*Any Woman Can*	12 July 1976	Gay Sweatshop on tour and at Kings Head
David Pownall/ Paines Plough	*Ladybird, Ladybird*	20 April 1976	Bush Theatre
Red Ladder Theatre Company	*Anybody Sweating?*	November 1976	Bradford
Gavin Richards/ John Fiske	*England Expects*	January 1976	Belt & Braces at Half Moon & on tour
Andy Smith	*Free Chicken Dinners*	1 March 1976	Soho Poly
Andy Smith	*Winter Visitors*	2 March 1976	Bush Theatre
Andy Smith	*Breakers Yard*	12 July 1976	Pirate Jenny, Kings Head Evening
Tom Stoppard	*Dirty Linen*	5 April 1976	Ambiance Lunch Hour Theatre
Tom Stoppard	*Albert's Bridge*	18 October 1976	Kings Head Lunchtime
David Storey	*Mothers Day*	22 September 1976	Royal Court Theatre
Mike Stott	*Lenz* (revival)	8 April 1976	Hampstead Theatre Club
Eric Sutton	*Happy Christmas, Miss Figgis*	6 December 1976	Soho Poly
William Tanner	*Tsafendes*	16 February 1976	Ambiance Lunch Hour Theatre
Ian Taylor	*A Bit in Between*	8 November 1976	Soho Poly

Peter Terson/Paul			
Joyce	*Love Us and Leave Us*	3 June 1976	Open Space
George Thatcher	*The Only Way Out* (revival)	29 July 1976	Royal Court Theatre Upstairs
Paul Thompson/			
Steve Gooch	*Made in Britain*	11 May 1976	Oxford Playhouse
Bill Tidy/Alan			
Plater	*The Fosdyke Saga*	30 November 1976	Bush Theatre
John Turner	*Jack in the Docks*	February 1976	The Combination at The Albany Empire
John Turner	*Karno's Army*	July 1976	The Combination at The Albany Empire
John Turner	*Beauty and the Beast*	December 1976	The Combination at The Albany Empire
Michael Wells	*The Great Ban*	12 January 1976	Ambiance Lunch Hour Theatre
Arnold Wesker	*Love Letters on Blue Paper*	January 1976	BBC TV
Snoo Wilson	*Soul of the White Ant*	2 February 1976	Soho Poly, later at The Bush (March)
Womens Theatre			
Group	*Work to Role*	11 January 1976	Tour, and Bush Theatre
Charles Wood	*Dingo*	1 June 1976	RSC, The Other Place, Stratford, then Warehouse, 26 January 1978
Phil Woods	*Johnny Boxer*	February 1976	Half Moon Theatre
Phil Woods	*Out For Nine*	1 May 1976	Half Moon Theatre

1977

Aitmatov/			
Mukhamedzhanov	*The Ascent of Mount Fuji*	2 June 1977	Hampstead Theatre Club
Nigel Baldwin	*Sudlow's Dawn*	1977	Royal Court Theatre Upstairs
Howard Barker	*Fair Slaughter*	13 June 1977	Royal Court Theatre
Howard Barker	*That Good Between Us*	28 July 1977	RSC Warehouse
Eric Bentley	*Are You Now Or Have You Ever Been?*	7 June 1977	Bush Theatre, then at Mayfair
Tony Bicat	*Devil's Island*	11 January 1977	Joint Stock on tour at Cardiff, then at Royal Court
Stephen Black	*The Pokey*	2 May 1977	Soho Poly
John Bowen	*The Waiting Room*	17 January 1977	Kings Head Lunchtime
Bertolt Brecht	*To Those Born Later*	1 June 1977	Cottesloe (National Theatre)
Howard Brenton	*Epsom Downs*	4 August 1977	Joint Stock at the Round House
Broadside Mobile Workers Theatre (by Kathleen McCreery with Portuguese Workers Coordinating Committee)	*We Have the Power of the Winds*	18 February 1977	Portugal/Chile/Britain: Three Day Cultural Event, Conway Hall, London
Alan Brown	*Skoolplay*	21 October 1977	Royal Court Theatre Upstairs
Tina Brown	*Happy Yellow*	17 May 1977	Bush Theatre
John Byrne	*Writers Cramp*	1 November 1977	Bush Theatre
Ken Campbell/ Theodore			
Sturgeon	*Psychosis Unclassified*	6 September 1977	Bush Theatre
CAST (with Roland Muldoon)	*Confessions of a Socialist*	1977/78	National tour
Jon Chadwick/ John Hoyland	*Tighten Your Belt*	15 March 1977	Foco Novo at Swansea and on tour
Caryl Churchill	*Traps*	27 January 1977	Royal Court Theatre Upstairs
Caryl Churchill (with Bryony Lavery, Michelene Wandor, David Bradford)	*Floorshow*	October 1977	Monstrous Regiment, North London Poly

The Combination	*Twenty-five Years Reign*	March 1977	The Albany Empire
The Combination	*A Nite at The Vulture Club*	October 1977	The Albany Empire
Paul Copley	*Pillion*	4 October 1977	Bush Theatre
Margaretta D'Arcy	*A Pinprick of History*	5 December 1977	Ambiance Lunch Hour Theatre
Margaretta D'Arcy/ John Arden (with Galway Theatre Workshop)	*Silence*	April 1977	Eyre Square, Galway
Margaretta D'Arcy/ John Arden (with Galway Theatre Workshop)	*Mary's Name*	May 1977	University College, Galway
Margaretta D'Arcy/ John Arden (with Galway Theatre Workshop)	*Blow-in Chorus for Liam Cosgrave*	June 1977	Eyre Square, Galway
David Edgar	*Wreckers*	10 February 1977	7:84 Theatre Company, Exeter, then at Half Moon (18 April)
David Edgar	*Our Own People*	November 1977	Pirate Jenny on tour and at Half Moon
Donna Franceschild	*The Cleaning Lady*	6 June 1977	Soho Poly
Gilly Fraser	*A Bit of Rough*	5 December 1977	Soho Poly
Gay Sweatshop (with Michelene Wandor)	*Care and Control*	1977	Gay Sweatshop on tour and at Half Moon
Pam Gems	*Queen Christina*	9 September 1977	RSC at The Other Place, Stratford
Steve Gooch	*Back Street Romeo*	7 March 1977	Half Moon Theatre
Noel Greig/Drew Griffiths	*As Time Goes By*	1977	Gay Sweatshop on tour
Michael Hastings	*For the West*	11 May 1977	Royal Court Theatre Upstairs
Robert Holman	*German Skerries*	25 January 1977	Bush Theatre
Hull Truck (with Mike Bradwell)	*Bed of Roses*	September 1977	Traverse Theatre, Edinburgh
Terry James	*Confession Fever*	28 November 1977	Wakefield Tricycle Company at Kings Head Evening
Stephen Jeffreys	*Like Dolls or Angels*	12 December 1977	Kings Head Lunchtime
Barrie Keeffe	*Gimme Shelter*	31 January 1977	Soho Poly, then at the Royal Court Theatre
Barrie Keeffe	*A Mad World, My Masters*	28 April 1977	Joint Stock at Young Vic
Barrie Keeffe	*Killing Time*	22 August 1977	Soho Poly
Barrie Keeffe	*Up the Truncheon*	August 1977	National Youth Theatre, Shaw Theatre
Barrie Keeffe	*Barbarians (Killing Time, Abide with Me, In the City)*	28 September 1977	Greenwich Theatre
Roy Kift	*Happy and Glorious*	11 July 1977	Ambiance Lunch Hour Theatre
David Lan	*The Winter Dancers*	11 June 1977	Royal Court Theatre Upstairs
Jacek Laskowski	*Silver Lining*	24 October 1977	Ambiance Lunch Hour Theatre
Bryony Lavery	*Grandmother Steps*	30 May 1977	Kings Head Lunchtime
Mike Leigh	*Abigail's Party*	18 April 1977	Hampstead Theatre Club
Hugh Leonard	*Da*	20 July 1977	Kings Head Evening
John McGrath	*Trembling Giant*	1977	7:84 Theatre Company tour, then at Royal Court
John McGrath	*Out of Our Heads* (revival)	1977	7:84 Theatre Company on tour, at Royal Court
John McGrath	*The Life and Times of Joe of England*	1977	7:84 Theatre Company tour
Frank Marcus	*Blind Date*	7 March 1977	Kings Head Lunchtime
Charles Marowitz	*Variations on The Merchant of Venice*	17 May 1977	Open Space Theatre
Dave Marson	*The Slave Camp*	24 May 1977	Half Moon Theatre
Harald Muéller	*Rosie* (translated: Steve Gooch)	25 July 1977	Bush Theatre, then at Half Moon

North West Spanner (with Ernie Dalton)	*Jubilations*	15 May 1977	West Indian Sports and Social Club, Manchester
North West Spanner (with Ernie Dalton)	*Sign Here*	19 July 1977	Tochin's Building Site, Manchester
North West Spanner (with Ernie Dalton)	*Out of Control*	30 December 1977	Francis Shaw Social Club, Manchester
Mary O'Malley	*Once a Catholic*	10 August 1977	Royal Court Theatre
Alun Owen	*Shelter*	17 January 1977	Kings Head Lunchtime
Stewart Parker	*The Actress and the Bishop*	6 December 1977	Kings Head Lunchtime
Stewart Parker	*Spokesong*	7 September 1976	Kings Head Evening
Stewart Parker	*Kingdom Come*	12 January 1977	Kings Head Evening
Alan Passes	*Death Raise*	3 October 1977	Soho Poly
John Petherbridge	*Bank Siege*	4 April 1977	Soho Poly
Phantom Captain	*Loaded Questions*	3 January 1977	Kings Head Evening
Phantom Captain	*The Second Changeness Congress*	20 September 1977	Kings Head Evening
Brian Phelan	*News*	12 September 1977	Soho Poly
Alan Plater/Bill Tidy	*Fosdyke 2*	29 November 1977	Bush Theatre
Alan Plater	*Drums Along the Ginnel*	30 May 1977	Ambiance Lunch Hour Theatre
Eileen Pollock	*Not So Green as its Cabbage*	11 March 1977	Belt & Braces at Jacksons Lane & on tour
Bernard Pomerance	*The Elephant Man*	4 October 1977	Foco Novo at Exeter, then at Hampstead Theatre (3 November)
Red Ladder Theatre Company	*Would Jubilee've It*	March 1977	Wakefield Labour Club
Gavin Richards	*A Day in the Life of the World*	23 July 1977	Belt & Braces at Collegiate College, Exeter & on tour
Gavin Richards	*Mrs Colly Pepper*	29 November 1977	Belt & Braces at St Lukes College, Exeter & on tour
James Robson	*Forgive Me Delilah*	7 March 1977	Soho Poly
James Robson	*Factory Birds*	4 November 1977	RSC Warehouse
David Rudkin	*The Sons of Light*	9 November 1977	RSC, The Other Place, Stratford
David Rudkin	*Sovereignty Under Elizabeth*	14 November 1977	Ambiance Lunch Hour Theatre
Ali Salim	*Caramba*	11 October 1977	TOCAD at Kings Head Lunchtime
Howard Schuman	*Censored Scenes from King Kong*	18 November 1977	Open Space Theatre
Shared Experience	*Recitals of Mystery, Violence and Desire*	12 April 1977	Kings Head Evening
Michael Sharp	*A Day Forever*	1 February 1977	Open Space Theatre
Michael Sharp	*Virgins, Vultures and Love*	14 November 1977	Soho Poly
Wallace Shawn	*A Thought in Three Parts*	24 February 1977	Joint Stock at ICA
Sam Shepard	*Curse of the Starving Class*	21 April 1977	Royal Court Theatre
Sam Shepard	*Suicide in B Flat*	17 October 1977	Open Space Theatre
Andy Smith	*Grand Larceny*	October 1977	Half Moon Theatre
Andy Smith	*In the Shadow of the Guillotine*	June 1977	The Combination at The Albany Empire
Andy Smith	*Dick Whittington or the City of Fear*	15 December 1977	Half Moon Theatre
William Tanner	*Patty Hearst*	10 January 1977	Ambiance Lunch Hour Theatre
C. P. Taylor	*Bandits*	3 August 1977	RSC Warehouse
Paul Thompson	*The Lorenzaccio Story*	21 July 1977	RSC, The Other Place, Stratford, then Warehouse 13 April 1978
Susan Todd/Ann Mitchell	*Kiss and Kill*	September 1977	Monstrous Regiment, Stage One, London
John Turner/Noel Greig	*Heroes*	December 1977	The Combination at The Albany Empire

Michelene Wandor	*Old Wives Tale*	21 March 1977	Soho Poly
Tim Webb	*Zeppelins Over Deptford*	February 1977	The Combination at The Albany Empire
Mike Weller	*Split*	19 July 1977	Open Space Theatre
Arnold Wesker	*The Journalists*	27 March 1977	Amateur production, Criterion Theatre, Coventry
Arnold Wesker	*The Wedding Feast*	20 January 1977	Leeds Playhouse
Nathaniel West/ Robert Walker	*A Cool Million*	6 July 1977	Half Moon Theatre, then Open Space 22 April 1978
E. A. Whitehead	*Mecca*	6 July 1977	Open Space Theatre
Heathcote Williams	*Hancock's Last Half Hour*	18 April 1977	Ambiance Lunch Hour Theatre
Heathcote Williams	*Playpen*	22 November 1977	Royal Court Theatre Upstairs
Lanford Wilson	*Ludlow Fair*	21 February 1977	Kings Head Lunchtime
Snoo Wilson	*Elijah Disappearing*	21 February 1977	Soho Poly
Snoo Wilson/Kevin Coyne	*England England*	8 August 1977	Jeanetta Cochrane Theatre
Snoo Wilson	*Vampire* (new version)	10 March 1977	Bush Theatre
T Bone Wilson	*Come Jubilee*	15 February 1977	Bush Theatre
Womens Theatre Group	*Out! On the Costa del Trico*	11 January 1977	On Tour and at Bush Theatre
Womens Theatre Group	*Pretty Ugly*	18 November 1977	National tour

1978

Michael Almaz	*Cut*	22 May 1978	Soho Poly Evening
Michael Almaz	*Letters From K*	22 May 1978	Soho Poly Evening
Janet Amsden	*Peril at St Agathas*	26 June 1978	Soho Poly
John Arden	*Pearl*	3 July 1978	BBC Radio
Pete Atkin	*A & R*	28 July 1978	RSC Warehouse
Ed. B.	*Freeze*	27 December 1978	Ambiance Lunch Hour Theatre
Nigel Baldwin	*Irish Eyes and English Tears*	12 July 1978	Royal Court Theatre Upstairs
Howard Barker	*The Love of a Good Man*	18 October 1978	Sheffield Crucible
Howard Barker	*The Hang of the Gaol*	15 December 1978	RSC Warehouse
Peter Barnes	*Laughter*	24 January 1978	Royal Court Theatre
Stephen Bill	*Girl Talk*	15 May 1978	Soho Poly
Belt & Braces	*Red Rock Revue*	30 September 1978	Birmingham Poly and on tour
Tony Bicat	*Zigomania*	21 March 1978	Bush Theatre
Jon Blair & Norman Fenton	*Steve Biko: A Miserable and Lonely Death*	5 February 1978	RSC Warehouse
Edward Bond	*The Bundle*	13 January 1978	RSC Warehouse
Edward Bond	*The Woman*	10 August 1978	Olivier Theatre, National Theatre
John Bowen	*Bondage*	10 April 1978	Soho Poly
Bertolt Brecht	*The Measures Taken* (revival)	8 November 1978	Kings Head Lunchtime
Bertolt Brecht	*Asturo Ui* (revival)	12 October 1978	Half Moon Theatre
Bertolt Brecht	*A Respectable Wedding*	12 December 1978	Open Space Theatre
Howard Brenton/ Trevor Griffiths with Ken Campbell & David Hare	*Deeds*	8 March 1978	Nottingham Playhouse
Howard Brenton	*The Churchill Play* (revival)	21 August 1978	RSC, The Other Place, Stratford
Broadside Mobile Workers Theatre (with Anti-Apartheid Movement)	*Apartheid – The British Connection*	11 March 1978	Haringey Anti-Apartheid Group
John Burrows	*Restless Natives*	April 1978	The Combination at The Albany Empire
John Byrne	*The Slab Boys*	18 October 1978	Royal Court Theatre Upstairs
Ken Campbell	*The Great Caper* (revival)	July 1978	Hull Truck at Gulbenkian Theatre, Newcastle

CAST (with Roland Muldoon)	*What Happens Next?*	1978/9 Tour	CAST on tour
Laurence Collinson	*One Penny For Israel*	19 February 1978	Ambiance Lunch Hour Theatre
Bill Colvill	*Mozzle and His Wage Packet*	28 February 1978	Half Moon Theatre
Covent Garden Community Theatre Project	*On the House*	22 November 1978	Kings Head Evening
Margaretta D'Arcy	*West of Ireland Women Speaking*	March 1978	Women's Arts Alliance, London
Margaretta D'Arcy/ John Arden	*Vandaleur's Folly*	1978	7:84 Theatre Company tour, University Theatre, Lancaster
Margaretta D'Arcy/ John Arden	*The Little Gray Home in the West*	4 May 1978	Reading at Sugawn Theatre, London
Andrew Davies	*The Short Sighted Bear*	29 May 1978	Soho Poly
Lawrence Dobie	*The Graveyard Shift*	11 December 1978	Soho Poly
Dogg's Troupe	*Trash Machine*	27 December 1978	Ambiance Lunch Hour Theatre
John Dowie	*Only Men Shave*	31 January 1978	Bush Theatre
David Edgar	*The Jail Diary of Albie Sachs*	16 June 1978	RSC Warehouse
David Edgar	*Mary Barnes*	31 August 1978	Birmingham Rep., then at Royal Court 10 January 1979
Peter Flannery	*Savage Amusement*	5 July 1978	RSC Warehouse
Dario Fo	*We Can't Pay, We Won't Pay*	16 May 1978	Half Moon Theatre
Gay Sweatshop (men)	*Warm*	1978	Gay Sweatshop tour
Gay Sweatshop	*Iceberg*	1978	Gay Sweatshop tour
Gay Sweatshop (women)	*What the Hell Is She Doing Here?*	1978	Gay Sweatshop tour
Jonathan Gems	*Rinnie Bootsie Tootie Fruitti*	20 July 1978	Kings Head Lunchtime
Jonathan Gems	*Shithouse of the August Moon*	23 January 1978	Kings Head Lunchtime
Pam Gems	*Piaf*	11 October 1978	RSC The Other Place, Stratford
Steve Gooch	*The Women Pirates: Ann Bonney and Mary Read*	31 July 1978	RSC, Aldwych Theatre
Steve Grant	*Media Hack*	17 February 1978	Soho Poly
Susan Griffin	*Voices*	12 February 1978	Half Moon Theatre
David Halliwell	*Prejudice*	2 October 1978	Crucible, Sheffield
David Hare	*Licking Hitler*	10 January 1978	BBC TV
David Hare	*Plenty*	12 April 1978	National Theatre (Lyttleton)
Michael Hastings	*Gloo Joo*	18 September 1978	Hampstead Theatre Club
Jim Hiley	*The Prodigal Father*	6 February 1978	Soho Poly
Robert Holman	*Outside The Whale*	21 February 1978	Bush Theatre
Hull Truck (with Mike Bradwell)	*A Bed Of Roses*	3 January 1978	Bush Theatre and at the Royal Court
Ron Hutchinson	*Says I, Says He*	18 January 1978	Royal Court Theatre Upstairs
Ron Hutchinson	*Eejits*	16 May 1978	Bush Theatre
Tunde Ikoli	*On The Out*	18 April 1978	Foco Novo at the Bush Theatre
Albert Innaurato	*The Transfiguration of Benno Blimpie*	27 September 1978	Bush Theatre
Barrie Keeffe	*Frozen Assets*	9 January 1978	RSC Warehouse
Tom Kempinski	*What About Bourneo*	1 May 1978	Kings Head Lunchtime
Jack Klaff	*Letters Alone*	30 June 1978	RSC Warehouse
David Lan	*Red Earth*	25 October 1978	ICA
Bryony Lavery and Monstrous Regiment	*Time Gentlemen Please*	12 October 1978	Birmingham Centre For The Arts
Bryony Lavery	*Helen And Her Friends*	31 July 1978	Kings Head Lunchtime
Stephen Lowe	*The Ragged Trousered Philanthropists*		
Doug Lucie	*The New Garbo*	14 September 1978	Joint Stock at Plymouth, then on tour
		7 November 1978	Hull Truck at Humberside Theatre Hull, then at Kings Head Evening
Eamonn McCann	*Mad Micks and Englishmen*	21 March 1978	Pirate Jenny at Half Moon

Allan McClelland	*The Dalkey Archive* (adapted from Flan O'Brien)	December 1978	Hull Truck at the Bush Theatre
Philip Magdalany	*Boo Hoo*	27 July 1978	Open Space
Frank Marcus	*The Ballad of Wilfred II*	24 October 1978	Ambiance Lunch Hour Theatre
Dave Marson	*Tigers in the Snow*	20 July 1978	Half Moon Theatre
David Mercer	*Cousin Vladimir*	22 September 1978	RSC, Aldwych Theatre
Bill Morrison	*Flying Blind*	20 June 1978	Royal Court Theatre
North West Spanner (with Ernie Dalton)	*Partisans*	13 October 1978	West End Community Centre, Ashton-under-Lyne
Mary O'Malley	*Look Out ... Here Comes Trouble!*	16 November 1978	RSC Warehouse
Alan Passes	*Spellbound*	1 February 1978	Common Stock at the Half Moon
Robert Patrick	*My Cup Runneth Over*	21 November 1978	Ambiance Lunch Hour Theatre
Harold Pinter	*The Examination*	12 March 1978	Ambiance Lunch Hour Theatre
Harold Pinter	*Betrayal*	15 November 1978	Lyttleton, National Theatre
Stephen Poliakoff	*Shout Across the River*	21 September 1978	RSC Warehouse
Red Ladder Theatre Company (Glen Park, Chris Rawlence, Steve Trafford)	*Taking Our Time*	17 January 1978	East Hunslet Labour Club, Leeds
Red Ladder Theatre Company	*Where There's Brass*	November 1978	Shipley Trades Hall, Shipley
David Rudkin	*The Sons of Light* (new version)	8 June 1978	RSC Warehouse
David Rudkin	*The Judgement on Hippolytus*	6 December 1978	RSC, The Other Place, Stratford
Steven Rumbelow/ Triple Action Theatre	*Orpheus*	20 March 1978	Open Space Theatre
James Saunders	*Bodies*	9 February 1978	Hampstead Theatre Club
James Saunders	*Player Piano* (based on novel by Kurt Vonnegut)	14 June 1978	Ambiance Lunch Hour Theatre
Peter Sheridan	*Emigrants*	18 September 1978	Royal Court Theatre Upstairs
Alan Sillitoe	*The Interview*	12 March 1978	Ambiance Lunch Hour Theatre
Colin Spencer	*Keep It In The Family*	20 November 1978	Soho Poly
Tom Stoppard	*Every Good Boy Deserves Favour*	14 June 1978	Mermaid Theatre
Mike Stott	*Comings and Goings*	9 November 1978	Hampstead Theatre Club
Eric Sutton	*Lushcrush*	18 September 1978	Soho Poly
Ian Taylor	*Diary of a Nobody*	26 September 1978	Kings Head Lunchtime
Ian Taylor	*Lip Service*	9 October 1978	Soho Poly
Peter Terson	*Twilight Joker*	27 February 1978	Soho Poly
Peter Terson	*Rattling the Railings*	27 February 1978	Soho Poly
Ernst Toller	*The Machine Wreckers*	27 November 1978	Half Moon Theatre
Juan Vera	*Alfredo Galvez Or Twelve Shifts of Gear*	22 June 1978	Half Moon Theatre
George F. Walker	*Zastrozzi*	18 December 1978	Kings Head Evening
Michelene Wandor	*Scissors*	2 April 1978	Ambiance Lunch Hour Theatre
Tim Webb	*Pyrates*	February 1978	The Combination at The Albany Empire
Mike Westbrook	*Jazz Cabaret*	4 July 1978	Open Space Theatre
Peter Whelan	*Captain Swing*	26 June 1978	RSC The Other Place, Stratford
Alan Williams	*The Cockroach That Ate Cincinatti*	October 1978	Hull Truck at ICA
Heathcote Williams	*The Immortalist*	27 June 1978	Kings Head Lunchtime
Nigel Williams	*Class Enemy*	9 March 1978	Royal Court Theatre Upstairs, then Royal Court, 4 April 1978
Snoo Wilson	*The Glad Hand*	11 May 1978	Royal Court Theatre
Snoo Wilson	*A Greenish Man*	15 November 1978	Bush Theatre
Womens Theatre Group (with Eileen Fairweather & Melissa Murray)	*Hot Spot*	9 October 1978	Womens Theatre Group on tour

Womens Theatre Group	*In Our Way*	15 March 1978	Womens Theatre Group on tour
Victoria Wood, Snoo Wilson, Ron Hutchinson, Ken Campbell, Dusty Hughes, Nigel Baldwin	*In At The Death*	13 July 1978	Bush Theatre
Phil Woods	*British Bull Dog*	30 October 1978	Soho Poly
Stephen Wyatt	*Lullaby for Mrs Bentley*	1 September 1978	Kings Head Lunchtime
Olwen Wymark	*Loved*	24 October 1978	Wakefield Tricycle Company at the Bush Theatre

Select Bibliography of Plays

(The arrangement follows the order of the chapters in the book. The only plays listed are those mentioned in the text as being by the writer or group named in the chapter heading.)

John Arden and Margaretta D'Arcy

Ars Longa, Vita Brevis: Cassell

Armstrong's Last Goodnight; The Business of Good Government; The Hero Rises Up; The Island of the Mighty; Left-Handed Liberty; The Royal Pardon; Serjeant Musgrave's Dance; The Workhouse Donkey: Eyre Methuen

Live Like Pigs; The Happy Haven; The Waters of Babylon: in *Three Plays*, Penguin

The Non-Stop Connolly Show: Pluto Press

Albert Hunt and the Bradford College of Art Theatre Group

John Ford's Cuban Missile Crisis: Methuen

Pip Simmons Theatre Group

Superman: in *New Short Plays 3*, Methuen

Edward Bond

Early Morning: Calder & Boyars. Also in *Plays: One*, Eyre Methuen

A-A-America! (includes *Stone*); *Bingo* (includes *Passion*); *The Bundle; The Fool; Lear; Narrow Road to the Deep North; The Pope's Wedding* (includes *Black Mass*); *Saved; The Sea; Spring Awakening* (translated from Wedekind); *The Woman*: Eyre Methuen

David Mercer

The Generations (includes *Where the Difference Begins; A Climate of Fear; The Birth of a Private Man*); *A Suitable Case for Treatment*: John Calder

After Haggerty; Cousin Vladimir; Flint; On the Eve of Publication and other plays (includes *The Cellar and the Almond Tree; Emma's Time*): Eyre Methuen

Arnold Wesker

The Friends; The Old Ones: Jonathan Cape, then Penguin

The Kitchen; The Wesker Trilogy (includes *Chicken Soup with Barley*;
Roots; I'm Talking About Jerusalem): Penguin, then Jonathan Cape

The Journalists: Writers and Readers Publishing Co-operative. Also in
Collected Plays Volume Four, Penguin

The Wedding Feast; The Merchant: both in *Collected Plays Volume Four*,
Penguin

John McGrath

Random Happenings in the Hebrides: Davis-Poynter

Events While Guarding the Bofors Gun: Methuen

Fish in the Sea; The Game's a Bogey; Little Red Hen; Yobbo Nowt:
Pluto Press

The Cheviot, the Stag and the Black, Black Oil: West Highland Publishing
Company, then Pluto Press

Hull Truck

Bridget's House: TQ Publications

David Edgar

Two Kinds of Angel: in *The London Fringe Theatre*, Burnham Press

Destiny; Wreckers: Eyre Methuen

Dick Deterred: Monthly Review Press

Trevor Griffiths

Occupations: Calder & Boyars

All Good Men; Comedians; The Party; Through the Night: Faber & Faber

Apricots; Thermidor: Pluto Press

Howard Brenton

Lay-By (written with others): Calder & Boyars

Brassneck (written with David Hare); *Christie in Love and other plays*
(includes *Heads; The Education of Skinny Spew*); *The Churchill Play*;
Epsom Downs; Plays for Public Places (includes *Gum and Goo; Wesley*;
Scott of the Antarctic); *Plays for the Poor Theatre* (includes *A Saliva
Milkshake; Gum and Goo; Christie in Love; Heads; The Education of
Skinny Spew*); *Revenge; The Romans in Britain*: Eyre Methuen

A Saliva Milshake: TQ Publications. Also in *Plays for the Poor Theatre*,
Eyre Methuen

Belt and Braces Roadshow

England Expects (by Gavin Richards): Journeyman Press

Barrie Keeffe

Barbarians (includes *Killing Time; Abide With Me; In the City*); *Frozen
Assets; Gimme Shelter* (includes *Gem; Gotcha; Getaway*); *A Mad World,
My Masters; Sus*: Eyre Methuen

Howard Barker

Stripwell (includes *Claw*); *That Good Between Us*; John Calder

Cheek: in *New Short Plays 3*, Methuen

Caryl Churchill
Owners: Methuen
Cloud Nine; *Light Shining in Buckinghamshire*; *Traps*: Pluto Press
Vinegar Tom: TQ Publications

David Hare
Lay-By (written with others): Calder & Boyars
Brassneck (written with Howard Brenton): Eyre Methuen
Fanshen; *Knuckle*; *Licking Hitler*; *Plenty*; *Teeth 'n' Smiles*: Faber & Faber

Index